SOCIAL WELFARE

FIGHTING POVERTY
AND HOMELESSNESS

ISSN 1937-3295

SOCIAL WELFARE

FIGHTING POVERTY AND HOMELESSNESS

Mark Lane

INFORMATION PLUS® REFERENCE SERIES
Formerly Published by Information Plus, Wylie, Texas

GALE
CENGAGE Learning®

Detroit • New York • San Francisco • New Haven, Conn • Waterville, Maine • London

Social Welfare: Fighting Poverty and Homelessness

Mark Lane

Kepos Media, Inc.: Steven Long and Janice Jorgensen, Series Editors

Project Editors: Elizabeth Manar, Kathleen J. Edgar, Kimberley McGrath

Rights Acquisition and Management: Leitha Etheridge-Sims

Composition: Evi Abou-El-Seoud, Mary Beth Trimper

Manufacturing: Rita Wimberley

For product information and technology assistance, contact us at
Gale Customer Support, 1-800-877-4253.
For permission to use material from this text or product,
submit all requests online at **www.cengage.com/permissions.**
Further permissions questions can be e-mailed to
permissionrequest@cengage.com

Cover photograph: © Sharon Day/Shutterstock.com.

While every effort has been made to ensure the reliability of the information presented in this publication, Gale, a part of Cengage Learning, does not guarantee the accuracy of the data contained herein. Gale accepts no payment for listing; and inclusion in the publication of any organization, agency, institution, publication, service, or individual does not imply endorsement of the editors or publisher. Errors brought to the attention of the publisher and verified to the satisfaction of the publisher will be corrected in future editions.

Gale
27500 Drake Rd.
Farmington Hills, MI 48331-3535

ISBN-13: 978-0-7876-5103-9 (set)   ISBN-10: 0-7876-5103-6 (set)
ISBN-13: 978-1-56995-792-9   ISBN-10: 1-56995-792-4

ISSN 1937-3295

This title is also available as an e-book.
ISBN-13: 978-1-56995-838-4 (set)
ISBN-10: 1-56995-838-6 (set)
Contact your Gale sales representative for ordering information.

Printed in the United States of America
1 2 3 4 5   17 16 15 14 13

TABLE OF CONTENTS

PREFACE

Social Welfare: Fighting Poverty and Homelessness is part of the *Information Plus Reference Series*. The purpose of each volume of the series is to present the latest facts on a topic of pressing concern in modern American life. These topics include the most controversial and studied social issues of the 21st century: abortion, animal rights, capital punishment, care of senior citizens, crime, the environment, health care, immigration, minorities, national security, water, women, youth, and many more. Even though this series is written especially for high school and undergraduate students, it is an excellent resource for anyone in need of factual information on current affairs.

By presenting the facts, it is the intention of Gale, Cengage Learning to provide its readers with everything they need to reach an informed opinion on current issues. To that end, there is a particular emphasis in this series on the presentation of scientific studies, surveys, and statistics. These data are generally presented in the form of tables, charts, and other graphics placed within the text of each book. Every graphic is directly referred to and carefully explained in the text. The source of each graphic is presented within the graphic itself. The data used in these graphics are drawn from the most reputable and reliable sources, such as from the various branches of the U.S. government and from private organizations and associations. Every effort was made to secure the most recent information available. Readers should bear in mind that many major studies take years to conduct and that additional years often pass before the data from these studies are made available to the public. Therefore, in many cases the most recent information available in 2013 is dated from 2010 or 2011. Older statistics are sometimes presented as well, if they are landmark studies or of particular interest and no more-recent information exists.

Although statistics are a major focus of the *Information Plus Reference Series*, they are by no means its only content. Each book also presents the widely held positions and important ideas that shape how the book's subject is discussed in the United States. These positions are explained in detail and, where possible, in the words of their proponents. Some of the other material to be found in these books includes historical background, descriptions of major events related to the subject, relevant laws and court cases, and examples of how these issues play out in American life. Some books also feature primary documents or have pro and con debate sections that provide the words and opinions of prominent Americans on both sides of a controversial topic. All material is presented in an evenhanded and unbiased manner; readers will never be encouraged to accept one view of an issue over another.

HOW TO USE THIS BOOK

Aid for the poor has long been a controversial topic in the United States. Most Americans agree that society should help those who have fallen on hard times, but there are many different opinions as to how this is best accomplished. The 1990s were a time of particularly heavy debate about this issue, and with the so-called Great Recession of 2007–09 and the passage of comprehensive health care reform in 2010, the second decade of the 21st century may be another period of debate and change in means-tested assistance. This volume also describes those who make use of the welfare system, why they use it, and what they get out of it.

Social Welfare: Fighting Poverty and Homelessness consists of eight chapters and three appendixes. Each chapter is devoted to a particular aspect of social welfare. For a summary of the information covered in each chapter, please see the synopses provided in the Table of Contents. Chapters generally begin with an overview of the basic facts and background information on the chapter's topic, then proceed to examine subtopics of particular interest. For example, Chapter 3, Public Programs to Fight Poverty, presents an overview of the welfare system as it was affected by the Personal Responsibility and Work Opportunity Reconciliation Act of 1996, the welfare reform effort enacted by Congress and President Bill Clinton. The chapter then discusses the welfare reform law itself, the individual safety-net programs as they have taken shape since welfare reform, and the ascendance of the welfare-to-work concept. Readers can find their way through each chapter by looking for the section and subsection headings, which are clearly set off from the text. They can also refer to the book's extensive Index if they already know what they are looking for.

Statistical Information

The tables and figures featured throughout *Social Welfare: Fighting Poverty and Homelessness* will be of particular use to readers in learning about this topic. These tables and figures represent an extensive collection of the most recent and valuable statistics on social welfare, as well as related issues—for example, graphics cover the amount of money spent each year for various government welfare programs, the demographics of poverty, the role of child support payments in preventing poverty, and the number of people without health insurance in the United States. Gale, Cengage Learning believes that making this information available to readers is the most important way to fulfill the goal of this book: to help readers understand the issues and controversies surrounding social welfare and reach their own conclusions.

Each table or figure has a unique identifier appearing above it for ease of identification and reference. Titles for the tables and figures explain their purpose. At the end of each table or figure, the original source of the data is provided.

To help readers understand these often complicated statistics, all tables and figures are explained in the text. References in the text direct readers to the relevant statistics. Furthermore, the contents of all tables and figures are fully indexed. Please see the opening section of the Index at the back of this volume for a description of how to find tables and figures within it.

Appendixes

Besides the main body text and images, *Social Welfare: Fighting Poverty and Homelessness* has three appendixes. The first is the Important Names and Addresses directory. Here, readers will find contact information for a number of government and private organizations that can provide further information on aspects of social welfare. The second appendix is the Resources section, which can also assist readers in conducting their own research. In this section the author and editors of *Social Welfare: Fighting Poverty and Homelessness* describe some of the sources that were most useful during the compilation of this book. The final appendix is the Index. It has been greatly expanded from previous editions and should make it even easier to find specific topics in this book.

ADVISORY BOARD CONTRIBUTIONS

The staff of Information Plus would like to extend its heartfelt appreciation to the Information Plus Advisory Board. This dedicated group of media professionals provides feedback on the series on an ongoing basis. Their comments allow the editorial staff who work on the project to continually make the series better and more user-friendly. The staff's top priority is to produce the highest-quality and most useful books possible, and the Information Plus Advisory Board's contributions to this process are invaluable.

The members of the Information Plus Advisory Board are:

- Kathleen R. Bonn, Librarian, Newbury Park High School, Newbury Park, California
- Madelyn Garner, Librarian, San Jacinto College, North Campus, Houston, Texas
- Anne Oxenrider, Media Specialist, Dundee High School, Dundee, Michigan
- Charles R. Rodgers, Director of Libraries, Pasco-Hernando Community College, Dade City, Florida
- James N. Zitzelsberger, Library Media Department Chairman, Oshkosh West High School, Oshkosh, Wisconsin

COMMENTS AND SUGGESTIONS

The editors of the *Information Plus Reference Series* welcome your feedback on *Social Welfare: Fighting Poverty and Homelessness*. Please direct all correspondence to:

Editors
Information Plus Reference Series
27500 Drake Rd.
Farmington Hills, MI 48331-3535

CHAPTER 1
POVERTY AND HOMELESSNESS IN THE UNITED STATES

The U.S. government, like the governments of other developed nations, administers a number of programs that are intended to provide for the basic needs of poor and disadvantaged citizens. These programs are collectively called social welfare programs, and can take a variety of forms, including direct financial payments, assistance with food purchases, housing aid, and free health care. Compared to other developed nations, the social welfare system in the United States is modest in scope, with eligibility requirements that frequently exclude all but the poorest of citizens and time limits that are meant to keep individuals and families from becoming permanently dependent on government aid.

Modern social welfare policy has its roots in the so-called English Poor Laws, which were first implemented during the late 16th century and then codified by Queen Elizabeth I (1533–1603) in the Act for the Relief of the Poor in 1601, which made local government authorities responsible for aiding the indigent. During the colonial period in U.S. history, social welfare policy represented an extension of the English Poor Laws, with programs and institutions created at the colonial rather than the federal level and with large variations in benefits and management from colony to colony. After U.S. independence, there remained questions about the constitutionality of the federal government's involvement in social welfare. It was only with establishment of the Freedmen's Bureau, which was created in 1865 to aid newly liberated slaves after the Civil War (1861–1865), that a precedent was established for the federal management of social welfare programs in emergency situations.

During the Great Depression (1929–1939), the U.S. national unemployment rate rose as high as 25%, and public opinion shifted markedly in favor of a federal social welfare system that would operate permanently, rather than only in emergency situations. President Franklin D. Roosevelt (1882–1945) laid the groundwork for the modern U.S. welfare system with his New Deal, which consisted of a set of laws that were passed between 1933 and 1938 to stabilize the country's economy and provide relief to the poor and unemployed. Among the most prominent New Deal programs were the Works Progress Administration, which employed many of those who had lost their jobs during the Depression in a wide variety of public works projects, and the Social Security Act, which established a permanent system of retirement benefits, unemployment insurance, and aid to poor and handicapped children. This last feature of the act, which established the federal Aid to Dependent Children program, was expanded during the 1960s, and the program was renamed Aid to Families with Dependent Children (AFDC). Roosevelt also established the first national food stamp program, which provided assistance with food purchases. This program was later discontinued before being revived in the 1960s, when the U.S. welfare system was expanded.

Besides the expansion of the AFDC and the reestablishment of a federal food assistance program, the 1960s saw the establishment of Medicare, which provides health care to retirees, and Medicaid, which provides health care to the poor and disabled. These were crucial parts of President Lyndon B. Johnson's (1908–1973) War on Poverty, which consisted of a set of legislative initiatives that grew out of the concern for social justice mobilized during the civil rights movement.

The poverty rate in the United States decreased substantially in the wake of Johnson's antipoverty initiatives, but public support for social programs waned in the decades that followed. Increasing opposition to social welfare programs culminated with the Personal Responsibility and Work Opportunity Act of 1996 (PRWORA), which was passed by the Republican-controlled U.S. House of Representatives and signed into law by the Democratic President Bill Clinton (1946–). The PRWORA replaced the AFDC, which offered open-ended support to impoverished families, with Temporary Assistance for Needy Families (TANF), which was intended to incentivize job-seeking by limiting the amount of time a recipient can participate in the program. Even though most of the funding for TANF comes from the federal government, as did the funding for the AFDC, states were granted wide latitude in deciding how to allocate benefits.

A major addition to the U.S. social welfare system came with the passage of the Affordable Care Act (ACA), which was signed by President Barack Obama (1961–) in 2010. Besides attempting to reform the market for health insurance and to control rapidly rising health care costs, the ACA was intended to provide health insurance to those who could not afford it. The law's provisions began to go into effect soon after its passage, with total implementation of the health care overhaul to be achieved by late 2014. Upon full implementation, the law is expected to result in dramatic increases in low-income Americans' access to health care.

THE FEDERAL DEFINITION OF POVERTY

Decisions about how to determine who is poor and deserving of government aid have inspired controversy at least since the time of the English Poor Laws. Many of the U.S. government's social welfare initiatives hinge on the official definition of poverty, with both the size of an individual's benefits and the overall scope of the programs hanging in the balance.

The federal government began measuring poverty in 1959. During President Johnson's national War on Poverty, researchers realized that few statistical tools were available to measure the number of Americans who continued to live in poverty in one of the most affluent nations in the world. To fight this so-called war, it had to be determined who was poor and why.

During the early 1960s Mollie Orshansky (1915–2006) of the Social Security Administration suggested that the poverty income level be defined as the income sufficient to purchase a minimally adequate amount of goods and services. The necessary data for defining and pricing a full market basket of goods were not available then, nor are they available now. However, Orshansky noted that in 1955 the U.S. Department of Agriculture (USDA) had published the Household Food Consumption Survey, which showed that an average family of three or more people spent approximately one-third of its after-tax income on food. She multiplied the USDA's 1961 economy food plan (a no-frills food basket meeting the then-recommended dietary allowances) by three.

Basically, this defined a poor family as any family or person whose after-tax income was not sufficient to purchase a minimally adequate diet if one-third of the income was spent on food. Differences were allowed for size of family, gender of the head of the household, and whether it was a farm or nonfarm family. The threshold (the level at which poverty begins) for a farm family was set at 70% of a nonfarm household. (The difference between farm and nonfarm households was eliminated in 1982.)

The poverty thresholds set by the U.S. Census Bureau are still based on the theoretical food budget. These thresholds are updated each year to reflect inflation. People with incomes below the applicable threshold are classified as living below the poverty level.

The Census Bureau's poverty thresholds are used for statistical purposes, such as the calculation of the number of poor in the United States. The U.S. Department of Health and Human Services (HHS) uses a simplified version of the Census Bureau's thresholds to arrive at a separate measure of poverty each year. These HHS poverty guidelines are used for administrative purposes by many federal agencies. The HHS uses them to determine Community Services Block Grants, Low-Income Home Energy Assistance Block Grants, and Head Start educational allotments. The guidelines are also the basis for funding the USDA's Supplemental Nutrition Assistance Program (formerly the Food Stamp Program), the National School Lunch Program, and the Special Supplemental Food Program for Women, Infants, and Children. The U.S. Department of Labor uses the guidelines to determine funding for the Job Corps and other employment and training programs under the Workforce Investment Act of 1998. Some state and local governments choose to use the federal poverty guidelines for some of their own programs, such as state health insurance programs and financial guidelines for child support enforcement.

The poverty guidelines vary by family size and composition. In 2013 a family of four living in the 48 contiguous states and the District of Columbia earning $23,550 or less annually was considered impoverished. (See Table 1.1.) A person living alone who earned less than $11,490 was considered poor, as was a family of eight members making less than $39,630. The poverty level is set higher for Alaska and Hawaii, in keeping with federal practices dating from the 1960s that reflect those states' higher cost of living relative to the 48 contiguous states and the District of Columbia.

TABLE 1.1

Poverty guidelines for the 48 contiguous states and the District of Columbia, 2013

Persons in family/household	Poverty guideline
1	$11,490
2	15,510
3	19,530
4	23,550
5	27,570
6	31,590
7	35,610
8	39,630

Note: For families/households with more than 8 persons, add $4,020 for each additional person.

SOURCE: "2013 Poverty Guidelines for the 48 Contiguous States and the District of Columbia," in "Annual Update of the HHS Poverty Guidelines," *Federal Register*, vol. 78, no. 16, January 24, 2013, http://www.gpo.gov/fdsys/pkg/FR-2013-01-24/pdf/2013-01422.pdf (accessed January 31, 2013)

THE HISTORICAL EFFORT TO REDUCE POVERTY

Since the late 1950s Americans have seen some successes and some failures in the battle against poverty. Table 1.2 provides historical data on those living below the federally established poverty level, and Figure 1.1 provides a graphic representation of the changes in the poverty rate between 1959 and 2011. Of the total population of nearly 176.6 million in 1959, 22.4%, or 39.5 million people, lived below the poverty level. After an initial decline through the 1960s and 1970s, the poverty rate began to increase during the early 1980s, coinciding

TABLE 1.2

Poverty status of people by family relationship, 1959–2011

[Numbers in thousands. People as of March of the following year.]

	All people			All families			People in families — Families with female householder no husband present			Unrelated individuals		
		Below poverty level			Below poverty level			Below poverty level			Below poverty level	
Year	Total	Number	Percent	Total	Number	Percent	Total	Number	Percent	Total	Number	Percent
All races												
2011	308,456	46,247	15.0	252,316	33,126	13.1	48,103	16,451	34.2	54,517	12,416	22.8
2010	306,130	46,343	15.1	250,200	33,120	13.2	46,454	15,911	34.3	54,250	12,449	22.9
2009	303,820	43,569	14.3	249,384	31,197	12.5	45,315	14,746	32.5	53,079	11,678	22.0
2008	301,041	39,829	13.2	248,301	28,564	11.5	44,027	13,812	31.4	51,534	10,710	20.8
2007	298,699	37,276	12.5	245,443	26,509	10.8	43,961	13,478	30.7	51,740	10,189	19.7
2006	296,450	36,460	12.3	245,199	25,915	10.6	43,223	13,199	30.5	49,884	9,977	20.0
2005	293,135	36,950	12.6	242,389	26,068	10.8	42,244	13,153	31.1	49,526	10,425	21.1
2004	290,617	37,040	12.7	240,754	26,544	11.0	42,053	12,832	30.5	48,609	9,926	20.4
2003	287,699	35,861	12.5	238,903	25,684	10.8	41,311	12,413	30.0	47,594	9,713	20.4
2002	285,317	34,570	12.1	236,921	24,534	10.4	40,529	11,657	28.8	47,156	9,618	20.4
2001	281,475	32,907	11.7	233,911	23,215	9.9	39,261	11,223	28.6	46,392	9,226	19.9
2000	278,944	31,581	11.3	231,909	22,347	9.6	38,375	10,926	28.5	45,624	8,653	19.0
1999	276,208	32,791	11.9	230,789	23,830	10.3	38,580	11,764	30.5	43,977	8,400	19.1
1998	271,059	34,476	12.7	227,229	25,370	11.2	39,000	12,907	33.1	42,539	8,478	19.9
1997	268,480	35,574	13.3	225,369	26,217	11.6	38,412	13,494	35.1	41,672	8,687	20.8
1996	266,218	36,529	13.7	223,955	27,376	12.2	38,584	13,796	35.8	40,727	8,452	20.8
1995	263,733	36,425	13.8	222,792	27,501	12.3	38,908	14,205	36.5	39,484	8,247	20.9
1994	261,616	38,059	14.5	221,430	28,985	13.1	37,253	14,380	38.6	38,538	8,287	21.5
1993	259,278	39,265	15.1	219,489	29,927	13.6	37,861	14,636	38.7	38,038	8,388	22.1
1992	256,549	38,014	14.8	217,936	28,961	13.3	36,446	14,205	39.0	36,842	8,075	21.9
1991	251,192	35,708	14.2	212,723	27,143	12.8	34,795	13,824	39.7	36,845	7,773	21.1
1990	248,644	33,585	13.5	210,967	25,232	12.0	33,795	12,578	37.2	36,056	7,446	20.7
1989	245,992	31,528	12.8	209,515	24,066	11.5	32,525	11,668	35.9	35,185	6,760	19.2
1988	243,530	31,745	13.0	208,056	24,048	11.6	32,164	11,972	37.2	34,340	7,070	20.6
1987	240,982	32,221	13.4	206,877	24,725	12.0	31,893	12,148	38.1	32,992	6,857	20.8
1986	238,554	32,370	13.6	205,459	24,754	12.0	31,152	11,944	38.3	31,679	6,846	21.6
1985	236,594	33,064	14.0	203,963	25,729	12.6	30,878	11,600	37.6	31,351	6,725	21.5
1984	233,816	33,700	14.4	202,288	26,458	13.1	30,844	11,831	38.4	30,268	6,609	21.8
1983	231,700	35,303	15.2	201,338	27,933	13.9	30,049	12,072	40.2	29,158	6,740	23.1
1982	229,412	34,398	15.0	200,385	27,349	13.6	28,834	11,701	40.6	27,908	6,458	23.1
1981	227,157	31,822	14.0	198,541	24,850	12.5	28,587	11,051	38.7	27,714	6,490	23.4
1980	225,027	29,272	13.0	196,963	22,601	11.5	27,565	10,120	36.7	27,133	6,227	22.9
1979	222,903	26,072	11.7	195,860	19,964	10.2	26,927	9,400	34.9	26,170	5,743	21.9
1978	215,656	24,497	11.4	191,071	19,062	10.0	26,032	9,269	35.6	24,585	5,435	22.1
1977	213,867	24,720	11.6	190,757	19,505	10.2	25,404	9,205	36.2	23,110	5,216	22.6
1976	212,303	24,975	11.8	190,844	19,632	10.3	24,204	9,029	37.3	21,459	5,344	24.9
1975	210,864	25,877	12.3	190,630	20,789	10.9	23,580	8,846	37.5	20,234	5,088	25.1
1974	209,362	23,370	11.2	190,436	18,817	9.9	23,165	8,462	36.5	18,926	4,553	24.1
1973	207,621	22,973	11.1	189,361	18,299	9.7	21,823	8,178	37.5	18,260	4,674	25.6
1972	206,004	24,460	11.9	189,193	19,577	10.3	21,264	8,114	38.2	16,811	4,883	29.0
1971	204,554	25,559	12.5	188,242	20,405	10.8	20,153	7,797	38.7	16,311	5,154	31.6
1970	202,183	25,420	12.6	186,692	20,330	10.9	19,673	7,503	38.1	15,491	5,090	32.9
1969	199,517	24,147	12.1	184,891	19,175	10.4	17,995	6,879	38.2	14,626	4,972	34.0
1968	197,628	25,389	12.8	183,825	20,695	11.3	18,048	6,990	38.7	13,803	4,694	34.0
1967	195,672	27,769	14.2	182,558	22,771	12.5	17,788	6,898	38.8	13,114	4,998	38.1
1966	193,388	28,510	14.7	181,117	23,809	13.1	17,240	6,861	39.8	12,271	4,701	38.3
1965	191,413	33,185	17.3	179,281	28,358	15.8	16,371	7,524	46.0	12,132	4,827	39.8
1964	189,710	36,055	19.0	177,653	30,912	17.4	(NA)	7,297	44.4	12,057	5,143	42.7
1963	187,258	36,436	19.5	176,076	31,498	17.9	(NA)	7,646	47.7	11,182	4,938	44.2
1962	184,276	38,625	21.0	173,263	33,623	19.4	(NA)	7,781	50.3	11,013	5,002	45.4
1961	181,277	39,628	21.9	170,131	34,509	20.3	(NA)	7,252	48.1	11,146	5,119	45.9
1960	179,503	39,851	22.2	168,615	34,925	20.7	(NA)	7,247	48.9	10,888	4,926	45.2
1959	176,557	39,490	22.4	165,858	34,562	20.8	(NA)	7,014	49.4	10,699	4,928	46.1

SOURCE: Adapted from "Table 2. Poverty Status of People by Family Relationship, Race, and Hispanic Origin: 1959 to 2011," in *Historical Poverty Tables—People*, U.S. Census Bureau, September 12, 2012, http://www.census.gov/hhes/www/poverty/data/historical/people.html (accessed January 15, 2013)

FIGURE 1.1

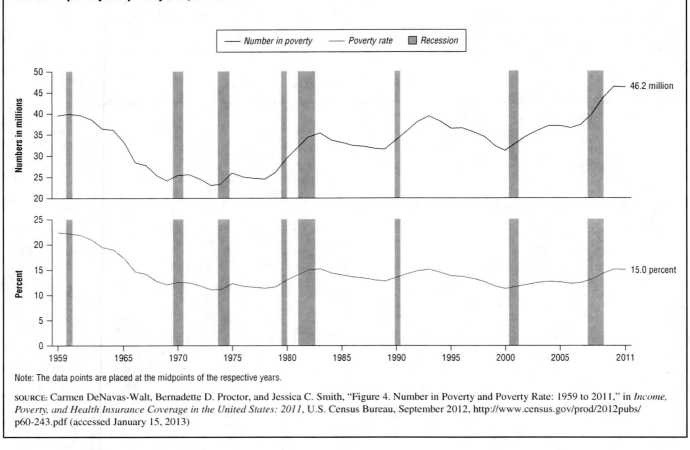

Number in poverty and poverty rate, 1959–2011

Note: The data points are placed at the midpoints of the respective years.

SOURCE: Carmen DeNavas-Walt, Bernadette D. Proctor, and Jessica C. Smith, "Figure 4. Number in Poverty and Poverty Rate: 1959 to 2011," in *Income, Poverty, and Health Insurance Coverage in the United States: 2011*, U.S. Census Bureau, September 2012, http://www.census.gov/prod/2012pubs/p60-243.pdf (accessed January 15, 2013)

with a downturn in household and family incomes for all Americans. The poverty rate rose steadily until it reached a 17-year high of 15.2% in 1983, a year during which the country was climbing out of a serious economic recession.

The percentage of Americans living in poverty then began dropping, falling to 12.8% in 1989. (See Table 1.2.) After that, the percentage increased again, reaching 15.1% in 1993. It then dropped to 11.3% in 2000; however, because the nation's economy faltered substantially during the so-called Great Recession, which lasted from December 2007 to June 2009, the poverty rate rose again to 15.1% in 2010 and remained at 15% in 2011. In *The Great Recession, Unemployment Insurance and Poverty* (April 2010, http://www.urban.org/uploadedpdf/412072_great_recession.pdf), Wayne Vroman of the Urban Institute explains the correlation between rising unemployment rates and rising poverty rates during this period. He puts these rates in historical perspective by noting that 2009 registered a weaker labor market than any year since World War II (1939–1945). Although the unemployment rate peaked at 10% in late 2009 and declined over the following three years, it remained high by historical

standards even though the country's economy had officially exited the recession. (See Table 1.3.)

Analysts believe the overall decline in poverty between 1959 and 2011 was due to both the growth in the economy and the success of some of the antipoverty programs that were instituted during the 1960s; yet not all demographic subcategories experienced the same level of change. For example, in *Income, Poverty, and Health Insurance Coverage in the United States: 2011* (September 2010, http://www.census.gov/prod/2010pubs/p60-238.pdf), Carmen DeNavas-Walt, Bernadette D. Proctor, and Jessica C. Smith of the Census Bureau note that the poverty rate of those aged 65 years and older had improved dramatically from 24.6% in 1970 to 8.7% in 2011. (See Figure 1.2.) For children under 18 years of age and for adults aged 18 to 64 years, however, the poverty rate increased substantially during this period.

RATIO OF INCOME TO POVERTY LEVELS

For purposes of analysis, the Census Bureau uses income-to-poverty ratios that are calculated by dividing income by the respective poverty threshold for each family size. The resulting number is then tabulated on a

TABLE 1.3

Unemployment rate, 1948–2012

[Seasonally adjusted]

Year	Jan	Feb	Mar	Apr	May	Jun	Jul	Aug	Sep	Oct	Nov	Dec
1948	3.4	3.8	4.0	3.9	3.5	3.6	3.6	3.9	3.8	3.7	3.8	4.0
1949	4.3	4.7	5.0	5.3	6.1	6.2	6.7	6.8	6.6	7.9	6.4	6.6
1950	6.5	6.4	6.3	5.8	5.5	5.4	5.0	4.5	4.4	4.2	4.2	4.3
1951	3.7	3.4	3.4	3.1	3.0	3.2	3.1	3.1	3.3	3.5	3.5	3.1
1952	3.2	3.1	2.9	2.9	3.0	3.0	3.2	3.4	3.1	3.0	2.8	2.7
1953	2.9	2.6	2.6	2.7	2.5	2.5	2.6	2.7	2.9	3.1	3.5	4.5
1954	4.9	5.2	5.7	5.9	5.9	5.6	5.8	6.0	6.1	5.7	5.3	5.0
1955	4.9	4.7	4.6	4.7	4.3	4.2	4.0	4.2	4.1	4.3	4.2	4.2
1956	4.0	3.9	4.2	4.0	4.3	4.3	4.4	4.1	3.9	3.9	4.3	4.2
1957	4.2	3.9	3.7	3.9	4.1	4.3	4.2	4.1	4.4	4.5	5.1	5.2
1958	5.8	6.4	6.7	7.4	7.4	7.3	7.5	7.4	7.1	6.7	6.2	6.2
1959	6.0	5.9	5.6	5.2	5.1	5.0	5.1	5.2	5.5	5.7	5.8	5.3
1960	5.2	4.8	5.4	5.2	5.1	5.4	5.5	5.6	5.5	6.1	6.1	6.6
1961	6.6	6.9	6.9	7.0	7.1	6.9	7.0	6.6	6.7	6.5	6.1	6.0
1962	5.8	5.5	5.6	5.6	5.5	5.5	5.4	5.7	5.6	5.4	5.7	5.5
1963	5.7	5.9	5.7	5.7	5.9	5.6	5.6	5.4	5.5	5.5	5.7	5.5
1964	5.6	5.4	5.4	5.3	5.1	5.2	4.9	5.0	5.1	5.1	4.8	5.0
1965	4.9	5.1	4.7	4.8	4.6	4.6	4.4	4.4	4.3	4.2	4.1	4.0
1966	4.0	3.8	3.8	3.8	3.9	3.8	3.8	3.8	3.7	3.7	3.6	3.8
1967	3.9	3.8	3.8	3.8	3.8	3.9	3.8	3.8	3.8	4.0	3.9	3.8
1968	3.7	3.8	3.7	3.5	3.5	3.7	3.7	3.5	3.4	3.4	3.4	3.4
1969	3.4	3.4	3.4	3.4	3.4	3.5	3.5	3.5	3.7	3.7	3.5	3.5
1970	3.9	4.2	4.4	4.6	4.8	4.9	5.0	5.1	5.4	5.5	5.9	6.1
1971	5.9	5.9	6.0	5.9	5.9	5.9	6.0	6.1	6.0	5.8	6.0	6.0
1972	5.8	5.7	5.8	5.7	5.7	5.7	5.6	5.6	5.5	5.6	5.3	5.2
1973	4.9	5.0	4.9	5.0	4.9	4.9	4.8	4.8	4.8	4.6	4.8	4.9
1974	5.1	5.2	5.1	5.1	5.1	5.4	5.5	5.5	5.9	6.0	6.6	7.2
1975	8.1	8.1	8.6	8.8	9.0	8.8	8.6	8.4	8.4	8.4	8.3	8.2
1976	7.9	7.7	7.6	7.7	7.4	7.6	7.8	7.8	7.6	7.7	7.8	7.8
1977	7.5	7.6	7.4	7.2	7.0	7.2	6.9	7.0	6.8	6.8	6.8	6.4
1978	6.4	6.3	6.3	6.1	6.0	5.9	6.2	5.9	6.0	5.8	5.9	6.0
1979	5.9	5.9	5.8	5.8	5.6	5.7	5.7	6.0	5.9	6.0	5.9	6.0
1980	6.3	6.3	6.3	6.9	7.5	7.6	7.8	7.7	7.5	7.5	7.5	7.2
1981	7.5	7.4	7.4	7.2	7.5	7.5	7.2	7.4	7.6	7.9	8.3	8.5
1982	8.6	8.9	9.0	9.3	9.4	9.6	9.8	9.8	10.1	10.4	10.8	10.8
1983	10.4	10.4	10.3	10.2	10.1	10.1	9.4	9.5	9.2	8.8	8.5	8.3
1984	8.0	7.8	7.8	7.7	7.4	7.2	7.5	7.5	7.3	7.4	7.2	7.3
1985	7.3	7.2	7.2	7.3	7.2	7.4	7.4	7.1	7.1	7.1	7.0	7.0
1986	6.7	7.2	7.2	7.1	7.2	7.2	7.0	6.9	7.0	7.0	6.9	6.6
1987	6.6	6.6	6.6	6.3	6.3	6.2	6.1	6.0	5.9	6.0	5.8	5.7
1988	5.7	5.7	5.7	5.4	5.6	5.4	5.4	5.6	5.4	5.4	5.3	5.3
1989	5.4	5.2	5.0	5.2	5.2	5.3	5.2	5.2	5.3	5.3	5.4	5.4
1990	5.4	5.3	5.2	5.4	5.4	5.2	5.5	5.7	5.9	5.9	6.2	6.3
1991	6.4	6.6	6.8	6.7	6.9	6.9	6.8	6.9	6.9	7.0	7.0	7.3
1992	7.3	7.4	7.4	7.4	7.6	7.8	7.7	7.6	7.6	7.3	7.4	7.4
1993	7.3	7.1	7.0	7.1	7.1	7.0	6.9	6.8	6.7	6.8	6.6	6.5
1994	6.6	6.6	6.5	6.4	6.1	6.1	6.1	6.0	5.9	5.8	5.6	5.5
1995	5.6	5.4	5.4	5.8	5.6	5.6	5.7	5.7	5.6	5.5	5.6	5.6
1996	5.6	5.5	5.5	5.6	5.6	5.3	5.5	5.1	5.2	5.2	5.4	5.4
1997	5.3	5.2	5.2	5.1	4.9	5.0	4.9	4.8	4.9	4.7	4.6	4.7
1998	4.6	4.6	4.7	4.3	4.4	4.5	4.5	4.5	4.6	4.5	4.4	4.4
1999	4.3	4.4	4.2	4.3	4.2	4.3	4.3	4.2	4.2	4.1	4.1	4.0
2000	4.0	4.1	4.0	3.8	4.0	4.0	4.0	4.1	3.9	3.9	3.9	3.9
2001	4.2	4.2	4.3	4.4	4.3	4.5	4.6	4.9	5.0	5.3	5.5	5.7
2002	5.7	5.7	5.7	5.9	5.8	5.8	5.8	5.7	5.7	5.7	5.9	6.0
2003	5.8	5.9	5.9	6.0	6.1	6.3	6.2	6.1	6.1	6.0	5.8	5.7
2004	5.7	5.6	5.8	5.6	5.6	5.6	5.5	5.4	5.4	5.5	5.4	5.4
2005	5.3	5.4	5.2	5.2	5.1	5.0	5.0	4.9	5.0	5.0	5.0	4.9
2006	4.7	4.8	4.7	4.7	4.6	4.6	4.7	4.7	4.5	4.4	4.5	4.4
2007	4.6	4.5	4.4	4.5	4.4	4.6	4.7	4.6	4.7	4.7	4.7	5.0
2008	5.0	4.9	5.1	5.0	5.4	5.6	5.8	6.1	6.1	6.5	6.8	7.3
2009	7.8	8.3	8.7	9.0	9.4	9.5	9.5	9.6	9.8	10.0	9.9	9.9
2010	9.8	9.8	9.9	9.9	9.6	9.4	9.5	9.5	9.5	9.5	9.8	9.3
2011	9.1	9.0	8.9	9.0	9.0	9.1	9.0	9.0	9.0	8.9	8.6	8.5
2012	8.3	8.3	8.2	8.1	8.2	8.2	8.2	8.1	7.8	7.9	7.8	7.8

SOURCE: "Unemployment Rate (Series ID LNS14000000)," in *Labor Force Statistics from the Current Population Survey*, U.S. Department of Labor, Bureau of Labor Statistics, http://data.bls.gov/timeseries/LNS14000000 (accessed February 8, 2013)

scale that includes three categories: poor, near-poor, and nonpoor. Poor people have a poverty ratio below 1.00. People above the poverty level are divided into two groups: the near-poor and the nonpoor. The near-poor have a poverty ratio between 1.00 and 1.24 (100% to 124% of the poverty level) and the nonpoor have an

FIGURE 1.2

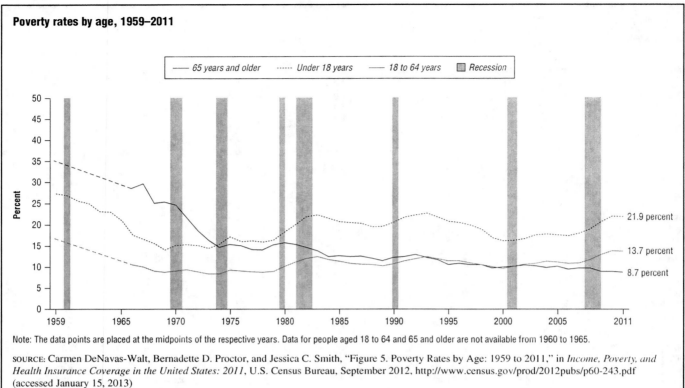

Poverty rates by age, 1959–2011

Note: The data points are placed at the midpoints of the respective years. Data for people aged 18 to 64 and 65 and older are not available from 1960 to 1965.

SOURCE: Carmen DeNavas-Walt, Bernadette D. Proctor, and Jessica C. Smith, "Figure 5. Poverty Rates by Age: 1959 to 2011," in *Income, Poverty, and Health Insurance Coverage in the United States: 2011*, U.S. Census Bureau, September 2012, http://www.census.gov/prod/2012pubs/p60-243.pdf (accessed January 15, 2013)

income-to-poverty ratio of 1.25 (125% of the poverty level) and above.

In 2011, 6.6% of the total U.S. population, or 20.4 million people, had income-to-poverty ratios under 0.5, or half of the poverty threshold. (See Table 1.4.) Fully 19.8% of the population, or 61 million people, were either poor or near-poor. Children were disproportionately poor. Even though children under the age of 18 years accounted for only 23.9% of the total U.S. population, they accounted for 35.6% of those living at half of the poverty threshold or below. Of the total number of poor and near-poor in 2011, children accounted for 33.8%. By contrast, adults aged 18 to 64 years, at 62% of the U.S. population, made up 59.8% of those living at half of the poverty threshold or below and 56.3% of the total number of poor and near-poor. Meanwhile, those aged 65 years or older were the least likely to be poor or near-poor. At 13.5% of the U.S. population, the elderly accounted for only 4.6% of those living at or below half of the poverty threshold and only 9.9% of the total number of poor and near-poor in 2011.

HOW ACCURATE IS THE POVERTY LEVEL?

Almost every year since the Census Bureau first defined the poverty level observers have been concerned about its accuracy. Since the early 1960s, when Orshansky defined the estimated poverty level based on an average family's food budget, living patterns have changed and food costs have become a smaller percentage of family spending. For example, the U.S. Bureau of Labor Statistics (BLS) reports in the press release "Consumer Expenditures—2011" (September 25, 2012, http://www.bls.gov/news.release/cesan.nr0.htm) that in 2011 the average family allocated 13% ($6,458) of its overall household spending on food. By contrast, housing accounted for 33.8% ($16,803) of family spending and transportation for 16.7% ($8,293). When taking into account the spending of only the lowest-earning 20% of American households, the relative weight of housing costs as an element of total spending increases. This group allocated 39.9% of its total spending in 2011 on housing. Based on these changes in consumption patterns, many analysts ask: Should the amount spent on food be multiplied by a factor higher than three to arrive at a more accurate definition of poverty? Or should the poverty level be based on housing, which is by far the most expensive need across all income brackets? Should it be based on some other set of factors?

Other critics of the official poverty measure point to its insensitivity to geographical differences. Housing costs vary widely between, for example, rural Nebraska and New York City, as do costs for other basic necessities, including food, utilities, health care, and transportation. Even within one state, the differences between rural, suburban, and urban costs of living can diverge widely. A family of four with an income approaching the official

TABLE 1.4

People with income below specified ratios of their poverty thresholds, by selected characteristics, 2011

[Numbers in thousands]

| Characteristic | Total | Income-to-poverty ratio | | | | | | | |
| | | Under 0.50 | | Under 1.25 | | Under 1.50 | | Under 2.00 | |
		Number	Percent	Number	Percent	Number	Percent	Number	Percent
All people	308,456	20,356	6.6	60,949	19.8	76,636	24.8	106,011	34.4
Age									
Under 18 years	73,737	7,252	9.8	20,611	28.0	25,039	34.0	32,678	44.3
18 to 64 years	193,213	12,164	6.3	34,312	17.8	42,872	22.2	59,369	30.7
65 years and older	41,507	940	2.3	6,025	14.5	8,725	21.0	13,965	33.6
Sex									
Male	150,990	8,948	5.9	27,150	18.0	34,443	22.8	48,587	32.2
Female	157,466	11,408	7.2	33,798	21.5	42,193	26.8	57,424	36.5
Race* and Hispanic origin									
White	241,334	13,311	5.5	41,626	17.2	53,355	22.1	75,669	31.4
White, not Hispanic	194,960	8,523	4.4	26,209	13.4	34,149	17.5	50,180	25.7
Black	39,609	5,055	12.8	13,448	34.0	16,006	40.4	20,307	51.3
Asian	16,086	880	5.5	2,618	16.3	3,271	20.3	4,686	29.1
Hispanic (any race)	52,279	5,466	10.5	17,415	33.3	21,677	41.5	28,740	55.0
Family status									
In families	252,316	13,763	5.5	43,865	17.4	55,965	22.2	79,133	31.4
Householder	80,529	4,092	5.1	12,500	15.5	16,069	20.0	23,194	28.8
Related children under 18	72,568	6,845	9.4	19,950	27.5	24,298	33.5	31,803	43.8
Related children under 6	23,860	2,822	11.8	7,393	31.0	8,820	37.0	11,318	47.4
In unrelated subfamilies	1,623	442	27.2	786	48.4	916	56.4	1,147	70.7
Unrelated individuals	54,517	6,151	11.3	16,297	29.9	19,755	36.2	25,730	47.2

*Federal surveys now give respondents the option of reporting more than one race. Therefore, two basic ways of defining a race group are possible. A group such as Asian may be defined as those who reported Asian and no other race (the race-alone or single-race concept) or as those who reported Asian regardless of whether they also reported another race (the race-alone-or-in-combination concept). This table shows data using the first approach (race alone). The use of the single-race population does not imply that it is the preferred method of presenting or analyzing data. The Census Bureau uses a variety of approaches. About 2.9 percent of people reported more than one race in Census 2010. Data for American Indians and Alaska Natives, Native Hawaiian and other Pacific Islanders, and those reporting two or more races are not shown separately.
Note: Details may not sum to totals because of rounding.

SOURCE: Adapted from Carmen DeNavas-Walt, Bernadette D. Proctor, and Jessica C. Smith, "Table 5. People with Income below Specified Ratios of Their Poverty Thresholds by Selected Characteristics: 2011," in *Income, Poverty, and Health Insurance Coverage in the United States: 2011*, U.S. Census Bureau, September 2012, http://www.census.gov/prod/2012pubs/p60-243.pdf (accessed January 15, 2013)

poverty measure of $23,550 would clearly be able to purchase more with that amount of money in rural Nebraska than in New York City, so why does the federal government define poverty identically for two such families?

Social changes, too, have altered the economic landscape in the 21st century, as critics of the official poverty measure point out. In families headed by two parents, both parents are far more likely to be working than they were a generation or two ago, and there is a much greater likelihood that a single parent, usually the mother, will be heading the family. Child care costs, which were of little concern during the 1950s, when stay-at home mothers were the norm, have become a major issue for working parents in the 21st century. Moreover, family life has become more complicated, with complex financial consequences arising as parents living in one household may pay child support to another or receive support payments from another. Such incomes and expenses are not factored into the official poverty measure, which obscures the overall portrait of the nation's poor.

Moreover, if the goal is to measure U.S. poverty accurately, these are not the only expenses and forms of

income that many analysts believe should be included in the poverty guidelines. The official poverty thresholds take into account only gross income, neglecting to account for that portion of income that must be spent on taxes and is therefore unavailable for spending on basic necessities. Even though many low-income Americans pay no federal income taxes, they are frequently still subject to state and payroll taxes. Additionally, the poverty guidelines take no account of expenses that are accrued in the process of working or of out-of-pocket medical spending. Medical spending, too, is subject to another variable: age. The young spend far less money on health care than the elderly. Therefore, many critics argue that a poverty measure that does not take into account the burden of medical spending for the elderly does not accurately reflect economic realities.

Forms of income that are not factored into the official poverty thresholds include the various in-kind (or noncash) benefits that households receive from government sources, many of which can be used to meet basic expenses. Even though some of these benefits, such as Medicaid, can be difficult to quantify, others, such as food assistance, have a more obvious cash value. Likewise,

TABLE 1.5

Official poverty measure vs. supplemental poverty measure

	Official poverty measure	Supplemental poverty measure
Measurement units	Families and unrelated individuals	All related individuals who live at the same address, including any coresident unrelated children who are cared for by the family (such as foster children) and any cohabitors and their children
Poverty threshold	Three times the cost of minimum food diet in 1963	The 33rd percentile of expenditures on food, clothing, shelter, and utilities (FCSU) of consumer units with exactly two children multiplied by 1.2
Threshold adjustments	Vary by family size, composition, and age of householder	Geographic adjustments for differences in housing costs and a three parameter equivalence scale for family size and composition
Updating thresholds	Consumer Price Index: all items	Five year moving average of expenditures on FCSU
Resource measure	Gross before-tax cash income	Sum of cash income, plus in-kind benefits that families can use to meet their FCSU needs, minus taxes (or plus tax credits), minus work expenses, minus out-of-pocket medical expenses

SOURCE: Kathleen Short, "Poverty Measure Concepts: Official and Supplemental," in *The Research Supplemental Poverty Measure: 2010*, U.S. Census Bureau, November 2011, http://www.census.gov/hhes/povmeas/methodology/supplemental/research/Short_ResearchSPM2010.pdf (accessed January 31, 2013)

many poor and near-poor families benefit from the Earned Income Tax Credit, an Internal Revenue Service provision that allows working people to deduct certain dollar amounts from their tax bills if their incomes fall below annually updated thresholds. The deducted amounts function in the same way as government assistance, many analysts argue, and should therefore be included in poverty measurements.

THE SUPPLEMENTAL POVERTY MEASURE

Kathleen Short of the Census Bureau explains in *The Research Supplemental Poverty Measure: 2010* (November 2011, http://www.census.gov/hhes/povmeas/methodology/supplemental/research/Short_ResearchSPM2010.pdf) that these widely publicized shortcomings in the official poverty measure led Congress to empower in 1990 the National Academy of Sciences (NAS) to study the efficacy of the official measure and to recommend alternatives. The NAS assembled the Panel on Poverty and Family Assistance, and the panel's 1995 report, *Measuring Poverty: A New Approach*, recommended the creation of an alternate poverty measure in order to address many of the previously mentioned weaknesses in the official guidelines. During the late 1990s the Census Bureau began incorporating a number of experimental poverty measures in some of its reports and data sets. Taking into account various shortcomings of the official poverty measures, the data revealed different portraits of the poor population.

After continued research and discussion over the following decade, the U.S. Interagency Technical Working Group (ITWG) outlined the characteristics of a Supplemental Poverty Measure (SPM) that it proposed to begin using alongside the official measure. The new SPM specifies a poverty threshold that accounts not only for food expenses multiplied by three but also for the amount that is spent on a basic bundle of food, clothing, shelter, and utilities, as well as for additional household needs. The SPM further takes into account the needs of different family types and the needs of households in different geographic locations. In calculating income thresholds, the SPM includes not only cash income from all sources but also the value of various forms of government assistance and tax credits; and it takes into consideration necessary household expenses including income taxes, payroll taxes, child care, child support payments, and health care costs. (See Table 1.5.)

The ITWG proposed that the SPM be included in official data released by the Census Bureau and the BLS, but strictly as a research tool. There were no plans to use it for the determination of funding for social welfare programs; rather, it was to supplement the portrait of poverty provided by the official measure. Full inclusion of the tool in Census Bureau and BLS publications and data sets was slated for 2011, but this timeline was delayed due to funding issues. As of 2013 the two agencies continued to publish preliminary findings applying the SPM to Census Bureau and BLS data as they awaited the resources to fully implement the new measures across the full range of their research into poverty.

These reports, such as Kathleen Short's *The Research Supplemental Poverty Measure: 2011* (November 2012, http://www.census.gov/hhes/povmeas/methodology/supplemental/research/Short_ResearchSPM2011.pdf), indicated that use of the SPM would provide a substantially different picture of the impoverished population than that rendered by use of the official measure. Whereas the official Census Bureau estimate of people in poverty was 46.6 million in 2011 (or 15.1% of the U.S. population), the SPM resulted in an estimate of 49.7 million poor people (or 16.1% of the U.S. population). (See Table 1.6.) Moreover, the composition of the poor population shifted in response to the new methods of calculation. Whereas the official measure yielded an estimate of 16.5 million children (22.3% of all U.S. children) living in poverty in 2011, the SPM yielded an estimate of 13.4 million poor children (18.1% of all U.S. children). The SPM shows significant increases, however, in the poverty rate for those aged 18 to 64 years. Whereas 26.5 million nonelderly adults (13.7% of the total number of people in that age group)

TABLE 1.6

Number and percentage of people in poverty using official poverty measure and supplemental poverty measure (SPM), 2011

[People as of March of the following year]

Characteristic	Number[a] (in thousands)	Official[a] Number Estimate	Official[a] Percent Estimate	SPM Number Estimate	SPM Percent Estimate	Difference Number	Difference Percent
All people	**308,827**	**46,618**	**15.1**	**49,695**	**16.1**	**3,077**	**1.0**
Sex							
Male	151,175	20,686	13.7	23,112	15.3	2,426	1.6
Female	157,653	25,932	16.4	26,583	16.9	651	0.4
Age							
Under 18 years	74,108	16,506	22.3	13,429	18.1	−3,077	−4.2
18 to 64 years	193,213	26,492	13.7	30,020	15.5	3,527	1.8
65 years and older	41,507	3,620	8.7	6,247	15.1	2,627	6.3
Type of unit							
In married couple unit	186,235	13,849	7.4	18,576	10.0	4,727	2.5
In female householder unit	63,347	18,773	29.6	18,996	30.0	223	0.4
In male householder unit	32,307	5,582	17.3	7,071	21.9	1,488	4.6
In new SPM unit	26,939	8,414	31.2	5,052	18.8	−3,362	−12.5
Race[b] and Hispanic origin							
White	241,586	31,101	12.9	34,427	14.3	3,326	1.4
White, not Hispanic	195,148	19,358	9.9	21,427	11.0	2,068	1.1
Black	39,696	11,016	27.8	10,214	25.7	−801	−2.0
Asian	16,094	1,981	12.3	2,719	16.9	738	4.6
Hispanic (any race)	52,358	13,323	25.4	14,670	28.0	1,347	2.6
Nativity							
Native born	268,851	39,022	14.5	39,368	14.6	346	0.1
Foreign born	39,976	7,596	19.0	10,327	25.8	2,731	6.8
Naturalized citizen	17,934	2,233	12.5	3,286	18.3	1,053	5.9
Not a citizen	22,042	5,363	24.3	7,041	31.9	1,678	7.6
Tenure							
Owner	206,718	16,217	7.8	19,978	9.7	3,761	1.8
Owner/mortgage	136,699	7,932	5.8	11,138	8.1	3,206	2.3
Owner/no mortgage/rent free	73,418	9,232	12.6	9,592	13.1	360	0.5
Renter	98,710	29,454	29.8	28,966	29.3	−488	−0.5
Residence							
Inside metropolitan statistical areas	261,455	38,502	14.7	43,322	16.6	4,820	1.8
Inside principal cities	100,302	20,127	20.1	21,748	21.7	1,621	1.6
Outside principal cities	161,153	18,375	11.4	21,574	13.4	3,199	2.0
Outside metropolitan statistical areas[c]	47,372	8,116	17.1	6,373	13.5	−1,743	−3.7
Region							
Northeast	55,035	7,266	13.2	8,262	15.0	996	1.8
Midwest	66,115	9,313	14.1	8,454	12.8	−860	−1.3
South	115,068	18,512	16.1	18,432	16.0	−79	−0.1
West	72,610	11,527	15.9	14,547	20.0	3,020	4.2
Health insurance coverage							
With private insurance	197,323	9,806	5.0	15,010	7.6	5,204	2.6
With public, no private insurance	62,891	23,077	36.7	19,677	31.3	−3,400	−5.4
Not insured	48,613	13,736	28.3	15,008	30.9	1,273	2.6
Work experience							
Total, 18 to 64 years	**193,213**	**26,492**	**13.7**	**30,020**	**15.5**	**3,527**	**1.8**
All workers	144,163	10,345	7.2	13,611	9.4	3,266	2.3
Worked full-time, year-round	97,443	2,732	2.8	4,983	5.1	2,252	2.3
Less than full-time, year-round	46,720	7,614	16.3	8,628	18.5	1,014	2.2
Did not work at least 1 week	49,049	16,147	32.9	16,409	33.5	262	0.5
Disability status[d]							
Total, 18 to 64 years	**193,213**	**26,492**	**13.7**	**30,020**	**15.5**	**3,527**	**1.8**
With a disability	14,968	4,313	28.8	4,133	27.6	−180	−1.2
With no disability	177,309	22,105	12.5	25,795	14.5	3,690	2.1

were living in poverty in 2011 according to the official measure, 30 million (15.5%) would be classified as poor according to the SPM. The increase among the elderly poor, when using the SPM instead of the official poverty measure, is even more pronounced. The official measure indicated that 3.6 million (8.7%) of those aged 65 years or older were poor in 2011, whereas the SPM indicated that 6.3 million (15.1%) were living in poverty.

TABLE 1.6

Number and percentage of people in poverty using official poverty measure and supplemental poverty measure (SPM), 2011 [CONTINUED]

[People as of March of the following year]

ªIncludes unrelated individuals under the age of 15.
ᵇFederal surveys now give respondents the option of reporting more than one race. Therefore, two basic ways of defining a race group are possible. A group such as Asian may be defined as those who reported Asian and no other race (the race-alone or single-race concept) or as those who reported Asian regardless of whether they also reported another race (the race-alone-or-in-combination concept). This table shows data using the first approach (race alone). The use of the single-race population does not imply that it is the preferred method of presenting or analyzing data. The Census Bureau uses a variety of approaches. About 2.9 percent of people reported more than one race in Census 2010. Data for American Indians and Alaska Natives, Native Hawaiians and other Pacific Islanders, and those reporting two or more races are not shown separately.
ᶜThe "Outside metropolitan statistical areas" category includes both micropolitan statistical areas and territory outside of metropolitan and micropolitan statistical areas.
ᵈThe sum of those with and without a disability does not equal the total because disability status is not defined for individuals in the armed forces.

SOURCE: Kathleen Short, "Table 1. Number and Percent of People in Poverty by Different Poverty Measures: 2011," in *Research Supplemental Poverty Measure: 2011*, U.S. Census Bureau, November 2012, http://www.census.gov/hhes/povmeas/methodology/supplemental/research/Short_ResearchSPM2011.pdf (accessed January 31, 2013)

A number of policy experts met the release of the SPM data with skepticism. In "The Supplemental Poverty Measure: Is Child Poverty Really Less of a Problem Than We Thought?" (August 3, 2012, http://www.cepr.net/index.php/blogs/cepr-blog/the-supplemental-poverty-measure-does-it-paint-a-more-accurate-picture-of-poverty), Shawn Fremstad of the Center for Economic and Policy Research takes aim at the decreases in child poverty resulting from use of the SPM. Arguing that the SPM accurately shows an increase in poverty among the elderly because of its inclusion of out-of-pocket medical expenses in its calculations, Fremstad maintains that comparable adjustments are needed in the calculation of child poverty to account for "children's basic needs for care and healthy development."

Mark Levinson of the Service Employees International Union makes a more fundamental case for the SPM's inadequacy in "Mismeasuring Poverty" (*American Prospect*, June 25, 2012). Faulting the official poverty measure for "setting the poverty bar so low that tens of millions of poor Americans are not accounted for," Levinson maintains that the SPM fails to fix this basic shortcoming. Noting that the original intent of President Johnson's War on Poverty was to aid "those whose basic needs exceed their means to satisfy them," he laments the fact that tens of millions of Americans fit this description and yet do not qualify for government assistance. In place of either the official poverty measure or the SPM, Levinson suggests that a more reasonable alternative would be a definition of poverty such as those used in European countries, where families earning less than 50% or 60% of the median income are considered to be poor.

THE U.S. POVERTY LINE IN A GLOBAL CONTEXT

Indeed, the poverty bar is set lower in the United States than in other comparably developed countries. Martin Ravallion of the International Monetary Fund's World Bank reports in "A Relative Question" (*Finance and Development*, vol. 49, no. 4, December 2012) that most high-income countries peg their poverty lines to average incomes, so that the poverty line rises as a country's economy grows. The rationale behind such systems is that one can feel poor in a rich country even when one's income is above the level required for basic subsistence, and that poverty describes a condition of having too little money to participate in society.

To assess poverty, the World Bank uses a figure called purchasing power parity (PPP), which compares the ability of people to purchase basic necessities in different places and at different times. The poverty line is far lower in less-developed and developing countries than it is in the United States. As of 2012, the government of China maintained a poverty line that was equivalent to PPP of $1.80 per day, or double its previous poverty line of $0.90 per day. China's poverty measure was little different from the average poverty line of the world's 20 poorest countries (PPP of $1.25 per day), which is considered the absolute poverty line, or the amount needed for basic survival in the developing world. Luxembourg, the nation with the highest poverty line in the world in 2012, classified those living on less than the PPP equivalent of $43 per day as poor. Even though U.S. citizens on average demonstrate consumption patterns similar to those in Luxembourg, meaning that participation in society would require roughly the same amount of income in both countries, the U.S. poverty line was equivalent to PPP of only $13 per day in 2012.

According to Ravallion, 22% of the world's population lived at or below the absolute poverty line of $1.25 per day in 2008. Even though this represented a tremendous decrease from the 52% of the world's population that were classified as living in absolute poverty in 1981, it still amounted to 1 billion people living in conditions that were far more dire than those experienced by any of the poor in the United States and western Europe, with the likely exception of the homeless.

INCOME INEQUALITY

Whether considered globally or nationally, there is no mistaking the relative nature of poverty. Although the official U.S. poverty measure does not account for an individual's or family's poverty in terms of the country's average income, researchers in the fields of anthropology, psychology, and economics have established that people judge their own level of welfare not in absolute terms but relative to the prosperity of their society as a whole. For this and other reasons, many policy experts are concerned about a growing body of evidence suggesting that the gap between the rich and the poor in the United States widened considerably at the end of the 20th century and the beginning of the 21st century.

The Census Bureau has released a number of studies that show a change in the distribution of wealth and earnings in the United States. Unlike many short-term economic changes that are often the product of normal economic cycles of growth and recession, these changes seem to indicate fundamental changes in American society.

Utilizing Census Bureau data, Arloc Sherman and Chad Stone of the Center on Budget and Policy Priorities explain in "Income Gaps between Very Rich and Everyone Else More Than Tripled in Last Three Decades, New Data Show" (June 25, 2010, http://www.cbpp.org/files/6-25-10inc.pdf) that the gaps between the richest 1% of Americans and the middle and poorest fifths of Americans more than tripled between 1979 and 2007. During this period average after-tax incomes for the top 1% rose by 281%, whereas the middle fifth of households saw their incomes increase by only 25% and the lowest fifth of households saw their incomes increase by only 16%. In 2007, 17.1% of all after-tax income was earned by the wealthiest 1% of Americans.

Census data on income and earnings provide additional information on income inequality. The accumulation of wealth by the highest quintile of earners, as Table 1.7 shows, proceeded most rapidly between 1977 and 2007, a period during which the richest 20% of Americans increased their share of all household income from 44% in 1977 to 49.7% in 2007. This upper quintile's accumulation of wealth did not dramatically accelerate relative to the other quintiles of earners during the Great Recession, but neither did the quintile lose ground; its share of all U.S. household income stood at 50% in 2008 and at 50.3% in 2009 and 2010. The trend toward further inequality continued after the recession, however. In 2011 the top quintile claimed 51.1% of all household income.

All other quintiles of income earners saw their shares of total income fall steadily between 1977 and 2007. (See Table 1.7.) The lowest quintile's share of income was 4.2% in 1977 and 3.4% in 2007; the second-lowest quintile claimed 10.2% of all income in 1977 and 8.7% in 2007; the middle quintile of earners took home 16.9% of all

income in 1977 and 14.8% in 2007; and the second-highest quintile's share was 24.7% in 1977 and 23.4% in 2007. Even though these declines slowed during and immediately after the Great Recession, the overall trend continued, with each of the lower four quintiles losing ground to the top quintile by 2011, when the bottom quintile earned 3.2% of all income, the second quintile 8.4%, the third quintile 14.3%, and the fourth quintile 23%.

Why Is the Income Gap Growing?

Many reasons exist to explain the growing inequality, although observers disagree about which are more important. One reason is that the proportion of the elderly population, which is likely to earn less, is growing. According to the Census Bureau, 26.8 million of 121.1 million households, or 22.2%, were headed by a householder 65 years of age or older in 2011. (See Table 1.8; a household may consist of a single individual or a group of related or unrelated people living together, whereas a family consists of related individuals.) The median (the middle value—half are higher and half are lower) household income of households headed by a person aged 65 years or older was $33,118, compared with a median household income of $55,640 for households headed by someone under the age of 65 years.

In addition, more people than in previous years were living in nonfamily situations (either alone or with nonrelatives). In 2011, 40.6 million of 121.1 million households, or 33.5%, were nonfamily households. (See Table 1.8.) These nonfamily households earned a median income of $30,221, compared with the $62,273 median income of family households.

The increase in the number of households headed by females and the increased labor force participation of women have also contributed to growing income inequality in the United States. In 2011, 15.7 million of 80.5 million family households, or 19.5%, were headed by women, and 21.3 million of 40.6 million nonfamily households, or 52.7%, were headed by women. (See Table 1.8.) Female-headed households typically earn significantly less than other types of households. The earnings of female-headed family households in 2011 were only 67.9% of the earnings of male-headed family households ($33,637 and $49,567, respectively) and only 45.4% of the earnings of married-couple households ($33,637 and $74,130, respectively). Meanwhile, female nonfamily householders earned 71.8% of male nonfamily householders ($25,492 and $35,482, respectively). On average, female full-time workers earned only 77% of what male full-time workers earned in 2011. (See Figure 1.3.)

Robert J. Gordon and Ian Dew-Becker of the National Bureau of Economic Research argue in *Controversies about the Rise of American Inequality: A Survey* (May 2008, http://papers.nber.org/papers/w13982) that the declining real value

TABLE 1.7

Household income dispersion, selected years, 1967–2011

[Income in 2011 Consumer Price Index Research Series Using Current Methods (CPI-U-RS) adjusted dollars]

Measures of income dispersion	2011	2010[a]	2009[b]	2008	2007	1997	1987[c]	1977	1967[c]
Measure									
Household income at selected percentiles									
10th percentile limit	12,000	12,235	12,709	12,703	13,192	12,875	11,812	11,839	9,597
20th percentile limit	20,262	20,631	21,446	21,636	22,010	21,517	20,454	19,385	17,663
50th (median)	50,054	50,831	52,195	52,546	54,489	51,704	49,358	45,884	42,056
80th percentile limit	101,582	103,184	104,857	104,710	108,473	99,900	91,596	81,138	69,710
90th percentile limit	143,611	143,154	144,317	144,467	147,523	136,454	120,840	103,485	88,551
95th percentile limit	186,000	186,178	188,744	188,027	191,997	176,817	153,271	128,469	111,866
Household income ratios of selected percentiles									
90th/10th	11.97	11.70	11.36	11.37	11.18	10.60	10.23	8.74	9.23
95th/20th	9.18	9.02	8.80	8.69	8.72	8.22	7.49	6.63	6.33
95th/50th	3.72	3.66	3.62	3.58	3.52	3.42	3.11	2.80	2.66
80th/50th	2.03	2.03	2.01	1.99	1.99	1.93	1.86	1.77	1.66
80th/20th	5.01	5.00	4.89	4.84	4.93	4.64	4.48	4.19	3.95
20th/50th	0.40	0.41	0.41	0.41	0.40	0.42	0.41	0.42	0.42
Mean household income of quintiles									
Lowest quintile	11,239	11,341	12,113	12,176	12,530	12,350	11,613	11,275	9,419
Second quintile	29,204	29,432	30,678	30,833	31,936	30,875	29,516	27,751	26,098
Third quintile	49,842	50,718	51,940	52,367	54,202	51,944	49,346	45,909	41,670
Fourth quintile	80,080	81,365	82,516	83,316	85,814	80,454	74,589	67,264	58,301
Highest quintile	178,020	174,734	179,142	178,685	182,203	171,527	141,848	119,948	104,920
Shares of household income of quintiles									
Lowest quintile	3.2	3.3	3.4	3.4	3.4	3.6	3.8	4.2	4.0
Second quintile	8.4	8.5	8.6	8.6	8.7	8.9	9.6	10.2	10.8
Third quintile	14.3	14.6	14.6	14.7	14.8	15.0	16.1	16.9	17.3
Fourth quintile	23.0	23.4	23.2	23.3	23.4	23.2	24.3	24.7	24.2
Highest quintile	51.1	50.3	50.3	50.0	49.7	49.4	46.2	44.0	43.6
Summary measures									
Gini index of income inequality	0.477	0.470	0.468	0.466	0.463	0.459	0.426	0.402	0.397
Mean logarithmic deviation of income	0.585	0.574	0.550	0.541	0.532	0.484	0.414	0.364	0.380
Theil	0.422	0.400	0.403	0.398	0.391	0.396	0.311	0.276	0.287
Atkinson:									
e = 0.25	0.101	0.097	0.097	0.096	0.095	0.094	0.077	0.069	0.071
e = 0.50	0.198	0.191	0.190	0.188	0.185	0.183	0.155	0.139	0.143
e = 0.75	0.300	0.293	0.288	0.285	0.281	0.272	0.238	0.213	0.220

[a]Implementation of Census 2010-based population controls.
[b]Medians are calculated using $2,500 income intervals. Beginning with 2009 income data, the Census Bureau expanded the upper income intervals used to calculate medians to $250,000 or more. Medians falling in the upper open-ended interval are plugged with "$250,000." Before 2009, the upper open-ended interval was $100,000 and a plug of "$100,000" was used.
[c]Implementation of a new Current Population Survey (CPS) American Savings Education Council processing system.

SOURCE: Adapted from Carmen DeNavas-Walt, Bernadette D. Proctor, and Jessica C. Smith, "Table A-2. Selected Measures of Household Income Dispersion: 1967–2011," in *Income, Poverty, and Health Insurance Coverage in the United States: 2011*, U.S. Census Bureau, September 2012, http://www.census.gov/prod/2012pubs/p60-243.pdf (accessed January 15, 2013).

of the minimum wage has contributed to income inequality, particularly for female workers, who are more likely than males to work for minimum wages; among men, the decline of unions has contributed to growing income inequality. Analysts also point to forces beyond government control. Chrystia Freeland observes in "Income Inequality Sheds Its Taboo Status" (*New York Times*, November 29, 2012) that most economists agree that the technology revolution and globalization, which have resulted in the loss of many of the highest-paying jobs available to those in the lower income quintiles, are important drivers of inequality. While incomes have stagnated for the lower quintiles, those at the extreme top of the income scale have seen unprecedented gains in their earnings. Freeland notes that as of 2012, "the wealth of the 400 richest Americans has increased more than fivefold over the past 20 years."

HOMELESSNESS

Homelessness is a complex social problem. Educators, sociologists, economists, and political scientists who have studied homelessness for decades agree that it is caused by a combination of poverty, misfortune, illness, and behavior. It is also evident that, for most people,

TABLE 1.8

Income and earnings summary measures by selected characteristics, 2010 and 2011

[Income in 2011 dollars. Households and people as of March of the following year.]

| Characteristic | 2010[a] | | 2011 | | Percentage change in real median income (2011 less 2010) |
	Number (thousands)	Median income (dollars) Estimate	Number (thousands)	Median income (dollars) Estimate	Estimate
Households					
All households	119,927	50,831	121,084	50,054	−1.5
Type of household					
Family households	79,539	63,331	80,506	62,273	−1.7
Married-couple	58,656	74,782	58,949	74,130	−0.9
Female householder, no husband present	15,235	32,978	15,669	33,637	2.0
Male householder, no wife present	5,648	51,384	5,888	49,567	−3.5
Nonfamily households	40,388	30,511	40,578	30,221	−0.9
Female householder	21,420	26,165	21,383	25,492	−2.6
Male householder	18,968	36,605	19,195	35,482	−3.1
Race[b] and Hispanic origin of householder					
White	96,306	53,340	96,964	52,214	−2.1
White, not Hispanic	83,314	56,178	83,573	55,412	−1.4
Black	15,265	33,137	15,583	32,229	−2.7
Asian	5,212	66,286	5,374	65,129	−1.7
Hispanic (any race)	14,435	38,818	14,939	38,624	−0.5
Age of householder					
Under 65 years	94,190	56,850	94,241	55,640	−2.1
15 to 24 years	6,231	29,114	6,180	30,460	4.6
25 to 34 years	19,487	51,450	19,846	50,774	−1.3
35 to 44 years	21,458	63,355	21,241	61,916	−2.3
45 to 54 years	24,767	64,307	24,195	63,861	−0.7
55 to 64 years	22,246	58,256	22,779	55,937	−4.0
65 years and older	25,737	32,454	26,843	33,118	2.0
Nativity of householder					
Native born	103,232	51,736	103,965	50,801	−1.8
Foreign born	16,695	45,354	17,119	44,431	−2.0
Naturalized citizen	8,568	54,616	8,874	51,926	−4.9
Not a citizen	8,127	37,561	8,246	37,894	0.9
Disability status of householder[c]					
Households with householder aged 18 to 64	93,997	56,916	94,050	55,683	−2.2
With disability	8,951	26,300	8,793	25,420	−3.3
Without disability	84,632	60,378	84,787	59,411	−1.6
Earnings of full-time, year-round workers					
Men with earnings	56,283	49,463	57,993	48,202	−2.5
Women with earnings	43,179	38,052	43,683	37,118	−2.5
Disability status					
Workers without disability, age 15 and over[c]					
Men with earnings	53,948	49,798	55,655	48,493	−2.6
Women with earnings	41,869	38,152	42,462	37,174	−2.6
Workers with disability, age 15 and over[c]					
Men with earnings	1,655	42,868	1,622	42,211	−1.5
Women with earnings	1,229	32,873	1,152	34,168	3.9

[a]Consistent with 2011 data through implementation of Census 2010-based population controls.
[b]Federal surveys now give respondents the option of reporting more than one race. Therefore, two basic ways of defining a race group are possible. A group such as Asian may be defined as those who reported Asian and no other race (the race-alone or single-race concept) or as those who reported Asian regardless of whether they also reported another race (the race-alone-or-in-combination concept). This table shows data using the first approach (race alone). The use of the single-race population does not imply that it is the preferred method of presenting or analyzing data. The Census Bureau uses a variety of approaches. About 2.9 percent of people reported more than one race in Census 2010. Data for American Indians and Alaska Natives, Native Hawaiians and other Pacific Islanders, and those reporting two or more races are not shown separately in this table.
[c]The sum of those with and without a disability does not equal the total because disability status is not defined for individuals in the armed forces.

SOURCE: Adapted from Carmen DeNavas-Walt, Bernadette D. Proctor, and Jessica C. Smith, "Table 1. Income and Earnings Summary Measures by Selected Characteristics: 2010 and 2011," in *Income, Poverty, and Health Insurance Coverage in the United States: 2011*, U.S. Census Bureau, September 2012, http://www.census.gov/prod/2012pubs/p60-243.pdf (accessed January 15, 2013)

homelessness is a temporary condition rather than a way of life and that the number of Americans who experience homelessness at some point in a given year has appreciably increased since the 1990s. Beyond these and other basic facts, however, the study of homelessness is complicated by methodological problems with counting the homeless and with disagreement over the definition of homelessness.

FIGURE 1.3

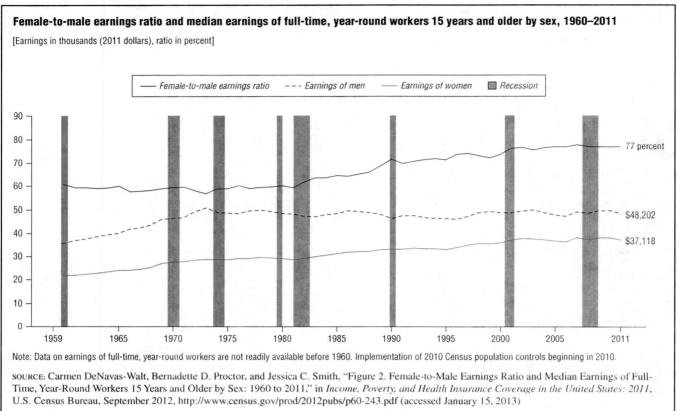

Female-to-male earnings ratio and median earnings of full-time, year-round workers 15 years and older by sex, 1960–2011

[Earnings in thousands (2011 dollars), ratio in percent]

Note: Data on earnings of full-time, year-round workers are not readily available before 1960. Implementation of 2010 Census population controls beginning in 2010.

SOURCE: Carmen DeNavas-Walt, Bernadette D. Proctor, and Jessica C. Smith, "Figure 2. Female-to-Male Earnings Ratio and Median Earnings of Full-Time, Year-Round Workers 15 Years and Older by Sex: 1960 to 2011," in *Income, Poverty, and Health Insurance Coverage in the United States: 2011*, U.S. Census Bureau, September 2012, http://www.census.gov/prod/2012pubs/p60-243.pdf (accessed January 15, 2013)

What Does It Mean to Be Homeless?

During a period of growing concern about homelessness in the mid-1980s, the first major piece of federal legislation aimed specifically at helping the homeless was adopted: the Stewart B. McKinney Homeless Assistance Act of 1987 (later renamed the McKinney-Vento Homeless Assistance Act). The act officially defines a homeless person as:

1. An individual who lacks a fixed, regular, and adequate nighttime residence; and

2. An individual who has a primary nighttime residence that is:

   A. A supervised publicly or privately operated shelter designed to provide temporary living accommodations (including welfare hotels, congregate shelters, and transitional housing for the mentally ill);

   B. An institution that provides a temporary residence for individuals intended to be institutionalized; or

   C. A public or private place not designed for, or ordinarily used as, a regular sleeping accommodation for human beings.

The government definition of a homeless person focuses on whether a person is housed. Broader definitions of homelessness take into account whether a person has a home. For example, Martha Burt et al. report in *Helping America's Homeless: Emergency Shelter or Affordable Housing?* (2001) that as late as 1980 the Census Bureau identified people who lived alone and did not have a "usual home elsewhere"—in other words, a larger family—as homeless. In this sense the term *home* describes living within a family, rather than having a roof over one's head.

Burt et al. also state that homeless people themselves, when interviewed during the 1980s and 1990s, drew a distinction between having a house and having a home. Even when homeless people had spent significant periods of time in a traditional shelter, such as an apartment or rented room, if they felt those houses were transitional or insecure, they identified themselves as having been homeless while living there. According to Burt et al., these answers "reflect how long they have been without significant attachments to people."

Burt et al. and other homeless advocates disagree with the narrow government definition of a homeless person, which focuses on a person's sleeping arrangements. They assert that the definition should be broadened to include groups of people who, while they may have somewhere to live, do not really have a home in the conventional sense. Considerable debate has resulted over expanding the classification to include people in situations such as the following:

- People engaging in prostitution who spend each night in a different hotel room, paid for by clients

- Children in foster or relative care

- People living in stable but inadequate housing (e.g., having no plumbing or heating)

- People "doubled up" in conventional dwellings for the short term (the Census Bureau defines doubled-up households as those including one or more person over the age of 18 years who is not enrolled in school and is not the householder, spouse, or cohabiting partner of the householder)

- People in hotels paid for by vouchers to the needy

- Elderly people living with family members because they cannot afford to live elsewhere

Official definitions are important because total counts of the homeless influence the levels of funding that Congress authorizes for homeless programs. With the availability of federal funds since the passage of the McKinney-Vento Homeless Assistance Act, institutional constituencies have formed that advocate for additional funding, an effort in which more expansive definitions are helpful.

Causes of Homelessness

In 2012 the U.S. Conference of Mayors, a nonpartisan organization of cities with populations higher than 30,000, surveyed the mayors of major cities on the extent and causes of urban homelessness and published the results in *Hunger and Homelessness Survey: A Status Report on Hunger and Homelessness in America's Cities, a 25-City Survey* (December 2012, http://usmayors.org/pressreleases/uploads/2012/1219-report-HH.pdf). The city officials surveyed identified the lack of affordable housing as the primary cause of homelessness, both among families with children and among homeless individuals. Among families, the other leading causes of homelessness in 2012 were (in descending order) poverty, unemployment, eviction, and domestic violence. Among individuals, the leading causes of homelessness after the lack of affordable housing were unemployment, poverty, mental illness, and substance abuse.

Jesse McKinley reports in "Cities Deal with a Surge in Shantytowns" (*New York Times*, March 25, 2009) that as a result of the foreclosure crisis, which began in 2007, tent cities sprang up in major cities around the nation. Public attention shifted to these modern-day "Hoovervilles" (shantytowns that arose during the Great Depression) after an episode of the *Oprah Winfrey Show* focused on a tent city in Sacramento, California, in March 2009. In "'American Dream' Withers as Tent Cities Mushroom in Promised Land" (*International Business Times*, November 21, 2010), Jijo Jacob notes that tent cities continued to be erected after the recession officially ended in June 2009. Jacob explains that continued high unemployment and surging foreclosures were feeding a growing homelessness rate. Jacob suggests that the crisis had not reached its peak;

the financial firm Moody's had reported earlier in 2010 that 15 million Americans owed more to the bank than their homes were worth. Jennifer Jiggetts notes in "Virginia Beach Tent Cities for Homeless Keep Popping Up" (*Virginian-Pilot* [Hampton Roads, VA], April 10, 2011) that despite the improving economy in 2011, the homeless problem was still persistent.

In "Homeless Rates in U.S. Held Level amid Recession, Study Says, but Big Gains Are Elusive" (*New York Times*, December 10, 2012), Annie Lowery reports that the U.S. Department of Housing and Urban Development (HUD) estimated that the overall number of the homeless did not rise over the course of the recession and its aftermath. In fact, the number of chronically homeless fell 19% between 2007 and 2012 as a result, most likely, of targeted government efforts to reduce that portion of the homeless population. It is further believed that the problem of temporary homelessness was alleviated during this period thanks to emergency stimulus funding passed by Congress to address the consequences of the Great Recession. Part of this funding aimed to identify those who were vulnerable to homelessness as a result of foreclosure and the lack of affordable housing, and to find new housing for them; HUD estimates that more than 1 million people avoided homelessness as a result of this program. Given the decrease in the number of chronically homeless, however, the relative steadiness of the overall homeless count suggests that the ranks of those who were forced into temporary homelessness by the economic downturn increased appreciably between 2007 and 2012, in spite of the success of the government's homeless prevention efforts. As the stimulus funding began to expire in 2012, experts feared that homelessness would increase in 2013 and beyond.

Additionally, it is clear that while there may not have been a pronounced increase in the absolute number of homeless individuals and households, millions of Americans lost their homes during the Great Recession. As Rakesh Kochhar and D'Vera Cohn of the Pew Research Center observe in *Fighting Poverty in a Bad Economy, Americans Move in with Relatives* (October 3, 2011, http://www.pewsocialtrends.org/2011/10/03/fighting-poverty-in-a-bad-economy-americans-move-in-with-relatives/), an unprecedented number of people left their own homes and moved in with family members between 2007 and 2009. During that time, according to the report's authors, the number of multigenerational households grew from 46.5 million to 51.4 million, for "the largest increase in modern history." While many advocates for the homeless would argue that such people should be counted among the homeless so that government aid might be more effective at meeting society's needs, these doubled-up families were not considered homeless.

Counting the Homeless

CENSUS BUREAU COUNTS. Crafting policies to combat homelessness depends heavily on the collection of reliable information regarding the number and attributes of the homeless population, but the very nature of homelessness makes accurate data collection difficult. Typically, researchers studying the U.S. population at large contact people in their homes using in-person or telephone surveys to obtain information regarding income, education levels, household size, ethnicity, and other demographic data. Homeless people cannot be counted at home, of course, and researchers have struggled to address this methodological shortcoming.

The Census Bureau, which is the source for much of the data that are used by lawmakers and policy experts, was subjected to harsh criticism by homeless advocates and others for apparent oversights in its counts of the homeless population for the 1990 Census. In "The 1990 Census Shelter and Street Night Enumeration" (March 1992, http://www.amstat.org/sections/srms/proceedings/papers/1992_029.pdf), Diane F. Barrett, Irwin Anolik, and Florence H. Abramson of the Census Bureau indicate that in March 1990 census officials, on what was known as Shelter and Street Night (S-Night), counted homeless people found in shelters, emergency shelters, shelters for abused women, shelters for runaway and neglected youth, low-cost motels, Young Men's Christian Associations and Young Women's Christian Associations, and subsidized units at motels. Additionally, they counted people found in the early morning hours sleeping in abandoned buildings, bus and train stations, all-night restaurants, parks, and vacant lots. The results of this count were released the following year in the Census Bureau publication "Count of Persons in Selected Locations Where Homeless Persons Are Found." Homeless advocates criticized the methods and results as inadequate and charged that they provided a low estimate of homeless people in the United States. According to Annetta C. Smith and Denise I. Smith of the Census Bureau in *Emergency and Transitional Shelter Population: 2000* (October 2001, http://www.census.gov/prod/2001pubs/censr01-2.pdf), the Census Bureau responded by emphasizing that S-Night "should not be used as a count of people experiencing homelessness." S-Night results were not a reflection of the prevalence of homelessness over a given year, but a count of homeless people identified during a single night, a snapshot, like the census itself.

The National Law Center on Homelessness and Poverty alleged that the methodology of the S-Night count was unconstitutional. In 1992 the law center, the Conference of Mayors, the cities of Baltimore, Maryland, and San Francisco, California, 15 local homeless organizations, and seven homeless people (the plaintiffs) filed suit in the federal district court in Washington, D.C. They charged the Census Bureau with excluding segments of the homeless population in the 1990 population count by not counting those in hidden areas and by not allocating adequate funds for S-Night.

In its suit the law center cited an internal Census Bureau memorandum that stated in part, "We know we will miss people by counting the 'open' rather than 'concealed' (two studies showed that about two-thirds of the street population sleep concealed)." Studies funded by the Census Bureau indicated that up to 70% of the homeless street population in Los Angeles, California, were missed, as were 32% in New Orleans, Louisiana, 47% in New York, New York, and 69% in Phoenix, Arizona. Advocates were greatly concerned that this underrepresentation would negatively affect the funding of homeless initiatives.

In 1994 the district court dismissed the case, ruling that the plaintiffs' case was without merit. The court ruled that failure to count all the homeless was not a failure to perform a constitutional duty because the Constitution does not give individuals a right to be counted or a right to a perfectly accurate census. The court stated that the "methods used by the Bureau on S-Night were reasonably designed to count as nearly as practicable all those people residing in the United States and, therefore, easily pass constitutional muster." In *National Law Center on Homelessness and Poverty v. Michael Kantor* (No. 94-5312 [1996]), the U.S. Court of Appeals upheld the district court's finding.

For the 2000 census, the Census Bureau undertook a special operation, called Service-Based Enumeration (SBE). Between March 27 and March 29, 2000, census workers focused solely on counting the homeless population at the locations where they were the most likely to be found. On specific nights, counts of those staying in emergency and transitional shelters, of homeless people taking advantage of soup kitchens, and of those staying in outdoor locations were done.

The SBE methods were considered to be an improvement over the methods that were used in the 1990 census. Homeless citizens and advocates alike expected to see an increase in the number of homeless people reported by the Census Bureau in the 2000 census as compared with the 1990 census. Expectations that the higher population counts would translate into higher funding levels for services to the homeless were also raised.

In 2001, however, the Census Bureau reported that it would not be releasing a specific homeless count because of the liability issues raised after the 1990 census. The Census Bureau stated that it would have only one category showing the number of people tabulated at "emergency and transitional shelters." This count was openly incomplete, relative to the overall homeless population. Other people falling under the federal definition of homelessness, such as people who were counted at domestic violence shelters, family crisis centers, soup kitchens, mobile food vans, and targeted nonsheltered outdoor locations (i.e., street people, car dwellers, and so on) during the March 2000 SBE night were to be included in the category of "other noninstitutional group quarters population." This category was overly inclusive; it included, for instance, students living in college dormitories. As a result, the homeless portion of the category could not be extracted.

The Census Bureau replicated the 2000 SBE count for the 2010 census. Enumerators counted the homeless residing in shelters on the night of May 29, interviewed people at soup kitchens and mobile food vans to determine their sheltered status on May 30, and counted people sleeping at preidentified outdoor locations on the night of May 31. As with the 2000 census, the Census Bureau declined to offer numbers purporting to represent the entire homeless population. In 2010, 209,325 Americans were counted as occupants of emergency and transitional shelters, as part of the 2010 SBE effort. (See Table 1.9.)

HUD COUNTS. HUD attempts to collect data that more accurately represent the U.S. homeless population at large. Since 1983 the agency has conducted national point-in-time (PIT) studies of the homeless. These studies, which are undertaken in collaboration with local government officials and shelters across the United States, are like the Census Bureau's SBE count, in that they determine the number of homeless people during a specific time period and at specific places. However, HUD's PIT counts make a greater effort at comprehensiveness; for example, the agency attempts to locate unsheltered as well as sheltered homeless people. Thus, they provide something closer to a more accurate snapshot of the American homeless population at a given moment in time.

HUD's assessment of the homeless population goes beyond PIT counts, as well. The department monitors the inventory of shelter beds to derive further information about the size of the homeless population and the nature of its needs. It also collaborates with state and municipal governments in the collection of longitudinal data about specific homeless populations. This longitudinal data, which is collected over time in an attempt to determine long-term patterns among the homeless, is stored in a database called the Homeless Management Information Systems (HMIS). PIT counts, shelter inventories, and HMIS data represent the three main data sets that are used by local governments, in partnership with HUD, to build a yearly portrait of the American homeless population. Each year HUD submits its findings in the *Annual Homeless Assessment Report* (*AHAR*) to Congress.

TABLE 1.9

Group quarters and emergency and transitional shelter populations, 2010

Sex and selected age group	Total population		Group quarters population		Emergency and transitional shelter population		
	Number	Percent	Number	Percent	Number	Percent	Percent of group quarters population
Both sexes	**308,745,538**	**100.0**	**7,987,323**	**100.0**	**209,325**	**100.0**	**2.6**
Male	151,781,326	49.2	4,858,210	60.8	129,969	62.1	2.7
Female	156,964,212	50.8	3,129,113	39.2	79,356	37.9	2.5
Both sexes, all ages	**308,745,538**	**100.0**	**7,987,323**	**100.0**	**209,325**	**100.0**	**2.6**
Under 18 years	74,181,467	24.0	260,586	3.3	42,290	20.2	16.2
18 to 64 years	194,296,087	62.9	6,269,031	78.5	161,578	77.2	2.6
65 years and over	40,267,984	13.0	1,457,706	18.3	5,457	2.6	0.4
Median age	37.2	(X)	28.8	(X)	39.2	(X)	(X)
Male, all ages	**151,781,326**	**100.0**	**4,858,210**	**100.0**	**129,969**	**100.0**	**2.7**
Under 18 years	37,945,136	25.0	165,477	3.4	21,325	16.4	12.9
18 to 64 years	96,473,230	63.6	4,239,142	87.3	104,834	80.7	2.5
65 years and over	17,362,960	11.4	453,591	9.3	3,810	2.9	0.8
Median age	35.8	(X)	29.5	(X)	43.9	(X)	(X)
Female, all ages	**156,964,212**	**100.0**	**3,129,113**	**100.0**	**79,356**	**100.0**	**2.5**
Under 18 years	36,236,331	23.1	95,109	3.0	20,965	26.4	22.0
18 to 64 years	97,822,857	62.3	2,029,889	64.9	56,744	71.5	2.8
65 years and over	22,905,024	14.6	1,004,115	32.1	1,647	2.1	0.2
Median age	38.5	(X)	25.4	(X)	29.7	(X)	(X)

(X) Not applicable.
Note: Percentages may not sum to 100.0 due to rounding.

SOURCE: Amy Symens Smith, Charles Holmberg, and Marcella Jones-Puthoff, "Table 1. Total, Group Quarters, and Emergency and Transitional Shelter Populations by Sex and Selected Age Groups: 2010," in *The Emergency and Transitional Shelter Population: 2010*, U.S. Census Bureau, September 2012, http://www.census.gov/prod/cen2010/reports/c2010sr-02.pdf (accessed February 2, 2013)

For the 2012 *AHAR*, HUD conducted its PIT count on a single night in January of that year. On that night, HUD estimated the U.S. homeless population was 633,782. (See Figure 1.4.) Of this total amount, 394,379 (62%) were homeless individuals, and 239,403 (38%) were members of homeless families. These numbers represented a slight decline of less than 0.5% in the homeless population over the previous year and a decline of 5.7% since 2007. The decline from 2007 to 2012 was more pronounced among homeless individuals (6.8%) than among persons in families (3.7%).

Of the 633,782 homeless Americans counted on that January night in 2012, 390,155 (62%) were living in emergency shelters or transitional housing, and 243,627 (38%) were in unsheltered locations. (See Figure 1.5.) The sheltered and unsheltered homeless populations were little changed from the 2011 PIT count. The number of sheltered homeless people had not appreciably changed between 2007 and 2012, although it did spike in 2009 and 2010, at 403,308 and 403,543, respectively. Meanwhile, the unsheltered homeless population dropped significantly between 2007 and 2012, falling from 280,487 to 243,627, for an overall decline of 13.1%.

FIGURE 1.4

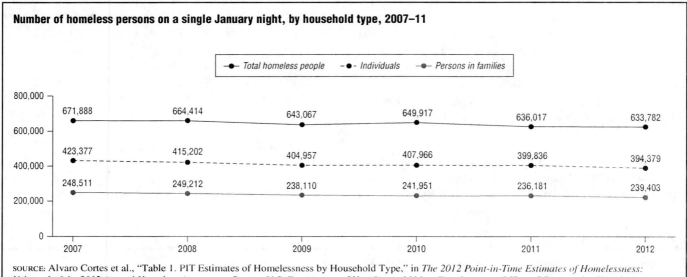

Number of homeless persons on a single January night, by household type, 2007–11

SOURCE: Alvaro Cortes et al., "Table 1. PIT Estimates of Homelessness by Household Type," in *The 2012 Point-in-Time Estimates of Homelessness: Volume I of the 2012 Annual Homeless Assessment Report*, U.S. Department of Housing and Urban Development, Office of Community Planning, November 2012, https://www.onecpd.info/resources/documents/2012AHAR_PITestimates.pdf (accessed January 15, 2013)

FIGURE 1.5

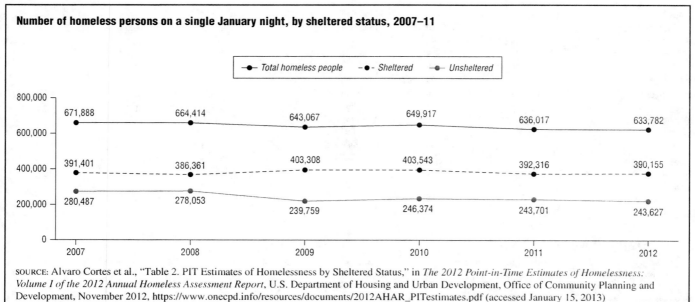

Number of homeless persons on a single January night, by sheltered status, 2007–11

SOURCE: Alvaro Cortes et al., "Table 2. PIT Estimates of Homelessness by Sheltered Status," in *The 2012 Point-in-Time Estimates of Homelessness: Volume I of the 2012 Annual Homeless Assessment Report*, U.S. Department of Housing and Urban Development, Office of Community Planning and Development, November 2012, https://www.onecpd.info/resources/documents/2012AHAR_PITestimates.pdf (accessed January 15, 2013)

FIGURE 1.6

Number of emergency, transitional, and permanent beds for homeless persons, 2007–12

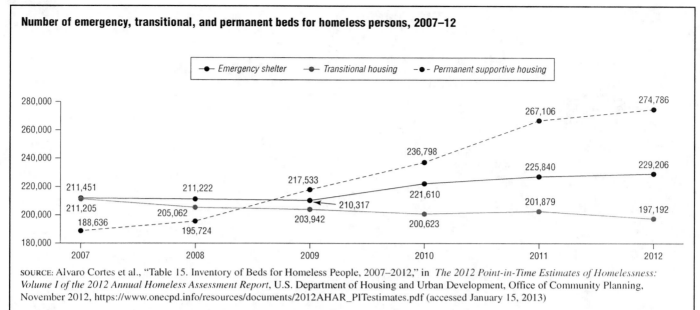

SOURCE: Alvaro Cortes et al., "Table 15. Inventory of Beds for Homeless People, 2007–2012," in *The 2012 Point-in-Time Estimates of Homelessness: Volume I of the 2012 Annual Homeless Assessment Report*, U.S. Department of Housing and Urban Development, Office of Community Planning, November 2012, https://www.onecpd.info/resources/documents/2012AHAR_PITestimates.pdf (accessed January 15, 2013)

Perhaps contributing to the decline in the unsheltered homeless population was an increase in the inventory of shelter beds and supportive housing facilities during the same period. HUD indicates that between 2007 and 2012 the overall number of shelter beds grew from 611,292 to 701,184, an increase of 89,892 (14.7%). (See Figure 1.6.) The number of emergency shelter beds increased from 211,451 in 2007 to 229,206 in 2012, an increase of 17,755 (8.4%). Meanwhile, there was a dramatic improvement in the availability of permanent supportive

housing facilities, which offer housing as well as support services to disabled homeless people on a permanent basis. Between 2007 and 2012 the inventory of permanent supportive housing beds in the United States grew from 188,636 to 274,786, an increase of 86,150 (45.7%). These gains were offset by a decline in the number of transitional housing beds, or housing options available to the homeless for up to 24 months. The inventory of beds classified as transitional housing fell from 211,205 in 2007 to 197,192 in 2012, representing a decrease of 14,013 (6.6%).

CHAPTER 2
WHO ARE THE POOR?

CHARACTERISTICS OF THE POOR

Carmen DeNavas-Walt, Bernadette D. Proctor, and Jessica C. Smith of the U.S. Census Bureau indicate in *Income, Poverty, and Health Insurance Coverage in the United States: 2011* (September 2012, http://www.census .gov/prod/2012pubs/p60-243.pdf) that in 2011, 46.2 million people, or 15% of the U.S. population, had income-to-poverty ratios under 1.00 and were therefore officially considered poor. As shown in Table 1.4 in Chapter 1, 60.9 million Americans, or 19.8% of the U.S. population, were poor or near-poor, meaning that they had income-to-poverty ratios of 1.25 or less.

Children under the age of 18 years were the most likely age group to be poor; 16.1 million (21.9%) of all Americans in this age group were poor in 2011. (See Table 2.1.) Approximately 26.5 million adults aged 18 to 64 years (13.7% of the total number in this age group) were poor, and 3.6 million Americans over the age of 65 years (8.7% of the total) were poor. Children were also more likely than those in other age groups to experience income-to-poverty ratios of 1.25 or less. In 2011, 28% (20.6 million) of all children under the age of 18 years were either poor or near-poor, compared with 17.8% (34.3 million) of adults aged 18 to 64 years and 14.5% (6 million) of adults aged 65 years and older. (See Table 1.4 in Chapter 1.) Children were also disproportionately represented among the desperately poor (those whose incomes fall below half of the poverty line); 9.8% (7.3 million) of all children were in this category in 2011, compared with 6.3% (12.2 million) of adults aged 18 to 64 years and 2.3% (940,000) of adults over the age of 65 years.

Even though poverty rates were high in the early 21st century, individuals were not necessarily trapped in poverty for long periods. Robin J. Anderson of the Census Bureau finds in *Dynamics of Economic Well-Being: Poverty, 2004–2006* (March 2011, http://www.census.gov/hhes/ www/poverty/publications/dynamics04/P70-123.pdf), the most recent longitudinal study of poverty available by the Census Bureau as of March 2013, that 28.9% of the U.S. population was in poverty for at least two months between January 2004 and December 2006, but that only 2.8% of the population was in poverty for the entire period. Of those who were in poverty between January and February 2004 at the start of the study period, about a quarter (23.1%) remained in poverty until the end of the study. However, more than half of people who exited poverty were still considered near-poor, with incomes of less than 150% of the poverty threshold.

Race and Ethnicity

Historically, poverty rates have been consistently lower for whites than for minorities in the United States. According to DeNavas-Walt, Proctor, and Smith, in 1959, 28.5 million (18.1%) whites lived below the poverty level, whereas 9.9 million (55.1%) African-Americans did. By 1970 the rate of poverty of white Americans had declined to 9.9%, where it remained for approximately the next 10 years. The poverty rate for African-Americans was more than three times that of whites in 1970, at 33.5%. By 2000, a year in which the U.S. economy was strong, 21.6 million whites (9.5%) lived in poverty, whereas 8 million African-Americans (22.5%) did.

In 2011 African-Americans and Hispanics continued to be disproportionately affected by poverty. In that year 9.8% of non-Hispanic whites were poor, compared with 27.6% of African-Americans and 25.3% of Hispanics. (See Table 2.1.) The poverty rates for all racial and ethnic groups had risen since 2008 as a result of the so-called Great Recession (which lasted from late 2007 to mid-2009) and unemployment, although they rose faster for these minority groups. Even though the recession had officially ended in 2009, unemployment remained high, as did the overall poverty rate and the poverty rates for minority groups.

TABLE 2.1

People in poverty, by selected characteristics, 2010 and 2011

[Numbers in thousands. People as of March of the following year.]

| Characteristic | 2010[a] | | | 2011 | | | Change in poverty (2011 less 2010)[b] | |
| | | Below poverty | | | Below poverty | | | |
	Total	Number	Percent	Total	Number	Percent	Number	Percent
People								
Total	306,130	46,343	15.1	308,456	46,247	15.0	−96	−0.1
Family status								
In families	250,200	33,120	13.2	252,316	33,126	13.1	6	−0.1
Householder	79,559	9,400	11.8	80,529	9,497	11.8	96	—
Related children under 18	72,581	15,598	21.5	72,568	15,539	21.4	−59	−0.1
Related children under 6	23,892	6,037	25.3	23,860	5,844	24.5	−193	−0.8
In unrelated subfamilies	1,680	774	46.1	1,623	705	43.4	−69	−2.6
Reference person	654	283	43.2	671	272	40.6	−10	−2.6
Children under 18	933	469	50.2	846	409	48.4	−60	−1.9
Unrelated individuals	54,250	12,449	22.9	54,517	12,416	22.8	−33	-0.2
Race[c] and Hispanic origin								
White	239,982	31,083	13.0	241,334	30,849	12.8	−234	−0.2
White, not Hispanic	194,783	19,251	9.9	194,960	19,171	9.8	−80	—
Black	39,283	10,746	27.4	39,609	10,929	27.6	183	0.2
Asian	15,611	1,899	12.2	16,086	1,973	12.3	74	0.1
Hispanic (any race)	50,971	13,522	26.5	52,279	13,244	25.3	−278	−1.2
Sex								
Male	149,737	20,893	14.0	150,990	20,501	13.6	−391	−0.4
Female	156,394	25,451	16.3	157,466	25,746	16.3	295	0.1
Age								
Under 18 years	73,873	16,286	22.0	73,737	16,134	21.9	−152	−0.2
18 to 64 years	192,481	26,499	13.8	193,213	26,492	13.7	−6	−0.1
65 years and older	39,777	3,558	8.9	41,507	3,620	8.7	62	−0.2
Nativity								
Native born	266,723	38,485	14.4	268,490	38,661	14.4	176	—
Foreign born	39,407	7,858	19.9	39,966	7,586	19.0	−272	−1.0
Naturalized citizen	17,344	1,954	11.3	17,934	2,233	12.5	279	1.2
Not a citizen	22,063	5,904	26.8	22,032	5,353	24.3	−551	−2.5
Region								
Northeast	54,710	7,038	12.9	54,977	7,208	13.1	170	0.2
Midwest	66,038	9,216	14.0	66,023	9,221	14.0	5	—
South	113,681	19,123	16.8	114,936	18,380	16.0	−743	−0.8
West	71,701	10,966	15.3	72,520	11,437	15.8	471	0.5
Residence								
Inside metropolitan statistical areas	258,366	38,466	14.9	261,155	38,202	14.6	−264	−0.3
Inside principal cities	98,816	19,532	19.8	100,183	20,007	20.0	475	0.2
Outside principal cities	159,550	18,933	11.9	160,973	18,195	11.3	−739	−0.6
Outside metropolitan statistical areas[d]	47,764	7,877	16.5	47,301	8,045	17.0	168	0.5
Work experience								
Total, 18 to 64 years	192,481	26,499	13.8	193,213	26,492	13.7	−6	−0.1
All workers	143,687	10,462	7.3	144,163	10,345	7.2	−117	−0.1
Worked full-time, year-round	95,697	2,600	2.7	97,443	2,732	2.8	132	0.1
Less than full-time, year-round	47,991	7,862	16.4	46,720	7,614	16.3	−248	−0.1
Did not work at least 1 week	48,793	16,037	32.9	49,049	16,147	32.9	110	0.1
Disability status[e]								
Total, 18 to 64 years	192,481	26,499	13.8	193,213	26,492	13.7	−6	−0.1
With a disability	14,974	4,196	28.0	14,968	4,313	28.8	117	0.8
With no disability	176,592	22,227	12.6	177,309	22,105	12.5	−122	−0.1

African-American and Hispanic children suffered even more disproportionately from poverty than African-American and Hispanic adults and seniors. In 2010, 39.2% of non-Hispanic African-Americans under the age of 18 years and 35% of Hispanics under the age of 18 years were poor, compared with only 12.4% of non-Hispanic white children in the same age group. (See Table 2.2.) Only 5.1% of non-Hispanic white children were desperately poor (having income-to-poverty ratios under 0.5, or half of the poverty threshold), compared with 15.1% of Hispanic children and 20.3% of non-Hispanic African-American children.

DeNavas-Walt, Proctor, and Smith indicate that 2 million Asian-Americans (12.3%) lived below the poverty line in 2011. (See Table 2.1.) The rate was substantially lower than

[Numbers in thousands. People as of March of the following year.]

—Represents or rounds to zero.
ªConsistent with 2011 data through implementation of Census 2010-based population controls.
ᵇDetails may not sum to totals because of rounding.
ᶜFederal surveys now give respondents the option of reporting more than one race. Therefore, two basic ways of defining a race group are possible. A group such as Asian may be defined as those who reported Asian and no other race (the race-alone or single-race concept) or as those who reported Asian regardless of whether they also another race (the race-alone-or-in-combination concept). This table shows data using the first approach (race alone). The use of the single-race population does not imply that it is the preferred method of presenting or analyzing data. The Census Bureau uses a variety of approaches. About 2.9 percent of people reported more than one race in Census 2010. Data for American Indians and Alaska Natives, Native Hawaiians and other Pacific Islanders, and those reporting two or more races are not shown separately.
ᵈThe "Outside metropolitan statistical areas" category includes both micropolitan statistical areas and territory outside of metropolitan and micropolitan statistical areas.
ᵉThe sum of those with and without a disability does not equal the total because disability status is not defined for individuals in the armed forces.

SOURCE: Adapted from Carmen DeNavas-Walt, Bernadette D. Proctor, and Jessica C. Smith, "Table 3. People in Poverty by Selected Characteristics: 2010 and 2011," in *Income, Poverty, and Health Insurance Coverage in the United States: 2011*, U.S. Census Bureau, September 2012, http://www.census.gov/prod/2012pubs/p60-243.pdf (accessed January 15, 2013)

it was in 1987, the first year that the Census Bureau kept statistics on Asian-Americans, when 16.1% lived below the poverty level. Even though the Asian-American poverty rate was higher than the non-Hispanic white rate, it rose more slowly as a result of the Great Recession and its aftermath. Whereas the non-Hispanic white poverty rate went from 8.6% in 2008 to 9.8% in 2011, the Asian-American rate rose from 11.8% to 12.3% during the same period.

The median (the middle value—half are higher and half are lower) household income reflects the disparity in poverty levels between different groups. In 2011 Asian-Americans had the highest median income among all racial and ethnic groups, at $67,885, whereas the median income for non-Hispanic whites was $55,305. (See Table 2.3.) African-Americans ($33,223), Native Americans and Alaskan Natives ($35,192), and Hispanics ($39,589) had the lowest median household incomes.

Age

CHILD POVERTY. The United States has historically had one of the highest rates of child poverty in the developed world. In *Relative Income Poverty among Children in Rich Countries* (January 2012, http://www.unicef-irc.org/publications/pdf/iwp_2012_01.pdf), Jonathan Bradshaw et al. analyze government data from the world's richest 35 countries to create a comparative portrait of child poverty in the developed world at various points between 2006 and 2011. Setting a poverty threshold (for the purposes of the study) of 50% of the median disposable income in each country (which is consistent with the standards of many international studies measuring poverty), the researchers find that the United States had the second-highest child poverty rate of the 35 countries surveyed, at 23.1%. (See Figure 2.1.) This percentage was significantly higher than that of countries such as Lithuania (15.4%), Italy (15.9%), Greece (16%), Spain (17.1%), Bulgaria (17.8%), and Latvia (18.8%). Only Romania's child poverty rate, at 25.5%, was higher. Iceland had the lowest child poverty rate in the

developed world, at 4.7%, followed by Finland (5.3%), Cyprus (6.1%), the Netherlands (6.1%), Norway (6.1%), Slovenia (6.3%), and Denmark (6.5%).

Bradshaw et al. also find that the U.S. government assistance and tax allowance programs do little to alleviate child poverty. With one of the lowest levels of government spending on family benefits and tax breaks, at slightly more than 0.5% of the gross domestic product (GDP; the total value of final goods and services that are produced within an economy in a given year), the United States accomplishes little in the way of alleviating child poverty. Countries that spend 2% or more of their GDP on family benefits and tax breaks, such as Australia, New Zealand, Hungary, and the United Kingdom, achieved reductions in child poverty of as much as 20% in the years measured. Ireland, which spent approximately 2.5% of its GDP on family benefits and tax breaks, saw reductions in child poverty of over 30%.

In 2010 U.S. children living with a female householder were particularly likely to live in poverty. Almost half (47.3%) of these children lived in poverty, compared with 11.6% of children living with married parents. (See Table 2.2.) Between 2007 and 2010, as a result of the Great Recession, the child poverty rate among female-headed households rose dramatically, from 43% to 47.3%. The rate among married-couple households increased substantially during this period as well, from 8.6% to 11.6%. Younger children living with single mothers were even more likely to be poor. Well over half (58.7%) of children aged five years and younger with female-householder parents were poor, as were 41.9% of children aged six to 17 years. More than half (52.8%) of non-Hispanic African-American children living in female-householder families were poor, and 57.5% of Hispanic children living in female-householder families were poor. Meanwhile, 36.1% of non-Hispanic white children living in female-householder families were poor.

TABLE 2.2

Percentage of children ages 0–17 living below selected poverty levels, by selected characteristics, selected years 1980–2010

Characteristic	1980	1985	1990	1995	2000	2005	2006	2007	2008	2009	2010
Below 100% poverty											
Total	**18.3**	**20.7**	**20.6**	**20.8**	**16.2**	**17.6**	**17.4**	**18.0**	**19.0**	**20.7**	**22.0**
Gender											
Male	18.1	20.3	20.5	20.4	16.0	17.4	17.2	17.9	18.8	20.4	22.2
Female	18.6	21.1	20.8	21.2	16.3	17.8	17.6	18.1	19.2	21.0	21.8
Age											
Ages 0–5	20.7	23.0	23.6	24.1	18.3	20.2	20.3	21.1	21.7	24.3	25.8
Ages 6–17	17.3	19.5	19.0	19.1	15.2	16.3	16.0	16.5	17.6	18.9	20.1
Race and Hispanic origin[a]											
White, non-Hispanic	11.8	12.8	12.3	11.2	9.1	10.0	10.0	10.1	10.6	11.9	12.4
Black, non-Hispanic	42.3	43.3	44.5	41.5	31.0	34.5	33.3	34.4	34.7	35.7	39.2
Hispanic	33.2	40.3	38.4	40.0	28.4	28.3	26.9	28.6	30.6	33.1	35.0
Region[b]											
Northeast	16.3	18.5	18.4	19.0	14.5	15.5	15.7	16.1	16.6	18.0	18.4
South	22.5	22.8	23.8	23.5	18.4	19.7	19.4	20.8	20.5	22.4	24.4
Midwest	16.3	20.7	18.8	16.9	13.1	15.9	16.3	16.6	18.7	19.6	20.4
West	16.1	19.3	19.8	22.1	16.9	17.5	16.6	16.3	18.6	21.0	22.2
Children in married-couple families, total	10.1	11.4	10.3	10.0	8.0	8.5	8.2	8.6	9.9	11.1	11.6
Ages 0–5	11.6	12.9	11.7	11.1	8.7	9.9	9.5	9.6	11.1	13.4	13.5
Ages 6–17	9.4	10.5	9.5	9.4	7.7	7.7	7.5	8.1	9.3	9.8	10.7
White, non-Hispanic	7.5	8.2	6.9	6.0	4.7	4.5	4.3	4.8	5.3	6.1	6.4
Black, non-Hispanic	19.7	17.2	17.8	12.0	8.5	12.4	11.8	11.0	11.0	14.5	16.0
Hispanic	23.0	27.2	26.6	28.4	20.8	20.1	18.5	19.4	22.2	24.0	25.2
Children in female-householder families, no husband present, total	51.4	54.1	54.2	50.7	40.5	43.1	42.4	43.0	43.9	45.1	47.3
Ages 0–5	65.4	65.7	65.9	61.9	50.7	52.9	53.0	54.0	54.0	54.8	58.7
Ages 6–17	46.2	49.1	48.4	45.2	36.3	38.9	37.7	37.9	39.1	40.5	41.9
White, non-Hispanic	38.6	39.1	41.4	34.9	29.3	33.8	33.6	32.9	33.1	35.1	36.1
Black, non-Hispanic	64.9	66.7	65.1	61.5	48.9	50.2	49.9	49.8	51.8	51.1	52.8
Hispanic	64.8	73.0	68.9	66.0	50.5	51.0	47.5	51.8	52.1	52.9	57.5
Below 50% poverty											
Total	**6.9**	**8.6**	**8.8**	**8.5**	**6.7**	**7.7**	**7.5**	**7.8**	**8.5**	**9.3**	**9.9**
Gender											
Male	6.9	8.6	8.8	8.4	6.6	7.3	7.5	7.8	8.4	9.0	10.0
Female	6.9	8.6	8.8	8.5	6.8	8.1	7.5	7.8	8.6	9.5	9.7
Age											
Ages 0–5	8.3	10.0	10.7	10.8	8.1	9.1	9.4	9.8	10.4	11.3	12.0
Ages 6–17	6.2	7.8	7.8	7.2	6.0	7.0	6.5	6.8	7.5	8.2	8.8
Race and Hispanic origin[a]											
White, non-Hispanic	4.3	5.0	5.0	3.9	3.7	4.1	4.3	4.3	4.5	5.0	5.1
Black, non-Hispanic	17.7	22.1	22.7	20.5	14.9	17.3	16.0	17.1	17.6	17.8	20.3
Hispanic	10.8	14.1	14.2	16.3	10.2	11.5	10.3	11.0	12.5	14.1	15.1
Region[b]											
Northeast	4.7	6.5	7.6	8.6	6.4	7.5	6.4	7.4	7.7	8.2	8.8
South	9.7	10.9	11.3	10.1	7.9	9.0	8.5	8.9	9.8	9.8	10.5
Midwest	6.3	9.5	8.9	6.6	5.5	6.5	7.3	7.4	8.4	9.7	9.7
West	5.1	5.6	6.1	7.8	6.2	7.0	6.8	6.7	7.1	8.8	9.8
Children in married-couple families, total	3.1	3.5	2.7	2.6	2.2	2.4	2.2	2.6	3.2	3.6	3.5
Ages 0–5	3.7	4.0	3.2	2.9	2.2	2.8	2.8	2.8	3.7	4.4	4.1
Ages 6–17	2.8	3.1	2.4	2.5	2.2	2.2	1.9	2.5	2.9	3.2	3.2
White, non-Hispanic	2.5	2.6	2.0	1.5	1.5	1.2	1.2	1.4	1.8	1.8	1.8
Black, non-Hispanic	4.2	5.2	3.9	2.5	2.9	4.5	2.8	4.3	4.4	5.7	5.8
Hispanic	6.2	7.4	6.7	8.6	4.5	5.2	4.7	5.5	6.2	7.5	7.5
Children in female-householder families, no husband present, total	22.3	27.0	28.7	24.4	19.7	22.5	21.6	21.7	23.0	23.2	25.5
Ages 0–5	31.4	35.8	37.7	34.3	28.4	29.4	29.7	30.5	31.3	30.4	33.3
Ages 6–17	18.8	23.2	24.2	19.7	16.1	19.6	18.0	17.7	19.0	19.8	21.8
White, non-Hispanic	15.3	17.5	21.1	14.5	13.4	16.4	17.0	16.7	15.9	17.6	18.6
Black, non-Hispanic	31.0	38.0	37.1	32.6	23.9	26.5	26.1	25.6	27.0	26.1	28.5
Hispanic	24.7	31.1	33.1	33.1	26.0	29.1	23.4	25.2	28.8	28.0	32.1

Not only are children overrepresented among the poor but also they arguably suffer more from the deprivations of poverty than do adults. Childhood poverty is a matter of great concern because strong evidence suggests that food insecurity and lack of good medical care caused by poverty can limit a child's physical and cognitive development. The higher incidence of poverty among children age five and younger is of particular concern to child

TABLE 2.2

Percentage of children ages 0–17 living below selected poverty levels, by selected characteristics, selected years 1980–2010 [CONTINUED]

Characteristic	1980	1985	1990	1995	2000	2005	2006	2007	2008	2009	2010
Below 150% poverty											
Total	**29.9**	**32.3**	**31.4**	**32.2**	**26.7**	**28.2**	**28.6**	**29.3**	**30.5**	**32.0**	**33.4**
Gender											
Male	29.6	32.2	31.3	31.7	26.6	28.0	28.4	29.2	30.4	31.9	33.5
Female	30.3	32.3	31.6	32.7	26.8	28.3	28.8	29.5	30.6	32.2	33.2
Age											
Ages 0–5	33.2	35.6	34.6	35.5	29.3	31.5	32.2	33.2	34.0	36.2	37.2
Ages 6–17	28.4	30.5	29.7	30.5	25.4	26.5	26.8	27.4	28.8	29.9	31.4
Race and Hispanic origin[a]											
White, non-Hispanic	21.7	22.6	21.4	20.1	16.4	17.2	17.7	17.8	19.0	19.8	20.6
Black, non-Hispanic	57.3	59.5	57.8	56.5	45.4	48.7	47.7	48.6	50.6	51.0	54.0
Hispanic	52.7	57.8	56.0	59.4	47.3	45.9	45.9	47.8	47.7	50.0	52.0
Region[b]											
Northeast	27.0	28.1	26.7	28.8	23.4	24.9	24.6	26.0	26.0	27.3	27.4
South	35.8	36.7	36.0	35.8	29.5	31.2	31.6	32.8	33.6	34.2	36.9
Midwest	26.0	31.0	28.7	26.8	21.8	25.0	26.5	26.3	28.7	30.5	30.8
West	27.9	30.4	31.4	35.0	29.3	28.8	28.7	29.0	30.5	33.4	34.2
Children in married-couple families, total	20.6	22.2	20.1	20.0	16.2	17.0	17.2	17.5	18.9	20.2	21.0
Ages 0–5	23.7	25.7	22.2	21.3	17.8	19.8	19.7	19.6	21.3	23.6	23.5
Ages 6–17	19.1	20.3	18.8	19.2	15.5	15.6	15.9	16.4	17.6	18.3	19.7
White, non-Hispanic	16.5	17.1	14.7	13.4	10.0	10.0	10.3	10.3	11.7	12.1	13.0
Black, non-Hispanic	34.6	37.1	31.6	25.3	20.0	22.9	22.2	20.3	23.0	26.0	27.0
Hispanic	43.4	47.3	46.6	49.8	39.4	38.5	37.4	38.9	38.6	41.1	42.6
Children in female-householder families, no husband present, total	66.7	68.1	67.6	65.7	57.6	58.9	59.6	60.5	61.6	61.4	63.3
Ages 0–5	79.1	77.4	77.1	75.3	67.2	68.8	69.6	71.2	70.8	70.3	73.0
Ages 6–17	62.0	64.1	62.9	61.0	53.7	54.7	55.2	55.6	57.2	57.2	58.7
White, non-Hispanic	53.6	54.4	56.1	50.1	45.1	47.8	49.1	49.3	50.2	49.9	50.2
Black, non-Hispanic	79.9	79.6	77.4	76.2	66.1	66.9	67.4	67.7	69.8	68.1	70.5
Hispanic	80.7	84.8	80.8	81.7	70.3	67.4	67.3	70.0	70.4	69.8	73.3
Below 200% poverty											
Total	**42.3**	**43.5**	**42.4**	**43.3**	**37.5**	**38.9**	**39.0**	**39.2**	**40.6**	**42.2**	**43.6**
Gender											
Male	42.3	43.2	42.5	43.1	37.5	38.6	38.8	39.1	40.4	41.9	43.6
Female	42.4	43.7	42.3	43.5	37.6	39.3	39.2	39.3	40.8	42.6	43.5
Age											
Ages 0–5	46.8	47.1	46.0	46.7	41.0	42.4	42.9	42.9	44.0	46.2	47.4
Ages 6–17	40.3	41.6	40.5	41.5	35.9	37.3	37.1	37.3	38.8	40.2	41.6
Race and Hispanic origin[a]											
White, non-Hispanic	33.8	33.6	32.3	30.5	25.5	26.2	26.3	26.2	27.3	28.7	29.2
Black, non-Hispanic	70.1	70.9	68.1	68.0	58.9	61.2	59.8	60.1	61.0	62.5	65.2
Hispanic	67.2	70.3	69.5	72.9	62.6	60.7	61.0	60.8	62.0	63.0	65.1
Region[b]											
Northeast	39.1	37.5	36.3	38.2	33.0	33.9	34.1	35.1	34.3	36.7	35.8
South	47.8	48.6	47.7	48.4	41.6	42.5	42.4	42.6	44.3	45.2	47.3
Midwest	39.1	42.5	39.6	36.9	31.2	35.3	35.9	36.4	38.4	40.2	40.9
West	40.5	41.7	42.7	46.1	40.5	40.5	40.1	39.4	41.1	43.3	45.3

advocates, given that the preschool years represent the most crucial period for brain development. In "Poverty during Early Childhood May Last a Lifetime" (*Discovery News*, February 22, 2010), Jessica Marshall reports on several studies that show that early childhood poverty actually causes changes in the brain that lead to problems in adulthood, including lower adult income.

Poverty is the largest predictor of child abuse and neglect, and children born into poverty, especially African-Americans and Hispanics, are disproportionately likely to end up in prison. The Children's Defense Fund argues in *America's Cradle to Prison Pipeline* (October 2007, http://www.childrensdefense.org/child-research-data-publications/data/cradle-prison-pipeline-report-2007-full-lowres.pdf) that poverty is the driving force behind what it calls the "Cradle to Prison Pipeline," a life cycle in which "so many poor and minority youths are and will remain trapped in a trajectory that leads to marginalized lives, imprisonment and premature death."

POVERTY AMONG THE ELDERLY. In contrast with children, senior citizens are underrepresented among the poor. DeNavas-Walt, Proctor, and Smith find that in 2011, 8.7% of

TABLE 2.2

Percentage of children ages 0–17 living below selected poverty levels, by selected characteristics, selected years 1980–2010 [CONTINUED]

Characteristic	1980	1985	1990	1995	2000	2005	2006	2007	2008	2009	2010
Children in married-couple families, total	33.2	33.9	31.4	31.1	26.4	27.0	26.7	26.3	28.4	30.0	30.8
Ages 0–5	38.1	38.1	34.5	33.2	29.2	30.2	30.1	29.0	31.3	33.7	33.5
Ages 6–17	30.8	31.6	29.6	29.9	25.1	25.4	24.9	25.0	26.9	28.0	29.3
White, non-Hispanic	28.3	27.8	25.4	23.3	18.2	18.1	17.7	17.4	19.0	20.3	20.6
Black, non-Hispanic	50.9	52.5	44.7	38.3	35.3	35.3	34.1	32.3	34.1	38.6	40.4
Hispanic	60.5	62.8	62.1	66.0	55.5	54.1	53.3	52.2	54.4	55.1	56.4
Children in female-householder families, no husband present, total	78.2	77.4	77.6	76.4	69.7	71.2	71.7	72.1	72.3	72.5	73.9
Ages 0–5	87.9	84.5	85.4	84.3	78.6	80.2	80.3	80.7	79.3	79.4	82.4
Ages 6–17	74.5	74.4	73.7	72.5	66.0	67.4	67.9	68.2	69.0	69.3	69.9
White, non-Hispanic	67.8	66.6	68.0	62.6	57.1	60.2	61.6	61.5	61.3	60.9	62.0
Black, non-Hispanic	89.1	87.1	85.7	86.9	78.4	78.8	78.9	79.0	79.5	79.3	80.2
Hispanic	87.3	89.9	89.1	88.6	82.5	80.6	80.1	81.3	80.6	81.0	83.8

[a]For race and Hispanic-origin data in this table: From 1980 to 2002, following the 1977 Office of Management and Budget (OMB) standards for collecting and presenting data on race, the Current Population Survey (CPS) asked respondents to choose one race from the following: white, black, American Indian or Alaskan Native, or Asian or Pacific Islander. An "Other" category was also offered. Beginning in 2003, the Current Population Survey (CPS) allowed respondents to select one or more race categories. All race groups discussed in this table from 2002 onward refer to people who indicated only one racial identity within the categories presented. For this reason data from 2002 onward are not directly comparable with data from earlier years. People who reported only one race are referred to as the race-alone population. The use of the race-alone population in this table does not imply that it is the preferred method of presenting or analyzing data. Data on race and Hispanic origin are collected separately. Persons of Hispanic origin may be of any race.

[b]Regions: Northeast includes CT, MA, ME, NH, NJ, NY, PA, RI, and VT. South includes AL, AR, DC, DE, FL, GA, KY, LA, MD, MS, NC, OK, SC, TN, TX, VA, and WV. Midwest includes IA, IL, IN, KS, MI, MN, MO, ND, NE, OH, SD, and WI. West includes AK, AZ, CA, CO, HI, ID, MT, NM, NV, OR, UT, WA, and WY.

Note: The 2004 data have been revised to reflect a correction to the weights in the 2005 Annual Social and Economic (ASEC) Supplement. Data for 1999, 2000, and 2001 use Census 2000 population controls. Data for 2000 onward are from the expanded (CPS) sample. The poverty level is based on money income and does not include noncash benefits, such as food stamps. Poverty thresholds reflect family size and composition and are adjusted each year using the annual average Consumer Price Index level. In 2010, the poverty threshold for a two-parent, two-child family was $22,113. The levels shown here are derived from the ratio of the family's income to the family's poverty threshold.

SOURCE: Adapted from "Table ECON1.A. Child Poverty: Percentage of Children Ages 0–17 Living below Selected Poverty Levels by Selected Characteristics, 1980–2010," in *America's Children in Brief: Key National Indicators of Well-Being, 2012*, Federal Interagency Forum on Child and Family Statistics, 2012, http://www.childstats.gov/americaschildren/tables.asp (accessed January 15, 2013)

TABLE 2.3

Median household income in the past 12 months, by race and Hispanic origin, 2011

	United States	
	Total	Median income (dollars)
Subject	Estimate	Estimate
Households	114,991,725	50,502
One race—		
White	78.0%	53,444
Black or African American	12.1%	33,223
American Indian and Alaska Native	0.7%	35,192
Asian	4.0%	67,885
Native Hawaiian and other Pacific Islander	0.1%	49,378
Some other race	3.3%	37,172
Two or more races	1.7%	44,115
Hispanic or Latino origin (of any race)	11.9%	39,589
White alone, not Hispanic or Latino	70.2%	55,305

SOURCE: Adapted from "S1903. Median Income in the Past 12 Months (in 2011 Inflation-Adjusted Dollars)," in *2011 American Community Survey 1-Year Estimates*, U.S. Census Bureau, 2012, http://factfinder2.census.gov/faces/tableservices/jsf/pages/productview.xhtml?pid=ACS_11_1YR_S1903&prodType=table (accessed January 15, 2013)

Social Security for the sharp decline in poverty among the elderly. Even though it was enacted in 1935, Social Security began paying substantially higher benefits in the era following World War II (1939–1945). Gary V. Engelhardt and Jonathan Gruber of the National Bureau of Economic Research maintain in *Social Security and the Evolution of Elderly Poverty* (May 2004, http://www.nber.org/papers/w10466.pdf) that increases in benefit levels between 1967 and 2000 account for the entirety of the reduction in poverty among the elderly.

Poverty rates among the elderly are the source of some dispute among analysts, however. Since the federal government's official poverty measure does not take into account out-of-pocket medical expenses, which are far higher on average for the elderly than for children and adults under the age of 65 years, many believe that the true poverty rate among the elderly is higher than Census Bureau estimates suggest. The Census Bureau has attempted to account for this issue in its formulation of the Supplemental Poverty Measure (SPM), which adjusts for expenses including out-of-pocket medical costs. According to Kathleen Short of the Census Bureau in *The Research Supplemental Poverty Measure: 2011* (November 2012, http://www.census.gov/hhes/povmeas/methodology/supplemental/research/Short_ResearchSPM2011.pdf), using the SPM to calculate poverty rates results in a poverty rate for the elderly of 15.1% in 2011, almost double the rate of elderly poverty

adults aged 65 years and older were poor, down from 8.9% the year before. (See Table 2.1.) Between 1959 and 2011 the number of people aged 65 years and older living in poverty dropped significantly, from a high of about 35% to current levels. (See Figure 1.2 in Chapter 1.) Most observers credit

FIGURE 2.1

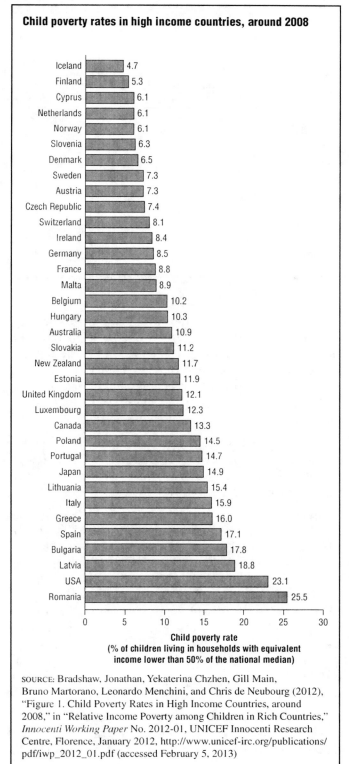

Child poverty rates in high income countries, around 2008

Country	Child poverty rate
Iceland	4.7
Finland	5.3
Cyprus	6.1
Netherlands	6.1
Norway	6.1
Slovenia	6.3
Denmark	6.5
Sweden	7.3
Austria	7.3
Czech Republic	7.4
Switzerland	8.1
Ireland	8.4
Germany	8.5
France	8.8
Malta	8.9
Belgium	10.2
Hungary	10.3
Australia	10.9
Slovakia	11.2
New Zealand	11.7
Estonia	11.9
United Kingdom	12.1
Luxembourg	12.3
Canada	13.3
Poland	14.5
Portugal	14.7
Japan	14.9
Lithuania	15.4
Italy	15.9
Greece	16.0
Spain	17.1
Bulgaria	17.8
Latvia	18.8
USA	23.1
Romania	25.5

Child poverty rate
(% of children living in households with equivalent
income lower than 50% of the national median)

SOURCE: Bradshaw, Jonathan, Yekaterina Chzhen, Gill Main, Bruno Martorano, Leonardo Menchini, and Chris de Neubourg (2012), "Figure 1. Child Poverty Rates in High Income Countries, around 2008," in "Relative Income Poverty among Children in Rich Countries," *Innocenti Working Paper* No. 2012-01, UNICEF Innocenti Research Centre, Florence, January 2012, http://www.unicef-irc.org/publications/pdf/iwp_2012_01.pdf (accessed February 5, 2013)

derived from the official measure (8.7%). (See Table 1.6 in Chapter 1.) Because there were no plans to use the SPM to administer government benefits as of 2013, it was unclear how or even if the disparity between the two measures of elderly poverty would affect public policy.

Urban Areas

According to the official poverty thresholds, people living in cities and rural areas experience poverty at similar rates, while suburban Americans are less likely than either to suffer from poverty. In 2011, 20% of people living in cities lived below the poverty line, as did 17% of rural Americans. (See Table 2.1.) However, only 11.3% of people who lived in suburban areas (inside metropolitan statistical areas but outside the densest population centers in those areas) lived below the poverty line.

Even though urban and rural areas have similar official poverty rates, there is substantial doubt about whether the two populations truly experience the same levels of poverty. Because of sometimes dramatic differences in the cost of living between rural and urban areas, which are not accounted for in the official poverty measure, the equivalence between these two rates has perhaps been overstated. The Census Bureau's SPM, which attempts to account for geographical variation in the cost of living, yields different rates of poverty than the official measure. Short indicates that according to the SPM, 21.7% of urban dwellers were poor in 2011, compared with 13.5% of rural Americans. The SPM also yields a higher rate of poverty among suburbanites, at 13.4%.

Family Status

In 2011 people living in families (13.1%) were much less likely than people living in unrelated subfamilies (43.4%) or in households with unrelated individuals (22.8%) to suffer from poverty. (See Table 2.1.) However, there was a major variation in the poverty rate between different family structures. Whereas 9.5 million families in the United States (11.8% of the total number of families) were living in poverty in 2011, families headed by married couples had the lowest poverty rate (6.2%). (See Table 2.4.) Almost one-third (31.2%) of families with a female householder (no husband present) were living in poverty, compared with 16.1% of households headed by a male with no wife present. Single parents were much more likely to have household incomes below the poverty line if they did not work full time.

SINGLE-PARENT FAMILIES. The proportion of single-parent families steadily increased between 1970 and the early 1990s, and the proportion of married-couple families correspondingly declined. Since then, the structure of U.S. households and families has remained relatively stable. According to the Census Bureau, there were 80.5 million families in the United States in 2012; of these, 58.9 million (73.2%) were headed by married couples. (See Table 2.5.) Of the remaining families, 5.9 million (7.3%) were single-parent households headed by men, and 15.7 million (19.5%) were single-parent households headed by women.

TABLE 2.4

Families in poverty, by type of family, 2010 and 2011

[Numbers in thousands. Families as of March of the following year.]

Characteristic	2010[a]			2011			Change in poverty (2011 less 2010)[b]	
		Below poverty			Below poverty			
	Total	Number	Percent	Total	Number	Percent	Number	Percent
Families								
Total	79,559	9,400	11.8	80,529	9,497	11.8	96	—
Type of family								
Married-couple	58,667	3,681	6.3	58,963	3,652	6.2	−29	−0.1
Female householder, no husband present	15,243	4,827	31.7	15,678	4,894	31.2	67	−0.4
Male householder, no wife present	5,649	892	15.8	5,888	950	16.1	58	0.3

—Represents or rounds to zero.
[a]Consistent with 2011 data through implementation of Census 2010-based population controls.
[b]Details may not sum to totals because of rounding.

SOURCE: Adapted from Carmen DeNavas-Walt, Bernadette D. Proctor, and Jessica C. Smith, "Table 4. Families in Poverty by Type of Family: 2010 and 2011," in *Income, Poverty, and Health Insurance Coverage in the United States: 2011*, U.S. Census Bureau, September 2012, http://www.census.gov/prod/2012pubs/p60-243.pdf (accessed January 15, 2013)

One factor in the rise of single-parent families is the rise in the divorce rate. Jason Fields of the Census Bureau indicates in *America's Families and Living Arrangements: 2003* (November 2004, http://www.census.gov/prod/2004pubs/p20-553.pdf) that in 1970 only 3.5% of men and 5.7% of women were separated or divorced. By 2012, 8.9% of men and 11.1% of women were divorced and had not remarried. (See Table 2.6.) The percentage of divorced women is consistently higher than the percentage of divorced men because divorced men are more likely to remarry, whereas divorced women are more likely to raise the children from the first marriage. As Table 2.7 shows, in 2009 there were an estimated 13.7 million custodial parents, or parents who were raising children in the absence of the second parent. Of these, 11.2 million were female, and 2.4 million were male; in other words, 82.2% of custodial parents were mothers.

Another reason for the rise in single-parent families is the rise in people who never marry yet still have children. According to the Census Bureau in *America's Families and Living Arrangements: 2003*, only 28.1% of males aged 15 years and older had never married in 1970; that figure stood at 34.2% by 2012. (See Table 2.6.) Likewise, the percentage of females aged 15 years and older who had never married rose from 22.1% in 1970 to 28.4% in 2012. The proportion of those who have never married has increased as young adults delay the age at which they marry. As Table 2.8 shows, the median age at first marriage, after remaining relatively stable between 1890 and 1970, rose dramatically for both men and women between 1970 and 2011. The median age of women at first marriage was 20.8 years in 1970 and 26.5 years in 2011; and the median age of men at first marriage was 23.2 years in 1970 and 28.7 years in 2011. In addition, the proportion of all households that were

unmarried-partner heterosexual households steadily rose between 1996 and 2010, from 2.9% to 6.4% of all households. As of 2012, there were 7.8 million households headed by opposite-sex unmarried couples; 3.2 million (40.4%) of these households had at least one biological child under the age of 18 years present. (See Table 2.9.)

Single-parent women were more likely than single-parent men to have never been married. In 2012, 47.4% of single mothers and 30.5% of single fathers had never been married. (See Table 2.10.)

African-American children are far more likely to live with a single parent than are non-Hispanic white or Hispanic children. In 2012, 4.5 million (34.9%) of a total 13 million African-American children (including those children who had both African-American and other racial characteristics) lived with married parents. Another 663,000 (5.1%) lived with unmarried parents who were both present; 6.4 million (49.3%) lived with their mother only; and 544,000 (4.2%) lived with their father only. (See Table 2.11.) In all, 53.5% of African-American children lived with one parent, and 32.9% lived with a single mother who had never been married.

By contrast, 10.4 million (59%) of a total 17.6 million Hispanic children lived with married parents, 4.9 million (28%) lived with their mother only, and 540,000 (3.1%) lived with their father only. (See Table 2.11.) An even smaller proportion of non-Hispanic white children lived with a single parent. In 2012, 28.8 million (73.7%) of a total 39.1 million non-Hispanic white children lived with married parents, 6.4 million (16.4%) lived with their mother only, and 1.7 million (4.3%) lived with their father only.

Moreover, in 2012 a higher percentage of African-American children than non-Hispanic white children or

TABLE 2.5

Households by type and selected characteristics, 2012

[Numbers in thousands]

	Total	Family households				Nonfamily households		
		Total	Married couple	Male householder	Female householder	Total	Male householder	Female householder
All households	121,084	80,506	58,949	5,888	15,669	40,578	19,195	21,383
Size of household								
One member	33,188	—	—	—	—	33,188	14,835	18,354
Two members	40,983	34,935	26,457	2,362	6,116	6,048	3,421	2,627
Three members	19,241	18,303	11,622	1,808	4,873	939	648	291
Four members	16,049	15,759	12,126	971	2,662	289	209	80
Five members	7,271	7,198	5,533	462	1,204	72	53	19
Six members	2,734	2,706	2,022	173	511	29	17	12
Seven or more members	1,617	1,604	1,190	112	303	13	13	0
Number of nonrelatives in household								
No nonrelatives	108,861	75,673	58,082	4,245	13,346	33,188	14,835	18,354
One nonrelative	10,211	4,163	675	1,385	2,104	6,048	3,421	2,627
Two nonrelatives	1,396	458	137	173	147	939	648	291
Three or more nonrelatives	615	212	56	85	71	403	292	111
Race of householder								
White alone	96,964	64,614	50,054	4,348	10,211	32,350	15,393	16,957
Black alone	15,583	9,651	4,361	956	4,334	5,933	2,661	3,271
Asian alone	5,374	4,149	3,298	320	531	1,225	598	628
All remaining single races and all race combinations	3,162	2,092	1,235	265	592	1,070	543	527
Hispanic origin of householder								
Hispanic[a]	14,939	11,585	7,222	1,277	3,086	3,353	1,818	1,535
White alone, non-Hispanic	83,573	54,146	43,376	3,231	7,539	29,426	13,792	15,635
Other non-Hispanic	22,572	14,774	8,351	1,380	5,043	7,798	3,585	4,213
White alone or combination householder								
White alone or in combination with one or more other races	98,551	65,642	50,700	4,443	10,500	32,908	15,660	17,249
Other	22,533	14,864	8,249	1,446	5,169	7,670	3,535	4,134
Black alone or combination householder								
Black alone or in combination with one or more other races	16,165	10,025	4,546	1,002	4,477	6,141	2,767	3,374
Other	104,919	70,481	54,403	4,886	11,192	34,438	16,429	18,009
Asian alone or combination householder								
Asian alone or in combination with one or more other races	5,705	4,342	3,435	334	573	1,362	677	685
Other	115,379	76,163	55,514	5,554	15,095	39,216	18,518	20,698
Marital status of householder								
Married, spouse present	58,949	58,949	58,949	—	—	—	—	—
Married, spouse absent[b]	2,057	910	—	263	647	1,146	671	475
Widowed	11,694	2,731	—	502	2,229	8,963	1,944	7,020
Divorced	18,801	7,007	—	1,833	5,174	11,794	5,934	5,860
Separated[c]	3,915	2,033	—	486	1,547	1,883	1,069	813
Never married	25,668	8,876	—	2,805	6,071	16,792	9,578	7,214
Tenure								
Own/buying	79,175	58,022	47,544	3,302	7,176	21,154	9,294	11,859
Rent	40,233	21,604	10,892	2,488	8,225	18,628	9,441	9,188
No cash rent	1,676	880	513	99	268	796	460	336

Dash ("—") represents or rounds to zero.
[a]Hispanics may be of any race.
[b]In past reports: Married spouse absent—other (excluding separated).
[c]In past reports: Married spouse absent—Separated.

SOURCE: "Table H1. Households by Type and Tenure of Householder for Selected Characteristics: 2012," in *America's Families and Living Arrangements: 2012*, U.S. Census Bureau, November 13, 2012, http://www.census.gov/hhes/families/data/cps2012.html (accessed January 15, 2013)

Hispanic children lived with neither parent. In that year, 853,000 (6.6%) African-American children, 563,000 (3.2%) Hispanic children, and 1.1 million (2.8%) non-Hispanic white children lived with neither parent. (See Table 2.11.) In part, this is because African-American children are more likely than children from other racial groups to live with grandparents without the presence of either parent; African-American children are also more likely than other children to live in foster care.

TABLE 2.6

Marital status of people aged 15 years and over, 2012

[Numbers in thousands, except for percentages]

All races	Total	Married spouse present	Married spouse absent	Widowed	Divorced	Separated	Never married	Total	Married spouse present	Married spouse absent	Widowed	Divorced	Separated	Never married
Both sexes				Number							Percent			
Total 15	247,573	122,095	3,568	14,058	24,911	5,668	77,273	100.0	49.3	1.4	5.7	10.1	2.3	31.2
Male														
Total 15	119,877	61,047	1,759	2,864	10,696	2,475	41,035	100.0	50.9	1.5	2.4	8.9	2.1	34.2
Female														
Total 15	127,695	61,047	1,809	11,193	14,215	3,193	36,238	100.0	47.8	1.4	8.8	11.1	2.5	28.4

Dash ("—") Represents or rounds to zero.
Note: Prior to 2001, this table included group quarters people. Hispanics may be of any race.

SOURCE: Adapted from "Table A1. Marital Status of People 15 Years and over, by Age, Sex, Personal Earnings, Race, and Hispanic Origin, 2012," in *America's Families and Living Arrangements: 2012*, U.S. Census Bureau, November 13, 2012, http://www.census.gov/hhes/families/data/cps2012.html (accessed January 15, 2013)

CHILD SUPPORT. Child support is becoming an increasingly important source of income for impoverished single parents because of the time limits in place for receiving cash assistance from the government. In *Custodial Mothers and Fathers and Their Child Support: 2009* (December 2011, http://www.census.gov/prod/2011 pubs/p60-240.pdf) Timothy S. Grall of the Census Bureau notes that in 2009, 50.6% of all custodial parents had either legally binding or informal child-support agreements in place. (See Table 2.7.) Likewise, 47% of custodial parents below the poverty line had agreements in place. Among custodial parents below the poverty line who received their full allotment of child-support payments, these payments represented 62.6% of their total income, on average.

A higher percentage of custodial mothers (54.9%) than fathers (30.4%) had custodial agreements in place in 2009. (See Table 2.7.) Both custodial mothers and fathers received, on average, far less than they were entitled to receive according to these agreements. The average amount of child support due to custodial mothers in 2009 was $5,997; they actually received an average of $3,702, or 61.7% of the total payments due them. The average amount of child support due to custodial fathers in 2007 was $5,601; they actually received an average of $3,059, or 54.6% of total payments due. Approximately 29.5% of custodial mothers and 27.1% of fathers with child-support agreements in place received no payments at all. Among custodial mothers and fathers living below the poverty line, the average award amount received was 52.9% of the total, and 33.7% of parents received no payments at all.

Studies indicate that a number of factors influence the rates of nonpayment of child support. Many researchers have focused specifically on fathers' willingness and ability to pay child support, since the overwhelming majority of custodial parents are mothers. According to Lenna Nepomnyaschy and Irwin Garfinkel in "Child Support Enforcement and Fathers' Contributions to Their Nonmarital Children" (*Social Service Review*, vol. 84, no. 3, September 2010), past studies have noted that a high level of trust between the parents correlates to higher levels of support payment. Additionally, fathers who have lived with the mother and child and fathers who maintain a regular visitation schedule with the child tend to satisfy their child-support obligations more fully than those who have not cohabited and/or do not regularly see their child. Studies also show that child-support payments sometimes decline over time, especially when fathers have new biological children and when mothers move on to new romantic relationships and/or have new biological children.

Child support can be either informal or formal. Informal child-support agreements, wherein the father gives the mother money and in-kind awards without any legal encumbrances, are common during the first 15 months after a child is born. Studies show that informal support tends to decline over time and that formal child-support agreements, which are legally enforceable, become more important sources of income for custodial mothers beginning at 45 months after the child's birth. Enforcement of formal child-support agreements varies by state. Whether strong child-support enforcement, as is common in some states, leads to better outcomes for custodial mothers and their children has not been established, in part because strong enforcement is associated with declines in informal support.

Custodial parents are more likely to be poor than other Americans, and custodial mothers are significantly more likely to be poor than custodial fathers. According to Grall, between 1993 and 2001 the percentage of

TABLE 2.7

Demographic characteristics of custodial parents by award status and payments received, 2009

[Numbers in thousands, as of spring 2010. Parents living with own children under 21 years of age whose other parent is not living in the home.]

		With child support agreements or awards									
					Due child support payments in 2009						
					Average due (in dollars)	Average received (in dollars)	Percent received	Received all payments		Did not receive payments	
Characteristic	Total	Total	Percent	Total				Total	Percent	Total	Percent
All custodial parents											
Total	13,672	6,914	50.6	5,897	5,955	3,634	61.0	2,428	41.2	1,724	29.2
Sex											
Male	2,435	740	30.4	619	5,601	3,059	54.6	211	34.1	168	27.1
Female	11,237	6,174	54.9	5,278	5,997	3,702	61.7	2,217	42.0	1,555	29.5
Age											
Under 30 years	3,304	1,458	44.1	1,210	3,881	2,180	56.2	444	36.7	391	32.3
30 to 39 years	4,924	2,667	54.2	2,357	5,529	2,825	51.1	880	37.3	720	30.5
40 years and over	5,444	2,789	51.2	2,330	5,208	2,330	44.7	1,104	47.4	612	26.3
Race and ethnicity[a]											
White alone	9,538	5,053	53.0	4,321	6,545	4,151	63.4	1,876	43.4	1,179	27.3
White alone, not Hispanic	7,127	3,976	55.8	3,410	6,754	4,136	61.2	1,517	44.5	927	27.2
Black alone	3,439	1,534	44.6	1,295	4,026	1,899	47.2	430	33.2	492	38.0
Hispanic (any race)	2,662	1,181	44.4	1,004	5,806	4,217	72.6	412	41.0	274	27.3
Current marital status[b]											
Married	2,515	1,320	52.5	1,152	5,536	3,429	61.9	527	45.7	288	25.0
Divorced	4,589	2,719	59.3	2,388	7,102	4,736	66.7	1,037	43.4	627	26.3
Separated	1,679	699	41.6	529	5,782	3,025	52.3	213	40.3	176	33.3
Never married	4,737	2,096	44.2	1,763	4,709	2,420	51.4	611	34.7	603	34.2
Educational attainment											
Less than high school diploma	1,998	844	42.2	708	4,528	1,939	42.8	214	30.2	291	41.1
High school graduate	4,555	2,129	46.7	1,796	5,728	3,335	58.2	740	41.2	486	27.1
Less than 4 years of college	4,825	2,656	55.0	2,289	6,038	3,975	65.8	1,107	48.4	555	24.2
Bachelor's degree or more	2,294	1,285	56.0	1,105	7,070	4,501	63.7	474	42.9	255	23.1
Selected characteristics											
Family income below 2009 poverty level	3,876	1,823	47.0	1,524	4,905	2,593	52.9	550	36.1	513	33.7
Worked full-time, year-round	6,772	3,545	52.3	3,078	6,129	3,382	55.2	1,306	42.4	868	28.2
Public assistance program participation[c]	5,149	2,495	48.5	2,093	5,104	2,931	57.4	771	36.8	671	32.1
With one child	7,819	3,584	45.8	2,996	5,537	3,387	61.2	1,241	41.4	838	28.0
With two or more children	5,853	3,330	56.9	2,901	6,387	3,889	60.9	1,186	40.9	885	30.5
Child had contact with other parent in 2009	9,138	4,979	54.5	4,301	6,070	4,262	70.2	2,043	47.5	1,014	23.6

[a]Includes those reporting one race alone and not in combination with any other race.
[b]Excludes 153,000 with marital status of widowed.
[c]Received either Medicaid, food stamps, public housing or rent subsidy, Temporary Assistance for Needy Families (TANF), or general assistance.

SOURCE: Timothy S. Grall, "Table 2. Demographic Characteristics of Custodial Parents by Award Status and Payments Received: 2009," in *Custodial Mothers and Fathers and Their Child Support: 2009*, U.S. Census Bureau, December 2011, http://www.census.gov/prod/2011pubs/p60-240.pdf (accessed January 15, 2013)

custodial parents and their children living below the poverty level declined from 33.3% to 23.4%, and then remained statistically unchanged between 2001 and 2007. (See Figure 2.2.) The Great Recession led to an increase in poverty among custodial parents, with the poverty rate among them rising to 28.3% by 2009, roughly twice the poverty rate among the U.S. population at large (14.3%) at that time. The poverty rate among custodial mothers was 30.4% in 2009, compared with 18.8% for custodial fathers. This disproportion in the poverty rates is compounded by the imbalance in the number of custodial mothers and fathers. In 2009 there were 11.2 million custodial mothers and 2.4 million custodial fathers; thus,

approximately 4.2 million custodial mothers lived below the poverty line, compared with approximately 458,000 custodial fathers.

By Race

As previously stated, the poverty rate differs among racial and ethnic groups. DeNavas-Walt, Proctor, and Smith find that in 2011 non-Hispanic whites had the lowest rate, at 9.8%, followed by Asian-Americans, at 12.3%. (See Table 2.1.) In contrast, more than a quarter of Hispanics (25.3%) and African-Americans (27.6%) lived in poverty. In addition, African-Americans and Hispanics were much more likely to be desperately poor or have incomes below

TABLE 2.8

Median age at first marriage, by sex, 1890–2011

Year	Men	Women
2011	28.7	26.5
2010	28.2	26.1
2009	28.1	25.9
2008	27.6	25.9
2007	27.5	25.6
2006	27.5	25.5
2005	27.1	25.3
2004	27.4	25.3
2003	27.1	25.3
2002	26.9	25.3
2001	26.9	25.1
2000	26.8	25.1
1999	26.9	25.1
1998	26.7	25.0
1997	26.8	25.0
1996	27.1	24.8
1995	26.9	24.5
1994	26.7	24.5
1993	26.5	24.5
1992	26.5	24.4
1991	26.3	24.1
1990	26.1	23.9
1989	26.2	23.8
1988	25.9	23.6
1987	25.8	23.6
1986	25.7	23.1
1985	25.5	23.3
1984	25.4	23.0
1983	25.4	22.8
1982	25.2	22.5
1981	24.8	22.3
1980	24.7	22.0
1979	24.4	22.1
1978	24.2	21.8
1977	24.0	21.6
1976	23.8	21.3
1975	23.5	21.1
1974	23.1	21.1
1973	23.2	21.0
1972	23.3	20.9
1971	23.1	20.9
1970	23.2	20.8
1969	23.2	20.8
1968	23.1	20.8
1967	23.1	20.6
1966	22.8	20.5
1965	22.8	20.6
1964	23.1	20.5
1963	22.8	20.5
1962	22.7	20.3
1961	22.8	20.3
1960	22.8	20.3
1959	22.5	20.2
1958	22.6	20.2
1957	22.6	20.3
1956	22.5	20.1
1955	22.6	20.2
1954	23.0	20.3
1953	22.8	20.2
1952	23.0	20.2
1951	22.9	20.4
1950	22.8	20.3
1949	22.7	20.3
1948	23.3	20.4
1947	23.7	20.5
1940	24.3	21.5
1930	24.3	21.3
1920	24.6	21.2
1910	25.1	21.6
1900	25.9	21.9
1890	26.1	22.0

TABLE 2.8

Median age at first marriage, by sex, 1890–2011 [CONTINUED]

Notes: Figures for 1947 to present are based on Current Population Survey data. Figures for years prior to 1947 are based on decennial censuses.

SOURCE: "Table MS-2. Estimated Median Age at First Marriage, by Sex: 1890 to the Present," U.S. Census Bureau, http://www.census.gov/population/socdemo/hh-fam/ms2.xls (accessed February 5, 2013)

0.50 of the poverty level; 12.8% of African-Americans and 10.5% of Hispanics were desperately poor in 2011. (See Table 1.4 in Chapter 1.) Non-Hispanic whites (4.4%) and Asian-Americans (5.5%) had much lower rates of desperate poverty.

Work Experience

The probability of a family living in poverty is influenced by three primary factors: the size of the family, the number of workers, and the characteristics of the wage earners. As the number of wage earners in a family increases, the probability of poverty declines. The likelihood of a second wage earner is greatest in families that are headed by married couples.

In 2010 most Americans aged 16 years and older worked at some point during the year (158.9 million of 239 million, or 66.5%). (See Table 2.12.) Approximately 8.1% of all Americans who worked at some point during the year lived in poverty, compared with 23% of those who did not work that year. The rate of poverty was higher in 2010 for those who worked only 26 weeks or less (20%) than for those who worked 27 weeks or more (7.2%). However, the poverty rate among individuals who worked 27 weeks or more was up significantly from 2007, when it was 5.1%. (See Table 2.13.)

Most poor children live in families in which one or more adults work. However, millions of working parents are not able to earn enough to lift their families out of poverty—even those who work full time all year.

Education

Not surprisingly, poverty rates drop sharply as years of schooling rise. The U.S. Bureau of Labor Statistics reports in *Highlights of Women's Earnings in 2011* (October 2012, http://www.bls.gov/cps/cpswom2011.pdf) that in 2011 the median weekly earnings for men aged 25 years and older who had not completed high school was $488; for women it was $395, or 80.9% of what their male peers earned. Men and women at this level of education collectively earned approximately two-fifths what their counterparts with bachelor's degrees or higher earned. Men with a four-year college degree earned a median of $1,332 per week, whereas women earned $998 (74.9% of what males earned). Those men and women who had a high school diploma but no college degree earned roughly half of what

TABLE 2.9

Opposite-sex unmarried couples, by selected characteristics, 2012

[Numbers in thousands]

	Total		No biological children		At least one biological child under 18, of either partner	
All opposite sex unmarried couples	**N**	**%**	**N**	**%**	**N**	**%**
Total	7,845	100.0	4,678	100.0	3,166	100.0
Age of male partner						
15–24 years	1,124	14.3	728	15.6	395	12.5
25–29 years	1,577	20.1	860	18.4	717	22.6
30–34 years	1,273	16.2	609	13.0	664	21.0
35–39 years	825	10.5	360	7.7	464	14.7
40–44 years	738	9.4	355	7.6	382	12.1
45–49 years	639	8.1	353	7.5	286	9.0
50–54 years	538	6.9	414	8.8	124	3.9
55–64 years	755	9.6	647	13.8	108	3.4
65+ years	378	4.8	352	7.5	26	0.8
Age of female partner						
15–24 years	1,723	22.0	1,004	21.5	719	22.7
25–29 years	1,677	21.4	905	19.4	771	24.4
30–34 years	1,046	13.3	428	9.1	619	19.5
35–39 years	706	9.0	263	5.6	443	14.0
40–44 years	696	8.9	356	7.6	340	10.8
45–49 years	612	7.8	457	9.8	155	4.9
50–54 years	490	6.2	401	8.6	89	2.8
55–64 years	646	8.2	623	13.3	23	0.7
65+ years	249	3.2	242	5.2	7	0.2
Age difference						
Male 10+ years older than female	852	10.9	464	9.9	388	12.2
Male 6–9 years older than female	1,010	12.9	552	11.8	458	14.5
Male 4–5 years older than female	850	10.8	473	10.1	377	11.9
Male 2–3 years older than female	1,386	17.7	791	16.9	595	18.8
Male and female within 1 year	2,234	28.5	1,408	30.1	826	26.1
Female 2–3 years older than male	526	6.7	336	7.2	190	6.0
Female 4–5 years older than male	303	3.9	180	3.9	123	3.9
Female 6–9 years older than male	364	4.6	246	5.3	118	3.7
Female 10+ years older than male	318	4.1	227	4.9	91	2.9
Race of male partner						
White alone—non-Hispanic	4,962	63.3	3,349	71.6	1,613	51.0
Black alone—non-Hispanic	1,009	12.9	534	11.4	475	15.0
Hispanic[a]	1,468	18.7	563	12.0	906	28.6
All remaining single races and all race combinations, non-Hispanic	405	5.2	233	5.0	172	5.4
Race of female partner						
White alone—non-Hispanic	5,072	64.7	3,368	72.0	1,704	53.8
Black alone—non-Hispanic	803	10.2	436	9.3	367	11.6
Hispanic[a]	1,446	18.4	553	11.8	894	28.2
All remaining single races and all race combinations, non-Hispanic	523	6.7	322	6.9	201	6.4
Race difference[b]						
Both white alone—non-Hispanic	4,472	57.0	3,024	64.6	1,448	45.7
Both black alone—non-Hispanic	738	9.4	399	8.5	338	10.7
Both other alone or any combination—non-Hispanic	244	3.1	135	2.9	109	3.5
Both Hispanic	1,103	14.1	358	7.7	745	23.5
Neither Hispanic	579	7.4	363	7.8	216	6.8
One Hispanic, other non-Hispanic	708	9.0	399	8.5	309	9.8
Race of male partner						
White alone	6,242	79.6	3,858	82.5	2,383	75.3
Black alone	1,094	13.9	554	11.8	541	17.1
Asian alone	197	2.5	114	2.4	83	2.6
All remaining single races and all race combinations	312	4.0	152	3.3	160	5.0

college-educated men and women did, and those with an associate's degree or some amount of college education had weekly earnings equaling roughly two-thirds the earnings of their counterparts with college degrees.

Education alone does not necessarily correlate with avoidance of poverty, however. Sophia Addy, Will Engelhardt, and Curtis Skinner indicate in the fact sheet "Basic Facts about Low-Income Children: Children under 18 Years,

TABLE 2.9

Opposite-sex unmarried couples, by selected characteristics, 2012 [CONTINUED]

[Numbers in thousands]

	Total		Presence of biological children			
			No biological children		At least one biological child under 18, of either partner	
All opposite sex unmarried couples	N	%	N	%	N	%
Race of female partner						
White alone	6,305	80.4	3,858	82.5	2,447	77.3
Black alone	920	11.7	466	10.0	454	14.3
Asian alone	253	3.2	159	3.4	93	3.0
All remaining single races and all race combinations	367	4.7	195	4.2	173	5.5
Race difference						
Both white alone	5,942	75.7	3,664	78.3	2,277	71.9
Both black alone	856	10.9	434	9.3	422	13.3
Both Asian alone	162	2.1	89	1.9	74	2.3
Both other alone or any comb.	167	2.1	71	1.5	97	3.1
Partners identify as different races	717	9.1	421	9.0	296	9.4
Origin of male partner						
Hispanic	1,468	18.7	563	12.0	906	28.6
Non-Hispanic	6,376	81.3	4,116	88.0	2,261	71.4
Origin of female partner						
Hispanic	1,446	18.4	553	11.8	894	28.2
Non-Hispanic	6,398	81.6	4,126	88.2	2,272	71.8
Origin difference						
Neither Hispanic	6,033	76.9	3,921	83.8	2,112	66.7
Both Hispanic	1,103	14.1	358	7.7	745	23.5
Male Hispanic, female not	365	4.7	205	4.4	160	5.1
Female Hispanic, male not	343	4.4	194	4.2	149	4.7
Labor force status of male partner						
Not in labor force	1,240	15.8	876	18.7	364	11.5
In labor force	6,605	84.2	3,803	81.3	2,802	88.5
Labor force status of female partner						
Not in labor force	2,096	26.7	1,091	23.3	1,005	31.7
In labor force	5,749	73.3	3,587	76.7	2,162	68.3
Labor force difference						
Both in labor force	5,090	64.9	3,159	67.5	1,931	61.0
Only male in labor force	1,515	19.3	643	13.8	872	27.5
Only female in labor force	658	8.4	428	9.1	231	7.3
Neither in labor force	581	7.4	448	9.6	133	4.2
Employment of male partner						
Not employed	1,978	25.2	1,271	27.2	707	22.3
Employed	5,867	74.8	3,407	72.8	2,459	77.7
Employment of female partner						
Not employed	2,684	34.2	1,386	29.6	1,298	41.0
Employed	5,160	65.8	3,292	70.4	1,868	59.0
Employment difference						
Both in labor force—both employed	4,199	53.5	2,695	57.6	1,505	47.5
Both in labor force—only male employed	398	5.1	197	4.2	201	6.3
Both in labor force—only female employed	391	5.0	219	4.7	172	5.4
Both in labor force—both unemployed	102	1.3	49	1.0	54	1.7
Male in labor force—male employed	1,270	16.2	516	11.0	754	23.8
Male in labor force—male unemployed	245	3.1	127	2.7	118	3.7
Female in labor force—female employed	571	7.3	378	8.1	192	6.1
Female in labor force—female unemployed	88	1.1	49	1.1	39	1.2
Not in labor force—not employed	581	7.4	448	9.6	133	4.2
Male education						
Not high school graduate	1,152	14.7	462	9.9	690	21.8
High school graduate	3,062	39.0	1,701	36.4	1,361	43.0
Some college	2,130	27.2	1,300	27.8	831	26.2
Bachelor's degree or higher	1,501	19.1	1,216	26.0	285	9.0

2011" (January 2013, http://www.nccp.org/publications/pdf/ text_1074.pdf) that a majority of children who live in low-income or poor families have parents without any college education. Among children living below the poverty line in 2011, 30% of parents had no high school diploma, and 31% had a high school diploma but no college education. Perhaps surprisingly, a substantial proportion (39%) of poor children had parents with some college education.

TABLE 2.9

Opposite-sex unmarried couples, by selected characteristics, 2012 [CONTINUED]

[Numbers in thousands]

	Total		Presence of biological children			
			No biological children		At least one biological child under 18, of either partner	
All opposite sex unmarried couples	N	%	N	%	N	%
Female education						
Not high school graduate	1,012	12.9	429	9.2	583	18.4
High school graduate	2,474	31.5	1,384	29.6	1,090	34.4
Some college	2,622	33.4	1,508	32.2	1,114	35.2
Bachelor's degree or higher	1,737	22.1	1,358	29.0	379	12.0
Education difference						
Neither has Bachelor's degree	5,571	71.0	2,945	62.9	2,627	83.0
One has Bachelor's degree, other has less	1,309	16.7	894	19.1	415	13.1
Both have Bachelor's degree or more	964	12.3	840	17.9	124	3.9
Personal earnings of male partner						
Under $5,000 or loss	335	4.3	181	3.9	153	4.8
Without income	1,385	17.7	939	20.1	446	14.1
$5,000 to $9,999	381	4.9	204	4.4	177	5.6
$10,000 to $14,999	527	6.7	298	6.4	229	7.2
$15,000 to $19,999	554	7.1	296	6.3	258	8.1
$20,000 to $24,999	619	7.9	342	7.3	276	8.7
$25,000 to $29,999	612	7.8	332	7.1	281	8.9
$30,000 to $39,999	1,041	13.3	588	12.6	453	14.3
$40,000 to $49,999	756	9.6	431	9.2	324	10.2
$50,000 to $74,999	965	12.3	606	13.0	358	11.3
$75,000 to $99,999	350	4.5	228	4.9	123	3.9
$100,000 and over	320	4.1	232	5.0	88	2.8
Personal earnings of female partner						
Under $5,000 or loss	504	6.4	239	5.1	265	8.4
Without income	2,130	27.2	1,126	24.1	1,004	31.7
$5,000 to $9,999	535	6.8	280	6.0	255	8.0
$10,000 to $14,999	629	8.0	362	7.7	267	8.4
$15,000 to $19,999	605	7.7	348	7.4	258	8.1
$20,000 to $24,999	583	7.4	353	7.6	230	7.3
$25,000 to $29,999	484	6.2	308	6.6	176	5.6
$30,000 to $39,999	925	11.8	626	13.4	299	9.4
$40,000 to $49,999	502	6.4	348	7.4	154	4.9
$50,000 to $74,999	625	8.0	444	9.5	181	5.7
$75,000 to $99,999	165	2.1	123	2.6	42	1.3
$100,000 and over	157	2.0	122	2.6	35	1.1
Personal earnings difference						
Male earns $50,000+ more	687	8.8	410	8.8	277	8.8
Male earns $30,000–$49,999 more	850	10.8	421	9.0	429	13.6
Male earns $10,000–$29,999 more	1,825	23.3	955	20.4	870	27.5
Male earns $5,000–$9,999 more	613	7.8	380	8.1	233	7.4
Male earns within $4,999 of female	1,912	24.4	1,252	26.8	660	20.8
Female earns $5,000–$9,999 more	409	5.2	230	4.9	178	5.6
Female earns $10,000–$29,999 more	1,000	12.7	638	13.6	362	11.4
Female earns $30,000–$49,999 more	303	3.9	218	4.7	85	2.7
Female earns $50,000+ more	246	3.1	174	3.7	71	2.2

Dash ("—") represents or rounds to zero.
Note: Excludes ever-married children under 18 years.
[a]Hispanics may be of any race.
[b]"White" refers to non-Hispanic white alone, "black" to non-Hispanic black alone, and "other" to non-Hispanic other alone or in comb.

SOURCE: "Table UC3. Opposite Sex Unmarried Couples by Presence of Biological Children under 18, and Age, Earnings, Education, and Race and Hispanic Origin of Both Partners: 2012," in *America's Families and Living Arrangements: 2012*, U.S. Census Bureau, November 13, 2012, http://www.census.gov/hhes/families/data/cps2012.html (accessed January 16, 2013).

GOVERNMENT ASSISTANCE

The demand for welfare assistance increased sharply during the 1990s. However, because of decreased funding and welfare reform measures that gave states more flexibility in dispersing benefits, a smaller proportion of eligible families actually received benefits. In the fact sheet "A Decade of Welfare Reform: Facts and Figures— Assessing the New Federalism" (June 2006, http://www.urban.org/UploadedPDF/900980_welfarereform.pdf), the Urban Institute explains that the number of eligible families enrolled in welfare programs decreased from 80% in 1996 to 48% in 2002. Some were ineligible because they had assets such as a car or a savings account that brought them above permitted limits. Others did not know they were

TABLE 2.10

Single-parent family groups with own children under 18, by marital status and demographic characteristics, 2012

[Numbers in thousands]

	All one-parent unmarried family groups		Maintained by father										Maintained by mother									
			Total		Never married		Divorced		Separated*		Widowed		Total		Never Married		Divorced		Separated*		Widowed	
	N	%	N	%	N	%	N	%	N	%	N	%	N	%	N	%	N	%	N	%	N	%
All family groups	12,279	100.0	1,956	100.0	598	30.5	869	44.4	394	20.1	96	4.9	10,322	100.0	4,892	47.4	3,186	30.9	1,900	18.4	345	3.3
Region																						
Northeast	2,014	16.4	281	100.0	107	38.0	114	40.5	55	19.6	5	1.8	1,734	100.0	856	49.4	489	28.2	339	19.5	50	2.9
Midwest	2,679	21.8	452	100.0	138	30.4	221	48.9	72	15.9	21	4.7	2,227	100.0	1,091	49.0	730	32.8	330	14.8	76	3.4
South	4,895	39.9	716	100.0	204	28.5	305	42.6	163	22.7	44	6.2	4,178	100.0	2,035	48.7	1,232	29.5	778	18.6	133	3.2
West	2,691	21.9	506	100.0	149	29.4	228	45.0	104	20.6	25	4.9	2,185	100.0	910	41.7	735	33.6	453	20.7	87	4.0
Size of family group																						
Two members	5,445	44.3	1,058	100.0	387	36.6	463	43.8	166	15.7	42	3.9	4,388	100.0	2,377	54.2	1,277	29.1	622	14.2	112	2.5
Three members	3,975	32.4	624	100.0	142	22.8	306	49.0	140	22.4	36	5.8	3,350	100.0	1,400	41.8	1,178	35.2	654	19.5	118	3.5
Four members	1,769	14.4	207	100.0	54	26.0	78	37.7	64	30.9	11	5.4	1,561	100.0	641	41.1	502	32.1	359	23.0	59	3.8
Five members	698	5.7	50	100.0	11	21.9	17	35.2	16	31.8	6	11.1	650	100.0	305	47.0	148	22.7	156	24.0	41	6.3
Six or more members	392	3.2	16	100.0	3	20.4	4	22.5	8	49.6	1	7.5	375	100.0	169	45.1	82	21.8	109	29.1	15	4.0
Age of reference person																						
Under 20 years	236	1.9	11	100.0	9	81.0	2	19.0	—	—	—	—	224	100.0	211	94.0	1	0.5	12	5.5	—	—
20–24 years	1,354	11.0	77	100.0	66	85.9	2	2.9	7	8.9	2	2.3	1,277	100.0	1,078	84.4	39	3.1	159	12.4	1	0.1
25–29 years	1,759	14.3	200	100.0	143	71.4	31	15.6	23	11.4	3	1.6	1,558	100.0	1,083	69.5	224	14.4	239	15.3	12	0.8
30–34 years	2,210	18.0	320	100.0	145	45.3	99	30.8	75	23.5	1	0.3	1,890	100.0	1,026	54.3	492	26.1	360	19.1	12	0.6
35–39 years	2,225	18.1	368	100.0	99	27.0	183	49.7	70	19.0	16	4.3	1,857	100.0	678	36.5	692	37.2	438	23.6	49	2.7
40–44 years	1,866	15.2	358	100.0	59	16.5	202	56.3	91	25.5	6	1.6	1,508	100.0	375	24.9	723	47.9	327	21.7	83	5.5
45–54 years	2,173	17.7	479	100.0	60	12.4	280	58.6	99	20.7	40	8.3	1,695	100.0	372	21.9	881	52.0	316	18.7	126	7.4
55+ years	457	3.7	146	100.0	18	12.2	70	48.0	29	20.0	29	19.8	312	100.0	69	22.0	133	42.7	48	15.3	62	19.9
Family income																						
Family income under $10,000	2,142	17.4	151	100.0	67	44.2	57	37.6	20	13.5	7	4.8	1,990	100.0	1,170	58.8	416	20.9	372	18.7	32	1.6
$10,000 to $14,999	1,043	8.5	101	100.0	29	28.9	38	37.4	30	30.0	4	3.7	942	100.0	509	54.1	206	21.9	200	21.2	27	2.8
$15,000 to $19,999	1,021	8.3	141	100.0	58	41.3	48	34.0	30	21.3	5	3.4	880	100.0	442	50.2	208	23.6	200	22.7	30	3.4
$20,000 to $24,999	1,040	8.5	148	100.0	57	38.7	38	25.5	35	23.6	18	12.2	892	100.0	457	51.2	248	27.8	167	18.8	20	2.2
$25,000 to $29,999	967	7.9	113	100.0	42	37.3	43	37.7	24	21.1	4	3.8	854	100.0	375	43.9	290	34.0	158	18.5	31	3.6
$30,000 to $39,999	1,617	13.2	268	100.0	77	28.8	125	46.5	58	21.8	8	2.8	1,350	100.0	582	43.1	471	34.9	247	18.3	50	3.7
$40,000 to $49,999	1,118	9.1	218	100.0	61	27.9	108	49.7	40	18.4	9	4.1	900	100.0	391	43.5	324	36.0	159	17.7	26	2.9
$50,000 to $74,999	1,748	14.2	437	100.0	111	25.3	227	51.9	82	18.7	17	4.0	1,311	100.0	499	38.1	532	40.6	221	16.8	59	4.5
$75,000 to $99,999	697	5.7	160	100.0	41	25.6	77	48.2	34	21.3	8	4.9	537	100.0	218	40.6	213	39.6	81	15.1	25	4.7
$100,000 and over	887	7.2	219	100.0	54	24.7	109	49.6	40	18.4	16	7.2	667	100.0	248	37.2	278	41.7	95	14.3	46	6.8
Poverty status																						
Below poverty level	4,311	35.1	352	100.0	131	37.2	122	34.7	85	24.1	14	4.0	3,960	100.0	2,225	56.2	839	21.2	808	20.4	88	2.2
At or above poverty level	7,968	64.9	1,606	100.0	467	29.1	747	46.5	310	19.3	82	5.1	6,362	100.0	2,667	41.9	2,346	36.9	1,092	17.2	257	4.0
Number of own children under 18																						
One own child under 18	6,872	56.0	1,256	100.0	434	34.6	547	43.6	214	17.0	61	4.9	5,616	100.0	2,860	50.9	1,731	30.8	824	14.7	201	3.6
Two own children under 18	3,603	29.3	531	100.0	124	23.3	259	48.7	123	23.2	25	4.8	3,073	100.0	1,283	41.8	1,036	33.7	660	21.5	94	3.0
Three own children under 18	1,282	10.4	147	100.0	33	22.3	53	36.5	51	34.7	10	6.5	1,136	100.0	485	42.7	344	30.3	271	23.9	36	3.2
Four or more own children under 18	521	4.2	24	100.0	7	30.3	10	41.1	7	28.6	—	—	497	100.0	264	53.1	74	14.9	145	29.2	14	2.8

TABLE 2.10

Single-parent family groups with own children under 18, by marital status and demographic characteristics, 2012 [CONTINUED]

[Numbers in thousands]

	All one-parent unmarried family groups		Maintained by father										Maintained by mother										
			Total		Never married		Divorced		Separated*		Widowed		Total		Never Married		Divorced		Separated*		Widowed	
	N	%	N	%	N	%	N	%	N	%	N	%	N	%	N	%	N	%	N	%	N	%
Own children 6–17 years																						
Without own children 6–17	3,020	24.6	367	100.0	230	62.7	85	23.1	47	12.8	5	1.4	2,653	100.0	1,981	74.6	326	12.3	331	12.5	15	0.6
One own child 6–17	5,563	45.3	1,052	100.0	271	25.7	514	48.9	211	20.1	56	5.3	4,511	100.0	1,773	39.3	1,695	37.6	837	18.6	206	4.6
Two own children 6–17	2,744	22.3	437	100.0	74	17.0	232	53.1	104	23.8	27	6.1	2,307	100.0	792	34.3	921	39.9	509	22.1	85	3.7
Three own children 6–17	743	6.0	95	100.0	21	22.0	35	36.7	31	32.5	8	8.8	649	100.0	253	39.1	210	32.4	159	24.5	27	4.1
Four or more own children 6–17	210	1.7	7	100.0	2	29.1	3	46.2	2	24.7	—	—	203	100.0	93	46.0	34	16.7	64	31.5	12	5.8
Own children 12–17 years																						
Without own children 12–17	6,565	53.5	958	100.0	425	44.3	352	36.7	162	16.9	19	2.0	5,606	100.0	3,414	60.9	1,177	21.0	926	16.5	89	1.6
One own child 12–17	4,342	35.4	799	100.0	154	19.3	415	51.9	171	21.4	59	7.4	3,543	100.0	1,108	31.3	1,487	42.0	755	21.3	193	5.4
Two own children 12–17	1,202	9.8	191	100.0	16	8.5	100	52.3	60	31.2	15	8.0	1,011	100.0	316	31.3	469	46.4	173	17.1	53	5.2
Three or more own children 12–17	170	1.4	8	100.0	2	30.2	2	28.6	2	19.2	2	22.0	162	100.0	53	32.9	52	32.0	46	28.4	11	6.7
Own children 6–11 years																						
Without own children 6–11	6,956	56.7	1,128	100.0	349	30.9	502	44.5	214	19.0	63	5.5	5,828	100.0	2,919	50.1	1,812	31.1	888	15.2	209	3.6
One own child 6–11	3,960	32.3	647	100.0	212	32.7	266	41.1	141	21.8	28	4.4	3,312	100.0	1,445	43.6	1,044	31.5	721	21.8	102	3.1
Two own children 6–11	1,186	9.7	161	100.0	29	17.8	94	58.4	33	20.5	5	3.2	1,025	100.0	445	43.4	310	30.2	240	23.4	30	3.0
Three or more own children 6–11	177	1.4	19	100.0	8	42.1	6	31.2	5	26.7	—	—	158	100.0	83	52.8	20	12.7	51	32.1	4	2.4
Own children under 6 years																						
Without own children under 6	7,442	60.6	1,432	100.0	324	22.6	722	50.5	296	20.7	90	6.3	6,009	100.0	2,051	34.1	2,485	41.3	1,171	19.5	302	5.0
One own child under 6	3,822	31.1	439	100.0	232	52.7	126	28.6	75	17.2	6	1.5	3,382	100.0	2,272	67.2	572	16.9	504	14.9	34	1.0
Two own children under 6	878	7.2	76	100.0	39	51.8	14	18.0	23	30.2	—	—	802	100.0	490	61.1	116	14.4	188	23.4	8	1.0
Three or more own children under 6	137	1.1	10	100.0	3	29.0	7	71.0	—	—	—	—	128	100.0	78	61.4	13	9.8	37	28.7	—	—
Own children under 3 years																						
Without own children under 3	9,864	80.3	1,756	100.0	468	26.6	834	47.5	361	20.6	93	5.3	8,108	100.0	3,271	40.3	2,954	36.4	1,554	19.2	329	4.1
One own child under 3	2,232	18.2	190	100.0	123	64.6	31	16.3	33	17.2	3	1.8	2,042	100.0	1,489	72.9	221	10.8	317	15.5	15	0.7
Two or more own children under 3	183	1.5	10	100.0	7	67.6	3	32.4	—	—	—	—	173	100.0	133	76.6	10	6.0	28	16.5	2	0.9
Age of own children																						
With own children under 18 years	12,279	100.0	1,957	100.0	598	30.5	869	44.4	394	20.1	96	4.9	10,323	100.0	4,892	47.4	3,186	30.9	1,900	18.4	345	3.3
Without own children under 12 years	3,634	29.6	746	100.0	116	15.5	412	55.2	161	21.6	57	7.7	2,889	100.0	814	28.2	1,397	48.4	491	17.0	187	6.5
With own children under 12 years	8,645	70.4	1,211	100.0	482	39.8	457	37.8	233	19.2	39	3.2	7,434	100.0	4,078	54.9	1,789	24.1	1,409	19.0	158	2.1
With own children under 6 years	7,442	60.6	1,432	100.0	324	22.6	722	50.5	296	20.7	90	6.3	6,009	100.0	2,051	34.1	2,485	41.3	1,171	19.5	302	5.0
Without own children under 6 years	4,837	39.4	524	100.0	274	52.2	146	27.9	98	18.7	6	1.2	4,311	100.0	2,840	65.9	700	16.2	729	16.9	42	1.0
With own children under 5 years	8,237	67.1	1,550	100.0	360	23.2	774	49.9	325	21.0	91	5.9	6,686	100.0	2,420	36.2	2,667	39.9	1,289	19.3	310	4.6
Without own children under 5 years	4,042	32.9	406	100.0	237	58.5	95	23.3	69	17.0	5	1.3	3,636	100.0	2,472	68.0	518	14.3	611	16.8	35	1.0
With own children under 3 years	9,864	80.3	1,756	100.0	468	26.6	834	47.5	361	20.6	93	5.3	8,108	100.0	3,271	40.3	2,954	36.4	1,554	19.2	329	4.1
Without own children under 3 years	2,415	19.7	200	100.0	130	64.8	34	17.1	33	16.4	3	1.7	2,214	100.0	1,621	73.2	231	10.4	346	15.6	16	0.7
With own children under 1 year	11,532	93.9	1,904	100.0	553	29.1	865	45.4	390	20.5	96	5.0	9,628	100.0	4,343	45.1	3,130	32.5	1,812	18.8	343	3.6
Without own children under 1 year	747	6.1	51	100.0	44	84.9	3	6.5	4	8.6	—	—	695	100.0	549	79.0	56	8.0	88	12.7	2	0.3
With own children 3–5 years	9,251	75.3	1,585	100.0	429	27.1	749	47.3	314	19.8	93	5.9	7,666	100.0	3,314	43.2	2,652	34.6	1,385	18.1	315	4.1
Without own children 3–5 years	3,027	24.7	371	100.0	168	45.4	120	32.2	80	21.6	3	0.8	2,656	100.0	1,578	59.4	533	20.1	515	19.4	30	1.1
Without own children 6–11 years	6,956	56.7	1,128	100.0	349	30.9	502	44.5	214	19.0	63	5.5	5,828	100.0	2,919	50.1	1,812	31.1	888	15.2	209	3.6

TABLE 2.10

Single-parent family groups with own children under 18, by marital status and demographic characteristics, 2012 [CONTINUED]

[Numbers in thousands]

	All one-parent unmarried family groups		Maintained by father										Maintained by mother										
			Total		Never married		Divorced		Separated*		Widowed		Total		Never Married		Divorced		Separated*		Widowed	
	N	%	N	%	N	%	N	%	N	%	N	%	N	%	N	%	N	%	N	%	N	%
Age of own children																						
With own children 6–11 years	5,323	43.3	827	100.0	248	30.0	366	44.2	180	21.7	33	4.0	4,495	100.0	1,973	43.9	1,374	30.6	1,012	22.5	136	3.0
Without own children 12–17 years	6,565	53.5	958	100.0	425	44.3	352	36.7	162	16.9	19	2.0	5,606	100.0	3,414	60.9	1,177	21.0	926	16.5	89	1.6
With own children 12–17 years	5,714	46.5	999	100.0	173	17.3	517	51.8	232	23.2	77	7.7	4,716	100.0	1,478	31.3	2,008	42.6	974	20.6	256	5.4
Without own children 6–17 years	3,020	24.6	367	100.0	230	62.7	85	23.1	47	12.8	5	1.4	2,653	100.0	1,981	74.6	326	12.3	331	12.5	15	0.6
With own children 6–17 years	9,259	75.4	1,590	100.0	368	23.1	784	49.3	347	21.8	91	5.7	7,669	100.0	2,911	38.0	2,859	37.3	1,569	20.5	330	4.3
Own children in specified age groups																						
Children in two or more age groups	4,683	38.1	522	100.0	116	22.3	226	43.2	148	28.3	32	6.2	4,160	100.0	1,731	41.6	1,279	30.7	978	23.5	172	4.1
Families with children 12–17 only	2,822	23.0	635	100.0	111	17.5	348	54.8	130	20.5	46	7.2	2,187	100.0	655	30.0	1,053	48.2	360	16.5	119	5.4
Families with children 6–11 only	2,195	17.9	469	100.0	161	34.3	216	46.1	79	16.9	13	2.7	1,727	100.0	789	45.7	578	33.5	316	18.3	44	2.5
Families with children 3–5 only	1,218	9.9	199	100.0	112	56.4	58	29.2	27	13.5	2	0.9	1,021	100.0	706	69.2	183	18.0	127	12.4	5	0.5
Families with children under 3 only	1,361	11.1	131	100.0	97	73.5	21	16.2	10	7.7	3	2.6	1,229	100.0	1,011	82.3	93	7.5	119	9.7	6	0.5
Under 6 only	3,020	24.6	367	100.0	230	62.7	85	23.1	47	12.8	5	1.4	2,653	100.0	1,981	74.6	326	12.3	331	12.5	15	0.6
Some under 6, some 6–17	1,817	14.8	159	100.0	44	27.7	62	39.0	52	32.5	1	0.8	1,658	100.0	860	51.8	374	22.6	397	24.0	27	1.6
6–17 only	7,442	60.6	1,432	100.0	324	22.6	722	50.5	296	20.7	90	6.3	6,009	100.0	2,051	34.1	2,485	41.3	1,171	19.5	302	5.0

Note: "Own children" exclude ever-married children under 18 years.
Dash ("—") Represents or rounds to zero.
*Includes 'Married spouse absent'

SOURCE: "Table FG6. One-Parent Unmarried Family Groups with Own Children under 18, by Marital Status of the Reference Person: 2012," in *America's Families and Living Arrangements: 2012*, U.S. Census Bureau, November 13, 2012. http://www.census.gov/hhes/families/data/cps2012.html (accessed January 16, 2013)

TABLE 2.11

Living arrangements of children and marital status of parents, by selected characteristics, 2012

[Numbers in thousands]

	Total	Living with both parents		Living with mother only					Living with father only					Living with neither parent
		Married to each other	Not married to each other	Married spouse absent	Widowed	Divorced	Separated	Never married	Married spouse absent	Widowed	Divorced	Separated	Never married	No parent present
All children	**73,817**	**47,330**	**2,937**	**1,029**	**601**	**5,383**	**2,621**	**8,356**	**146**	**148**	**1,278**	**495**	**858**	**2,634**
Male	37,770	24,284	1,555	526	286	2,766	1,336	4,130	92	68	747	260	454	1,267
Female	36,047	23,046	1,382	503	315	2,617	1,285	4,226	54	80	531	235	404	1,368
Both sexes														
Total	**73,817**	**47,330**	**2,937**	**1,029**	**601**	**5,383**	**2,621**	**8,356**	**146**	**148**	**1,278**	**495**	**858**	**2,634**
Age of child														
Under 1 year	3,903	2,442	467	44	2	65	66	653	2	—	3	3	54	102
1–2 years	8,034	5,136	717	97	18	199	209	1,247	6	4	38	23	100	240
3–5 years	12,358	7,954	655	188	33	607	414	1,722	14	4	133	69	184	380
6–8 years	12,182	7,812	430	197	75	771	476	1,471	20	11	234	89	160	435
9–11 years	12,269	8,003	277	173	110	1,022	518	1,233	30	27	240	88	145	405
12–14 years	12,348	7,874	225	162	147	1,314	450	1,101	34	43	296	124	131	446
15–17 years	12,722	8,108	167	168	216	1,405	488	929	40	59	333	98	85	628
Race														
White alone	54,259	38,004	2,035	624	426	3,970	1,789	3,686	114	101	1,018	371	541	1,578
Black alone	11,166	3,734	520	266	93	933	599	3,797	10	31	133	75	223	752
Asian alone	3,628	2,988	98	70	29	107	68	112	17	9	21	13	22	74
All remaining single races and all race combinations	4,765	2,603	284	70	54	373	165	761	5	7	106	35	73	230
Race														
Hispanic*	17,570	10,364	1,178	346	128	1,198	972	2,281	50	32	145	100	213	563
White alone, Non-Hispanic	39,062	28,806	1,075	309	336	2,964	963	1,850	69	77	893	286	343	1,091
All remaining single races and all race combinations, non-hispanic	17,186	8,160	684	374	137	1,220	686	4,225	27	39	240	109	303	981
Race														
White alone or in combination with one or more other races	57,529	39,869	2,237	668	454	4,246	1,880	4,198	117	101	1,081	394	573	1,711
Other	16,288	7,460	701	361	147	1,137	741	4,158	29	47	197	101	285	924
Race														
Black alone or in combination with one or more other races	13,012	4,537	663	290	104	1,094	649	4,276	10	31	161	86	256	853
Other	60,805	42,792	2,275	739	497	4,289	1,972	4,081	136	117	1,116	409	602	1,781
Race														
Asian alone or in combination with one or more other races	4,542	3,657	129	84	33	179	83	168	20	9	39	18	28	95
Other	69,275	43,673	2,809	945	568	5,204	2,538	8,188	126	139	1,239	476	830	2,539
Presence of siblings														
None	15,458	7,212	829	191	110	1,298	405	2,578	28	46	473	126	388	1,772
One sibling	28,648	19,629	1,035	358	212	2,232	924	2,673	53	56	518	202	279	478
Two siblings	17,920	12,478	612	213	144	1,278	677	1,713	39	40	215	137	136	238
Three siblings	7,645	5,127	327	151	101	411	380	920	11	5	53	29	52	78
Four siblings	2,487	1,629	109	71	15	109	138	355	14	1	4	—	1	40
Five or more siblings	1,659	1,255	26	45	20	55	97	117	—	—	14	—	2	29

TABLE 2.11

Living arrangements of children and marital status of parents, by selected characteristics, 2012 (CONTINUED)

[Numbers in thousands]

	Total	Living with both parents		Living with mother only					Living with father only					Living with neither parent
		Married to each other	Not married to each other	Married spouse absent	Widowed	Divorced	Separated	Never married	Married spouse absent	Widowed	Divorced	Separated	Never married	No parent present
Presence of parent's unmarried partner														
Child's parent does not have opposite sex partner	68,600	47,330	226	975	549	4,693	2,467	7,539	131	143	964	429	520	2,634
Child's parent has opposite sex partner	5,217	—	2,712	55	52	690	154	818	15	5	314	65	338	—
Partner is also other parent	2,712	—	2,712	—	—	—	—	—	—	—	—	—	—	—
Partner is not other parent	2,505	—	—	55	52	690	154	818	15	5	314	65	338	—
Highest education of either parent														
No parents present	2,634		—	—	—	—	—	—	—	—	—	—	—	2,634
Less than 9th grade	2,609	1,604	111	90	52	129	234	259	16	12	10	38	55	—
9th to 12th grade, no diploma	5,034	1,910	335	178	61	379	364	1,515	14	10	102	68	97	—
High school graduate	16,101	8,168	1,018	276	147	1,336	840	3,159	65	70	456	185	380	—
Some college or AA degree	20,360	12,287	1,041	303	185	2,198	842	2,716	23	28	396	106	234	—
Bachelor's degree	15,743	13,043	342	127	121	959	248	505	15	8	235	54	87	—
Prof. or graduate degree	11,336	10,317	89	55	35	382	93	202	13	20	79	44	5	—
Poverty status														
Below 100% of poverty	16,397	5,155	1,344	556	178	1,679	1,246	4,493	44	22	196	103	221	1,160
100% to 199% of poverty	16,471	9,162	832	262	194	1,498	843	2,172	28	51	314	156	264	695
200% of poverty and above	40,949	33,012	761	211	229	2,206	532	1,691	74	76	768	235	374	780
100 percent of poverty														
Below 100% of poverty	16,397	5,155	1,344	556	178	1,679	1,246	4,493	44	22	196	103	221	1,160
100% of poverty and above	57,420	42,174	1,593	473	423	3,704	1,375	3,863	102	126	1,082	392	637	1,475
125 percent of poverty														
Below 125% of poverty	20,850	7,463	1,609	645	246	2,077	1,486	5,173	54	32	237	138	320	1,370
125% of poverty and above	52,967	39,867	1,328	385	355	3,306	1,135	3,183	92	116	1,041	357	538	1,265

Dash "—" represents or rounds to zero.
Note: Excludes children in group quarters, and those who are a family reference person or spouse.
*Hispanics may be of any race.

SOURCE: Adapted from "Table C3. Living Arrangements of Children under 18 Years and Marital Status of Parents, by Age, Sex, Race, and Hispanic Origin and Selected Characteristics of the Child for All Children: 2012," in *America's Families and Living Arrangements: 2012*, U.S. Census Bureau, November 13, 2012, http://www.census.gov/hhes/families/data/cps2012.html (accessed January 16, 2013)

FIGURE 2.2

Poverty status of custodial parents, 1993–2009

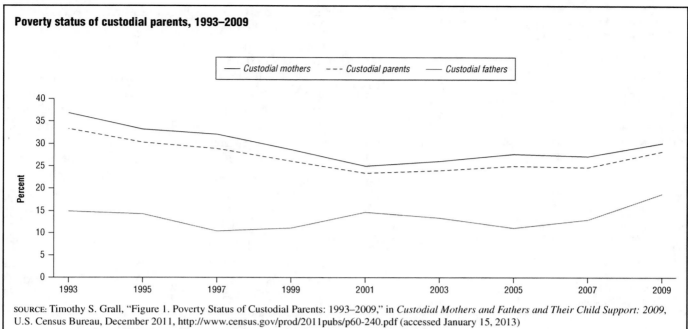

SOURCE: Timothy S. Grall, "Figure 1. Poverty Status of Custodial Parents: 1993–2009," in *Custodial Mothers and Fathers and Their Child Support: 2009*, U.S. Census Bureau, December 2011, http://www.census.gov/prod/2011pubs/p60-240.pdf (accessed January 15, 2013)

TABLE 2.12

Poverty status and work experience of people in families and unrelated individuals, 2010

[Numbers in thousands]

Poverty status and work experience	Total people	In married-couple families				In families maintained by women			In families maintained by men			Unrelated individuals
		Husbands	Wives	Related children under 18 years	Other relatives	House holder	Related children under 18 years	Other relatives	House holder	Related children under 18 years	Other relatives	
Total												
All people[a]	238,999	57,367	57,978	5,459	20,771	15,001	2,327	12,937	5,538	573	6,177	54,871
With labor force activity	158,882	44,428	36,992	1,228	13,097	10,533	405	7,638	4,293	105	3,960	36,202
1 to 26 weeks	12,023	1,546	2,570	780	2,381	733	240	1,028	211	55	375	2,103
27 or more weeks	146,859	42,882	34,422	448	10,716	9,799	165	6,609	4,082	50	3,585	34,099
With no labor force activity	80,116	12,939	20,985	4,230	7,674	4,468	1,922	5,299	1,244	468	2,217	18,669
At or above poverty level												
All people[a]	207,693	53,826	54,390	5,010	19,488	10,261	1,501	10,435	4,660	444	5,507	42,172
With labor force activity	145,964	42,377	35,919	1,192	12,634	7,959	344	6,744	3,769	96	3,692	31,237
1 to 26 weeks	9,616	1,359	2,307	761	2,252	298	199	849	149	48	309	1,085
27 or more weeks	136,348	41,018	33,613	431	10,382	7,661	144	5,896	3,621	48	3,383	30,152
With no labor force activity	61,730	11,449	18,470	3,818	6,854	2,302	1,157	3,691	891	348	1,815	10,934
Below poverty level												
All people[a]	31,306	3,541	3,588	449	1,283	4,739	826	2,502	878	129	670	12,700
With labor force activity	12,919	2,051	1,073	36	463	2,574	61	893	524	9	268	4,965
1 to 26 weeks	2,407	186	263	19	128	436	41	180	63	7	66	1,018
27 or more weeks	10,512	1,864	810	17	335	2,138	21	714	461	—	202	3,947
With no labor force activity	18,387	1,490	2,515	413	820	2,166	765	1,609	354	120	402	7,734
Rate[b]												
All people[a]	13.1	6.2	6.2	8.2	6.2	31.6	35.5	19.3	15.8	22.5	10.9	23.1
With labor force activity	8.1	4.6	2.9	2.9	3.5	24.4	15.2	11.7	12.2	8.8	6.8	13.7
1 to 26 weeks	20.0	12.1	10.2	2.4	5.4	59.4	17.0	17.5	29.6	12.0	17.7	48.4
27 or more weeks	7.2	4.3	2.4	3.9	3.1	21.8	12.5	10.8	11.3	c	5.6	11.6
With no labor force activity	23.0	11.5	12.0	9.8	10.7	48.5	39.8	30.4	28.4	25.6	18.1	41.4

[a]Data on families include primary families that own or rent the housing unit as well as related and unrelated subfamilies that reside with them.
[b]Number below the poverty level as a percent of the total.
[c]Data not shown where base is less than 80,000.
Note: Dash represents or rounds to zero.

SOURCE: "Table 6. People in Families and Unrelated Individuals: Poverty Status and Work Experience, 2010," in *A Profile of the Working Poor, 2010*, U.S. Department of Labor, U.S. Bureau of Labor Statistics, March 2012, http://www.bls.gov/cps/cpswp2010.pdf (accessed January 16, 2013)

TABLE 2.13

Poverty status of persons and primary families in the labor force for 27 or more weeks, 2007–10

[Numbers in thousands]

Characteristic	2007	2008	2009	2010
Total persons[a]	146,567	147,838	147,902	146,859
In poverty	7,521	8,883	10,391	10,512
Working—poor rate	5.1	6.0	7.0	7.2
Unrelated individuals	33,226	32,785	33,798	34,099
In poverty	2,558	3,275	3,947	3,947
Working—poor rate	7.7	10.0	11.7	11.6
Primary families[b]	65,158	65,907	65,467	64,931
In poverty	4,169	4,538	5,193	5,269
Working—poor rate	6.4	6.9	7.9	8.1

[a]Includes persons in families, not shown separately.
[b]Primary families with at least one member in the labor force for more than half the year.
Note: Updated population controls are introduced annually with the release of January data.

SOURCE: "Table A. Poverty Status of Persons and Primary Families in the Labor Force for 27 Weeks or More, 2007–2010," in *A Profile of the Working Poor, 2010*, U.S. Department of Labor, U.S. Bureau of Labor Statistics, March 2012, http://www.bls.gov/cps/cpswp2010.pdf (accessed January 16, 2013)

eligible for benefits, and some knew they were eligible but chose not to accept benefits or thought the effort was not worth the amount of benefits they would receive.

The Great Recession increased the number of people receiving means-tested benefits. The American Recovery and Reinvestment Act, which was signed by President Barack Obama (1961–) in February 2009, contained provisions for a $5 billion contingency fund for Temporary Assistance for Needy Families programs under which states could receive up to 80% of the cost of spending increases in fiscal years 2009 and 2010. The act also allocated an additional $500 million to support participation in the Supplemental Nutrition Assistance Program (SNAP). The act authorized an increase in SNAP benefits to families of up to 113.6% of the value of the Thrifty Food Plan (a plan that serves as the basis for maximum food stamp allotments).

Who Receives Benefits?

The Census Bureau reports that in 2011, 99.7 million people, or 32.3% of the total U.S. population, lived in households that received some form of means-tested assistance (assistance based on income below a certain amount). (See Table 2.14.) This number was up substantially from 2006, before the recession began, when 77.1 million people (26% of the total U.S. population) lived in households that received these benefits. In 2011 approximately 46.2 million people were living below the poverty level, up substantially from 36.5 million in 2006. (See Table 2.15.) Of those living in poverty in 2011, 34.4 million (74.3%) were receiving some form of means-tested aid.

Certain types of households were more likely than others to receive means-tested assistance in 2011. Nine out of 10 (90.3%) poor families with children under the age of 18 years received government assistance. (See Table 2.15.) Poor families with children under the age of 18 years headed by a single mother were the most likely to receive government assistance; 93.4% of these families received some form of government assistance. In fact, over three-quarters (75.8%) of all families (not just those in poverty) with children under the age of 18 years headed by a single mother received some form of means-tested assistance in 2011. By comparison, 61.3% of families with children under the age of 18 years headed by a single father and 35.2% of married-couple families received means-tested assistance in that year. (See Table 2.14.)

In 2011 a slightly higher proportion of females (33.6%) than males (30.9%) lived in a household that received means-tested assistance or welfare benefits of any kind. (See Table 2.14.) About 53 million females received program assistance in 2011, compared with 46.7 million males. Among those living below the poverty level, 19.3 million women, or 75.1%, received benefits during some part of the year, compared with 15 million males, or 73.4%. (See Table 2.15.)

One reason for the larger percentage of females receiving assistance is that women are more likely to live in a family without a spouse present. DeNavas-Walt, Proctor, and Smith indicate that another reason is that women, on average, earned only 77% of what men earned in 2011. Age may also play a role in the higher number of women in poverty; there are far more elderly women than men. Another reason is that fewer single mothers participate in the workforce permanently and full time than do single fathers. Grall reports that 76% of custodial mothers worked either full or part time that year, whereas 85.1% of custodial fathers did. Grall suggests one reason that might be part of the cause of this disparity: Custodial mothers were more likely than custodial fathers to have two or more children living with them (44.1% and 37.1%, respectively).

Nearly half (47.8%) of children under the age of 18 years lived in households that received means-tested assistance in 2011. (See Table 2.14.) Approximately 36.5% of young adults aged 18 to 24 years lived in households that received means-tested assistance, as did 33.5% of adults aged 25 to 34 years, 31.4% of adults aged 35 to 44 years, 25.1% of adults aged 45 to 54 years, 21.8% of adults aged 55 to 59 years, and 20.6% of adults aged 60 to 64 years. Nearly one out of five (19.2%) people aged 65 years and older received means-tested assistance.

LENGTH OF TIME IN POVERTY
Entering and Exiting Poverty

For most poor Americans poverty is not a static condition. Some people near the poverty level improve

TABLE 2.14

Program participation status of households for all income levels, 2011

[Numbers in thousands. People who lived with someone (a nonrelative or a relative) who received aid. Not every person tallied here received the aid themselves.]

Both sexes

All races / All income levels	Total	In household that received means-tested assistance		In household that received means-tested assistance excluding school lunch		In household that received means-tested cash assistance		In household that received food stamps		In household in which one or more persons were covered by Medicaid		Lived in public or authorized housing	
		Number	Percent	Number	Percent	Number	Percent	Number	Percent	Number	Percent	Number	Percent
Total[a]	**308,456**	**99,691**	**32.3**	**90,398**	**29.3**	**21,725**	**7.0**	**40,235**	**13.0**	**78,819**	**25.6**	**11,675**	**3.8**
Under 18 years	73,737	35,236	47.8	30,906	41.9	5,999	8.1	15,680	21.3	28,747	39.0	4,076	5.5
18 to 24 years	30,140	10,999	36.5	10,048	33.3	2,268	7.5	4,599	15.3	8,526	28.3	1,349	4.5
25 to 34 years	41,219	13,813	33.5	12,762	31.0	2,582	6.3	6,004	14.6	11,242	27.3	1,490	3.6
35 to 44 years	39,927	12,556	31.4	10,980	27.5	2,351	5.9	4,368	10.9	9,761	24.4	1,067	2.7
45 to 54 years	43,955	11,032	25.1	10,046	22.9	3,023	6.9	4,058	9.2	8,453	19.2	1,095	2.5
55 to 59 years	20,470	4,459	21.8	4,306	21.0	1,565	7.6	1,697	8.3	3,476	17.0	517	2.5
60 to 64 years	17,501	3,610	20.6	3,523	20.1	1,359	7.8	1,265	7.2	2,778	15.9	470	2.7
65 years and over	41,507	7,987	19.2	7,828	18.9	2,578	6.2	2,565	6.2	5,837	14.1	1,612	3.9
65 to 74 years	23,383	4,370	18.7	4,257	18.2	1,441	6.2	1,456	6.2	3,264	14.0	777	3.3
75 years and over	18,123	3,617	20.0	3,571	19.7	1,138	6.3	1,109	6.1	2,573	14.2	834	4.6
Male													
Total	**150,990**	**46,722**	**30.9**	**42,218**	**28.0**	**9,949**	**6.6**	**18,092**	**12.0**	**36,804**	**24.4**	**4,649**	**3.1**
Under 18 years	37,711	18,008	47.8	15,752	41.8	3,032	8.0	8,023	21.3	14,648	38.8	2,048	5.4
18 to 24 years	15,160	5,108	33.7	4,583	30.2	1,027	6.8	1,931	12.7	3,833	25.3	519	3.4
25 to 34 years	20,464	6,044	29.5	5,647	27.6	1,118	5.5	2,351	11.5	4,850	23.7	454	2.2
35 to 44 years	19,677	5,694	28.9	5,018	25.5	1,062	5.4	1,863	9.5	4,443	22.6	379	1.9
45 to 54 years	21,490	5,193	24.2	4,730	22.0	1,357	6.3	1,785	8.3	3,989	18.6	401	1.9
55 to 59 years	9,879	2,023	20.5	1,933	19.6	690	7.0	720	7.3	1,558	15.8	197	2.0
60 to 64 years	8,278	1,603	19.4	1,569	19.0	633	7.6	499	6.0	1,251	15.1	150	1.8
65 years and over	18,332	3,049	16.6	2,985	16.3	1,029	5.6	921	5.0	2,233	12.2	502	2.7
65 to 74 years	10,980	1,837	16.7	1,790	16.3	627	5.7	558	5.1	1,362	12.4	295	2.7
75 years and over	7,353	1,212	16.5	1,195	16.3	402	5.5	363	4.9	871	11.8	206	2.8
Female													
Total	**157,466**	**52,969**	**33.6**	**48,179**	**30.6**	**11,777**	**7.5**	**22,143**	**14.1**	**42,015**	**26.7**	**7,026**	**4.5**
Under 18 years	36,026	17,229	47.8	15,154	42.1	2,967	8.2	7,657	21.3	14,099	39.1	2,028	5.6
18 to 24 years	14,980	5,890	39.3	5,464	36.5	1,241	8.3	2,668	17.8	4,693	31.3	831	5.5
25 to 34 years	20,755	7,769	37.4	7,114	34.3	1,464	7.1	3,654	17.6	6,392	30.8	1,036	5.0
35 to 44 years	20,251	6,861	33.9	5,962	29.4	1,289	6.4	2,505	12.4	5,318	26.3	688	3.4
45 to 54 years	22,465	5,839	26.0	5,316	23.7	1,666	7.4	2,273	10.1	4,463	19.9	694	3.1
55 to 59 years	10,592	2,436	23.0	2,373	22.4	874	8.3	977	9.2	1,918	18.1	320	3.0
60 to 64 years	9,223	2,007	21.8	1,954	21.2	725	7.9	766	8.3	1,527	16.6	319	3.5
65 years and over	23,174	4,937	21.3	4,843	20.9	1,550	6.7	1,644	7.1	3,604	15.6	1,110	4.8
65 to 74 years	12,404	2,533	20.4	2,467	19.9	814	6.6	898	7.2	1,902	15.3	482	3.9
75 years and over	10,771	2,405	22.3	2,376	22.1	736	6.8	746	6.9	1,702	15.8	628	5.8

TABLE 2.14

Program participation status of households for all income levels, 2011 [CONTINUED]

[Numbers in thousands. People who lived with someone (a nonrelative or a relative) who received aid. Not every person tallied here received the aid themselves.]

Both sexes

All races All income levels	Total	In household that received means-tested assistance		In household that received means-tested assistance excluding school lunch		In household that received means-tested cash assistance		In household that received food stamps		In household in which one or more persons were covered by Medicaid		Lived in public or authorized housing	
		Number	Percent	Number	Percent	Number	Percent	Number	Percent	Number	Percent	Number	Percent
Household relationship													
Total[a]	308,456	99,691	32.3	90,398	29.3	21,725	7.0	40,235	13.0	78,819	25.6	11,675	3.8
65 years and over	41,507	7,987	19.2	7,828	18.9	2,578	6.2	2,565	6.2	5,837	14.1	1,612	3.9
In families[b]	252,316	85,630	33.9	76,688	30.4	17,758	7.0	33,468	13.3	69,003	27.3	8,467	3.4
Householder	80,529	23,516	29.2	21,280	26.4	5,166	6.4	9,200	11.4	18,737	23.3	2,592	3.2
Under 65 years	66,098	20,991	31.8	18,820	28.5	4,304	6.5	8,359	12.6	16,802	25.4	2,345	3.5
65 years and over	14,431	2,525	17.5	2,460	17.0	863	6.0	841	5.8	1,936	13.4	247	1.7
Related children under 18 years[e]	72,568	34,499	47.5	30,250	41.7	5,868	8.1	15,337	21.1	28,132	38.8	4,032	5.6
Under 6 years	23,860	11,798	49.4	11,016	46.2	2,127	8.9	5,926	24.8	10,320	43.3	1,569	6.6
6 to 17 years	48,708	22,701	46.6	19,234	39.5	3,741	7.7	9,411	19.3	17,812	36.6	2,463	5.1
Own children 18 years and over[d]	26,879	9,513	35.4	8,652	32.2	2,569	9.6	3,429	12.8	7,546	28.1	791	2.9
In married-couple families[f]	187,474	47,296	25.2	41,976	22.4	8,329	4.4	13,827	7.4	37,917	20.2	2,381	1.3
Husbands[f]	58,963	11,749	19.9	10,589	18.0	2,307	3.9	3,311	5.6	9,288	15.8	688	1.2
Under 65 years	46,118	10,133	22.0	9,007	19.5	1,758	3.8	2,892	6.3	8,064	17.5	522	1.1
65 years and over	12,846	1,616	12.6	1,582	12.3	550	4.3	419	3.3	1,224	9.5	165	1.3
Wives[f]	58,963	11,749	19.9	10,589	18.0	2,307	3.9	3,311	5.6	9,288	15.8	688	1.2
Under 65 years	48,895	10,558	21.6	9,419	19.3	1,902	3.9	3,010	6.2	8,405	17.2	551	1.1
65 years and over	10,069	1,192	11.8	1,170	11.6	405	4.0	301	3.0	882	8.8	137	1.4
Related children under 18 years[e]	48,840	17,216	35.2	14,812	30.3	2,092	4.3	5,575	11.4	13,877	28.4	790	1.6
Under 6 years	16,266	5,822	35.8	5,321	32.7	747	4.6	2,161	13.3	4,997	30.7	346	2.1
6 to 17 years	32,574	11,394	35.0	9,492	29.1	1,345	4.1	3,414	10.5	8,881	27.3	444	1.4
Own children 18 years and over[d]	16,641	4,607	27.7	4,135	24.9	1,132	6.8	1,148	6.9	3,763	22.6	174	1.0
In families with male householder, no spouse present	16,739	7,701	46.0	6,929	41.4	1,682	10.0	3,022	18.1	6,082	36.3	519	3.1
Householder	5,888	2,530	43.0	2,287	38.8	529	9.0	977	16.6	1,969	33.4	182	3.1
Under 65 years	5,315	2,309	43.4	2,071	39.0	441	8.3	871	16.4	1,807	34.0	166	3.1
65 years and over	573	221	38.5	216	37.6	87	15.2	106	18.5	161	28.2	16	2.7
Related children under 18 years[e]	4,786	2,933	61.3	2,550	53.3	467	9.8	1,258	26.3	2,363	49.4	195	4.1
Under 6 years	1,582	1,107	69.9	1,056	66.7	178	11.2	551	34.8	973	61.5	70	4.4
6 to 17 years	3,204	1,827	57.0	1,494	46.6	289	9.0	707	22.1	1,389	43.4	125	3.9
Own children 18 years and over[d]	1,959	706	36.0	663	33.8	225	11.5	298	15.2	537	27.4	46	2.4
In families with female householder, no spouse present	48,103	30,633	63.7	27,784	57.8	7,747	16.1	16,619	34.5	25,005	52.0	5,567	11.6
Householder	15,678	9,237	58.9	8,404	53.6	2,330	14.9	4,912	31.3	7,481	47.7	1,723	11.0
Under 65 years	13,705	8,374	61.1	7,574	55.3	2,044	14.9	4,549	33.2	6,795	49.6	1,646	12.0
65 years and over	1,972	863	43.8	830	42.1	286	14.5	363	18.4	686	34.8	76	3.9
Related children under 18 years[e]	18,942	14,350	75.8	12,888	68.0	3,309	17.5	8,505	44.9	11,892	62.8	3,047	16.1
Under 6 years	6,012	4,870	81.0	4,640	77.2	1,202	20.0	3,214	53.5	4,350	72.4	1,152	19.2
6 to 17 years	12,930	9,481	73.3	8,248	63.8	2,107	16.3	5,290	40.9	7,542	58.3	1,894	14.7

TABLE 2.14

Program participation status of households for all income levels, 2011 [CONTINUED]

[Numbers in thousands. People who lived with someone (a nonrelative or a relative) who received aid. Not every person tallied here received the aid themselves.]

Both sexes

All races / All income levels	Total	In household that received means-tested assistance		In household that received means-tested assistance excluding school lunch		In household that received means-tested cash assistance		In household that received food stamps		In household in which one or more persons were covered by Medicaid		Lived in public or authorized housing	
		Number	Percent	Number	Percent	Number	Percent	Number	Percent	Number	Percent	Number	Percent
Own children 18 years and over[a]	8,279	4,201	50.7	3,853	46.5	1,212	14.6	1,983	23.9	3,246	39.2	570	6.9
In unrelated subfamilies[c]	1,623	994	61.2	892	55.0	160	9.8	506	31.2	829	51.1	58	3.6
Under 18 years	846	537	63.5	482	57.0	93	10.9	277	32.8	454	53.7	31	3.7
Under 6 years	286	204	71.6	201	70.3	43	15.0	127	44.4	192	67.1	15	5.3
6 to 17 years	560	333	59.4	282	50.3	50	8.9	151	26.9	262	46.8	16	2.9
18 years and over	777	457	58.7	410	52.7	67	8.6	229	29.4	375	48.3	27	3.4
Unrelated individuals[d]	54,517	13,067	24.0	12,817	23.5	3,808	7.0	6,261	11.5	8,987	16.5	3,151	5.8
Male	26,906	6,304	23.4	6,139	22.8	1,847	6.9	2,915	10.8	4,428	16.5	1,209	4.5
Under 65 years	22,837	5,452	23.9	5,291	23.2	1,595	7.0	2,618	11.5	3,876	17.0	912	4.0
Living alone	11,398	1,996	17.5	1,995	17.5	746	6.5	1,079	9.5	1,182	10.4	668	5.9
65 years and over	4,069	852	20.9	848	20.8	251	6.2	297	7.3	551	13.6	297	7.3
Living alone	3,462	686	19.8	686	19.8	178	5.2	237	6.8	406	11.7	287	8.3
Female	27,611	6,763	24.5	6,678	24.2	1,961	7.1	3,346	12.1	4,559	16.5	1,942	7.0
Under 65 years	18,663	4,813	25.8	4,728	25.3	1,444	7.7	2,607	14.0	3,329	17.8	1,102	5.9
Living alone	10,013	2,210	22.1	2,210	22.1	769	7.7	1,377	13.8	1,329	13.3	892	8.9
65 years and over	8,948	1,950	21.8	1,950	21.8	517	5.8	738	8.3	1,230	13.7	839	9.4
Living alone	8,369	1,787	21.3	1,787	21.3	457	5.5	685	8.2	1,088	13.0	833	10.0

Notes: Poverty in the United States is measured by comparing family income with one of 48 poverty thresholds—the dollar amounts used to determine who is poor. The poverty thresholds vary by size of family and the ages of the members.
[a]Universe: All people except unrelated individuals under age 15 (such as foster children). Since the Current Population Survey asks income questions only to people age 15 and over, if a child under age 15 is not part of a family by birth, marriage, or adoption, we do not know their income and cannot determine whether or not they are poor. Those people are excluded from the totals so as not to affect the percentages.
[b]People in families: People who are related to the householder by birth, marriage, or adoption. People who are related to each other but not to the householder are counted elsewhere (usually as unrelated subfamilies).
[c]People in unrelated subfamilies: People who are not related to the householder, but who are related to each other, either as a married couple or as a parent-child relationship with an unmarried child under 18.
[d]Unrelated individuals: People who are not in primary families (the householder's family) or unrelated subfamilies.
[e]People in families with related children: People living in a family where at least one member is a related child—a person under 18 who is related to the householder but is not the householder or spouse.
[f]In married-couple families the householder may be either the husband or the wife.
[g]Own children: Sons and daughters, including stepchildren and adopted children, of the householder.
New race categories: The 2003 Census Population Survey (CPS) asked respondents to choose one or more races. White alone refers to people who reported white and did not report any other race category. The use of this single-race population does not imply that it is the preferred method of presenting or analyzing data. The Census Bureau uses a variety of approaches. About 2.6 percent of people reported more than one race in 2000.
Black alone refers to people who reported black and did not report any other race category.
Asian alone refers to people who reported Asian and did not report any other race category.

SOURCE: "POV26. Program Participation Status of Household-Poverty Status of People: 2011, All Races—All Income Levels," in *Current Population Survey (CPS), 2012 Annual Social and Economic Supplement*, U.S. Census Bureau, September 12, 2012, http://www.census.gov/hhes/www/cpstables/032012/pov/POV26_001.htm (accessed January 16, 2013)

TABLE 2.15

Program participation status of household for persons below poverty level, 2011

[Numbers in thousands. People who lived with someone (a nonrelative or a relative) who received aid. Not every person tallied here received the aid themselves.]

Both sexes

All races Below poverty levels	Total	In household that received means-tested assistance		In household that received means-tested assistance excluding school lunch		In household that received means-tested cash assistance		In household that received food stamps		In household in which one or more persons were covered by Medicaid		Lived in public or authorized housing	
		Number	Percent	Number	Percent	Number	Percent	Number	Percent	Number	Percent	Number	Percent
Total[a]	**46,247**	**34,378**	**74.3**	**32,496**	**70.3**	**9,140**	**19.8**	**22,556**	**48.8**	**28,336**	**61.3**	**7,102**	**15.4**
Under 18 years	16,134	14,508	89.9	13,544	83.9	3,369	20.9	10,035	62.2	12,605	78.1	3,046	18.9
18 to 24 years	6,209	4,008	64.6	3,823	61.6	927	14.9	2,518	40.6	3,147	50.7	809	13.0
25 to 34 years	6,537	4,718	72.2	4,520	69.1	1,176	18.0	3,197	48.9	4,015	61.4	903	13.8
35 to 44 years	4,873	3,737	76.7	3,422	70.2	923	18.9	2,229	45.7	3,005	61.7	605	12.4
45 to 54 years	4,795	3,268	68.2	3,136	65.4	1,154	24.1	2,125	44.3	2,518	52.5	654	13.6
55 to 59 years	2,181	1,325	60.8	1,304	59.8	548	25.1	841	38.6	972	44.6	293	13.4
60 to 64 years	1,898	1,022	53.8	1,004	52.9	393	20.7	630	33.2	752	39.6	245	12.9
65 years and over	3,620	1,793	49.5	1,742	48.1	649	17.9	980	27.1	1,322	36.5	547	15.1
65 to 74 years	1,739	957	55.0	924	53.2	344	19.8	542	31.2	722	41.6	280	16.1
75 years and over	1,882	836	44.4	817	43.4	306	16.2	437	23.2	600	31.9	267	14.2
Male													
Total	**20,501**	**15,038**	**73.4**	**14,158**	**69.1**	**3,927**	**19.2**	**9,721**	**47.4**	**12,325**	**60.1**	**2,728**	**13.3**
Under 18 years	8,132	7,342	90.3	6,832	84.0	1,677	20.6	5,073	62.4	6,335	77.9	1,516	18.6
18 to 24 years	2,722	1,648	60.5	1,554	57.1	397	14.6	989	36.3	1,238	45.5	267	9.8
25 to 34 years	2,516	1,601	63.6	1,537	61.1	358	14.2	1,033	41.1	1,293	51.4	196	7.8
35 to 44 years	2,046	1,505	73.6	1,388	67.9	383	18.7	840	41.0	1,234	60.3	176	8.6
45 to 54 years	2,138	1,379	64.5	1,318	61.6	463	21.7	858	40.1	1,056	49.4	222	10.4
55 to 59 years	960	562	58.5	548	57.1	242	25.2	345	35.9	420	43.7	114	11.9
60 to 64 years	854	450	52.7	443	51.9	185	21.7	273	32.0	325	38.1	74	8.7
65 years and over	1,134	552	48.6	538	47.4	220	19.4	311	27.4	424	37.4	163	14.4
65 to 74 years	638	336	52.8	330	51.7	123	19.2	182	28.5	269	42.2	99	15.5
75 years and over	497	215	43.3	208	41.9	98	19.7	129	25.9	155	31.1	64	13.0
Female													
Total	**25,746**	**19,340**	**75.1**	**18,338**	**71.2**	**5,214**	**20.3**	**12,834**	**49.8**	**16,011**	**62.2**	**4,374**	**17.0**
Under 18 years	8,002	7,166	89.5	6,712	83.9	1,692	21.1	4,963	62.0	6,269	78.3	1,530	19.1
18 to 24 years	3,487	2,361	67.7	2,268	65.0	530	15.2	1,529	43.9	1,909	54.8	542	15.5
25 to 34 years	4,021	3,117	77.5	2,983	74.2	818	20.3	2,164	53.8	2,722	67.7	707	17.6
35 to 44 years	2,827	2,231	78.9	2,034	72.0	540	19.1	1,389	49.1	1,770	62.6	429	15.2
45 to 54 years	2,656	1,889	71.1	1,818	68.5	691	26.0	1,267	47.7	1,462	55.0	432	16.3
55 to 59 years	1,221	763	62.5	756	61.9	306	25.0	496	40.6	552	45.2	179	14.6
60 to 64 years	1,045	572	54.7	561	53.7	208	19.9	357	34.1	427	40.9	172	16.4
65 years and over	2,486	1,241	49.9	1,204	48.4	429	17.3	669	26.9	899	36.1	383	15.4
65 to 74 years	1,101	620	56.3	595	54.0	221	20.1	360	32.7	453	41.2	181	16.4
75 years and over	1,385	621	44.8	609	44.0	208	15.0	308	22.3	445	32.1	203	14.6

TABLE 2.15

Program participation status of household for persons below poverty level, 2011 [CONTINUED]

[Numbers in thousands. People who lived with someone (a nonrelative or a relative) who received aid. Not every person tallied here received the aid themselves.]

Both sexes

All races / Below poverty levels	Total	In household that received means-tested assistance		In household that received means-tested assistance excluding school lunch		In household that received means-tested cash assistance		In household that received food stamps		In household in which one or more persons were covered by Medicaid		Lived in public or authorized housing	
		Number	Percent	Number	Percent	Number	Percent	Number	Percent	Number	Percent	Number	Percent
Household relationship													
Total[a]	46,247	34,378	74.3	32,496	70.3	9,140	19.8	22,556	48.8	28,336	61.3	7,102	15.4
65 years and over	3,620	1,793	49.5	1,742	48.1	649	17.9	980	27.1	1,322	36.5	547	15.1
In families[b]	33,126	27,458	82.9	25,702	77.6	6,767	20.4	18,431	55.6	23,218	70.1	5,408	16.3
Householder	9,497	7,427	78.2	6,999	73.7	1,913	20.1	4,999	52.6	6,235	65.7	1,574	16.6
Under 65 years	8,765	7,043	80.3	6,636	75.7	1,788	20.4	4,766	54.4	5,954	67.9	1,505	17.2
65 years and over	731	385	52.6	363	49.7	125	17.1	233	31.9	280	38.3	69	9.4
Related children under 18 years[e]	15,539	14,028	90.3	13,100	84.3	3,257	21.0	9,765	62.8	12,180	78.4	3,009	19.4
Under 6 years	5,844	5,299	90.7	5,095	87.2	1,276	21.8	3,812	65.2	4,793	82.0	1,169	20.0
6 to 17 years	9,695	8,729	90.0	8,005	82.6	1,981	20.4	5,953	61.4	7,388	76.2	1,840	19.0
Own children 18 years and over[d]	2,814	2,318	82.4	2,178	77.4	648	23.0	1,472	52.3	1,824	64.8	400	14.2
In married-couple families[f]	13,907	10,412	74.9	9,665	69.5	2,121	15.3	6,273	45.1	8,660	62.3	1,079	7.8
Husbands[f]	3,652	2,411	66.0	2,265	62.0	543	14.9	1,446	39.6	1,981	54.2	275	7.5
Under 65 years	3,141	2,211	70.4	2,070	65.9	465	14.8	1,328	42.3	1,818	57.9	234	7.4
65 years and over	511	200	39.1	195	38.2	79	15.5	118	23.1	163	31.9	41	8.1
Wives[f]	3,652	2,411	66.0	2,265	62.0	543	14.9	1,446	39.6	1,981	54.2	275	7.5
Under 65 years	3,279	2,277	69.4	2,137	65.2	476	14.5	1,358	41.4	1,877	57.2	246	7.5
65 years and over	373	134	35.9	129	34.5	67	18.1	88	23.5	105	28.1	29	7.8
Related children under 18 years[e]	5,332	4,553	85.4	4,198	78.7	745	14.0	2,817	52.8	3,880	72.8	443	8.3
Under 6 years	1,963	1,667	84.9	1,593	81.2	287	14.6	1,087	55.4	1,497	76.3	173	8.8
6 to 17 years	3,369	2,886	85.7	2,605	77.3	458	13.6	1,729	51.3	2,383	70.7	270	8.0
Own children 18 years and over[d]	940	750	79.8	686	73.0	191	20.3	415	44.1	603	64.1	76	8.1
In families with male householder, no spouse present	2,768	2,182	78.8	2,032	73.4	518	18.7	1,442	52.1	1,797	64.9	217	7.8
Householder	950	713	75.0	667	70.2	161	17.0	465	49.0	580	61.0	74	7.8
Under 65 years	925	690	74.6	644	69.6	157	17.0	449	48.6	563	60.9	70	7.6
65 years and over	25	23	91.9	23	91.9	4	16.5	16	62.9	17	66.5	4	14.0
Related children under 18 years[e]	1,181	1,045	88.5	967	81.9	211	17.9	718	60.8	898	76.0	103	8.7
Under 6 years	442	405	91.6	394	89.2	81	18.4	302	68.4	357	80.7	37	8.5
6 to 17 years	739	640	86.6	573	77.6	130	17.6	416	56.3	541	73.1	65	8.8
Own children 18 years and over[d]	208	158	76.0	153	73.4	55	26.2	100	47.9	133	63.6	14	7.0
In families with female householder, no spouse present	16,451	14,863	90.3	14,004	85.1	4,128	25.1	10,716	65.1	12,761	77.6	4,113	25.0
Householder	4,894	4,304	87.9	4,067	83.1	1,208	24.7	3,088	63.1	3,674	75.1	1,225	25.0
Under 65 years	4,627	4,097	88.6	3,879	83.8	1,158	25.0	2,970	64.2	3,536	76.4	1,193	25.8
65 years and over	267	206	77.2	188	70.5	51	19.1	118	44.2	137	51.5	32	12.0
Related children under 18 years[e]	9,026	8,429	93.4	7,935	87.9	2,301	25.5	6,230	69.0	7,403	82.0	2,463	27.3
Under 6 years	3,440	3,227	93.8	3,108	90.4	908	26.4	2,422	70.4	2,939	85.4	958	27.9
6 to 17 years	5,586	5,203	93.1	4,827	86.4	1,394	24.9	3,808	68.2	4,464	79.9	1,505	26.9
Own children 18 years and over[d]	1,665	1,409	84.6	1,339	80.4	402	24.1	957	57.5	1,089	65.4	309	18.6

TABLE 2.15

Program participation status of household for persons below poverty level, 2011 [CONTINUED]

[Numbers in thousands. People who lived with someone (a nonrelative or a relative) who received aid. Not every person tallied here received the aid themselves.]

Both sexes

All races / Below poverty levels	Total	In household that received means-tested assistance		In household that received means-tested assistance excluding school lunch		In household that received means-tested cash assistance		In household that received food stamps		In household in which one or more persons were covered by Medicaid		Lived in public or authorized housing	
		Number	Percent	Number	Percent	Number	Percent	Number	Percent	Number	Percent	Number	Percent
In unrelated subfamilies[c]	705	580	82.4	541	76.8	128	18.1	382	54.3	520	73.8	47	6.7
Under 18 years	409	345	84.4	322	78.8	80	19.6	224	54.6	313	76.5	26	6.3
Under 6 years	192	158	82.4	156	81.4	40	20.6	119	61.8	147	76.8	13	7.0
6 to 17 years	217	187	86.2	166	76.5	41	18.8	105	48.3	165	76.2	13	5.8
18 years and over	295	235	79.6	219	74.0	47	16.0	159	53.8	207	70.2	21	7.1
Unrelated individuals[d]	12,416	6,340	51.1	6,253	50.4	2,246	18.1	3,742	30.1	4,598	37.0	1,647	13.3
Male	5,451	2,734	50.2	2,688	49.3	996	18.3	1,605	29.4	2,010	36.9	622	11.4
Under 65 years	4,926	2,457	49.9	2,412	49.0	878	17.8	1,458	29.6	1,801	36.6	513	10.4
Living alone	2,022	1,014	50.1	1,012	50.1	441	21.8	683	33.8	662	32.8	374	18.5
65 years and over	525	277	52.8	275	52.5	118	22.5	147	28.0	209	39.8	110	20.9
Living alone	413	218	52.9	218	52.9	86	20.9	122	29.5	156	37.8	103	24.8
Female	6,965	3,606	51.8	3,565	51.2	1,250	17.9	2,137	30.7	2,588	37.2	1,025	14.7
Under 65 years	5,303	2,831	53.4	2,790	52.6	988	18.6	1,741	32.8	2,026	38.2	716	13.5
Living alone	2,309	1,365	59.1	1,365	59.1	577	25.0	959	41.5	886	38.4	591	25.6
65 years and over	1,662	775	46.6	775	46.6	262	15.8	396	23.8	562	33.8	309	18.6
Living alone	1,536	715	46.5	715	46.5	244	15.9	369	24.0	509	33.1	308	20.1

Notes: Poverty in the United States is measured by comparing family income with one of 48 poverty thresholds—the dollar amounts used to determine who is poor. The poverty thresholds vary by size of family and the ages of the members.

[a]Universe: All people except unrelated individuals under age 15 (such as foster children). Since the Current Population Survey asks income questions only to people age 15 and over, if a child under age 15 is not part of a family by birth, marriage, or adoption, we do not know their income and cannot determine whether or not they are poor. Those people are excluded from the totals so as not to affect the percentages.

[b]People in families: People who are related to the householder by birth, marriage, or adoption. People who are related to each other but not to the householder are counted elsewhere (usually as unrelated subfamilies).

[c]People in unrelated subfamilies: People who are not related to the householder, but who are related to each other, either as a married couple or as a parent-child relationship with an unmarried child under 18.

[d]Unrelated individuals: People who are not in primary families (the householder's family) or unrelated subfamilies.

[e]People in families with related children: People living in a family where at least one member is a related child—a person under 18 who is related to the householder but is not the householder or spouse.

[f]In married-couple families the householder may be either the husband or the wife.

[g]Own children: Sons and daughters, including stepchildren and adopted children, of the householder.

New race categories: The 2003 Current Population Survey (CPS) asked respondents to choose one or more races. White alone refers to people who reported white and did not report any other race category. The use of this single-race population does not imply that it is the preferred method of presenting or analyzing data. The Census Bureau uses a variety of approaches. About 2.6 percent of people reported more than one race in 2000. Black alone refers to people who reported black and did not report any other race category. Asian alone refers to people who reported Asian and did not report any other race category.

SOURCE: "POV26. Program Participation Status of Household—Poverty Status of People: 2011, All Races—Below Poverty Levels," in *Current Population Survey (CPS), 2012 Annual Social and Economic Supplement*, U.S. Census Bureau, September 12, 2012, http://www.census.gov/hhes/www/cpstables/032012/pov/POV26_002.htm (accessed January 16, 2013)

their economic status within two years or less, whereas others at near-poverty levels become poor through economic catastrophes, such as an illness or job loss. Most data collected by the Census Bureau reflect a single point in time; in other words, they show how many people are in poverty or participating in a means-tested government program in a certain month. These surveys, however, do not reflect the dynamic nature of poverty for individual people and families.

The Census Bureau collects longitudinal information (measurements over time for specific individuals or families) about poverty and government program participation rates in its Survey of Income and Program Participation (SIPP). This makes it possible to measure the movement of individuals and families into and out of poverty (entry and exit rates), the duration of poverty spells (the number of months in poverty for those who were not poor during the first interview month, but who became poor at some point during the study), and the length of time individuals and families use government programs.

Anderson uses data from the 2004 SIPP panel to examine poverty in the period from January 2004 to December 2006. Anderson focuses on monthly measures of poverty and distinguishes between short- and long-term poverty. As shown in Figure 2.3, the episodic (monthly) poverty rate is significantly higher than the annual poverty rate. In 2006 the episodic poverty rate hovered around 20%, whereas the annual poverty rate was about half that. Other highlights of the survey include:

- Nearly three out of 10 (28.9%) people were poor for at least two months in the three years between 2004 and 2006. (See Figure 2.3.)

- Approximately 2.8% of the population was chronically poor. That is, the population was poor during all 36 months from January 2004 to December 2006.

- About 23.1% of people in poverty in January and February 2004 remained in poverty for the entire study period.

- Nonelderly adults were more likely than children or the elderly to exit poverty.

- Children had the highest entry rates into poverty and, along with retirement-age adults, had a low exit rate.

- About half (47.7%) of all poverty spells lasted two to four months, whereas 12.4% lasted more than two years.

RACE. Anderson notes that of the poor in 2004, non-Hispanic whites (49.6%) were more likely to have left poverty by 2006 than either African-Americans (29.5%) or Hispanics (42.1%). (See Figure 2.4.) Also, non-Hispanic whites who were not poor at the beginning of the study period were less likely to have entered poverty by 2006 than African-Americans or Hispanics. (See Figure 2.5.)

FIGURE 2.3

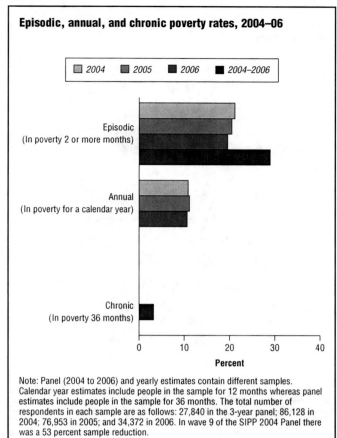

Episodic, annual, and chronic poverty rates, 2004–06

Note: Panel (2004 to 2006) and yearly estimates contain different samples. Calendar year estimates include people in the sample for 12 months whereas panel estimates include people in the sample for 36 months. The total number of respondents in each sample are as follows: 27,840 in the 3-year panel; 86,128 in 2004; 76,953 in 2005; and 34,372 in 2006. In wave 9 of the SIPP 2004 Panel there was a 53 percent sample reduction.

SOURCE: Robin J. Anderson, "Figure 1b. Selected Poverty Rates: 2004–2006," in *Dynamics of Economic Well-Being: Poverty, 2004–2006*, U.S. Census Bureau, March 2011, http://www.census.gov/hhes/www/poverty/publications/dynamics04/P70-123.pdf (accessed February 6, 2013)

Figure 2.6 shows the proportion of the entire population, the episodically poor population, and the chronically poor population made up of white, African-American, and other racial groups. Even though whites made up 80.7% of the total population, they made up only 72.5% of the episodically poor population and only 54.5% of the chronically poor population. In contrast, African-Americans made up 12.5% of the total population, but 19.6% of the episodically poor population and 37.6% of the chronically poor population. Therefore, African-Americans are disproportionally represented among the poor, especially among the chronically poor.

AGE. The elderly and children are less likely to exit poverty than are people of other ages. About 32.2% of the elderly and 37.6% of children under the age of 18 years who were poor in 2004 were able to escape poverty by 2006. (See Figure 2.4.) In contrast, adults aged 18 to 64 years were the most likely to escape poverty—45.8% moved out of poverty. However, children under the age of 18 years were much more likely to enter poverty at some point during the study period than were adults of any age. (See Figure 2.5.)

FIGURE 2.4

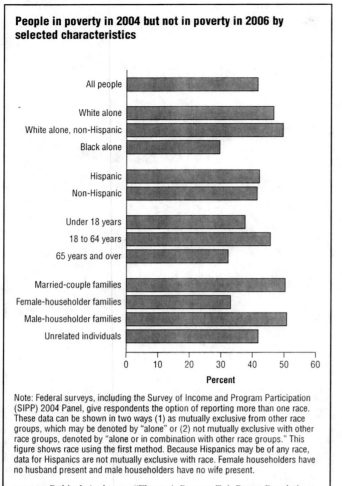

People in poverty in 2004 but not in poverty in 2006 by selected characteristics

Note: Federal surveys, including the Survey of Income and Program Participation (SIPP) 2004 Panel, give respondents the option of reporting more than one race. These data can be shown in two ways (1) as mutually exclusive from other race groups, which may be denoted by "alone" or (2) not mutually exclusive with other race groups, denoted by "alone or in combination with other race groups." This figure shows race using the first method. Because Hispanics may be of any race, data for Hispanics are not mutually exclusive with race. Female householders have no husband present and male householders have no wife present.

SOURCE: Robin J. Anderson, "Figure 4. Poverty Exit Rates: People in Poverty in 2004 but Not in Poverty in 2006 by Selected Characteristics," in *Dynamics of Economic Well-Being: Poverty, 2004–2006*, U.S. Census Bureau, March 2011, http://www.census.gov/hhes/www/poverty/publications/dynamics04/P70-123.pdf (accessed February 6, 2013)

FIGURE 2.5

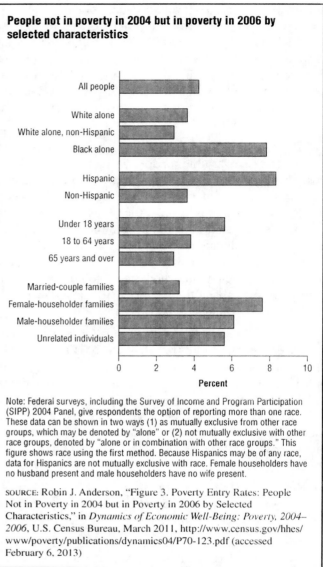

People not in poverty in 2004 but in poverty in 2006 by selected characteristics

Note: Federal surveys, including the Survey of Income and Program Participation (SIPP) 2004 Panel, give respondents the option of reporting more than one race. These data can be shown in two ways (1) as mutually exclusive from other race groups, which may be denoted by "alone" or (2) not mutually exclusive with other race groups, denoted by "alone or in combination with other race groups." This figure shows race using the first method. Because Hispanics may be of any race, data for Hispanics are not mutually exclusive with race. Female householders have no husband present and male householders have no wife present.

SOURCE: Robin J. Anderson, "Figure 3. Poverty Entry Rates: People Not in Poverty in 2004 but in Poverty in 2006 by Selected Characteristics," in *Dynamics of Economic Well-Being: Poverty, 2004–2006*, U.S. Census Bureau, March 2011, http://www.census.gov/hhes/www/poverty/publications/dynamics04/P70-123.pdf (accessed February 6, 2013)

Figure 2.6 shows the proportion of the entire population, the episodically poor population, and the chronically poor population made up of different age groups. Children are disproportionally represented among the poor. Even though they made up 26.1% of the population as a whole, they represent 32.8% of the episodically poor population and 44.9% of the chronically poor population. Adults aged 18 to 64 years were underrepresented among the poor, especially among the chronically poor, whereas adults aged 65 years and older, who often live on fixed incomes, were underrepresented among the episodically poor.

FAMILY STATUS. According to Anderson, poor families headed by married couples were much more likely than other poor family types to have left poverty by 2006, underscoring how having two potential wage earners in a family helps protect a family from poverty. Of the poor families headed by married couples in 2004, 50.3% were able to escape poverty by 2006. (See Figure 2.4.) Only 33% of the poor families headed by women recovered from poverty by 2006. Families headed by married couples were also significantly less likely to have entered poverty by 2006. (See Figure 2.5.) With at least two adults in the household, these families are more likely to have at least one person working than a family headed by a single person.

Figure 2.6 shows the proportion of the entire population, the episodically poor population, and the chronically poor population made up of unrelated individuals, female-householder families, male-householder families, and married-couple families. Female-householder families, which make up 14.4% of households in 2006, were overrepresented among the poor; they made up 25.8% of the episodically poor households and 49.9% of the chronically poor households. In contrast, married-couple families made up 65.9% of all households, but only 47.7% of the episodically poor households and only 17% of the chronically poor households.

FIGURE 2.6

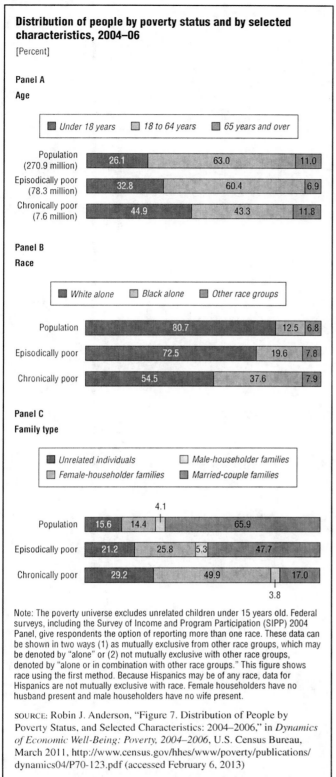

Distribution of people by poverty status and by selected characteristics, 2004–06

[Percent]

Panel A
Age

- Under 18 years
- 18 to 64 years
- 65 years and over

	Under 18	18 to 64	65+
Population (270.9 million)	26.1	63.0	11.0
Episodically poor (78.3 million)	32.8	60.4	6.9
Chronically poor (7.6 million)	44.9	43.3	11.8

Panel B
Race

- White alone
- Black alone
- Other race groups

	White	Black	Other
Population	80.7	12.5	6.8
Episodically poor	72.5	19.6	7.8
Chronically poor	54.5	37.6	7.9

Panel C
Family type

- Unrelated individuals
- Female-householder families
- Male-householder families
- Married-couple families

	Unrelated individuals	Female-householder	Male-householder	Married-couple
Population	15.6	14.4	4.1	65.9
Episodically poor	21.2	25.8	5.3	47.7
Chronically poor	29.2	49.9	3.8	17.0

Note: The poverty universe excludes unrelated children under 15 years old. Federal surveys, including the Survey of Income and Program Participation (SIPP) 2004 Panel, give respondents the option of reporting more than one race. These data can be shown in two ways (1) as mutually exclusive from other race groups, which may be denoted by "alone" or (2) not mutually exclusive with other race groups, denoted by "alone or in combination with other race groups." This figure shows race using the first method. Because Hispanics may be of any race, data for Hispanics are not mutually exclusive with race. Female householders have no husband present and male householders have no wife present.

SOURCE: Robin J. Anderson, "Figure 7. Distribution of People by Poverty Status, and Selected Characteristics: 2004–2006," in *Dynamics of Economic Well-Being: Poverty, 2004–2006*, U.S. Census Bureau, March 2011, http://www.census.gov/hhes/www/poverty/publications/dynamics04/P70-123.pdf (accessed February 6, 2013).

Having a Job Does Not Guarantee Escape from Poverty

The working poor are those people who participated in the labor force for at least 27 weeks (either working or looking for work) and who lived in families with incomes below the official poverty level. Approximately 10.5 million workers in 2010 (7.2% of individuals aged 16 years and older in the labor force) found that their jobs did not provide enough income to keep them out of poverty. (See Table 2.16.)

In 2010, 5.2 million working women and 5.3 million working men had incomes below the poverty level. (See Table 2.16.) Because there were fewer women in the labor force, working women had a higher poverty rate (7.6%) than working men (6.7%). Approximately 7.7 million (73.5%) of the working poor were white, 3 million (28.6%) were Hispanic, 2.1 million (20.2%) were African-American, and 339,000 (3.2%) were Asian-American. Even though whites constituted the bulk of the working poor, African-Americans and Hispanics experienced poverty while employed at much higher rates than whites. In 2010, 12.6% of African-Americans in the labor force were below the poverty line, as were 14.1% of Hispanics, compared with 6.5% of whites and 4.8% of Asian-Americans.

Workers between the ages of 16 and 24 years were much more likely to be in poverty than older workers in 2010. Approximately 14.4% of workers aged 16 to 19 and 15.5% of workers aged 20 to 24 did not make enough income to rise above the poverty line, compared with 9.2% of workers between the ages of 25 and 34 years and 7.3% of workers aged 35 to 44. (See Table 2.16.) Much of the reason for this is that many younger workers are still in school and/or work at part-time or entry-level jobs that often do not pay well. In general, as age increases, the likelihood of being both in the labor force and poor decreases.

Educational levels typically correlate directly with the risk of poverty among workers. Among workers in the labor force for at least 27 weeks in 2010, 21.4% of those with less than a high school diploma fell below the poverty level, compared with 9.2% of high school graduates. (See Table 2.17.) Far lower poverty rates were reported for workers with an associate's degree (4.5%) or a four-year college degree (2.1%). African-American and Hispanic workers, regardless of education levels, had higher poverty rates than white workers. Women had a higher poverty rate than men at all educational levels and among all race and ethnic groups. The highest poverty rate (36.2%) was for African-American women workers without a high school diploma.

In 2010 working families headed by married couples without children were less likely than other family types to be poor (1.9%). (See Table 2.18.) The presence of children under the age of 18 years increased the married-couple poverty rate to 7.3%, reflecting the added monetary burdens of raising children and the decreased likelihood that a family will have two adults working full time. Single women with children were the most likely to be living in poverty (28.2%), although a significant portion of single men with children were among the working poor (18%).

TABLE 2.16

Poverty status of people in the labor force for 27 weeks or more, by age, sex, race, and Hispanic origin, 2010

[Numbers in thousands]

Age and sex	Total	White	Black or African American	Asian	Hispanic or Latino ethnicity	Total	White	Black or African American	Asian	Hispanic or Latino ethnicity	Total	White	Black or African American	Asian	Hispanic or Latino ethnicity
						Below poverty level					Rate[a]				
Total, 16 years and older	**146,859**	**119,582**	**16,827**	**7,063**	**21,283**	**10,512**	**7,728**	**2,120**	**339**	**3,010**	**7.2**	**6.5**	**12.6**	**4.8**	**14.1**
16 to 19 years	3,140	2,621	329	72	571	452	326	101	7	125	14.4	12.4	30.6	[b]	21.8
20 to 24 years	13,300	10,669	1,795	449	2,546	2,057	1,531	429	43	421	15.5	14.3	23.9	9.5	16.5
25 to 34 years	32,561	25,743	4,216	1,661	6,127	3,005	2,132	670	89	954	9.2	8.3	15.9	5.4	15.6
35 to 44 years	32,056	25,461	3,884	1,948	5,467	2,353	1,778	428	87	862	7.3	7.0	11.0	4.5	15.8
45 to 54 years	34,721	28,539	3,870	1,636	4,068	1,689	1,258	314	66	454	4.9	4.4	8.1	4.0	11.2
55 to 64 years	24,066	20,426	2,197	1,049	1,943	814	604	148	43	162	3.4	3.0	6.8	4.1	8.3
65 years and older	7,015	6,122	536	247	560	143	99	30	5	32	2.0	1.6	5.5	2.1	5.8
Men, 16 years and older	**78,626**	**65,229**	**7,848**	**3,759**	**12,653**	**5,299**	**4,166**	**816**	**167**	**1,817**	**6.7**	**6.4**	**10.4**	**4.4**	**14.4**
16 to 19 years	1,577	1,317	153	37	328	206	164	27	4	74	13.1	12.5	17.9	[b]	22.5
20 to 24 years	7,035	5,720	862	253	1,547	908	718	160	12	211	12.9	12.6	18.5	4.8	13.6
25 to 34 years	17,908	14,446	2,031	926	3,857	1,568	1,228	226	51	615	8.8	8.5	11.1	5.5	15.9
35 to 44 years	17,362	14,146	1,784	1,022	3,275	1,242	1,023	161	33	549	7.2	7.2	9.0	3.2	16.8
45 to 54 years	18,223	15,244	1,790	854	2,255	890	674	150	45	268	4.9	4.4	8.4	5.2	11.9
55 to 64 years	12,627	10,900	987	526	1,081	408	305	75	19	80	3.2	2.8	7.6	3.6	7.4
65 years and older	3,893	3,455	240	141	311	77	54	16	3	20	2.0	1.6	6.7	2.2	6.4
Women, 16 years and older	**68,234**	**54,353**	**8,979**	**3,304**	**8,630**	**5,213**	**3,561**	**1,304**	**173**	**1,193**	**7.6**	**6.6**	**14.5**	**5.2**	**13.8**
16 to 19 years	1,563	1,304	177	35	244	246	162	74	3	51	15.7	12.4	41.7	[b]	20.9
20 to 24 years	6,265	4,950	933	196	999	1,149	813	269	30	210	18.3	16.4	28.8	15.5	21.0
25 to 34 years	14,652	11,296	2,185	735	2,270	1,437	904	444	38	339	9.8	8.0	20.3	5.2	15.0
35 to 44 years	14,694	11,314	2,099	927	2,192	1,111	756	267	54	314	7.6	6.7	12.7	5.8	14.3
45 to 54 years	16,498	13,295	2,079	782	1,814	799	584	163	21	186	4.8	4.4	7.9	2.7	10.2
55 to 64 years	11,439	9,526	1,209	524	862	406	299	73	24	81	3.5	3.1	6.0	4.6	9.4
65 years and older	3,122	2,667	297	105	249	66	45	14	—	12	2.1	1.7	4.6	1.9	4.9

[a]Number below the poverty level as a percent of the total in the labor force for 27 or more weeks.

[b]Data not shown where base is less than 80,000.

Note: Estimates for the race groups shown (white, black or African American, and Asian) do not sum to totals because data are not presented for all races. Persons whose ethnicity is identified as Hispanic or Latino may be of any race. Dash represents or rounds to zero.

SOURCE: "Table 2. People in the Labor Force for 27 or More Weeks: Poverty Status by Age, Sex, Race, and Hispanic or Latino Ethnicity, 2010," in *A Profile of the Working Poor, 2010,* U.S. Department of Labor, U.S. Bureau of Labor Statistics, March 2012, http://www.bls.gov/cps/cpswp2010.pdf (accessed January 16, 2013)

TABLE 2.17

Poverty status by educational attainment, race and Hispanic origin, and sex, 2010

[Numbers in thousands]

Educational attainment, race, and Hispanic or Latino ethnicity	Total	Men	Women	Below poverty level Total	Below poverty level Men	Below poverty level Women	Rate[a] Total	Rate[a] Men	Rate[a] Women
Total, 16 years and older	**146,859**	**78,626**	**68,234**	**10,512**	**5,299**	**5,213**	**7.2**	**6.7**	**7.6**
Less than a high school diploma	13,471	8,600	4,870	2,883	1,719	1,164	21.4	20.0	23.9
Less than 1 year of high school	4,396	2,950	1,445	1,082	715	367	24.6	24.2	25.4
1–3 years of high school	7,448	4,627	2,821	1,526	838	688	20.5	18.1	24.4
4 years of high school, no diploma	1,627	1,023	604	275	166	109	16.9	16.2	18.1
High school graduates, no college[b]	41,848	24,145	17,703	3,850	1,936	1,913	9.2	8.0	10.8
Some college or associate's degree	43,276	21,012	22,264	2,770	1,115	1,655	6.4	5.3	7.4
Some college, no degree	28,240	14,140	14,100	2,091	855	1,236	7.4	6.0	8.8
Associate's degree	15,036	6,872	8,164	678	260	419	4.5	3.8	5.1
Bachelor's degree and higher[c]	48,265	24,869	23,396	1,009	529	480	2.1	2.1	2.1
White, 16 years and older	**119,582**	**65,229**	**54,353**	**7,728**	**4,166**	**3,561**	**6.5**	**6.4**	**6.6**
Less than a high school diploma	10,902	7,161	3,740	2,270	1,445	825	20.8	20.2	22.1
Less than 1 year of high school	3,761	2,597	1,164	927	641	286	24.7	24.7	24.6
1–3 years of high school	5,914	3,763	2,152	1,135	664	471	19.2	17.6	21.9
4 years of high school, no diploma	1,227	802	425	208	140	68	17.0	17.5	16.0
High school graduates, no college[b]	33,764	19,801	13,962	2,705	1,453	1,252	8.0	7.3	9.0
Some college or associate's degree	34,992	17,355	17,637	1,963	847	1,116	5.6	4.9	6.3
Some college, no degree	22,651	11,608	11,044	1,496	656	840	6.6	5.7	7.6
Associate's degree	12,341	5,748	6,593	467	191	276	3.8	3.3	4.2
Bachelor's degree and higher[c]	39,924	20,911	19,013	789	421	368	2.0	2.0	1.9
Black or African American, 16 years and older	**16,827**	**7,848**	**8,979**	**2,120**	**816**	**1,304**	**12.6**	**10.4**	**14.5**
Less than a high school diploma	1,595	879	715	439	181	259	27.6	20.6	36.2
Less than 1 year of high school	263	156	108	92	45	47	34.9	28.7	44.0
1–3 years of high school	1,077	593	483	300	126	175	27.9	21.2	36.1
4 years of high school, no diploma	255	130	125	47	10	37	18.5	8.1	29.4
High school graduates, no college[b]	5,654	3,024	2,630	901	367	533	15.9	12.1	20.3
Some college or associate's degree	5,806	2,405	3,400	656	213	443	11.3	8.9	13.0
Some college, no degree	3,948	1,681	2,267	485	158	326	12.3	9.4	14.4
Associate's degree	1,858	724	1,134	171	55	116	9.2	7.6	10.3
Bachelor's degree and higher[c]	3,772	1,539	2,233	124	55	69	3.3	3.6	3.1
Asian, 16 years and older	**7,063**	**3,759**	**3,304**	**339**	**167**	**173**	**4.8**	**4.4**	**5.2**
Less than a high school diploma	542	289	253	71	37	34	13.1	12.7	13.4
Less than 1 year of high school	250	117	133	33	13	20	13.2	10.7	15.4
1–3 years of high school	203	120	83	31	17	14	15.2	14.3	16.5
4 years of high school, no diploma	89	51	38	7	7	—	[d]	[d]	[d]
High school graduates, no college[b]	1,370	701	670	114	57	57	8.3	8.2	8.5
Some college or associate's degree	1,350	708	642	74	28	47	5.5	3.9	7.3
Some college, no degree	871	466	405	53	21	32	6.1	4.5	8.0
Associate's degree	480	242	237	21	7	14	4.5	2.9	6.0
Bachelor's degree and higher[c]	3,800	2,061	1,739	80	45	35	2.1	2.2	2.0
Hispanic or Latino ethnicity, 16 years and older	**21,283**	**12,653**	**8,630**	**3,010**	**1,817**	**1,193**	**14.1**	**14.4**	**13.8**
Less than a high school diploma	6,281	4,269	2,012	1,557	1,025	532	24.8	24.0	26.5
Less than 1 year of high school	3,190	2,189	1,001	822	564	258	25.8	25.8	25.8
1–3 years of high school	2,451	1,649	803	595	370	225	24.3	22.4	28.0
4 years of high school, no diploma	640	431	208	140	90	50	21.9	20.9	23.9
High school graduates, no college[b]	6,741	4,205	2,536	923	550	372	13.7	13.1	14.7
Some college or associate's degree	5,125	2,629	2,496	413	180	233	8.1	6.8	9.4
Some college, no degree	3,573	1,924	1,649	313	148	165	8.8	7.7	10.0
Associate's degree	1,552	705	847	100	32	69	6.5	4.5	8.1
Bachelor's degree and higher[c]	3,136	1,551	1,586	117	62	55	3.7	4.0	3.5

[a]Number below the poverty level as a percent of the total in the labor force for 27 or more weeks.
[b]Includes people with a high school diploma or equivalent.
[c]Includes people with bachelor's, master's, professional, and doctoral degrees.
[d]Data not shown where base is less than 80,000.
Note: Estimates for the race groups shown (white, black or African American, and Asian) do not sum to totals because data are not presented for all races. Persons whose ethnicity is identified as Hispanic or Latino may be of any race. Dash represents or rounds to zero.

SOURCE: "Table 3. People in the Labor Force for 27 or More Weeks: Poverty Status by Educational Attainment, Race, Hispanic or Latino Ethnicity, and Sex, 2010," in *A Profile of the Working Poor, 2010*, U.S. Department of Labor, U.S. Bureau of Labor Statistics, March 2012, http://www.bls.gov/cps/cpswp2010.pdf (accessed January 16, 2013)

Finally, the labor market plays a major role in whether a working family lives in poverty. Three major labor market problems contributed to poverty among workers in 2010: unemployment, low earnings, and involuntary part-time employment. Only 0.8% of workers who did not suffer from any of these problems were poor in 2010. (See Table 2.19.) By

TABLE 2.18

Poverty status of families, by presence of related children and work experience of family members, 2010

[Numbers in thousands]

Characteristic	Total families	At or above poverty level	Below poverty level	Rate*
Total primary families	**64,931**	**59,662**	**5,269**	**8.1**
With related children under 18 years	34,722	30,299	4,424	12.7
Without children	30,209	29,363	846	2.8
With one member in the labor force	27,726	23,403	4,322	15.6
With two or more members in the labor force	37,206	36,259	947	2.5
With two members	31,186	30,375	811	2.6
With three or more members	6,020	5,884	136	2.3
Married-couple families	**48,427**	**46,167**	**2,260**	**4.7**
With related children under 18 years	24,518	22,724	1,794	7.3
Without children	23,908	23,443	465	1.9
With one member in the labor force	16,288	14,651	1,637	10.1
Husband	11,589	10,310	1,279	11.0
Wife	4,052	3,755	296	7.3
Relative	647	585	62	9.6
With two or more members in the labor force	32,139	31,516	623	1.9
With two members	27,197	26,653	544	2.0
With three or more members	4,942	4,863	79	1.6
Families maintained by women	**11,678**	**9,211**	**2,466**	**21.1**
With related children under 18 years	7,793	5,597	2,196	28.2
Without children	3,885	3,615	270	7.0
With one member in the labor force	8,452	6,232	2,221	26.3
Householder	7,003	5,063	1,940	27.7
Relative	1,450	1,169	281	19.4
With two or more members in the labor force	3,225	2,980	246	7.6
Families maintained by men	**4,827**	**4,284**	**543**	**11.2**
With related children under 18 years	2,411	1,978	433	18.0
Without children	2,416	2,306	110	4.5
With one member in the labor force	2,986	2,521	465	15.6
Householder	2,448	2,059	390	15.9
Relative	537	462	75	13.9
With two or more members in the labor force	1,841	1,763	78	4.2

*Number below the poverty level as a percent of the total in the labor force for 27 or more weeks.
Note: Data relate to primary families with at least one member in the labor force for 27 or more weeks.

SOURCE: "Table 5. Primary Families: Poverty Status, Presence of Related Children, and Work Experience of Family Members in the Labor Force for 27 or More Weeks, 2010," in *A Profile of the Working Poor, 2010*, U.S. Department of Labor, U.S. Bureau of Labor Statistics, March 2012, http://www.bls.gov/cps/cpswp2010.pdf (accessed January 16, 2013)

contrast, 22.1% of low-paid workers were in poverty. Unemployment accounted for the poverty of 8.6% of workers, and involuntary part-time work for 2.4%. However, it was the combination of two or more factors that had the most devastating effect on families. Among workers who experienced unemployment and low earnings, 40.5% were in poverty, as were 40.1% of those who experienced unemployment, low earnings, and involuntary part-time employment.

TABLE 2.19

Poverty status and labor market problems of full-time wage and salary workers, 2010

[Numbers in thousands]

Labor market problems	Total	At or above poverty level	Below poverty level	Rate[a]
Total, full-time wage and salary workers	**109,077**	**104,938**	**4,139**	**3.8**
No unemployment, involuntary part-time employment, or low earnings[b]	87,455	86,788	667	0.8
Unemployment only	7,668	7,008	659	8.6
Involuntary part-time employment only	2,816	2,749	68	2.4
Low earnings only	6,624	5,162	1,462	22.1
Unemployment and involuntary part-time employment	1,369	1,251	117	8.6
Unemployment and low earnings	1,812	1,079	734	40.5
Involuntary part-time employment and low earnings	809	587	222	27.5
Unemployment, involuntary part-time employment, and low earnings	524	314	210	40.1
Unemployment (alone or with other problems)	11,373	9,653	1,721	15.1
Involuntary part-time employment (alone or with other problems)	5,519	4,901	618	11.2
Low earnings (alone or with other problems)	9,770	7,141	2,628	26.9

[a]Number below the poverty level as a percent of the total in the labor force for 27 or more weeks.
[b]The low-earnings threshold in 2010 was $320.94 per week.

SOURCE: "Table 8. People in the Labor Force for 27 or More Weeks: Poverty Status and Labor Market Problems of Full-Time Wage and Salary Workers, 2010," in *A Profile of the Working Poor, 2010*, U.S. Department of Labor, U.S. Bureau of Labor Statistics, March 2012, http://www.bls.gov/cps/cpswp2010.pdf (accessed January 16, 2013)

CHAPTER 3
PUBLIC PROGRAMS TO FIGHT POVERTY

The federal government and individual states use many methods and administer a variety of assistance programs to combat poverty, by helping those whose incomes are below the poverty line as well as those who are at risk of poverty. These programs are often collectively referred to as welfare. Some, such as Temporary Assistance for Needy Families (TANF), which offers cash assistance to the poor, are designed to help people improve their situation and escape poverty. A number of programs, including the Supplemental Nutrition Assistance Program (SNAP, or the food stamp program) are designed to help those in poverty meet their basic needs. The Supplemental Security Income (SSI) program, meanwhile, provides assistance to people who have conditions that make it difficult for them to earn a living. In addition to welfare programs, the government has established policies such as the minimum wage and unemployment compensation that are intended to help people avoid poverty in the first place.

The first comprehensive welfare programs were established during the 1930s, and the overall welfare system was supplemented substantially in the 1960s. The most important change to the welfare system enacted since that time is the Personal Responsibility and Work Opportunity Reconciliation Act (PRWORA). First enacted in 1996 and renewed since, the PRWORA replaced a welfare system that was based primarily on the Aid to Families with Dependent Children (AFDC) program with one centered on TANF. Critics of the AFDC asserted that the system produced welfare dependency rather than temporary assistance to help recipients move into a job and off welfare. TANF was specifically designed to limit the amount of time individuals could receive benefits and to require them to work. The intention of the law was to reduce the number of people receiving welfare by bringing them into the workforce and out of poverty. The PRWORA also changed some other welfare programs to place greater

emphasis on these priorities. In "Policy Basics: An Introduction to TANF" (March 19, 2009, http://www.cbpp.org/cms/index.cfm?fa=view&id=936), Liz Schott of the Center on Budget and Policy Priorities (CBPP) notes that additional work requirements for TANF recipients put in place by the Deficit Reduction Act of 2005 further reduced the TANF caseload.

According to the U.S. Department of Health and Human Services (HHS) and the Census Bureau, the TANF caseload fell from a monthly average of 4.4 million families in 1996 to an average of 1.9 million families in 2010, a drop of 57%. (See Table 3.1.) This represents the largest welfare caseload decline in history. Observers agreed that some of the decline, especially in the first five years after welfare reform, was the result not necessarily of the reform itself but of a strong economy in which unemployment was about 4%. For example, a study conducted by the City University of New York and cited by the HHS in *Temporary Assistance for Needy Families Program (TANF): Fourth Annual Report to Congress* (April 2002) attributes 60% of the reductions in caseloads to welfare reform and 20% to the effects of a robust economy.

Critics of the PRWORA frequently suggest that the reduction in welfare caseloads, especially in the years since 2001, does not represent the large-scale movement of poor families from the welfare rolls into the labor force but represents, instead, the descent of many needy families further into poverty. In "Chart Book: TANF at 16" (August 22, 2012, http://www.cbpp.org/cms/index.cfm?fa=view&id=3566), the CBPP maintains that in the early years after welfare reform, there was an unprecedented movement of single mothers off of the welfare rolls and into the labor force, and that the trend was particularly pronounced among women without high school diplomas. Poverty began increasing in 2000, however, and unemployment rose in the years that followed even though the overall economy was growing. Then,

TABLE 3.1

Trends in the cash welfare caseload, 1961–2011

[Numbers in thousands]

Year	Families	Recipients	Adults	Children	As a percent of total children[a]	As a percent of all poor children[b]
1961	873	3,363	765	2,598	3.7	14.3
1962	939	3,704	860	2,844	4.0	15.7
1963	963	3,945	988	2,957	4.1	17.4
1964	1,010	4,195	1,050	3,145	4.3	18.6
1965	1,060	4,422	1,101	3,321	4.5	21.5
1966	1,096	4,546	1,112	3,434	4.7	26.5
1967	1,220	5,014	1,243	3,771	5.2	31.2
1968	1,410	5,702	1,429	4,274	5.9	37.8
1969	1,696	6,689	1,716	4,973	6.9	49.7
1970	2,207	8,462	2,250	6,212	8.6	57.7
1971	2,763	10,242	2,808	7,435	10.4	68.5
1972	3,048	10,944	3,039	7,905	11.1	74.9
1973	3,148	10,949	3,046	7,903	11.2	79.9
1974	3,219	10,847	3,041	7,805	11.2	75.0
1975	3,481	11,319	3,248	8,071	11.8	71.2
1976	3,565	11,284	3,302	7,982	11.8	76.2
1977	3,568	11,015	3,273	7,743	11.6	73.9
1978	3,517	10,551	3,188	7,363	11.2	72.8
1979	3,509	10,312	3,130	7,181	11.0	68.0
1980	3,712	10,774	3,355	7,419	11.5	63.2
1981	3,835	11,079	3,552	7,527	11.7	59.2
1982	3,542	10,358	3,455	6,903	10.8	49.6
1983	3,686	10,761	3,663	7,098	11.1	50.1
1984	3,714	10,831	3,687	7,144	11.2	52.3
1985	3,701	10,855	3,658	7,198	11.3	54.4
1986	3,763	11,038	3,704	7,334	11.5	56.0
1987	3,776	11,027	3,661	7,366	11.5	56.4
1988	3,749	10,915	3,586	7,329	11.4	57.8
1989	3,798	10,992	3,573	7,419	11.5	57.9
1990	4,057	11,695	3,784	7,911	12.1	57.9
1991	4,497	12,930	4,216	8,715	13.2	59.8
1992	4,829	13,773	4,470	9,303	13.9	59.9
1993	5,012	14,205	4,631	9,574	14.1	60.0
1994	5,033	14,161	4,593	9,568	13.9	61.7
1995	4,791	13,418	4,284	9,135	13.1	61.5
1996	4,434	12,321	3,928	8,600	12.3	58.7
1997	3,740	10,376	2,595	6,273	10.0	50.1
1998	3,050	8,347	2,074	5,319	8.1	42.9
1999	2,578	6,924	1,820	4,807	6.7	39.4
2000	2,303	6,143	1,655	4,479	6.1	38.1
2001	2,192	5,717	1,514	4,195	5.7	35.3
2002	2,187	5,609	1,479	4,119	5.6	33.6
2003	2,180	5,490	1,416	4,063	5.5	31.3
2004	2,153	5,342	1,362	3,969	5.4	30.2
2005	2,061	5,028	1,261	3,756	5.1	28.9
2006	1,906	4,582	1,120	3,453	4.6	26.7
2007	1,730	4,075	956	3,119	4.2	23.2
2008	1,701	4,005	946	3,059	4.1	21.6
2009	1,838	4,371	1,074	3,296	4.4	21.2
2010	1,919	4,598	1,163	3,435	4.6	20.9
2011	1,908	4,559	1,150	3,409	4.6	20.9

[a]Child recipients in the 50 states and District of Columbia divided by the number of resident children in the 50 states and District of Columbia.
[b]Child recipients in the 50 states and District of Columbia divided by the number of children (persons under the age of 18) in poverty as measured by the U.S. Census Bureau.

SOURCE: "Table 7-9. Trends in the Cash Welfare Caseload: 1961 to 2011," in *Background Material and Data on the Programs within the Jurisdiction of the Committee on Ways and Means (Green Book)*, U.S. House of Representatives Committee on Ways and Means, 2012, http://greenbook.waysandmeans.house .gov/sites/greenbook.waysandmeans.house.gov/files/2012/documents/Table%207-9%20TANF.pdf (accessed February 7, 2013)

with the so-called Great Recession that lasted from late 2007 to the summer of 2009, unemployment and poverty rates reached levels not seen since the early 1980s. The employment gains among impoverished single mothers disappeared during this time, but TANF caseloads did not grow proportionately.

By design TANF does not respond to worsening economic conditions, so it did little to alleviate poverty during the Great Recession and its prolonged aftermath. The administration of President Barack Obama (1961–) responded to the economic crisis by passing the American Recovery and Reinvestment Act (ARRA), which was signed into law in February 2009. The law provided, among many other measures meant to stimulate the economy, additional TANF resources to states through an emergency contingency fund that helps the states assist poor families during the recession while leaving the basic principles of TANF in place. Nevertheless, LaDonna Pavetti, Danilo Trisi, and Liz Schott of the CBPP find in *TANF Responded Unevenly to Increase in Need during Downturn: Findings Suggest Needed Improvements When Program Reauthorized* (January 25, 2011, http://www .cbpp.org/files/1-25-11tanf.pdf) that TANF caseloads increased by only 13% during the recession, even as the number of unemployed people doubled. During the Great Recession, unemployment rose from less than 5% in 2007 to a peak of 10% in 2009; and it remained well above historic norms, at 7.8%, at the end of 2012. (See Table 1.3 in Chapter 1.) Because TANF benefits are tied to work requirements, however, a situation in which no jobs are available also creates circumstances in which few people qualify for TANF benefits. By contrast SNAP, or the food stamp program, which is also designed to help those below the poverty line, is highly responsive to fluctuating numbers of poor people, and its caseload grew by 45% during the recession, roughly in proportion with the rising numbers of the unemployed.

TANF's responsiveness to economic fluctuations is further limited by the fact that states have wide latitude in administering benefits. States have no obligation to increase caseloads even when the level of need among their residents increases, so in 22 states TANF had small caseload increases or caseload declines during the recession. Though the recession's effects on poor Americans remained pronounced well beyond its official end, Congress failed to act on President Obama's request to renew the emergency TANF funding, and this supplemental funding was discontinued on September 30, 2010.

There was widespread consensus among advocates for the poor that, as a result of such circumstances, TANF was not meeting the needs of impoverished Americans. As Figure 3.1 shows, in 1996, 68 of 100 poor families were receiving cash assistance under AFDC, but by 2010 only 27 of every 100 poor families were receiving cash

assistance under TANF. Moreover, as the CBPP points out in "TANF at 16," even those who receive TANF benefits cannot meet their most basic needs. In 2011 benefits were less than half of the federal poverty level in all 50 states, and in 15 states TANF benefits amounted to only 10% to 20% of the federal poverty level. (See Figure 3.2.)

THE PERSONAL RESPONSIBILITY AND WORK OPPORTUNITY RECONCILIATION ACT

The following pages discuss the specific provisions of PRWORA.

Title I: Block Grants

Under the PRWORA, each state receives a single block grant (a lump sum of money). States have considerable control over how they implement the programs that are covered by the block grant, but the act requires that:

- Families on welfare for five cumulative years no longer receive further cash assistance. States can set shorter time limits and can exempt up to 20% of their caseload from the time limits.

- To count toward meeting the work requirement, a state must require individuals to participate in employment (public or private), on-the-job training, community service, work experience, vocational training (up to 12 months), or child care for other workers for at least 20 hours per week. State and local communities are responsible for the development of work, whether by creating community service jobs or by providing income subsidies or hiring incentives for potential employers.

- Unmarried parents under the age of 18 years must live with an adult or with adult supervision and must participate in educational or job training to receive benefits. In addition, the law encourages second-chance homes to provide teen parents with the skills

FIGURE 3.1

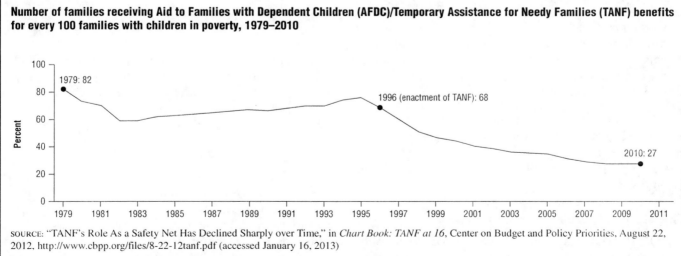

Number of families receiving Aid to Families with Dependent Children (AFDC)/Temporary Assistance for Needy Families (TANF) benefits for every 100 families with children in poverty, 1979–2010

SOURCE: "TANF's Role As a Safety Net Has Declined Sharply over Time," in *Chart Book: TANF at 16*, Center on Budget and Policy Priorities, August 22, 2012, http://www.cbpp.org/files/8-22-12tanf.pdf (accessed January 16, 2013)

FIGURE 3.2

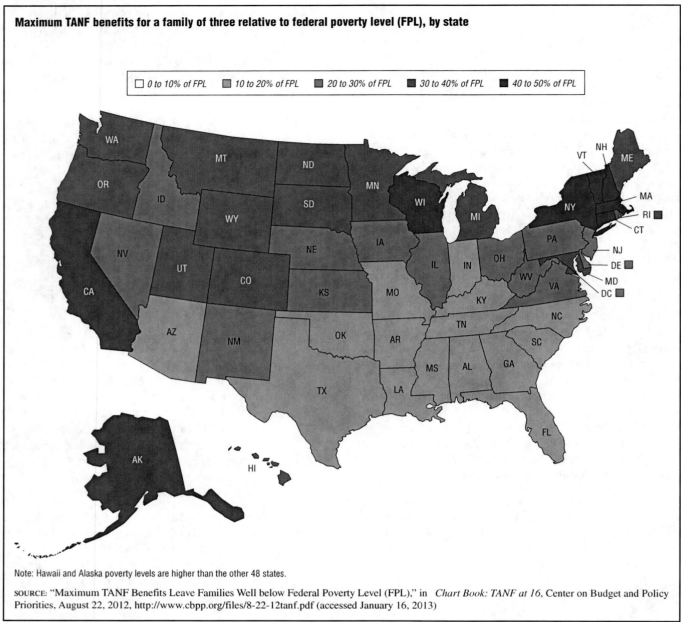

Maximum TANF benefits for a family of three relative to federal poverty level (FPL), by state

☐ *0 to 10% of FPL* ▨ *10 to 20% of FPL* ▨ *20 to 30% of FPL* ▨ *30 to 40% of FPL* ■ *40 to 50% of FPL*

Note: Hawaii and Alaska poverty levels are higher than the other 48 states.

SOURCE: "Maximum TANF Benefits Leave Families Well below Federal Poverty Level (FPL)," in *Chart Book: TANF at 16*, Center on Budget and Policy Priorities, August 22, 2012, http://www.cbpp.org/files/8-22-12tanf.pdf (accessed January 16, 2013)

and support they need. The law also provides $50 million per year in new funding for state abstinence education activities that are geared toward discouraging teen pregnancy through abstinence rather than through birth control.

None of the block grant funds can be used for adults who have been on welfare for over five years or who do not work after receiving benefits for two years. However, states are given some flexibility in how they spend their TANF funds.

Title II: Supplemental Security Income

The PRWORA redefined the term *disability* for children who receive SSI. A child is considered disabled if he

or she has a medically determinable physical or mental impairment that results in marked and severe functional limitations that have lasted or can be expected to last at least 12 months or that can be expected to cause death. The PRWORA removed "maladaptive behavior" as a medical criterion from the listing of impairments used for evaluating mental disabilities in children.

Title III: Child Support

To be eligible for federal funds, each state must operate a Child Support Enforcement program that meets federal guidelines. The state must establish centralized registries of child support orders and centers for the collection and disbursement of child support payments, and parents must sign their child support rights over to the state to be eligible for TANF benefits. The state must also establish enforcement methods, such as revoking the driver's and professional licenses of delinquent parents. The Administration for Children and Families (ACF) notes in the fact sheet "Office of Child Support Enforcement (OCSE)" (http://www.acf.hhs.gov/programs/css/resource/ocse-fact-sheet) that in FY 2011 the program handled 17.3 million cases at a cost of $4 billion.

To receive full benefits, a mother must cooperate with state efforts to establish paternity. She may be denied assistance if she refuses to disclose the father.

Title IV: Restricting Welfare and Public Benefits for Noncitizens

The PRWORA originally severely limited or banned benefits to most legal immigrants who entered the country on or after August 22, 1996, when the bill became law. Ineligibility continued for a five-year period or until the legal immigrants attained citizenship. In addition, states had the option of withholding eligibility for Medicaid, TANF, and other social services from legal immigrants already residing in the United States.

Illegal immigrants no longer had any entitlement to benefit programs, such as TANF or Medicaid. They could receive emergency medical care, short-term disaster relief, immunizations, and treatment for communicable diseases (in the interest of public health). They could also use community services such as soup kitchens and shelters, some housing programs, and school lunches/breakfasts if their children were eligible for free public education. States have established programs to verify the legal residence of immigrants before paying benefits and may elect to deny Special Supplemental Food Program for Women, Infants, and Children benefits and other child nutrition programs to illegal immigrants.

The Balanced Budget Act of 1997 and the Noncitizen Technical Amendment Act of 1998 invested $11.5 billion to restore disability and health benefits to 380,000 legal immigrants who were in the United States before the PRWORA became law in August 1996. The Balanced Budget Act also extended the SSI and Medicaid eligibility period for refugees and people seeking asylum from five years after entry to seven years to give these residents more time to naturalize.

Title V: Child Protection

The PRWORA gave states the authority to use current federal funds to pay for foster care for children in child care institutions. It extended the enhanced federal match for statewide automated child welfare information systems through 1997 and appropriated $6 million per year (FYs 1996 to 2002) for a national random sample study of abused and neglected children.

Title VI: Child Care

The law required that states maintain spending for child care for low-income families at the level of FY 1994 or FY 1995, whichever was greater, to be eligible for federally matched funds. Mandatory funding was set at $13.9 billion through June 30, 2004, with states receiving an estimated $1.2 billion per year before matching began. The remainder of the funds was available for state matching at the Medicaid rate.

As Liz Schott, LaDonna Pavetti, and Ife Finch of the CBPP write in "How States Have Spent Federal and State Funds under the TANF Block Grant" (August 7, 2012, http://www.cbpp.org/cms/index.cfm?fa=view&id=3808), the child care portion of TANF was one of the program's bright spots in the early years after welfare reform. Federal and state spending on child care rose from $1.1 billion in 1997 to $5.9 billion in 2000. Spending remained stagnant over the following 11 years, however, fluctuating between $5 billion and $6 billion. When taking inflation into account, the 2011 spending total of $5.5 billion represented a 29% decline from the 2000 figure of $5.9 billion.

As under previous laws, states must establish standards for the prevention and control of infectious diseases, such as immunization programs, and for building codes and physical safety in child care institutions. Child care workers must also receive minimal training in health and safety. However, many low-income people rely on informal sources of child care, including relatives and friends.

Pamela Holcomb et al. of the Urban Institute indicate in *Child Care Subsidies and TANF: A Synthesis of Three Studies on Systems, Policies, and Parents* (2006, http://www.urban.org/UploadedPDF/311302_synthesis.pdf) that despite increased federal funding for child care, the need outweighed the resources that were available under the law. As a result of more parents working while still on welfare or leaving welfare to work, the critical need for child care became more pronounced in the years after welfare reform.

The U.S. Government Accountability Office (GAO) finds in *Child Care: Multiple Factors Could Have Contributed to the Recent Decline in the Number of Children Whose Families Receive Subsidies* (May 2010, http://www.gao.gov/new.items/d10344.pdf) that between 2006 and 2008 the average number of children served by the Child Care and Development Block Grant had decreased by about 170,000, or 10%. The GAO also reports that the percentage of eligible children whose families received child care subsidies had declined. Only about a third or fewer eligible children received subsidies between 2004 and 2007. The GAO indicates that several reasons might account for this decline, including state policy allocating resources to other areas, decreased numbers of regulated child care providers, as well as a decreased demand for child care due to unemployment and reduced hours caused by the recession.

Title VII: Child Nutrition Programs

The PRWORA continued existing child nutrition programs, such as the National School Lunch Program and the School Breakfast Program. However, maximum reimbursement was reduced for the Summer Food Service Program and for some institutional food programs. States were allowed to decide whether to include or exclude legal immigrants from these programs. According to the U.S. Department of Agriculture (USDA), in *FY 2013 Budget Summary and Annual Performance Plan* (http://www.obpa.usda.gov/budsum/FY13budsum.pdf), the number of children participating in the school lunch and breakfast programs rose steadily between 2008, when 30.9 million children ate free lunches every day and 8.7 million ate free breakfasts, and 2012, when those numbers stood at 32 million and 12.7 million, respectively. For 2013, the agency expected approximately 32.4 million children per day to participate in the National School Lunch Program and 13.1 children per day to participate in the School Breakfast Program. The budget for Child Nutrition Programs rose accordingly during this time, from $17.5 billion in 2011 to $19.9 billion in 2013.

Title VIII: Supplemental Nutrition Assistance Program

The PRWORA reduced maximum benefits for the food stamp program, which became known, in 2008, as SNAP. The act set SNAP benefits at the level of the Thrifty Food Plan, an index set by the USDA that reflects the amount of money needed to purchase food to meet minimal nutrition requirements. Benefits were indexed to the rate of inflation so that they increase as inflation rises.

The law also restructured the way certain expenses and earnings were counted in establishing eligibility for food stamps. Under the PRWORA, when recipients' benefits are calculated, their countable monthly income is reduced by several deductions, including a standard deduction, a deduction for excessively high shelter expenses, a dependent care deduction, and medical expenses for the elderly and disabled. These deductions raised food stamp allotments.

In response to the severe economic recession that began in 2007, President Obama signed the ARRA in February 2009. According to the USDA in the memo "Economic Stimulus—Adjustments to the Maximum Supplemental Nutrition Assistance Program (SNAP) Monthly Allotments" (February 18, 2009, http://www.fns.usda.gov/snap/rules/Memo/2009/021809.pdf), the act increased SNAP benefits by 13.6% over the June value of the Thrifty Food Plan. Maximum monthly benefits for a family of four in the continental United States increased

to $668; the maximum monthly allotment for a family of three increased to $526. The ARRA increases in SNAP monthly benefits were set to expire on October 31, 2013.

By law, all SNAP recipients who are 18 to 50 years old and without children (known as able-bodied adults without dependents [ABAWD]) must work at least part time or be limited to three months of assistance in a 36-month period. Recipients who were in a workfare program (a welfare program that usually requires recipients to perform public-service duties) for 30 days but lost their placement may qualify for an additional three months of food assistance. (This provision was revised to allow states to exempt 15% of ABAWD recipients from this restriction.)

Reauthorization of the PRWORA

The PRWORA was reauthorized through 2010 when President George W. Bush (1946–) signed the Deficit Reduction Act in February 2006. The CBPP explains in *Implementing the TANF Changes in the Deficit Reduction Act: "Win-Win" Solutions for Families and States* (February 2007, http://www.cbpp.org/files/2-9-07tanf.pdf) that this bill did not increase funding for TANF programs; however, it did make the eligibility requirements more strict. The basic TANF block grant did not increase with inflation but remained capped at $16 billion. Thus, actual TANF funding has measurably decreased since that time. The reauthorization bill required 50% of TANF recipients to work in 2006, increasing by 5% each year to 70% in 2010. Funding for child care was set at $2 billion for each year between 2006 and 2010. Child support enforcement funding was reduced. Drug testing became required for every TANF applicant and recipient. Finally, the bill allowed TANF funds to be used to promote the value of marriage through public advertising and high school and adult classes and mentoring programs.

Although the law was scheduled for full-scale reauthorization in 2010, which would have entailed opportunities to enhance or alter its components, as of 2013 Congress instead passed short-term funding extensions, leaving the 2006 update of the law intact.

ELIGIBILITY FOR TANF AND BENEFIT PAYMENTS

Under TANF, states decide how much to aid a needy family. No federal guidelines exist for determining eligibility, and no requirement mandates that states aid all needy families. TANF does not require states to have a need standard or a gross income limit, as the AFDC did, but many states base their TANF programs in part on their earlier practices.

The maximum benefit is the amount paid to a family with no countable income. (Federal law specifies what income counts toward figuring benefits and what income, such as child support, is to be disregarded by the state.) The maximum benefit is to be paid only to those families that comply with TANF's work requirements or other program requirements established by the state, such as parental and personal responsibility rules.

Even though most states vary benefits according to family size, some eliminate or restrict benefit increases due to the birth of a new child to a recipient already receiving benefits. Instead, benefits depend on family size at the time of enrollment in 16 states. Idaho pays a flat monthly grant that is the same regardless of family size. Wisconsin pays benefits based on work activity of the recipient and not on family size. Five states provide an increase in benefits to TANF families following the birth of an additional child.

As Table 3.2 shows, most states have not changed their maximum benefit levels appreciably since 1996, despite the major changes brought about by the PRWORA, and despite the fact that inflation means that these steady amounts represent yearly reductions in benefits. The average (mean) maximum TANF benefit for a family of three was $394 in 1996 and $436 in 2011. Had benefit levels kept pace with inflation, the average maximum TANF award would have been approximately $558 in 2011. The average maximum AFDC benefit of $394 in 1996 represented an income of 34.9% of the poverty level for a family of three. In 2011 a family of three that collected the average maximum TANF monthly benefit of $436 per month would have had an annual income of $5,232, only 26.8% of the poverty level. (See Table 1.1 in Chapter 1.)

Many families receiving TANF benefits are also eligible for SNAP. A single benefit determination is made for both cash and food assistance. Whereas the eligibility and benefit amounts for TANF are determined by the states, SNAP eligibility and benefit amounts are determined by federal law and are consistent in all states.

SNAP benefits, which are administered by the USDA, are not counted in determining the TANF cash benefit. However, TANF benefits are considered part of a family's countable income in determining SNAP benefits, which are reduced $0.30 for each dollar of countable income. Therefore, SNAP benefits are, on average, higher in states with lower TANF benefits and vice versa; but compared with TANF, there is less variation in benefit levels from state to state. In 2012 the average monthly SNAP benefits per household were lowest in Oregon ($233.54), Minnesota ($235.94), and Massachusetts ($237.93). (See Table 3.3.) Alaska ($409.13) and Hawaii ($427.08) were the states with the highest average monthly SNAP benefits. (Poverty guidelines are higher in these two states because the costs of living there have historically been higher than in the lower 48 states.) U.S. territories such as Guam ($662.10) and the Virgin Islands ($416.58) also had high levels of SNAP benefits, due not only to high levels

TABLE 3.2

Maximum TANF benefits for a family of three, by state, selected years 1996–2011

[July. Families with no income.]

State	1996	2001	2006	2011
Alabama	$164	$164	$215	$215
Alaska	$923	$923	$923	$923
Arizona	$347	$347	$347	$278
Arkansas	$204	$204	$204	$204
California	$596			
Nonexempt	—	$645	$704	$638
Exempt	—	$720	$786	$714
Colorado	$356	$356	$356	$462
Connecticut	$543	$543	$543	$576
Delaware	$338	$338	$338	$338
D.C.	$415	$379	$407	$428
Florida	$303	$303	$303	$303
Georgia	$280	$280	$280	$280
Hawaii	$712	$570[a]	$570[a]	$610[b]
Idaho	$317	$293	$309	$309
Illinois	$377	$377	$396	$432
Indiana	$288	$288	$288	$288
Iowa	$426	$426	$426	$426
Kansas	$429	$429	$429	$429
Kentucky	$262	$262	$262	$262
Louisiana	$190	$240	$240	$240
Maine	$418	$461	$485	$485
Maryland	$373	$439	$490	$574
Massachusetts				
Exempt	$579	$633	$633	$633
Nonexempt	$565	$618	$618	$618
Michigan	$459	$459[c]	$489[c]	$492
Minnesota	$532	$532	$532	$532
Mississippi	$120	$170	$170	$170
Missouri	$292	$292	$292	$292
Montana	$425	$494	$442	$504
Nebraska	$364	$364	$364	$364
Nevada	$348	$348	$348	$383
New Hampshire	$550	$600	$625	$675
New Jersey	$424	$424	$424	$424
New Mexico	$389	$389	$389	$313
New York	$577	$577	$691	$788
North Carolina	$272	$272	$272	$272
North Dakota	$431	$477	$477	$427
Ohio	$341	$373	$410	$434
Oklahoma	$307	$292	$292	$292
Oregon	$460	$503	$514	$549
Pennsylvania	$403	$403	$403	$403
Rhode Island	$554	$554	$554	$554
South Carolina	$200	$203	$240	$216
South Dakota	$430	$430	$508	$555
Tennessee	$185	$185[d]	$185[d]	$185[d]
Texas	$188	$201	$223	$260
Utah	$426	$474	$474	$498
Vermont	$597	$629	$640	$640
Virginia	$291	$320	$320	$320
Washington	$546	$546	$546	$478
West Virginia	$253	$453	$340	$340
Wisconsin	$518			
W-2 transition	—	$628	$628	$628
Community service jobs	—	$673	$673	$673
Trial jobs/unsubsidezed employment	—	—[e]	—[e]	—[e]
Wyoming	$360	$340	$340	$577
Mean[f]	**$394**	**$409**	**$417**	**$436**
Median[f]	**$377**	**$389**	**$396**	**$429**

of poverty but also to differences in the administration of their social welfare systems relative to the 50 states. Other states with high SNAP benefit levels included California ($332.08), Colorado ($305.27), Louisiana ($305.50), and South Dakota ($305.71).

[July. Families with no income.]

TANF = Temporary Assistance for Needy Families.

Note: Maximum benefits are calculated assuming that the unit contains one adult and two children not subject to a family cap, has no special needs, pays for shelter, and lives in the most populated area of the state.

[a]Applies to units that have received assistance for two or more months in a lifetime. For units applying for their first or second months of benefits, the maximum monthly benefit for a family of three is $712.

[b]Applies to units that have received assistance for two or more months in a lifetime. For units applying for their first or second months of benefits, the maximum monthly benefit for a family of three is $763.

[c]Applies to units that have at least one employable adult. For units where all adults either receive Social Security insurance or are exempt from work requirements for reasons other than caring for a child under 3 months old, the maximum monthly benefit for a family of three is $477.

[d]For units where the caretaker is over 60, disabled, caring full time for a disabled family member, or excluded from the assistance unit, the maximum monthly benefit for a family of three is $232.

[e]The benefits in these components are based on the wages earned by individual recipients.

[f]The calculations include only one value per state (the policy affecting the largest percentage of the caseload).

SOURCE: David Kassabian, Anne Whitesell, and Erika Huber, "Table L5. Maximum Monthly Benefit for a Family of Three with No Income, 1996–2011 (July)," in *Welfare Rules Databook: State TANF Policies as of July 2011*, The Urban Institute, August 2012, http://www.urban.org/UploadedPDF/412641-Welfare-Rules-Databook-2011.pdf (accessed January 16, 2013)

THE WELFARE-TO-WORK CONCEPT

TANF recipients are expected to participate in work activities while receiving benefits. After 24 months of assistance, states must require recipients to work at least part time to continue to receive cash benefits. States are permitted to exempt certain groups of people from the work-activity requirements, including parents of very young children (up to one year) and disabled adults. TANF defines the work activities that count when determining a state's work participation rate.

As part of their plans, states must require parents to work after two years of receiving benefits. In 2000 states were required to have 40% of all parents and at least one adult in 90% of all two-parent families engaged in a work activity for a minimum of 20 hours per week for single parents and 35 hours per week for at least one adult in two-parent families. This work requirement became stricter with the 2006 reauthorization of the PRWORA, which required 50% of all single-parent TANF recipients to work in 2006, increasing by 5% each year to 70% in 2010.

TANF recipients required to work must spend a minimum number of hours per week engaged in one of the following activities:

- An unsubsidized job (no government help)
- A subsidized private job
- A subsidized public job

- Work experience
- On-the-job training
- Job search and job readiness (a usual maximum of six weeks total)
- Community service
- Vocational educational training (a 12-month maximum)
- Job skills training
- Education related to employment
- High school or a general equivalency diploma completion
- Providing child care for a community service participant

Additional provisions apply to young parents who are under the age of 20 years and are either household heads or married and who lack a high school diploma. They are considered "engaged in work" if they either maintain satisfactory attendance in high school (no hours specified) or participate in education directly related to work (20 hours per week).

PRWORA imposed strict limits on the number of TANF recipients who may get work credit through participation in education and training. No more than 30% of TANF families who are counted as engaged in work may consist of people who are participating in vocational educational training. Vocational educational training is the only creditable work activity not explicitly confined to high school dropouts.

In 2012 the states of Utah and Nevada appealed to the federal government, requesting that certain of the TANF work requirements be waived because the rigidity of the rules was making it increasingly difficult for them to fulfill the spirit of the law, which was to help people find permanent jobs. The rules relating to job training, educational programs, and work in government-subsidized jobs, for example, made it difficult for states to help TANF recipients simultaneously meet the PRWORA work requirements and prepare themselves for the forms of long-term employment that would lift them out of poverty for good. In July 2012 HHS granted the states waivers provided they devised better solutions for helping TANF benefit recipients find permanent jobs. This established a path for other states to address deficiencies in the work requirements and propose alternative plans.

Finding and Creating Jobs for TANF Recipients

Job availability is one of the most difficult challenges that states face when moving recipients from welfare to work. The national unemployment rate fell from a high of 7.5% in 1992 to 4% in 2000, before hovering between 4% and 6% through 2007. Although the overall U.S. economy grew between 2001 and 2007, incomes were stagnant for

TABLE 3.3

Supplemental Nutrition Assistance Program (SNAP) average monthly benefit per household, by state, fiscal years (FY) 2008–12

[Data as of March 8, 2013]

State/territory	Fiscal year 2008	Fiscal year 2009	Fiscal year 2010	Fiscal year 2011	Fiscal year 2012
Alabama	238.74	288.33	296.32	307.35	281.33
Alaska	357.45	430.24	436.40	419.10	409.13
Arizona	249.00	299.21	301.14	295.25	293.29
Arkansas	227.80	275.19	289.44	285.67	277.68
California	273.04	325.19	340.90	334.92	332.08
Colorado	247.63	302.70	325.09	317.73	305.27
Connecticut	196.86	249.36	263.07	262.18	264.11
Delaware	220.89	267.36	282.40	276.50	271.42
District of Columbia	196.15	234.88	247.22	251.12	243.85
Florida	198.73	246.94	268.56	258.62	255.24
Georgia	254.89	302.81	313.54	305.11	295.57
Guam	604.01	685.23	694.93	678.77	662.10
Hawaii	315.10	394.20	430.04	431.82	427.08
Idaho	237.89	307.48	318.49	313.02	299.54
Illinois	240.32	285.85	299.40	290.33	285.17
Indiana	240.50	296.39	309.35	303.08	299.86
Iowa	216.53	258.11	280.10	272.70	259.30
Kansas	205.23	252.06	272.91	271.62	266.15
Kentucky	217.92	264.36	279.87	275.25	268.71
Louisiana	262.96	307.50	303.21	297.31	305.50
Maine	189.17	245.01	259.83	252.36	239.38
Maryland	215.37	262.53	275.27	262.74	255.26
Massachusetts	183.47	229.53	238.54	240.76	237.93
Michigan	212.38	252.86	270.43	271.43	268.60
Minnesota	195.58	237.96	248.19	236.99	235.94
Mississippi	219.65	268.98	284.52	281.14	275.44
Missouri	216.14	263.06	277.56	276.16	275.89
Montana	221.22	274.02	287.64	281.96	272.67
Nebraska	225.21	259.78	280.66	280.55	279.71
Nevada	209.90	256.39	267.87	264.88	258.81
New Hampshire	190.45	251.24	255.39	250.43	246.17
New Jersey	210.62	257.53	282.65	272.77	271.07
New Mexico	234.23	286.76	299.42	294.07	290.26
New York	206.82	267.54	283.92	278.56	274.94
North Carolina	219.58	267.69	282.46	269.70	257.95
North Dakota	226.30	276.40	290.76	286.57	277.11
Ohio	236.44	288.95	303.22	293.68	286.76
Oklahoma	232.02	278.22	298.40	290.04	282.26
Oregon	185.74	228.81	237.85	236.13	233.54
Pennsylvania	206.79	250.80	262.61	270.45	265.86
Rhode Island	216.06	275.54	271.85	265.08	252.97
South Carolina	230.34	275.99	291.21	285.56	278.39
South Dakota	248.20	300.09	318.48	310.00	305.71
Tennessee	226.33	272.23	285.58	279.18	271.50
Texas	257.03	309.84	322.62	310.50	300.39
Utah	234.20	297.64	309.45	299.09	297.67
Vermont	187.42	233.56	244.13	243.04	238.53
Virginia	206.99	260.05	277.19	273.48	265.90
Virgin Islands	378.22	447.73	439.79	426.30	416.58
Washington	193.95	232.26	243.41	245.70	241.96
West Virginia	204.08	246.53	261.99	257.90	254.22
Wisconsin	198.22	241.25	263.00	251.50	243.92
Wyoming	229.95	276.22	297.54	288.77	288.64
Total	**226.60**	**275.51**	**289.60**	**283.99**	**278.48**

Notes: The following outlying areas receive Nutrition Assistance Grants which provide benefits analogous to the Supplemental Nutrition Assistance Program: Puerto Rico, American Samoa, and the Northern Marianas. Annual averages are total benefits divided by total annual household participation. All data are subject to revision.

SOURCE: "Supplemental Nutrition Assistance Program: Average Monthly Benefit per Household," in *Program Data: Supplemental Nutrition Assistance Program*, U.S. Department of Agriculture, Food and Nutrition Service, March 8, 2013, http://www.fns.usda.gov/pd/19SNAPavg$HH.htm (accessed March 25, 2013)

low-wage workers, and poverty rates were on the rise, suggesting that most of the growth in the U.S. economy during this time benefited those at the top of the income scale. The severe recession that began in 2007 dramatically worsened the unemployment situation and resulted in a poverty rate not seen in decades. The unemployment rate peaked at 10% in 2009, its highest level since 1983. (See Table 1.3 in Chapter 1.) In an environment characterized by high unemployment, welfare recipients, typically among the least-qualified candidates for jobs based on their employment histories, are at a pronounced disadvantage in the labor pool.

Moreover, even when the national unemployment rate is low, unemployment in some areas of the country might be much higher, and the skill level of unemployed people may not match the skills that are required for available jobs. Welfare recipients often lack job skills and work experience. If suitable jobs cannot be found, states must create work-activity placements and may use TANF block grant funds to do so.

Welfare agencies have had to change their focus and train staff to function more as job developers and counselors than as caseworkers. They make an initial assessment of recipients' skills as required by TANF. They may then develop personal responsibility plans for recipients, identifying what is needed (e.g., training, job-placement services, and support services) to move them into the workforce.

States have developed a variety of approaches to finding and creating job opportunities. Even though most rely on existing unemployment offices, many states have tried other options to help recipients find work:

- Collaboration with the business community to develop strategies that provide recipients with the skills and training employers want

- Use of several types of subsidies for employers who hire welfare recipients directly (subsidizing wages, providing tax credits to employers, and subsidizing workers' compensation and unemployment compensation taxes)

- Targeting state jobs for welfare recipients

- Financial encouragement for entrepreneurship and self-employment

- Creation of community service positions, often within city departments, such as parks and libraries (recipients usually participate in this workfare as a condition of continuing to receive benefits rather than wages)

However, when the economy slows and the unemployment rate climbs, fewer jobs exist for former welfare recipients. In his testimony before the U.S. Senate's Committee on Finance, Gordon L. Berlin (September 21, 2010, http://www.mdrc.org/sites/default/files/Rethinking%20 Welfare%20in%20the%20Great%20Recession.pdf), the president of MDRC, a nonprofit social policy research organization, stated that "the Great Recession has been an unprecedented test of antipoverty programs like TANF, demonstrating the limits of a social safety net built predominantly around work when unemployment is high."

The ARRA provided an additional emergency contingency fund of $2 billion. Several states created jobs programs or expanded existing jobs programs with this additional funding. The CBPP (http://www.cbpp.org/) provides several examples, including:

- Ohio created a subsidized jobs program that provided work for 1,500 parents and 8,000 youth across the state

- A Pennsylvania program subsidized 12,000 private- and public-sector jobs to provide employment for parents and youth

- Illinois created Put Illinois to Work, a program that subsidizes jobs for unemployed parents and youth

These programs and others were significantly jeopardized when Congress opted not to extend funding beyond September 30, 2010. The Illinois program, for example, which gave program participants real-world job training and experience, ended in January 2011.

Support Services Necessary for Moving Recipients to Work

Low-income adults and public assistance recipients face multiple barriers to working that put them at a disadvantage relative to other participants in the labor market. These barriers, such as a lack of basic skills and access to quality jobs, child care, and transportation, dramatically affect the ability of impoverished Americans to move from the welfare rolls to the labor force. This section addresses federal efforts to remove some of these barriers.

CHILD CARE. Access to affordable child care is one critical element in encouraging low-income parents to seek and keep jobs. In its white paper, "Child Care Subsidy Policy: Access to What?" (September 2012, http://www.naccrra.org/sites/default/files/publications/naccrra _publications/2012/subsidy_white_paper-_finalsept_2012 .pdf) Child Care Aware of America (formerly the National Association of Child Care Resource and Referral Agencies, a leading nonprofit devoted to extending access to affordable child care) noted that in 2011 the average yearly cost for full-time infant care in a child care center ranged from $4,600 in Mississippi to $15,000 in Massachusetts. The full-time costs for a four-year-old ranged from $3,900 in Mississippi to $11,700 in Massachusetts. Full-time infant care in an accredited home-based business ranged from $4,500 in South Carolina to $10,400 in New York, and full-time four-year-old care in a home-based business ranged from $4,100 in South Carolina to $9,600 in New York. These costs, according to Child Care Aware, meant that full-time child care in a licensed center or home-based business was out of reach not only for families living in poverty but also for families living at twice the poverty level in 2011. A family of three living at 200% of poverty in Massachusetts, for example, would have had to pay approximately 40% of its income to obtain full-time infant care in a licensed center.

The 1996 welfare reform law created a block grant to states for child care. The amount of the block grant was equivalent to what states received under the AFDC. However, states that maintain the amount that they spent for child care under the AFDC are eligible for additional matching funds. The block grant and the supplemental matching funds are referred to as the Child Care Development Fund (CCDF). In addition, states were given the option of transferring some of their TANF funds to the CCDF or spending them directly on child care services.

Because states can use TANF funds for child care, they have more flexibility to design child care programs, not only for welfare recipients but also for working-poor families who may need child care support to continue working and stay off welfare. States determine who is eligible for child care support, how much those parents will pay (often using a sliding fee scale), and the amount the state will reimburse providers of subsidized care. Children under the age of 13 years are eligible for child care subsidies; depending on the state, families with incomes up to 85% of the state's median income for a family of that size are eligible, although few states guarantee payments to all eligible families. For example, the Urban Institute notes in "The CCDF Policies Database Book of Tables: Key Cross-State Variations in CCDF Policies as of October 1, 2011" (October 2012, http://www.urban.org/UploadedPDF/412707-The-CCDF-Policies-Database-Book-of-Tables.pdf), that in 2011, waiting lists for child care subsidies existed in 31 states.

In "Characteristics of Families Served by Child Care and Development Fund (CCDF) Based on Preliminary FY2010 Data" (September 19, 2012, http://www.acf.hhs.gov/programs/occ/resource/characteristics-of-families-served-by-child-care-and-development-fund-ccdf), the ACF's Office of Child Care reports that in FY 2010 states provided child care subsidies to approximately 1.7 million low-income children in 998,600 families. If other funding sources (such as TANF direct spending on child care and other state and federal grants) are included in the calculation, the number of children who received subsidized child care was approximately 2.6 million. Of the children who received subsidies through CCDF, 66% were cared for in a child care center, 24% in family child care homes, 5% in the child's own home, and 5% in a group home. Nearly half (49%) of the families served under the program had incomes below the poverty level, 27% had incomes between 100% and 150% of poverty, and 13% had incomes above 150% of poverty.

TRANSPORTATION AND ACCESS TO JOBS. Transportation is another critical factor facing welfare recipients moving into a job. Recipients without a car must depend on public transportation. Yet, according to the U.S. Department of Transportation (DOT), in "Use of TANF, WtW, and Job Access Funds for Transportation" (October 2, 2012, http://www.fta.dot.gov/3715.html), two out of three new jobs are in suburban areas, often outside the range of public transportation, whereas three out of four welfare recipients live in rural areas or in central cities. Even when jobs are accessible to public transportation,

many day care centers and schools are not. Some jobs require weekend or night-shift work, when public transportation schedules are limited. Even for those recipients with cars, the expense of gas and repairs can deplete earnings. For low-income rural families, many of these problems are even more forbidding, due to a lack of any public transportation options.

To promote employment, TANF's vehicle asset limits are broader than they were under the AFDC. Each state has the flexibility to determine its own vehicle asset level, but all states have chosen to increase the limit for the value of the primary automobile in the family beyond that set under the AFDC. According to the USDA's Food and Nutrition Service (October 2010, http://www.fns.usda.gov/snap/rules/Memo/2000/TANFVehTable.htm), 36 states entirely exclude the value of one vehicle per household, and 13 of these exclude the value of all vehicles. The remaining states offer exemptions for vehicle values ranging from $1,500 (Georgia) to $15,000 (Minnesota), with some specifying different exemption amounts for a first and a second vehicle and some tying exemptions to the condition that the vehicle be used for work or other essential functions.

The DOT notes that states use a variety of approaches to provide transportation for TANF recipients moving into the workforce, such as:

- Reimbursing work-related transportation expenses (automobile expenses or public transportation)

- Providing financial assistance in the form of loans or grants to purchase or lease an automobile

- Filling transit service gaps, such as new routes or extended hours

- Providing transit alternatives, such as vanpools or shuttle services

- Offering entrepreneurial opportunities for recipients to become transportation providers

- Transferring TANF funds to the Social Services Block Grant to develop the transportation infrastructure for the working poor in rural areas and inner cities

GOVERNMENT PROGRAMS TO COMBAT HUNGER
Supplemental Nutrition Assistance Program

SNAP (previously called the Food Stamp Program), administered by the USDA, is the largest food assistance program in the United States. SNAP is designed to help low-income families purchase a nutritionally adequate, low-cost diet. Generally, SNAP may only be used to buy food to be prepared at home. It cannot be used for alcohol, tobacco, or hot foods that are intended to be consumed immediately, such as restaurant or delicatessen food.

SNAP calculates 30% of each recipient family's earnings and then issues enough food credits to make up the difference between that amount and the amount that is needed to buy an adequate diet. These monthly allotments are usually provided electronically through an electronic benefit transfer, a debit card that is similar to a bank card. The cash value of these benefits is based on the size of the household and how much the family earns. Households without an elderly or disabled member generally must have a monthly total (gross) cash income at or below 130% of the poverty level and may not have liquid assets (cash, savings, or other assets that can be easily sold) of more than $2,000. (If the household has a member aged 60 years or older, the asset limit is $3,000.) The net monthly income limit (gross income minus any approved deductions for child care, some housing costs, and other expenses) must be 100% or less of the poverty level, or $1,921 per month for a family of four between October 2012 and September 2013. (See Table 3.4.)

With some exceptions, SNAP is automatically available to Supplemental Security Income and TANF recipients. SNAP benefits are higher in states with lower TANF benefits because those benefits are considered a part of a family's countable income. To receive SNAP, certain household members must register for work, accept suitable job offers, or fulfill work or training requirements (such as looking or training for a job).

Even though the federal government sets guidelines and provides funding, SNAP is actually administered by the states. State agencies certify eligibility as well as calculate and issue benefit allotments. Most often, the welfare agency and staff that administer the TANF and Medicaid programs also run SNAP. The program operates in all 50 states, the District of Columbia, Guam, and the Virgin Islands. (Puerto Rico is covered under a separate nutrition-assistance program.)

Except for some small differences in Alaska, Hawaii, and the territories, the program is run the same way throughout the United States. The states pay 50% of the administrative costs, and the federal government pays 100% of SNAP benefits and the other 50% of the administrative costs.

Unlike TANF, SNAP is responsive to fluctuations in unemployment and the poverty level, with participation increasing in times of economic distress and decreasing as unemployment and poverty rates fall. In 2000, at a time of economic expansion and low unemployment, the federal government paid $15 billion in SNAP benefits. In 2012, as the U.S. economy continued to suffer the aftereffects of the Great Recession, the federal government spent $74.6 billion on SNAP benefits, or an estimated average monthly benefit of $133.41 per recipient. (See Table 3.5.) The American Recovery and Reinvestment Act supplemented SNAP's structural responsiveness to economic crisis by providing an additional $500 million to support participation in the program and by increasing benefit levels to 113.6% of the value of the Thrifty Food Plan (a plan that serves as the basis for maximum food allotments).

National School Lunch and School Breakfast Programs

The National School Lunch Program (NSLP) and the School Breakfast Program (SBP) provide federal cash and commodity support to participating public and private schools and to nonprofit residential institutions that serve meals to children. Children from households with incomes at or below 130% of the poverty line receive free meals. Children from households with incomes between 130% and 185% of the poverty level receive meals at a reduced price (no more than $0.40). Table 3.6 shows the income eligibility guidelines, based on the poverty guidelines, effective from July 1, 2012, to June 30, 2013. The levels were higher in Alaska and Hawaii than in the 48 contiguous states, the District of Columbia, Guam, and other U.S. territories. Children in TANF families are automatically eligible to receive free breakfasts and lunches. Almost 90% of federal funding for the NSLP is used to subsidize free and reduced-price lunches for low-income children.

The NSLP, which was created in 1946 under the National School Lunch Act, supplies subsidized lunches to children in almost all schools and in 6,000 residential and day care institutions. During the 1996–97 school year the USDA changed certain policies so that school meals would meet the recommendations of the Dietary Guidelines for America, the federal standards for what constitutes a healthy diet. The program has grown steadily

TABLE 3.4

Income chart for SNAP eligibility, 2012–13

[Oct. 1, 2012 through Sept. 30, 2013]

Household size	Gross monthly income (130 percent of poverty)	Net monthly income (100 percent of poverty)
1	$1,211	$931
2	1,640	1,261
3	2,069	1,591
4	2,498	1,921
5	2,927	2,251
6	3,356	2,581
7	3,785	2,911
8	4,214	3,241
Each additional member	+429	+330

Note: Gross income means a household's total, nonexcluded income, before any deductions have been made. Net income means gross income minus allowable deductions. SNAP gross and net income limits are higher in Alaska and Hawaii. SNAP = Supplemental Nutrition Assistance Program.

SOURCE: "Income," in *Supplemental Nutrition Assistance Program: Eligibility*, U.S. Department of Agriculture, Food and Nutrition Service, January 15, 2013, http://www.fns.usda.gov/snap/applicant_recipients/eligibility.htm (accessed January 23, 2013)

TABLE 3.5

SNAP participation and costs, 1969–2012

[Data as of March 8, 2013]

Fiscal year	Average participation	Average benefit per person[a]	Total benefits	All other costs[b]	Total costs
	Thousands	Dollars	Millions of dollars		
1969	2,878	6.63	228.80	21.70	250.50
1970	4,340	10.55	549.70	27.20	576.90
1971	9,368	13.55	1,522.70	53.20	1,575.90
1972	11,109	13.48	1,797.30	69.40	1,866.70
1973	12,166	14.60	2,131.40	76.00	2,207.40
1974	12,862	17.61	2,718.30	119.20	2,837.50
1975	17,064	21.40	4,385.50	233.20	4,618.70
1976	18,549	23.93	5,326.50	359.00	5,685.50
1977	17,077	24.71	5,067.00	394.00	5,461.00
1978	16,001	26.77	5,139.20	380.50	5,519.70
1979	17,653	30.59	6,480.20	459.60	6,939.80
1980	21,082	34.47	8,720.90	485.60	9,206.50
1981	22,430	39.49	10,629.90	595.40	11,225.20
1982[c]	21,717	39.17	10,208.30	628.40	10,836.70
1983	21,625	42.98	11,152.30	694.80	11,847.10
1984	20,854	42.74	10,696.10	882.60	11,578.80
1985	19,899	44.99	10,743.60	959.60	11,703.20
1986	19,429	45.49	10,605.20	1,033.20	11,638.40
1987	19,113	45.78	10,500.30	1,103.90	11,604.20
1988	18,645	49.83	11,149.10	1,167.70	12,316.80
1989	18,806	51.71	11,669.78	1,231.81	12,901.59
1990	20,049	58.78	14,142.79	1,304.47	15,447.26
1991	22,625	63.78	17,315.77	1,431.50	18,747.27
1992	25,407	68.57	20,905.68	1,556.66	22,462.34
1993	26,987	67.95	22,006.03	1,646.94	23,652.97
1994	27,474	69.00	22,748.58	1,744.87	24,493.45
1995	26,619	71.27	22,764.07	1,856.30	24,620.37
1996	25,543	73.21	22,440.11	1,890.88	24,330.99
1997	22,858	71.27	19,548.86	1,958.68	21,507.55
1998	19,791	71.12	16,890.49	2,097.84	18,988.32
1999	18,183	72.27	15,769.40	2,051.52	17,820.92
2000	17,194	72.62	14,983.32	2,070.70	17,054.02
2001	17,318	74.81	15,547.39	2,242.00	17,789.39
2002	19,096	79.67	18,256.20	2,380.82	20,637.02
2003	21,250	83.94	21,404.28	2,412.01	23,816.28
2004	23,811	86.16	24,618.89	2,480.14	27,099.03
2005	25,628	92.89	28,567.88	2,504.24	31,072.11
2006	26,549	94.75	30,187.35	2,715.72	32,903.06
2007	26,316	96.18	30,373.27	2,801.21	33,174.48
2008	28,223	102.19	34,608.40	3,033.64	37,642.04
2009	33,490	125.31	50,359.92	3,261.59	53,621.50
2010	40,302	133.79	64,702.16	3,611.00	68,313.17
2011	44,709	133.85	71,810.92	3,906.47	75,717.39
2012	46,609	133.41	74,619.46	3,803.31	78,422.77

SNAP = Supplemental Nutritional Assistance Program.
All data are subject to revision.
[a]Represents average monthly benefits per person.
[b]Includes the federal share of state administrative expenses, nutrition education, and employment and training programs. Also includes other federal costs (e.g., benefit and retailer redemption and monitoring, payment accuracy, electronic benefits transfer (EBT) systems, program evaluation and modernization, program access, health and nutrition pilot projects).
[c]Puerto Rico initiated food stamp operations during fiscal year 1975 and participated through June of fiscal year 1982. A separate nutrition assistance grant began in July 1982.

SOURCE: "Supplemental Nutrition Assistance Program Participation and Costs," in *Supplemental Nutrition Assistance Program: Program Data*, U.S. Department of Agriculture, Food and Nutrition Service, March 8, 2013, http://www.fns.usda.gov/pd/SNAPsummary.htm (accessed March 26, 2013)

since its introduction. In 2012 the program served free lunches to 18.7 million children and reduced-price lunches to another 2.7 million. (See Table 3.7.)

The SBP, which was created under the Child Nutrition Act of 1966, serves far fewer students than does the NSLP. The SBP also differs from the NSLP in that most schools offering the program are in low-income areas, and the children who participate in the program are mainly from low- and moderate-income families. In 2012 the program served free breakfasts to 9.8 million children and reduced-price breakfasts to another 1 million. (See Table 3.8.)

In December 2010 President Obama signed the Healthy, Hunger-Free Kids Act into law. This act upgraded nutritional standards for school meal programs and required schools to make information on the nutritional quality of meals available to parents. The act provided several ways to certify additional children for the free and reduced meal programs, including using Medicaid data to directly certify children rather than relying on

TABLE 3.6

Income eligibility guidelines for free and reduced-price meals, 2012–13

Effective from July 1, 2012 to June 30, 2013

Household size	Federal poverty guidelines Annual	Reduced price meals—185%					Free meals—130%				
		Annual	Monthly	Twice per month	Every two weeks	Weekly	Annual	Monthly	Twice per month	Every two weeks	Weekly
48 contiguous states, District of Columbia, Guam, and territories											
1	11,170	20,665	1,723	862	795	398	14,521	1,211	606	559	280
2	15,130	27,991	2,333	1,167	1,077	539	19,669	1,640	820	757	379
3	19,090	35,317	2,944	1,472	1,359	680	24,817	2,069	1,035	955	478
4	23,050	42,643	3,554	1,777	1,641	821	29,965	2,498	1,249	1,153	577
5	27,010	49,969	4,165	2,083	1,922	961	35,113	2,927	1,464	1,351	676
6	30,970	57,295	4,775	2,388	2,204	1,102	40,261	3,356	1,678	1,549	775
7	34,930	64,621	5,386	2,693	2,486	1,243	45,409	3,785	1,893	1,747	874
8	38,890	71,947	5,996	2,998	2,768	1,384	50,557	4,214	2,107	1,945	973
For each add'l family member, add	3,960	7,326	611	306	282	141	5,148	429	215	198	99
Alaska											
1	13,970	25,845	2,154	1,077	995	498	18,161	1,514	757	699	350
2	18,920	35,002	2,917	1,459	1,347	674	24,596	2,060	1,025	946	473
3	23,870	44,160	3,680	1,840	1,699	850	31,031	2,586	1,293	1,194	597
4	28,820	53,317	4,444	2,222	2,051	1,026	37,466	3,123	1,562	1,441	721
5	33,770	62,475	5,207	2,604	2,403	1,202	43,901	3,659	1,830	1,689	845
6	38,720	71,632	5,970	2,985	2,756	1,378	50.336	4,195	2,098	1,936	968
7	43,670	80,790	6,733	3,367	3,108	1,554	56,771	4,731	2,366	2,184	1,092
8	48,620	89,947	7,496	3,748	3460	1,730	63,206	5,268	2,634	2,431	1,216
For each add'l family member, add	4,950	9,168	764	382	353	177	6,435	537	269	248	124
Hawaii											
1	12,860	23,791	1,933	992	916	458	16,718	1,394	697	643	322
2	17,410	32,209	2,685	1,343	1,239	620	22,633	1,887	944	871	436
3	21,960	40,626	3,386	1,693	1,563	782	28,548	2,379	1,190	1,098	549
4	26,510	49,044	4,087	2,044	1,887	944	34,463	2,872	1,436	1,326	663
5	31,060	57,461	4,789	2,395	2,211	1,106	40,378	3,365	1,683	1,553	777
6	35,610	65,879	5,490	2,745	2,534	1,267	46,293	3,858	1,929	1,781	891
7	40,160	74,296	6,192	3,096	2,858	1,429	52,209	4,351	2,176	2,008	1,004
8	44,710	82,714	6,893	3,447	3,182	1,591	58,123	4,844	2,422	2,236	1,118
For each add'l family member, add	4,550	8,418	702	351	324	162	5,915	493	247	228	114

SOURCE: "Income Eligibility Guidelines," in "Child Nutrition Programs—Income Eligibility Guidelines," *Federal Register*, vol. 77, no. 57, March 23, 2012, http://www.gpo.gov/fdsys/pkg/FR-2012-03-23/pdf/2012-7036.pdf (accessed January 23, 2013)

paper applications or using census data in high-poverty communities to certify schoolwide income eligibility. In addition, the act expanded the school meal program to after-school meals through the existing Child and Adult Care Food Program providers across the nation.

Special Supplemental Food Program for Women, Infants, and Children

The Special Supplemental Food Program for Women, Infants, and Children (WIC) provides food assistance as well as nutrition counseling and health services to low-income pregnant women, to women who have just given birth and their babies, and to low-income children up to five years old. Participants in the program must have incomes at or below 185% of the poverty level (all but five states use this cutoff level) and must be nutritionally at risk.

As explained by the Child Nutrition Act of 1966, nutritional risk includes abnormal nutritional conditions, medical conditions related to nutrition, health-impairing dietary deficiencies, or conditions that might predispose a person to

these conditions. Pregnant women may receive benefits throughout their pregnancies and for up to six months after childbirth or up to one year for nursing mothers.

Those receiving WIC benefits get supplemental food each month in the form of actual food items or, more commonly, vouchers (coupons) for the purchase of specific items at the store. Permitted foods contain high amounts of protein, iron, calcium, vitamin A, and vitamin C. Items that may be purchased include milk, cheese, eggs, infant formula, cereals, and fruit or vegetable juices. Mothers participating in WIC are encouraged to breast-feed their infants if possible, but state WIC agencies will provide formula for mothers who choose to use it.

The USDA estimates that the national average monthly cost of a WIC food package in FY 2010 was $45.04 per participant, including food and administrative costs. (See Table 3.9.) The federal government spent an estimated $6.9 billion to operate WIC in 2012, and the program served approximately 8.9 million women, infants,

TABLE 3.7

National school lunch program participation and lunches served, 1969–2012

Fiscal year	Average participation				Total lunches served	Percent free/reduced price of total
	Free	Reduced price	Full price	Total		
	Millions					%
1969	2.9	*	16.5	19.4	3,368.2	15.1
1970	4.6	*	17.8	22.4	3,565.1	20.7
1971	5.8	0.5	17.8	24.1	3,848.3	26.1
1972	7.3	0.5	16.6	24.4	3,972.1	32.4
1973	8.1	0.5	16.1	24.7	4,008.8	35.0
1974	8.6	0.5	15.5	24.6	3,981.6	37.1
1975	9.4	0.6	14.9	24.9	4,063.0	40.3
1976	10.2	0.8	14.6	25.6	4,147.9	43.1
1977	10.5	1.3	14.5	26.2	4,250.0	44.8
1978	10.3	1.5	14.9	26.7	4,294.1	44.4
1979	10.0	1.7	15.3	27.0	4,357.4	43.6
1980	10.0	1.9	14.7	26.6	4,387.0	45.1
1981	10.6	1.9	13.3	25.8	4,210.6	48.6
1982	9.8	1.6	11.5	22.9	3,755.0	50.2
1983	10.3	1.5	11.2	23.0	3,803.3	51.7
1984	10.3	1.5	11.5	23.4	3,826.2	51.0
1985	9.9	1.6	12.1	23.6	3,890.1	49.1
1986	10.0	1.6	12.2	23.7	3,942.5	49.1
1987	10.0	1.6	12.4	23.9	3,939.9	48.6
1988	9.8	1.6	12.8	24.2	4,032.9	47.4
1989	9.7	1.6	12.9	24.2	4,004.9	47.2
1990	9.8	1.7	12.6	24.1	4,009.0	48.3
1991	10.3	1.8	12.2	24.2	4,050.7	50.4
1992	11.2	1.7	11.7	24.6	4,101.4	53.1
1993	11.7	1.7	11.4	24.9	4,137.7	54.8
1994	12.2	1.8	11.3	25.3	4,201.6	55.9
1995	12.4	1.9	11.4	25.7	4,253.3	56.4
1996	12.6	2.0	11.3	25.9	4,313.2	56.9
1997	12.9	2.1	11.3	26.3	4,409.0	57.6
1998	13.0	2.2	11.4	26.6	4,425.0	57.8
1999	13.0	2.4	11.6	27.0	4,513.6	57.6
2000	13.0	2.5	11.9	27.3	4,575.0	57.1
2001	12.9	2.6	12.0	27.5	4,585.2	56.8
2002	13.3	2.6	12.0	28.0	4,716.6	57.6
2003	13.7	2.7	11.9	28.4	4,762.9	58.5
2004	14.1	2.8	12.0	29.0	4,842.4	59.1
2005	14.6	2.9	12.2	29.6	4,976.4	59.4
2006	14.8	2.9	12.4	30.1	5,027.9	59.3
2007	15.0	3.1	12.6	30.6	5,071.3	59.3
2008	15.4	3.1	12.5	31.0	5,208.6	60.1
2009	16.3	3.2	11.9	31.3	5,186.1	62.6
2010	17.6	3.0	11.1	31.8	5,278.3	65.3
2011	18.3	2.7	10.8	31.8	5,274.4	66.6
2012	18.7	2.7	10.2	31.6	5,210.9	68.2

Notes: Fiscal year 2012 data are preliminary; all data are subject to revision. Participation data are 9-month averages (summer months are excluded).
*Included with free meals.

SOURCE: "National School Lunch Program: Participation and Lunches Served," U.S. Department of Agriculture, Food and Nutrition Service, January 4, 2013, http://www.fns.usda.gov/pd/slsummar.htm (accessed January 23, 2013)

TABLE 3.8

National school breakfast program participation and meals served, 1969–2012

Fiscal years	Total participation[a]				Meals served	Free/reduced price of total meals
	Free	Reduced price	Paid	Total		
	Millions					Percent
1969	—	—	—	0.22	39.70	71.0
1970	—	—	—	0.45	71.80	71.5
1971	0.60	[b]	0.20	0.80	125.50	76.3
1972	0.81	[b]	0.23	1.04	169.30	78.5
1973	0.99	[b]	0.20	1.19	194.10	83.4
1974	1.14	[b]	0.24	1.37	226.70	82.8
1975	1.45	0.04	0.33	1.82	294.70	82.1
1976	1.76	0.06	0.37	2.20	353.60	84.2
1977	2.02	0.11	0.36	2.49	434.30	85.7
1978	2.23	0.16	0.42	2.80	478.80	85.3
1979	2.56	0.21	0.54	3.32	565.60	84.1
1980	2.79	0.25	0.56	3.60	619.90	85.2
1981	3.05	0.25	0.51	3.81	644.20	86.9
1982	2.80	0.16	0.36	3.32	567.40	89.3
1983	2.87	0.15	0.34	3.36	580.70	90.3
1984	2.91	0.15	0.37	3.43	589.20	89.7
1985	2.88	0.16	0.40	3.44	594.90	88.6
1986	2.93	0.16	0.41	3.50	610.60	88.7
1987	3.01	0.17	0.43	3.61	621.50	88.4
1988	3.03	0.18	0.47	3.68	642.50	87.5
1989	3.11	0.19	0.51	3.81	658.45	86.8
1990	3.30	0.22	0.55	4.07	707.49	86.7
1991	3.61	0.25	0.58	4.44	771.86	87.3
1992	4.05	0.26	0.61	4.92	852.43	88.0
1993	4.41	0.28	0.66	5.36	923.56	87.9
1994	4.76	0.32	0.75	5.83	1,001.52	87.4
1995	5.10	0.37	0.85	6.32	1,078.92	86.8
1996	5.27	0.41	0.90	6.58	1,125.74	86.5
1997	5.52	0.45	0.95	6.92	1,191.21	86.5
1998	5.64	0.50	1.01	7.14	1,220.90	86.1
1999	5.72	0.56	1.09	7.37	1,267.62	85.4
2000	5.73	0.61	1.21	7.55	1,303.35	84.2
2001	5.80	0.67	1.32	7.79	1,334.51	83.2
2002	6.03	0.70	1.41	8.15	1,404.76	82.9
2003	6.22	0.74	1.47	8.43	1,447.90	82.8
2004	6.52	0.80	1.58	8.90	1,524.91	82.4
2005	6.80	0.86	1.70	9.36	1,603.88	82.1
2006	6.99	0.92	1.86	9.76	1,663.07	81.2
2007	7.15	0.98	1.99	10.12	1,713.96	80.6
2008	7.48	1.04	2.08	10.61	1,812.46	80.6
2009	7.99	1.07	2.01	11.08	1,866.68	82.1
2010	8.68	1.05	1.94	11.67	1,968.04	83.5
2011	9.20	0.98	2.00	12.17	2,048.15	83.7
2012	9.76	1.04	2.04	12.84	2,142.16	84.2

Notes: Fiscal year 2012 data are preliminary; all data are subject to revision.
[a]Nine month average: October–May plus September.
[b]Included with free participation.

SOURCE: "National School Breakfast Program Participation and Meals Served," U.S. Department of Agriculture, Food and Nutrition Service, January 4, 2013, http://www.fns.usda.gov/pd/sbsummar.htm (accessed January 23, 2013)

and children. WIC works in conjunction with the Farmers' Market Nutrition Program, which was established in 1992, to provide WIC recipients with increased access, in the form of vouchers, to fresh fruits and vegetables.

OTHER PUBLIC PROGRAMS TO FIGHT POVERTY

Unemployment Insurance

The federal government and the states combine to offer a system of unemployment insurance, often called unemployment compensation, that provides a temporary source of income to those who have lost their jobs. In addition to giving workers support as they seek new jobs, unemployment compensation is intended to exert a stabilizing influence on the economy. When workers lose their jobs, unemployment benefits allow them to continue satisfying their consumer needs, which keeps demand for goods and services from dropping precipitately in times of economic crisis or stagnation.

The unemployment insurance system was designed in 1935 during the administration of President Franklin

TABLE 3.9

Special Supplemental Food Program for Women, Infants, and Children (WIC) program participation and costs, 1974–2012

[Data as of January 4, 2013]

| Fiscal year | Total participation* | Program costs | | | Average monthly food cost per person |
| | | Food | NSA | Total 1 | |
	Thousands	Millions of dollars			Dollars
1974	88	8.2	2.2	10.4	15.68
1975	344	76.7	12.6	89.3	18.58
1976	520	122.3	20.3	142.6	19.60
1977	848	211.7	44.2	255.9	20.80
1978	1,181	311.5	68.1	379.6	21.99
1979	1,483	428.6	96.8	525.4	24.09
1980	1,914	584.1	140.5	727.7	25.43
1981	2,119	708.0	160.6	871.6	27.84
1982	2,189	757.6	190.5	948.8	28.83
1983	2,537	901.8	221.3	1,126.0	29.62
1984	3,045	1,117.3	268.8	1,388.1	30.58
1985	3,138	1,193.2	294.4	1,489.3	31.69
1986	3,312	1,264.4	316.4	1,582.9	31.82
1987	3,429	1,344.7	333.1	1,679.6	32.68
1988	3,593	1,434.8	360.6	1,797.5	33.28
1989	4,119	1,489.4	416.5	1,910.9	30.13
1990	4,517	1,636.8	478.7	2,122.4	30.20
1991	4,893	1,751.9	544.0	2,301.0	29.84
1992	5,403	1,960.5	632.7	2,600.6	30.24
1993	5,921	2,115.1	705.6	2,828.6	29.77
1994	6,477	2,325.2	834.4	3,169.3	29.92
1995	6,894	2,511.6	904.6	3,436.2	30.36
1996	7,186	2,689.9	985.1	3,695.4	31.19
1997	7,407	2,815.5	1,008.2	3,843.8	31.68
1998	7,367	2,808.1	1,061.4	3,890.4	31.76
1999	7,311	2,851.6	1,063.9	3,938.1	32.50
2000	7,192	2,853.1	1,102.6	3,982.1	33.06
2001	7,306	3,007.9	1,110.6	4,149.4	34.31
2002	7,491	3,129.7	1,182.3	4,339.8	34.82
2003	7,631	3,230.3	1,260.0	4,524.4	35.28
2004	7,904	3,562.0	1,272.4	4,887.3	37.55
2005	8,023	3,602.8	1,335.5	4,992.6	37.42
2006	8,088	3,598.2	1,402.6	5,072.7	37.07
2007	8,285	3,881.1	1,479.0	5,409.6	39.04
2008	8,705	4,534.0	1,607.6	6,188.8	43.40
2009	9,122	4,640.9	1,788.0	6,471.6	42.40
2010	9,175	4,562.8	1,907.9	6,682.8	41.44
2011	8,961	5,018.2	1,961.7	7,169.6	46.67
2012	8,908	4,814.8	1,942.0	6,850.7	45.04

Note: Participation data are annual averages (6 months in fiscal year 1974; 12 months all subsequent years).
NSA = Nutrition Services and Administrative costs.

SOURCE: "WIC Program Participation and Costs," U.S. Department of Agriculture, Food and Nutrition Service, January 4, 2013, http://www.fns.usda.gov/pd/wisummary.htm (accessed January 23, 2013)

Roosevelt (1882–1945) with the intent of giving states wide latitude in operating their own programs. For the basic system, states set their own eligibility criteria and benefit levels with minimal intervention so long as they operate within broad federal guidelines. The federal government pays for administrative costs, but the states manage their own funds for actual payments to those who have lost their jobs. Both state and federal spending on unemployment compensation is generated via taxes on employers, but economists note that this money ultimately comes from the workers themselves, since employers reduce the wages they pay in proportion to the taxes they are required to contribute to unemployment insurance funds. Most states offer up to 26 weeks of unemployment insurance benefits, although the duration of benefits is often shorter due to irregularities in an individual's employment history. Qualifying workers typically receive approximately half of the amount of money they made on the job.

The general criteria for unemployment compensation eligibility are consistent across the states. A qualifying worker must have met certain thresholds for the amount of time on the job and the income generated during that time, and s/he must have lost the job through no fault of his/her own. Additionally, the person must be ready and willing to work, and s/he must be actively seeking a new job. Unemployment insurance is not intended to cover numerous classes of workers, including self-employed workers, temporary workers, and those who voluntarily leave their jobs.

Different states interpret these general criteria very differently, however. In some states it is more difficult for employees to prove that they were fired through no fault of their own than in other, more pro-worker states. The period of employment used to calculate eligibility and benefits varies by state, compensation levels vary by state, and the degree to which part-time workers are covered varies by state. According to Chad Stone and William Chen of the CBPP ("Introduction to Unemployment Insurance," February 6, 2013, http://www.cbpp.org/cms/index.cfm?fa=view&id=1466#_ftnref7), since the 1990s basic unemployment compensation has provided support for fewer than half of unemployed workers. Stone and Chen point to a "growing percentage of unemployed workers who meet the basic criteria described above yet fail to satisfy their *state*'s eligibility criteria established decades ago (in a very different labor market)."

In addition to the basic unemployment insurance system, there is a permanent Extended Benefits (EB) program that covers workers for an additional period in states whose job markets are poor. The length of the extension of benefits varies based on the state's unemployment rate and the laws governing its unemployment insurance program. Historically EB is funded by both the federal government and the states, and the program operates even when the overall national economy is strong. With the Great Recession and the passage of the ARRA in 2009, however, the federal government began fully funding the EB program. This measure was intended to be temporary, but as of 2013 it remained in effect, in part because many states were struggling to keep their unemployment insurance funds solvent in the protracted aftermath of the Great Recession.

Additionally, the federal government has created numerous other temporary programs meant to supplement the basic state programs during periods of high unemployment nationwide. In 2008 Congress created the Emergency Unemployment Compensation (EUC) program to respond to the massive job losses during the Great Recession. Because of lingering unemployment even after the recession officially ended in mid-2009, EUC was repeatedly reauthorized, and it remained in operation through 2013. In states with particularly high unemployment during the Great Recession and its aftermath, some workers were able to collect benefits for as long as 99 weeks. As the unemployment rate climbed from below 5% in 2007 to a peak of 10% in 2009, the average duration of a worker's unemployment compensation rose from 15 weeks to almost 20 weeks, according to statistics available at the website of the U.S. Department of Labor's Employment and Training Administration (http://www.ows.doleta.gov/unemploy/chartbook.asp).

Federal Minimum Wage

The federal minimum wage dates back to the passage of the Fair Labor Standards Act of 1938, which established basic national standards for minimum wages, overtime pay, and the employment of child workers. (The minimum wage is a cash wage only and does not include any fringe benefits. Consequently, the total compensation for minimum-wage workers is even lower than the total compensation for higher-paid workers, who generally receive some kind of benefits besides wages. Most minimum-wage workers do not receive any benefits.) The provisions of the act have been extended to cover many other areas of employment since 1938.

The first minimum wage instituted in 1938 was $0.25 per hour. (See Table 3.10.) It gradually increased over the

TABLE 3.10

Federal minimum wage rates under the Fair Labor Standards Act, 1938–2013

Effective date	1938 Act[a]	1961 Amendments[b]	1966 & Subsequent amendments[c] Nonfarm	Farm
Oct. 24, 1938	$0.25			
Oct. 24, 1939	$0.30			
Oct. 24, 1945	$0.40			
Jan. 25, 1950	$0.75			
Mar. 1, 1956	$1.00			
Sept. 3, 1961	$1.15	$1.00		
Sept. 3, 1963	$1.25			
Sept. 3, 1964		$1.15		
Sept. 3, 1965		$1.25		
Feb. 1, 1967	$1.40	$1.40	$1.00	$1.00
Feb. 1, 1968	$1.60	$1.60	$1.15	$1.15
Feb. 1, 1969			$1.30	$1.30
Feb. 1, 1970			$1.45	
Feb. 1, 1971			$1.60	
May 1, 1974	$2.00	$2.00	$1.90	$1.60
Jan. 1, 1975	$2.10	$2.10	$2.00	$1.80
Jan. 1, 1976	$2.30	$2.30	$2.20	$2.00
Jan. 1, 1977			$2.30	$2.20
Jan. 1, 1978	$2.65 for all covered, nonexempt workers			
Jan. 1, 1979	$2.90 for all covered, nonexempt workers			
Jan. 1, 1980	$3.10 for all covered, nonexempt workers			
Jan. 1, 1981	$3.35 for all covered, nonexempt workers			
Apr. 1, 1990[d]	$3.80 for all covered, nonexempt workers			
Apr. 1, 1991	$4.25 for all covered, nonexempt workers			
Oct. 1, 1996[e]	$4.75 for all covered, nonexempt workers			
Sept. 1, 1997	$5.15 for all covered, nonexempt workers			
Jul. 24, 2007	$5.85 for all covered, nonexempt workers			
Jul. 24, 2008	$6.55 for all covered, nonexempt workers			
Jul. 24, 2009	$7.25 for all covered, nonexempt workers			

[a]The 1938 Act was applicable generally to employees engaged in interstate commerce or in the production of goods for interstate commerce.
[b]The 1961 Amendments extended coverage primarily to employees in large retail and service enterprises as well as to local transit, construction, and gasoline service station employees.
[c]The 1966 Amendments extended coverage to state and local government employees of hospitals, nursing homes, and schools, and to laundries, dry cleaners, and large hotels, motels, restaurants, and farms. Subsequent amendments extended coverage to the remaining federal, state and local government employees who were not protected in 1966, to certain workers in retail and service trades previously exempted, and to certain domestic workers in private household employment.
[d]Grandfather Clause: Employees who do not meet the tests for individual coverage, and whose employers were covered by the Fair Labor Standards Act, on March 31, 1990, and fail to meet the increased annual dollar volume (ADV) test for enterprise coverage, must continue to receive at least $3.35 an hour.
[e]A subminimum wage—$4.25 an hour—is established for employees under 20 years of age during their first 90 consecutive calendar days of employment with an employer.

SOURCE: "Federal Minimum Wage Rates under the Fair Labor Standards Act," U.S. Department of Labor, Wage and Hour Division, http://www.dol.gov/whd/minwage/chart.pdf (accessed January 16, 2013)

years, reaching $4.25 in 1991. In July 1996 Congress passed legislation that raised the minimum wage to $5.15 in 1997 by means of two $0.45 increases. In July 2007 the minimum wage was raised to $5.85, in July 2008 it was raised to $6.55, and in July 2009 it was raised to $7.25. As of 2013, a person working 40 hours per week for 50 weeks per year at minimum wage ($7.25 per hour) would gross $290 per week, or $14,500 per year, an income below the poverty level for a family of two ($15,510 in 2013) and substantially below the poverty level for a family of three ($19,530). (See Table 1.1 in Chapter 1.)

WHO WORKS FOR MINIMUM WAGE? Even though workers must receive at least the minimum wage for most jobs, there are some exceptions in which a person may be paid less than the minimum wage. Full-time students working on a part-time basis in the service and retail industries or at the students' academic institution, certain disabled people, and workers who are "customarily and regularly" tipped may receive less than the minimum wage. According to the Bureau of Labor Statistics (BLS), in *Characteristics of Minimum Wage Workers: 2011* (March 2, 2012, http://www.bls.gov/cps/minwage 2011.pdf), approximately 1.7 million people earned exactly the federal minimum wage in 2011, and approximately 2.2 million earned below the minimum. The number of those earning exactly the minimum wage was substantially higher than in 2009, when the figure stood at 980,000 workers, whereas the number of those making below minimum wage had declined, from 2.6 million in 2009. Workers making at or below the minimum wage were particularly concentrated in the South; 8% to 10% of hourly-wage workers in Georgia, Mississippi, and Texas made the minimum wage or less.

The BLS also notes that in 2011, 22% of workers in the leisure and hospitality industry made at or below the minimum wage; these workers constituted approximately half of the total number of workers who made the minimum wage or less. The bulk of these workers were restaurant workers who received tips in addition to their hourly wages. Additionally, part-time workers (2.5 million) were far more likely to make the minimum wage or less than were full-time workers (1.3 million).

Young workers hold minimum-wage jobs at rates that are disproportionate with their numbers as a share of the overall labor force. Half of the total number of workers making the minimum wage or less in 2011 were under age 25, even though this age group represented only one-fifth of the 73.9 million U.S. workers who were paid by the hour. The pool of workers making the minimum wage or less was disproportionately female: 2.4 million such workers were women, and 1.4 million were men. About 3 million of the total number of workers being paid at or below the minimum wage were white; 720,000 were Hispanic or Latino; 577,000

were African-American; and 99,000 were Asian-American. (See Table 3.11.)

Supplemental Security Income

SSI is a means-tested income assistance program authorized in 1972 by Title XVI of the Social Security Act. The SSI program replaced the combined federal-state programs of Old Age Assistance, Aid to the Blind, and Aid to the Permanently and Totally Disabled in the 50 states and the District of Columbia. However, these programs still exist in the U.S. territories of Guam, Puerto Rico, and the Virgin Islands. Since the first payments in 1974, SSI has provided monthly cash payments to needy aged, blind, and disabled individuals who meet the eligibility requirements. States may supplement the basic federal SSI payment.

A number of requirements must be met to receive financial benefits from SSI. First, a person must meet the program criteria for age, blindness, or disability. The aged, or elderly, are people 65 years and older. To be considered legally blind, a person must have vision of 20/200 or less in the better eye with the use of corrective lenses, have tunnel vision of 20 degrees or less (can only see a small area straight ahead), or have met state qualifications for the earlier Aid to the Blind program. A person is disabled if he or she cannot earn money at a job because of a physical or mental illness or injury that may cause his or her death, or if the condition lasts for 12 months or longer. Those who met earlier state Aid to the Permanently Disabled requirements may also qualify for assistance.

Unmarried children under the age of 18 (or age 22 if a full-time student) may qualify for SSI if they have a medically determinable physical or mental impairment that substantially reduces their ability to function independently or to engage in age-appropriate activities. This impairment must be expected to last for a continuous period of more than 12 months or to result in death.

Because SSI is a means-tested benefit, a person's income and property must be counted before he or she can receive benefits. In "2013 Social Security Changes" (October 16, 2012, http://www.socialsecurity.gov/press office/factsheets/colafacts2013.htm), the Social Security Administration indicates that in 2013 individuals and couples receiving Social Security benefits could not earn more than $710 and $1,066 per month, respectively. In addition, all but six states (Arkansas, Arizona, Mississippi, North Dakota, Tennessee, and West Virginia) pay a supplement to federal SSI beneficiaries. All forms of income are counted in determining benefits, and in some cases the income of non-recipients with whom beneficiaries live is counted. To receive benefits in 2013, a person could have no more than $2,000 worth of property, and a couple could have no more than $3,000 worth of property

TABLE 3.11

Workers paid hourly rates at or below minimum wage, by selected characteristics, 2011

| | Number of workers (in thousands) | | | | Percent distribution | | | | Percent of workers paid hourly rates | | |
| | | At or below minimum wage | | | | At or below minimum wage | | | | At or below minimum wage | |
Characteristic	Total paid hourly rates	Total	At minimum wage	Below minimum wage	Total paid hourly rates	Total	At minimum wage	Below minimum wage	Total	At minimum wage	Below minimum wage
Age and sex											
Total, 16 years and over	73,926	3,829	1,677	2,152	100.0	100.0	100.0	100.0	5.2	2.3	2.9
16 to 24 years	14,436	1,896	893	1,003	19.5	49.5	53.2	46.6	13.1	6.2	6.9
16 to 19 years	3,936	899	491	408	5.3	23.5	29.3	19.0	22.8	12.5	10.4
25 years and over	59,490	1,933	784	1,149	80.5	50.5	46.8	53.4	3.2	1.3	1.9
Men, 16 years and over	36,457	1,433	648	785	49.3	37.4	38.6	36.5	3.9	1.8	2.2
16 to 24 years	7,290	787	388	399	9.9	20.6	23.1	18.5	10.8	5.3	5.5
16 to 19 years	1,872	373	212	161	2.5	9.7	12.6	7.5	19.9	11.3	8.6
25 years and over	29,167	647	260	387	39.5	16.9	15.5	18.0	2.2	0.9	1.3
Women, 16 years and over	37,469	2,395	1,029	1,366	50.7	62.5	61.4	63.5	6.4	2.7	3.6
16 to 24 years	7,147	1,109	505	604	9.7	29.0	30.1	28.1	15.5	7.1	8.5
16 to 19 years	2,064	526	279	247	2.8	13.7	16.6	11.5	25.5	13.5	12.0
25 years and over	30,323	1,286	524	762	41.0	33.6	31.2	35.4	4.2	1.7	2.5
Race, sex, and Hispanic or Latino ethnicity											
White[a]	59,314	3,006	1,258	1,748	80.2	78.5	75.0	81.2	5.1	2.1	2.9
Men	29,743	1,108	484	624	40.2	28.9	28.9	29.0	3.7	1.6	2.1
Women	29,571	1,898	774	1,124	40.0	49.6	46.2	52.2	6.4	2.6	3.8
Black or African American[a]	9,523	577	324	253	12.9	15.1	19.3	11.8	6.1	3.4	2.7
Men	4,252	222	117	105	5.8	5.8	7.0	4.9	5.2	2.8	2.5
Women	5,271	356	208	148	7.1	9.3	12.4	6.9	6.8	3.9	2.8
Asian[a]	3,037	99	36	63	4.1	2.6	2.1	2.9	3.3	1.2	2.1
Men	1,425	41	13	28	1.9	1.1	0.8	1.3	2.9	0.9	2.0
Women	1,612	58	23	35	2.2	1.5	1.4	1.6	3.6	1.4	2.2
Hispanic or Latino[a]	13,264	720	340	380	17.9	18.8	20.3	17.7	5.4	2.6	2.9
Men	7,703	326	154	172	10.4	8.5	9.2	8.0	4.2	2.0	2.2
Women	5,561	394	186	208	7.5	10.3	11.1	9.7	7.1	3.3	3.7
Full- and part-time status and sex											
Full-time workers[b]	53,594	1,274	522	752	72.5	33.3	31.1	34.9	2.4	1.0	1.4
Men	29,292	501	205	296	39.6	13.1	12.2	13.8	1.7	0.7	1.0
Women	24,302	773	317	456	32.9	20.2	18.9	21.2	3.2	1.3	1.9
Part-time workers[b]	20,199	2,545	1,153	1,392	27.3	66.5	68.8	64.7	12.6	5.7	6.9
Men	7,103	932	443	489	9.6	24.3	26.4	22.7	13.1	6.2	6.9
Women	13,096	1,615	711	904	17.7	42.2	42.4	42.0	12.3	5.4	6.9

[a]Estimates for the above race groups (white, black or African American, and Asian) do not sum to totals because data are not presented for all races. Persons whose ethnicity is identified as Hispanic or Latino may be of any race.
[b]The distinction between full- and part-time workers is based on hours usually worked. These data will not sum to totals because full- or part-time status on the principal job is not identifiable for a small number of multiple jobholders. Full time is 35 hours or more per week; part time is less than 35 hours.
Note: Data exclude all self-employed persons whether or not their businesses are incorporated.

SOURCE: "Table 1. Employed Wage and Salary Workers Paid Hourly Rates with Earnings at or below the Prevailing Federal Minimum Wage by Selected Characteristics, 2011 Annual Averages," in *Characteristics of Minimum Wage Workers: 2011*, U.S. Department of Labor, Bureau of Labor Statistics, March 2, 2012, http://bls.gov/cps/minwage2011.pdf (accessed January 16, 2013)

(mainly in savings accounts or in stocks and bonds). Not included in countable resources are the person's home, car, and household items.

Tax Relief for the Poor

Both conservatives and liberals hailed the Tax Reform Act of 1986 as a major step toward relieving the tax burden of low-income families, one group of Americans whose wages and benefits have been eroding since 1979. The law enlarged and inflation-proofed the Earned Income Tax Credit (EITC), which provides a refundable tax credit that both offsets taxes and often operates as a wage supplement. Only those who work can qualify. The amount is determined, in part, by how much each qualified individual or family earns. It is also adjusted to the size of the family. To be eligible for the family EITC, workers must live with their children, who must be under 19 years old or full-time students under 24 years old.

The maximum credit for Tax Year 2012 was $475 for taxpayers with no children, $3,169 for taxpayers with one child, $5,236 for taxpayers with two children, and $5,891 for taxpayers with three or more children. Families received less if their income was low because they were also eligible for public assistance. A family of four received the maximum benefit if its earnings were slightly below the poverty line, but many families well above the poverty line received some credit. Individuals with no children were eligible for the EITC if their incomes were less than $13,980, and childless married couples who filed taxes jointly were eligible at an income level of $19,190 or less. With one child, a single parent qualified with an income of less than $36,920 and a married couple with an income of less than $42,130; with two children, a single parent qualified with an income of less than $41,952 and a married couple with an income of less than $47,162; and with three or more children, a single parent qualified with an income of less than $45,060 and a married couple with an income of less than $50,270.

The largest EITC benefits go to families that no longer need welfare. The gradual phase-out and avail-ability of the EITC at above-poverty income levels help stabilize a parent's employment by providing additional money to cover expenses that are associated with work-ing, such as child care and transportation. Research finds that the EITC has been an effective work incentive and has significantly increased work participation among single mothers.

Those who do not owe income tax, or who owe an amount smaller than the credit, receive a check directly from the Internal Revenue Service for the credit due them. Most recipients claim the credit when they file an income tax form. In 2012 U.S. taxpayers filed 26.5 million EITC claims for tax year 2011, for a total credit amount of $60.7 billion. The average credit amount per tax return was $2,200. (See Table 3.12.)

Even though the Tax Reform Act of 1986 has helped ease the burden of federal taxes, most of the poor still pay a substantial share of their income in state and local taxes. To address the needs of such low-income families, 24 states and the District of Columbia have enacted a state EITC to supplement the federal credit, as the CBPP reports in "Policy Basics: State Earned Income Tax Credits" (December 5, 2012, http://www.cbpp.org/cms/index.cfm?fa=view&id=2506).

TABLE 3.12

Earned Income Tax Credit (EITC) claims and dollar values, by state

State	Number of EITC claims	Total EITC amount	Average EITC amount
National	26.5 M	$60.7 B	$2,200
Alabama	526.8 K	$1.38 B	$2,622
Alaska	47.5 K	$94 M	$1,970
Arizona	549.6 K	$1.32 B	$2,398
Arkansas	304.3 K	$740 M	$2,431
California	2.99 M	$6.84 B	$2,290
Colorado	345 K	$719 M	$2,083
Connecticut	206 K	$415 M	$2,015
Delaware	70 K	$154 M	$2,195
District of Columbia	51 K	$111 M	$2,176
Florida	2 M	$4.66 B	$2,332
Georgia	1.1 M	$2.74 B	$2,550
Hawaii	108 K	$227 M	$2,100
Idaho	133 K	$290 M	$2,186
Illinois	1 M	$2.35 B	$2,323
Indiana	545 K	$1.22 B	$2,231
Iowa	207 K	$425 M	$2,051
Kansas	214 K	$466 M	$2,174
Kentucky	401 K	$905 M	$2,255
Louisiana	527 K	$1.38 B	$2,615
Maine	100 K	$192 M	$1,928
Maryland	395 K	$861 M	$2,180
Massachusetts	386 K	$752 M	$1,950
Michigan	820 K	$1.86 B	$2,265
Minnesota	338 K	$673 M	$1,993
Mississippi	405 K	$1.08 B	$2,674
Missouri	515 K	$1.16 B	$2,258
Montana	81 K	$161 M	$1,997
Nebraska	134 K	$287 M	$2,139
Nevada	227 K	$516 M	$2,275
New Hampshire	78 K	$144 M	$1,850
New Jersey	563 K	$1.22 B	$2,169
New Mexico	213 K	490 M	$2,300
New York	1.7 M	$3.75 B	$2,212
North Carolina	907 K	$2.14 B	$2,356
North Dakota	43 K	$83 M	$1,959
Ohio	952 K	$2.13 B	$2,238
Oklahoma	339 K	$792 M	$2,337
Oregon	270 K	$541 M	$2,000
Pennsylvania	905 K	$1.87 B	$2,070
Rhode Island	79 K	$171 M	$2,147
South Carolina	490 K	$1.18 B	$2,402
South Dakota	63 K	$130 M	$2,053
Tennessee	654 K	$1.55 B	$2,372
Texas	2.57 M	$6.92 B	$2,575
Utah	191 K	$429 M	$2,245
Vermont	45 K	$80 M	$1,793
Virginia	593 K	$1.29 B	$2,181
Washington	432 K	$885 M	$2,047
West Virginia	157 K	$329 M	$2,096
Wisconsin	383 K	$790 M	$2,062
Wyoming	37 K	$71 M	$1,937

K = thousands
M = millions
B = billions

SOURCE: "EITC Statistics," in *EITC Central*, Internal Revenue Service, June 2012, http://www.eitc.irs.gov/central/eitcstats/ (accessed January 16, 2013)

CHAPTER 4

WHO RECEIVES GOVERNMENT BENEFITS?

A variety of government programs exist to assist low-income and impoverished families as well as those unable to work either permanently, due to disability, or temporarily, due to job loss. Means-tested assistance programs (programs that are based on earning below a certain threshold), such as Temporary Assistance for Needy Families (TANF) and the Supplemental Nutrition Assistance Program (SNAP), provide the most assistance to the largest proportion of impoverished families, and they are particularly important sources of support for children. Supplemental Security Income (SSI), meanwhile, provides assistance to disabled Americans of all ages. Other forms of government assistance, such as unemployment compensation and tax credits, are aimed specifically at working Americans. Collectively, these programs represent an important safety net for a wide variety of the country's citizens.

Although assumptions about aid recipients' unwillingness to work are common, a sizable proportion of even the poorest welfare beneficiaries typically derive some amount of their income through work. In fact, as Arloc Sherman, Robert Greenstein, and Kathy Ruffing of the Center on Budget and Policy Priorities (CBPP) report in "Contrary to 'Entitlement Society' Rhetoric, over Nine-Tenths of Entitlement Benefits Go to Elderly, Disabled, or Working Households" (February 10, 2012, http://www.cbpp.org/files/2-10-12pov.pdf), 91% of the recipients of government aid in 2010 were either elderly, disabled, or employed. "People who are neither elderly nor disabled—and do not live in a working household—received only 9 percent of the benefits" from entitlement programs in 2010, the CBPP authors write. (See Figure 4.1.)

This chapter focuses on the populations that benefit from the most prominent antipoverty programs in the U.S. social welfare system: TANF, SNAP, unemployment compensation, and SSI.

TEMPORARY ASSISTANCE FOR NEEDY FAMILIES

In its 2012 report to Congress on the TANF program ("Temporary Assistance for Needy Families Program [TANF]: Ninth Report to Congress," June 1, 2012, http://www.acf.hhs.gov/programs/ofa/resource/ninth-report-to-congress), the U.S. Department of Health and Human Services' Office of Family Assistance (OFA) describes the TANF caseload as of the end of fiscal year 2009. A monthly average of 1.7 million families, according to the OFA, participated in TANF in 2009; among those families, there were an estimated 973,580 adults and 3.1 million children. With an average monthly caseload of 532,907, California accounted for 31% of the total U.S. TANF caseload, followed by New York, with a monthly caseload of 116,693. The national TANF caseload consisted in almost equal parts of whites (31.2%), African-Americans (33.3%), and Hispanics (28.8%); 85.9% of adult TANF recipients were female, and 14.1% were male.

There are three basic types of TANF cases: single-parent cases, two-parent cases, and child-only cases (cases in which no adult in the household is a recipient of TANF benefits). As Pamela J. Loprest of the Urban Institute writes in "How Has the TANF Caseload Changed over Time?" (March 8, 2012, http://www.urban.org/Uploaded PDF/412565-How-Has-the-TANF-Caseload-Changed-Over-Time.pdf), the proportion of each case type in the overall caseload has changed substantially in the years since the 1996 passage of the Personal Responsibility and Work Opportunity Reconciliation Act (PRWORA), which replaced Aid to Families with Dependent Children (AFDC) with TANF. In 1997 single-parent families accounted for 72% of the caseload, child-only TANF cases for approximately 20%, and two-parent families for about 7%. By 2009 single-parent households represented approximately 47% of the national caseload, child-only cases represented 48% of the caseload, and two-parent families represented 5% of the caseload.

FIGURE 4.1

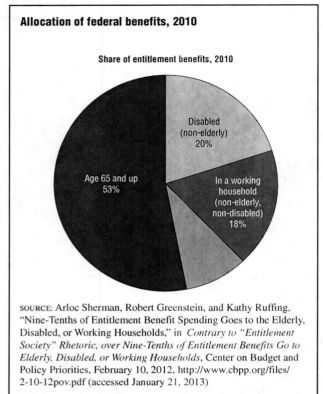

Allocation of federal benefits, 2010

Share of entitlement benefits, 2010

- Age 65 and up 53%
- Disabled (non-elderly) 20%
- In a working household (non-elderly, non-disabled) 18%

SOURCE: Arloc Sherman, Robert Greenstein, and Kathy Ruffing, "Nine-Tenths of Entitlement Benefit Spending Goes to the Elderly, Disabled, or Working Households," in *Contrary to "Entitlement Society" Rhetoric, over Nine-Tenths of Entitlement Benefits Go to Elderly, Disabled, or Working Households*, Center on Budget and Policy Priorities, February 10, 2012, http://www.cbpp.org/files/2-10-12pov.pdf (accessed January 21, 2013)

TABLE 4.1

Families receiving TANF, by state, fiscal year 2010

	Fiscal year 2010 caseload	% change from fiscal year 1997
Alabama	21,221	−38.5
Alaska	3,305	−72.5
Arizona	32,473	−40.7
Arkansas	8,547	−59.1
California	576,150	−29.4
Colorado	11,521	−61.5
Connecticut	17,268	−69.1
Delaware	5,157	−47.2
Dist. of Columbia	8,745	−63.7
Florida	58,267	−65.8
Georgia	20,572	−80.6
Hawaii	9,725	−54.3
Idaho	1,731	−73.2
Illinois	22,188	−88.8
Indiana	36,214	−19.0
Iowa	21,570	−25.2
Kansas	14,588	−27.8
Kentucky	30,209	−53.7
Louisiana	10,593	−81.3
Maine	14,778	−20.0
Maryland	24,543	−58.6
Massachusetts	53,914	−30.9
Michigan	68,233	−55.0
Minnesota	23,837	−55.3
Mississippi	12,092	−68.6
Missouri	38,902	−45.8
Montana	3,752	−57.8
Nebraska	8,661	−37.5
Nevada	10,271	−13.8
New Hampshire	6,173	−24.0
New Jersey	33,471	−64.9
New Mexico	19,797	−26.6
New York	155,530	−59.5
North Carolina	24,471	−75.3
North Dakota	2,035	−51.5
Ohio	103,030	−44.7
Oklahoma	9,420	−68.9
Oregon	30,207	25.5
Pennsylvania	51,883	−68.3
Rhode Island	7,445	−62.4
South Carolina	18,481	−46.0
South Dakota	3,231	−36.7
Tennessee	62,253	−11.6
Texas	50,618	−75.8
Utah	6,817	−44.3
Vermont	3,163	−61.7
Virginia	37,163	−31.0
Washington	69,125	−25.7
West Virginia	9,737	−71.1
Wisconsin	21,982	−43.5
Wyoming	327	−88.3
Total U.S.	**1,910,680**	**−51.5**

TANF = Temporary Assistance for Needy Families.

SOURCE: Pamela J. Loprest, "Table 1. Change in Families Receiving TANF, 1997–2010," in *How Has the TANF Caseload Changed over Time?* The Urban Institute, March 2012, http://urban.org/UploadedPDF/412565-How-Has-the-TANF-Caseload-Changed-Over-Time.pdf (accessed January 21, 2013)

These changes in the caseload composition do not correspond to increases in the child-only caseload, however, but to massive declines in the overall caseload. As Table 4.1 shows, the overall TANF caseload declined by 51.5% between 1997 and 2010, with declines in individual states ranging from 11.6% (Tennessee) to 88.8% (Illinois). In 35 states the TANF caseload decreased during this time by more than 40%; and only one state, Oregon, saw its caseload increase. Likewise, the absolute number of child-only TANF cases declined, from 978,000 in 1996 to 831,100 in 2009. The percentage of child-only cases, however, steadily rose relative to the other types of cases. Numerous adults became ineligible for TANF during this time, due to rising incomes, work requirements, benefit time limits, and other factors related both to changes in the economy and to welfare reform. Many of the households that received child-only benefits likely included an adult TANF recipient whose eligibility expired, who no longer qualified for benefits, or who had chosen not to enroll due to the eligibility restrictions. Child-only cases are subject to fewer eligibility restrictions and time limits than adult cases, so much of the changing composition of the TANF caseload reflects the fact that the need for assistance has remained relatively constant even though many adults have been removed from the welfare rolls.

Who Receives TANF Benefits?

The demographic characteristics of the adult TANF caseload have not changed dramatically since the passage of welfare reform. This contradicts the conventional wisdom prior to 1996, when many believed that the TANF work incentives would lead those adults most able and willing to work to exit the system, leaving a recipient population that was less capable of work and therefore demographically altered. As Loprest observes, however, the lack of demographic alteration in the TANF caseload may reflect the fact that many who left the welfare rolls

Who Receives Government Benefits?

did not find work. In other words, the same subpopulations continued to need government assistance both before and after welfare reform, even as the overall number of cash assistance recipients declined as a result of work requirements, time limits, and other rules.

Specifically, the distribution of the adult TANF caseload among different age groups remained relatively constant between the late 1990s and 2009, as Table 4.2 shows. In 1998, 6.1% of adult TANF recipients were under the age of 20; 8% were under age 20 in 2009. By far the largest share of adult recipients were between the ages of 20 and 39 in both years (75.2% and 76%, respectively), and the proportion of TANF recipients over the age of 39 declined slightly, from 18.6% to 16%. The proportion of Hispanics in the overall caseload rose appreciably, from 20% in 1998 to 24.2% in 2009, as did the proportion of Native Americans, from 1.6% to 5.3%. The proportion of African-Americans declined, from 37.1% in 1998 to 34.1% in 2009, and the proportion of whites remained relatively constant, at 35.6% and 35.4%. In 1998, 42.4% of adult TANF recipients had one child, 29.6% had two children, and 26.3% had three or more children. In 2009 these figures stood at 50.8%, 26.9%, and 20.4%.

Children who receive TANF benefits, either as part of the family of an adult TANF recipient or under a child-only designation, are overwhelmingly young. In 2009 about 73% of TANF children were age 11 or younger, whereas less than 10% were age 16 or older. Children two years old and younger represented 16% of the child caseload, and children between two and five years old represented 27% of the caseload. These percentages have remained relatively constant since 2000, as Table 4.3 shows. Hispanic children constituted 33.5% of the TANF caseload in 2009; 33.1% were African-American, and 26.1% were white. A small fraction (1.4%) of TANF children were qualified immigrants, as opposed to U.S. citizens.

Approximately 17% of TANF families had income from other sources in 2009. Those who had such income made a monthly average of $683 beyond their TANF benefits. About 9% of TANF families had income from child support, with an average monthly payment of $227, and 10% had cash assets. Those with cash on hand, in bank accounts, or in other investment vehicles constituted 10% of TANF families; assets held by these families averaged $220. Nearly one-quarter (23.5%) of TANF adults were employed, a dramatic increase over the 1992 AFDC employment rate of 6.6% but a decrease from the peak TANF employment rate of 27.6% in 1999. (See Table 4.4.)

Duration of TANF Benefits

According to Loprest of the Urban Institute, the majority of adult TANF recipients collect benefits for short periods. Setting aside child-only cases, which

TABLE 4.2

Characteristics of adult TANF recipients, fiscal years 1998 and 2009

	Fiscal year 1998	Fiscal year 2009
Age of adult recipients		
Under 20	6.1	8.0
20–39	75.2	76.0
Over 39	18.6	16.0
Gender of adult recipients		
Female	—[b]	85.9
Male	—[b]	14.1
Ethnicity/race of adult recipients		
Hispanic[a]	20.0	24.2
White	35.6	35.4
African American	37.1	34.1
Native American	1.6	5.3
Unknown	0.5	1.0
Marital status of adult recipients		
Single	52.5	69.5
Married	16.4	14.4
Separated/widowed/divorced	21.2	16.0
Citizenship of adult recipients		
U.S. citizen	88.1	91.2
Qualified alien	11.0[c]	7.1
Unknown	0.9	1.7
Employment status of adult recipients		
Employed	22.8	23.5
Unemployed	45.0	47.3
Not in labor force	28.3	29.2
Years of education of adult recipients		
No formal education	—[d]	5.3
1–11 years	42.6	36.4
12 or more years	46.0	58.0
Unknown	11.4[d]	0.4
Age of youngest child		
Unborn	—[e]	0.8
Under 1	11.0	15.3
1–5 years	45.1	41.0
6–19 years	42.0	42.1
Unknown	1.8[e]	0.7
Number of recipient children[f]		
Average	2.0	1.8
One	42.4	50.8
Two	29.6	26.9
Three or more	26.3	20.4
Unknown	1.8	1.8

TANF = Temporary Assistance for Needy Families.
[a]Can be of any race.
[b]Data not available.
[c]Fiscal year 1998 data do not distinguish between qualified and nonqualified aliens.
[d]Fiscal year 1998 data combine no formal education and unknown level of educaiton.
[e]Fiscal year 1998 data combine unborn children with unknown age of child.
[f]For all TANF families, including child only.

SOURCE: Pamela J. Loprest, "Table 2. Characteristics of Adult TANF Recipients (Percent)," in *How Has the TANF Caseload Changed over Time?* The Urban Institute, March 2012, http://urban.org/UploadedPDF/412565-How-Has-the-TANF-Caseload-Changed-Over-Time.pdf (accessed January 21, 2013)

generally are not subject to time limits, 41% of TANF recipients in 2009 had been collecting benefits for less than a year, and 23% of beneficiaries had been collecting benefits for less than two years; 12% of the overall caseload consisted of adults who had been receiving benefits for more than four years.

TABLE 4.3

Trend in TANF children, by age group, fiscal years 2000–09

	Under 2	2–5	6–11	12–15	16–19
2000	13.1%	25.6%	36.2%	17.4%	7.6%
2001	13.4%	24.9%	35.8%	18.4%	7.5%
2002	14.6%	25.1%	34.4%	18.3%	7.6%
2003	14.6%	25.4%	33.4%	18.8%	7.7%
2004	14.7%	25.7%	32.2%	19.4%	8.0%
2005	14.5%	25.0%	31.8%	19.9%	8.8%
2006	14.5%	25.5%	31.1%	19.7%	9.2%
2007	15.4%	25.3%	30.5%	19.2%	9.5%
2008	16.0%	25.5%	30.4%	18.5%	9.5%
2009	16.1%	26.9%	29.9%	17.9%	9.2%

TANF = Temporary Assistance for Needy Families.

SOURCE: "Table D. Trend in TANF Recipient Children by Age Group FY 2002 (sic)–FY 2009," in *Temporary Assistance for Needy Families Program (TANF): Ninth Report to Congress*, U.S. Department of Health and Human Services, Administration for Children and Families, Office of Family Assistance, June 1, 2012, http://www.acf.hhs.gov/programs/ofa/resource/ninth-report-to-congress (accessed January 21, 2013)

TABLE 4.4

Trend in employment rate of TANF recipients, fiscal years 1992–2009

	Employment rate
1992	6.6%
1993	6.9%
1994	8.3%
1995	9.3%
1996	11.3%
1997	13.2%*
1998	22.8%
1999	27.6%
2000	26.4%
2001	26.7%
2002	25.3%
2003	22.9%
2004	22.0%
2005	23.2%
2006	21.6%
2007	24.9%
2008	25.9%
2009	23.5%

TANF = Temporary Assistance for Needy Families.
AFDC = Aid to Families with Dependent Children.
*Based on AFDC data from the first three quarters of fiscal year 1997.

SOURCE: "Table E. Trend in Employment Rate of TANF Adult Recipients, FY 1992–FY 2009," in *Temporary Assistance for Needy Families Program (TANF): Ninth Report to Congress*, U.S. Department of Health and Human Services, Administration for Children and Families, Office of Family Assistance, June 1, 2012, http://www.acf.hhs.gov/programs/ofa/resource/ninth-report-to-congress (accessed January 21, 2013)

The PRWORA limited the duration that a family can collect TANF benefits to a lifetime maximum of 60 months, and states have the freedom to set shorter maximum time limits. As Liz Schott and LaDonna Pavetti of the CBPP write in "Many States Cutting TANF Benefits Harshly Despite High Unemployment and Unprecedented Need" (October 3, 2011, http://www.cbpp.org/files/5-19-11tanf.pdf), fiscal pressures at the state level

during the so-called Great Recession led to numerous cuts in TANF benefits, including reductions in the program time limits. For example, in 2010 Arizona cut its TANF time limit from the federally established 60 months to 36 months, before further shortening the lifetime maximum period to 24 months in 2011. California, which is home to 31% of the entire TANF caseload, shortened its time limit from 60 to 48 months in 2011, as well. As Schott and Pavetti write, "The TANF block grant has been in place long enough for us to know that families who reach time limits are among the most vulnerable families. They are far more likely than other TANF recipients to face employment barriers such as physical and mental health problems and to have lower levels of education that significantly reduce their chances of finding jobs."

SUPPLEMENTAL NUTRITION ASSISTANCE PROGRAM

In the years since the passage of the PRWORA in 1996, SNAP (previously called the Food Stamp Program) has increasingly functioned as a central part of the U.S. welfare system. As the scope of AFDC/TANF, formerly the centerpiece of the national safety net, contracted during the late 1990s and first years of the 21st century and then showed limited response to increasing levels of poverty during the Great Recession, SNAP became increasingly important to impoverished Americans.

SNAP is overseen by the U.S. Department of Agriculture (USDA) and is the largest of 15 food and nutrition assistance programs in the United States. SNAP issues an electronic debit card that may be used at more than 230,000 participating U.S. grocery stores to buy food that is prepared at home. The value of the benefits varies according to family size and household income: maximum amounts for October 2012 through September 2013 ranged from $200 per month for one person to $1,202 for a family of eight. (See Table 4.5.) Unlike other social welfare programs, however, SNAP is available to non-elderly adults, non-disabled adults, and childless adults.

Whereas TANF's prominence relative to other safety-net programs has dramatically declined since the passage of welfare reform legislation, SNAP, which is designed to meet fluctuations in need that arise with changing economic circumstances, has grown significantly since the 1980s. As Figure 4.2 shows, the number of SNAP beneficiaries declined from 1985 to 1989, grew rapidly during the early 1990s before peaking in 1994, and then declined again through 2000. Beginning in 2001, the number of SNAP households grew each year through 2011, and it grew especially rapidly during the period 2007 through 2011, as a result of the Great Recession, the effects of which lingered long after its official end in 2009. Indeed, more so than any other safety-net program with the exception, perhaps, of unemployment compensation, SNAP's size has corresponded to fluctuations in major economic indicators such as the unemployment rate and the poverty rate. As Sheila Zedlewski, Elaine Waxman, and Craig Gundersen of the Urban Institute observe in "SNAP's Role in the Great Recession and Beyond" (July 2012, http://www.urban.org/Uploaded PDF/412613-SNAPs-Role-in-the-Great-Recession-and-Beyond.pdf), "SNAP does more than combat hunger. It is an antipoverty program, a work support, a promoter of health and nutrition, and an automatic stabilizer in recessions—filling in the gaps that other safety net programs leave behind."

SNAP is without a doubt the most important program to that portion of the population that experiences food insecurity. This group includes most people living below the poverty line as well as many whose incomes are marginally higher than the poverty line.

Measuring the Need for Food Assistance

During the 1980s a number of studies found that some Americans, especially children, were suffering from hunger. Many observers did not believe these reports or thought they had been exaggerated. In 1984 a Task Force on Food Assistance appointed by President Ronald Reagan (1911–2004) found that it could not determine the extent of hunger in the United States because there was no agreed-on way to measure it.

COMMUNITY CHILDHOOD HUNGER IDENTIFICATION PROJECT. In response, the Food Research and Action Center (FRAC), an advocacy group for the poor, launched the Community Childhood Hunger Identification Project (CCHIP) to determine the extent of hunger in the United States. The first FRAC survey conducted

TABLE 4.5

SNAP maximum benefits, 2012–13

[Allotments for households in the 48 contiguous states and the District of Columbia. October 2012 through September 2013.]

People in household	Maximum monthly allotment
1	$200
2	$367
3	$526
4	$668
5	$793
6	$952
7	$1,052
8	$1,202
Each additional person	$150

Notes: SNAP = Supplemental Nutrition Assistance Program. The amount of benefits the household gets is called an allotment. The net monthly income of the household is multiplied by 0.3, and the result is subtracted from the maximum allotment for the household size to find the household's allotment. This is because SNAP households are expected to spend about 30 percent of their resources on food.

SOURCE: "Benefits," in *Supplemental Nutrition Assistance Program: Eligibility*, U.S. Department of Agriculture, Food and Nutrition Service, January 15, 2013, http://www.fns.usda.gov/snap/applicant_recipients/eligibility.htm (accessed January 23, 2013)

FIGURE 4.2

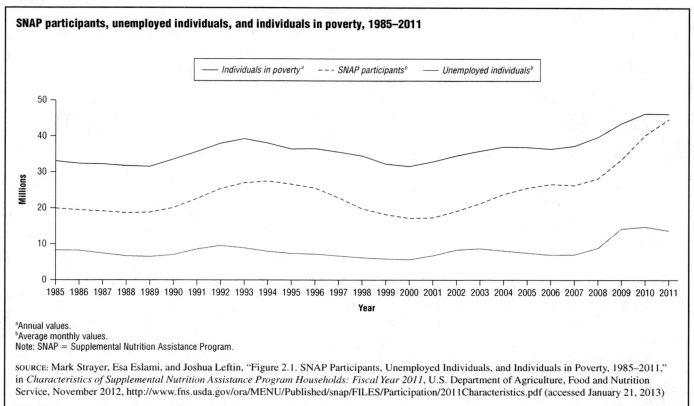

SNAP participants, unemployed individuals, and individuals in poverty, 1985–2011

[a]Annual values.
[b]Average monthly values.
Note: SNAP = Supplemental Nutrition Assistance Program.

SOURCE: Mark Strayer, Esa Eslami, and Joshua Leftin, "Figure 2.1. SNAP Participants, Unemployed Individuals, and Individuals in Poverty, 1985–2011," in *Characteristics of Supplemental Nutrition Assistance Program Households: Fiscal Year 2011*, U.S. Department of Agriculture, Food and Nutrition Service, November 2012, http://www.fns.usda.gov/ora/MENU/Published/snap/FILES/Participation/2011Characteristics.pdf (accessed January 21, 2013)

interviews in 2,335 households with incomes at or below 185% of the poverty level and with at least one child under the age of 12 years. The results of this survey, as reported by Cheryl A. Wehler et al. in *Community Childhood Hunger Identification Project: A Survey of Childhood Hunger in the United States* (1991), indicated that 32% of U.S. households with incomes at or below 185% of the poverty level experienced hunger. At least one child out of every eight under the age of 12 years suffered from hunger. Another 40% of low-income children were at risk for hunger.

Between 1992 and 1994 FRAC sponsored a second round of CCHIP surveys in nine states and the District of Columbia (5,282 low-income families with at least one child aged 12 years and younger). For the purposes of its report, FRAC defined hunger as food insufficiency (skipping meals, eating less, or running out of food) that occurred because of limited household resources. The results were reported by Wehler et al. in *Community Childhood Hunger Identification Project: A Survey of Childhood Hunger in the United States* (1995). FRAC concluded in the 1995 CCHIP survey that about 4 million children aged 12 years and younger experienced hunger for one or more months during the previous year. Another 9.6 million children were at risk of becoming hungry.

The 1995 CCHIP survey studied one child in each household (the child with the most recent birthday) and found that, in comparison with non-hungry children, hungry children were:

- More than three times as likely to suffer from unwanted weight loss
- More than four times as likely to suffer from fatigue
- Almost three times as likely to suffer from irritability
- More than three times as likely to have frequent headaches
- Almost one and a half times as likely to have frequent ear infections
- Four times as likely to suffer from concentration problems
- Almost twice as likely to have frequent colds

Based on the findings from the 1991 and 1995 CCHIP surveys, FRAC concluded that even though federal food programs are targeted to households most in need, a common barrier to program participation is a lack of information, particularly about eligibility guidelines. FRAC contended that if federal, state, and local governments made a greater effort to ensure that possible recipients were aware of their eligibility for food programs, such as the Special Supplemental Food Program for Women, Infants, and Children and the School Breakfast Program, there would be a large drop in hunger in the United States.

NATIONAL SURVEY OF AMERICAN FAMILIES. In 1997 the Urban Institute conducted the National Survey of American Families (NSAF; 2006, http://www.urban.org/center/anf/snapshots.cfm). Nearly half of low-income families (those with family incomes up to 200% of the federal poverty line) who were interviewed in 1997 reported that the food they purchased ran out before they got money to buy more, or they worried they would run out of food. Four out of five of these families with food problems reported suffering actual food shortages, and one out of five worried about food shortages. More children than adults lived in families that worried about or had trouble affording food—54% of low-income children experienced this problem. The NSAF was repeated in 1999, and families reported fewer problems affording food than in 1997. Four out of 10 low-income families were either concerned about or had difficulty affording food, down about 10% from 1997. However, approximately half of all low-income children still lived in families with difficulties affording food or had concern about the lack of food.

A third NSAF was conducted in 2002, and the results were released in 2004. According to Sandi Nelson of the Urban Institute in "Trends in Parents' Economic Hardship" (March 2004, http://www.urban.org/UploadedPDF/310970_snapshots3_no21.pdf), the 2002 report showed that 51.3% of low-income parents and 59.4% of single parents experienced food hardship. The report also indicated that the gains made between 1997 and 1999 had been erased.

FEDERAL GOVERNMENT SURVEYS. Since 1995 the USDA's Food and Nutrition Service and the Census Bureau have conducted annual surveys of food security, low food security (or food insecurity), and very low food security (previously called hunger). (Food-secure households are those that have access at all times to enough food for an active, healthy life. Low-food-security households are uncertain of having, or unable to acquire, enough food to meet basic needs at all times during the year.) Figure 4.3 shows the breakdown of U.S. households by food security status as of 2011.

Alisha Coleman-Jensen et al. of the USDA's Economic Research Service write in *Household Food Security in the United States, 2011* (September 2012, http://www.ers.usda.gov/media/884525/err141.pdf) that the agency uses 18 questions to assess a family's level of food security (Questions 11–18 were asked only if the household included children aged 17 or younger):

1. "We worried whether our food would run out before we got money to buy more." Was that often, sometimes, or never true for you in the last 12 months?

2. "The food that we bought just didn't last, and we didn't have money to get more." Was that often,

FIGURE 4.3

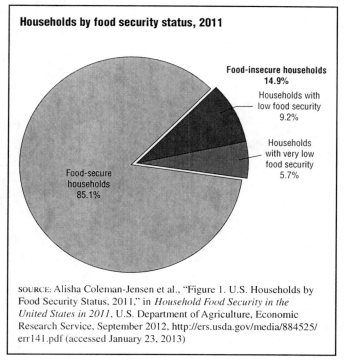

Households by food security status, 2011

Food-insecure households
14.9%

Households with
low food security
9.2%

Households
with very low
food security
5.7%

Food-secure
households
85.1%

SOURCE: Alisha Coleman-Jensen et al., "Figure 1. U.S. Households by Food Security Status, 2011," in *Household Food Security in the United States in 2011*, U.S. Department of Agriculture, Economic Research Service, September 2012, http://ers.usda.gov/media/884525/err141.pdf (accessed January 23, 2013)

sometimes, or never true for you in the last 12 months?

3. "We couldn't afford to eat balanced meals." Was that often, sometimes, or never true for you in the last 12 months?

4. In the last 12 months, did you or other adults in the household ever cut the size of your meals or skip meals because there wasn't enough money for food? (Yes/No)

5. (If yes to question 4) How often did this happen—almost every month, some months but not every month, or in only one or two months?

6. In the last 12 months, did you ever eat less than you felt you should because there wasn't enough money for food? (Yes/No)

7. In the last 12 months, were you ever hungry, but didn't eat, because there wasn't enough money for food? (Yes/No)

8. In the last 12 months, did you lose weight because there wasn't enough money for food? (Yes/No)

9. In the last 12 months, did you or other adults in your household ever not eat for a whole day because there wasn't enough money for food? (Yes/No)

10. (If yes to question 9) How often did this happen—almost every month, some months but not every month, or in only one or two months?

11. "We relied on a few kinds of low-cost food to feed our children because we were running out of money to buy food." Was that often, sometimes, or never true for you in the last 12 months?

12. "We couldn't feed our children a balanced meal, because we couldn't afford that." Was that often, sometimes, or never true for you in the last 12 months?

13. "The children were not eating enough because we just couldn't afford enough food." Was that often, sometimes, or never true for you in the last 12 months?

14. In the last 12 months, did you ever cut the size of any of the children's meals because there wasn't enough money for food? (Yes/No)

15. In the last 12 months, were the children ever hungry but you just couldn't afford more food? (Yes/No)

16. In the last 12 months, did any of the children ever skip a meal because there wasn't enough money for food? (Yes/No)

17. (If yes to question 16) How often did this happen—almost every month, some months but not every month, or in only one or two months?

18. In the last 12 months did any of the children ever not eat for a whole day because there wasn't enough money for food? (Yes/No)

Figure 4.4 shows that the levels of food insecurity steadily rose from 1999 to 2004, but dropped in 2005 before rising again. Food insecurity rose precipitously, however, between 2007 and 2011 as a result of the rising unemployment and poverty rates associated with the Great Recession. The prevalence rate of very low food security rose appreciably between 1999 and 2011, as well. (Households with very low food security often worry that their food will run out, report that their food does run out before they have money to buy more, cannot afford to eat balanced meals, often have adults who skip meals because there is not enough money for food, and report that they eat less than they should because of a lack of money.) In 2011, 14.9% of U.S. households reported some level of food insecurity during the year; 9.2% of U.S. households reported low food security, and 5.7% reported having very low food security. (See Figure 4.4.)

Poor and low-income households were more likely to experience food insecurity and very low food security during the year than were households with higher incomes. Coleman-Jensen et al. indicate that in 2011, 23.2% of households with an income below the poverty line reported low food security, and 17.9% of households reported very low food security. Moreover, food insecurity did not decrease substantially until households reached income levels well above the poverty line. Among households under 130% of the poverty line, 21.5% experienced low food security, and 16.1% experienced very low food security. Among households under

FIGURE 4.4

Trends in prevalence of household food insecurity, 1995–2011

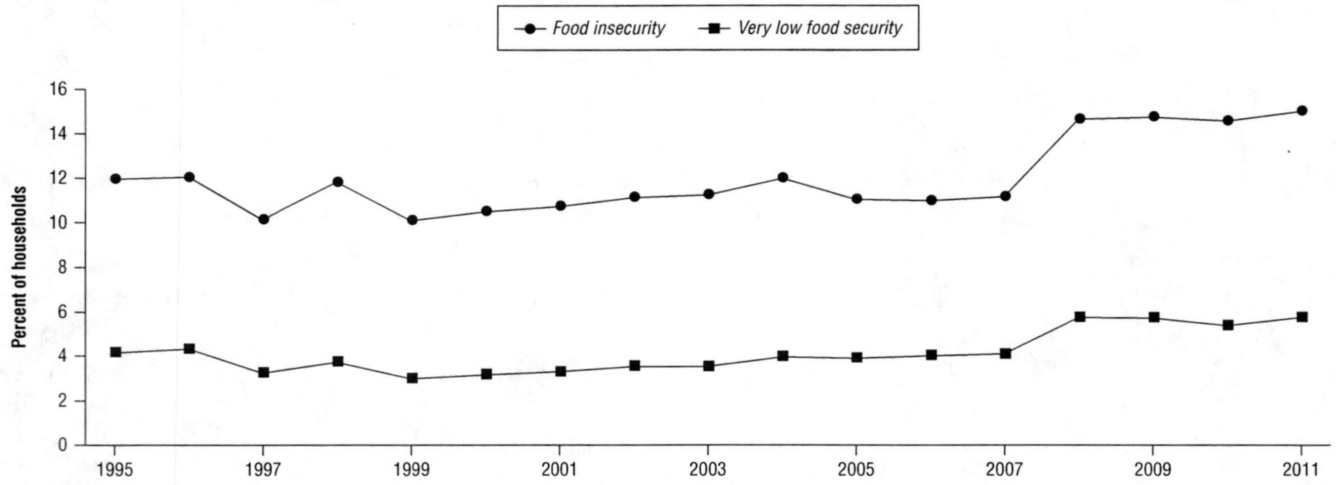

Note: Prevalence rates for 1996 and 1997 were adjusted for the estimated effects of differences in data collection screening protocols used in those years.

SOURCE: Alisha Coleman-Jensen et al., "Figure 3. Trends in the Prevalence of Food Insecurity and Very Low Food Security in U.S. Households, 1995–2011," in *Household Food Security in the United States in 2011*, U.S. Department of Agriculture, Economic Research Service, September 2012, http://ers.usda.gov/media/884525/err141.pdf (accessed January 23, 2013)

185% of poverty, 20.3% experienced low food security, and 14.2% experienced very low food security. These three categories of households represented 69.2 million of the total 119.5 million U.S. households surveyed—a number that does not include homeless families and that, therefore, likely underestimates the total amount of food insecurity. (See Table 4.6.)

Who Receives SNAP Benefits?

Although not all food-insecure households participate in SNAP, the two population sets overlap considerably. Mark Strayer, Esa Eslami, and Joshua Leftin of the USDA's Food and Nutrition Service (FNS) provide detailed information about SNAP recipients in "Characteristics of Supplemental Nutrition Assistance Program Households: Fiscal Year 2011" (November 2012, http://www.fns.usda.gov/ora/MENU/Published/snap/FILES/Participation/2011Characteristics.pdf). According to the authors, during an average month in 2011 approximately 44.7 million people in 21.1 million households received SNAP benefits. SNAP households received, on average, $284 worth of benefits per month. More than four out of five (83%) of SNAP households lived below the federal poverty line, and 43% lived at half the poverty line or below. One-fifth (20%) of SNAP households had no gross income, and 39% had no net income. Three out of 10 SNAP households (31%; 6.4 million out of 20.8 million) had income from a job, 20% (4.2 million) had income from SSI, 22% (4.7 million) had income from Social Security, 8% (1.6 million) had income from

TANF, and 4% (844,000) received general assistance. (See Table 4.7. Note that there are slight discrepancies between some of FNS data and the data in Table 4.7 and other graphics, due to the agency's use of two different data sets. The data sets are consistent with one another in spite of the small variations in absolute numbers.)

The composition of SNAP participant households has changed along with the absolute number of households, as Table 4.8 shows. In 1989, 7.1% of SNAP households had zero gross income, and 18.3% had zero net income. Meanwhile, in 1989, 41.9% of SNAP households received cash assistance through AFDC/TANF. The dramatic increase in the percentage of SNAP households with zero gross income (20% in 2011) and zero net income (39% in 2011) corresponds with a dramatic decline in the percentage of SNAP households receiving cash assistance through TANF. Only 7.6% of SNAP recipients were also TANF participants in 2011. Other notable changes in the composition of the SNAP caseload include an increase in the percentage of households with earned income, from 19.6% of households in 1989 to 30.5% in 2011; an increase in the proportion of disabled individuals, from 9.1% to 20.2%; and a decline in the proportion of households with children, from 60.4% to 47.1%.

In 2011, 15.3 million (34.6%) of SNAP's 44 million individual recipients were non-Hispanic whites, 10.2 million (23%) were African-American, and 6.8 million (15.4%) were Hispanic. Slightly more than 1.1 million Asian-Americans and 1.6 million Native Americans

TABLE 4.6

Households by food security status and selected characteristics, 2011

Category	Total[a]	Food secure			Food insecure					
					All		With low food security		With very low food security	
	1,000	1,000	Percent		1,000	Percent	1,000	Percent	1,000	Percent
All households	119,484	101,631	85.1		17,853	14.9	11,014	9.2	6,839	5.7
Household composition										
With children <18 yrs	38,803	30,814	79.4		7,989	20.6	5,750	14.8	2,239	5.8
With children <6 yrs	17,281	13,494	78.1		3,787	21.9	2,884	16.7	903	5.2
Married-couple families	25,421	21,879	86.1		3,542	13.9	2,671	10.5	871	3.4
Female head, no spouse	9,690	6,124	63.2		3,566	36.8	2,452	25.3	1,114	11.5
Male head, no spouse	3,055	2,295	75.1		760	24.9	532	17.4	228	7.5
Other household with child[b]	638	517	81.0		121	19.0	96	15.0	25	3.9
With no children <18 yrs	80,681	70,817	87.8		9,864	12.2	5,264	6.5	4,600	5.7
More than one adult	47,863	43,103	90.1		4,760	9.9	2,778	5.8	1,982	4.1
Women living alone	18,021	15,205	84.4		2,816	15.6	1,387	7.7	1,429	7.9
Men living alone	14,796	12,508	84.5		2,288	15.5	1,099	7.4	1,189	8.0
With elderly	30,099	27,579	91.6		2,520	8.4	1,589	5.3	931	3.1
Elderly living alone	11,402	10,400	91.2		1,002	8.8	579	5.1	423	3.7
Race/ethnicity of households										
White, non-Hispanic	83,304	73,823	88.6		9,481	11.4	5,689	6.8	3,792	4.6
Black, non-Hispanic	14,765	11,066	74.9		3,699	25.1	2,155	14.6	1,544	10.5
Hispanic[c]	14,410	10,629	73.8		3,781	26.2	2,583	17.9	1,198	8.3
Other	7,005	6,113	87.3		892	12.7	587	8.4	305	4.4
Household income-to-poverty ratio										
Under 1.00	15,557	9,164	58.9		6,393	41.1	3,616	23.2	2,777	17.9
Under 1.30	22,168	13,825	62.4		8,343	37.6	4,763	21.5	3,580	16.1
Under 1.85	31,437	20,593	65.5		10,844	34.5	6,376	20.3	4,468	14.2
1.85 and over	62,244	57,888	93.0		4,356	7.0	2,938	4.7	1,418	2.3
Income unknown	25,802	23,149	89.7		2,653	10.3	1,700	6.6	953	3.7
Area of residence[d]										
Inside metropolitan area	99,835	84,999	85.1		14,836	14.9	9,163	9.2	5,673	5.7
In principal cities[e]	33,515	27,597	82.3		5,918	17.7	3,646	10.9	2,272	6.8
Not in principal cities	49,253	42,770	86.8		6,483	13.2	4,013	8.1	2,470	5.0
Outside metropolitan area	19,649	16,632	84.6		3,017	15.4	1,851	9.4	1,166	5.9
Census geographic region										
Northeast	21,650	18,736	86.5		2,914	13.5	1,777	8.2	1,137	5.3
Midwest	26,359	22,798	86.5		3,561	13.5	2,141	8.1	1,420	5.4
South	44,772	37,618	84.0		7,154	16.0	4,431	9.9	2,723	6.1
West	26,703	22,478	84.2		4,225	15.8	2,665	10.0	1,560	5.8

[a]Totals exclude households for which food security status is unknown because they did not give a valid response to any of the questions in the food security scale. In 2011, these exclusions represented 405,000 households (0.3 percent of all households).
[b]Households with children in complex living arrangements, e.g., children of other relatives or unrelated roommate or boarder.
[c]Hispanics may be of any race.
[d]Metropolitan area residence is based on 2003 Office of Management and Budget delineation.
[e]Households within incorporated areas of the largest cities in each metropolitan area. Residence inside or outside of principal cities is not identified for about 17 percent of households in metropolitan statistical areas.

SOURCE: Alisha Coleman-Jensen et al., "Table 2. Households by Food Security Status and Selected Household Characteristics, 2011," in *Household Food Security in the United States in 2011*, U.S. Department of Agriculture, Economic Research Service, September 2012, http://ers.usda.gov/media/884525/err141 .pdf (accessed January 23, 2013)

received SNAP benefits, accounting for 2.6% and 3.6% of the overall SNAP population. (See Table 4.9.) Nearly 20 million (45.1%) of SNAP's 44 million individual recipients were under age 18, and 20.4 million (46.3%) were nonelderly adults. These nonelderly adults were split almost equally between those aged 18 to 35 (10.6 million) and those aged 36 to 59 (9.8 million). Almost 3.8 million (8.5%) SNAP recipients were aged 60 or older. Except among children, where male participants slightly outnumbered female participants (10.1 million versus 9.8 million), women were substantially more likely to receive SNAP benefits than men. Nearly 7 million women aged 18 to 35 received SNAP benefits, compared with 3.7 million men; 5.7 million women aged 36 to 59 received benefits, compared with 4.1 million men; and 2.5 million women aged 60 and older received benefits, compared with 1.3 million men.

According to Zedlewski, Waxman, and Gunderson of the Urban Institute, SNAP was responsible, between 2000 and 2009, for an average annual decrease in the poverty rate of 4.4% and an average annual decrease in the child poverty rate of 5.6%. More pronounced than its effects on moving individuals out of poverty, however, was SNAP's ability to ameliorate the depth and severity of poverty. Most families do not exit poverty as a result

TABLE 4.7

Characteristics of SNAP recipient households, 2011

Households with:	All households		Earned income		Social Security		Households with countable: Social Security Income (SSI)		Zero gross income		TANF		General assistance	
	Number (000)	Percent	Number (000)	Percent	Number (000)	Percent	Number (000)	Percent	Number (000)	Percent	Number (000)	Percent	Number (000)	Percent
Total[a]	**20,803**	**100.0**	**6,351**	**100.0**	**4,660**	**100.0**	**4,195**	**100.0**	**4,151**	**100.0**	**1,591**	**100.0**	**844**	**100.0**
Children	9,794	47.1	4,816	75.8	910	19.5	1,118	26.6	1,216	29.3	1,540	96.8	182	21.6
Single-adult household	5,477	26.3	2,201	34.7	535	11.5	635	15.1	782	18.8	956	60.1	115	13.7
Multiple-adult household	3,026	14.5	1,811	28.5	351	7.5	453	10.8	277	6.7	335	21.1	49	5.9
Married head household	1,873	9.0	1,197	18.8	190	4.1	236	5.6	180	4.3	161	10.1	22	2.7
Other multiple-adult Household	1,154	5.5	615	9.7	162	3.5	216	5.2	97	2.3	174	10.9	27	3.2
Children only	1,290	6.2	804	12.7	24	0.5	30	0.7	157	3.8	249	15.7	17	2.1
Elderly individuals	3,426	16.5	199	3.1	2,322	49.8	1,386	33.0	224	5.4	47	2.9	144	17.1
Living alone	2,730	13.1	88	1.4	1,849	39.7	1,125	26.8	210	5.1	2	0.1	108	12.8
Not living alone	696	3.3	111	1.7	473	10.2	261	6.2	14	0.3	44	2.8	36	4.3
Disabled nonelderly individuals[b]	4,199	20.2	457	7.2	2,127	45.6	2,894	69.0	0	0.0	284	17.9	173	20.5
Living alone	2,382	11.5	96	1.5	1,317	28.3	1,538	36.7	0	0.0	2	0.1	83	9.8
Not living alone	1,816	8.7	360	5.7	810	17.4	1,356	32.3	—	—	283	17.8	90	10.7
Other households[c]	5,033	24.2	1,209	19.0	38	0.8	0	0.0	2,718	65.5	41	2.6	425	50.4
Single-person household	4,545	21.8	950	15.0	23	0.5	0	0.0	2,600	62.6	27	1.7	408	48.4
Multi-person household	488	2.3	260	4.1	15	0.3	—	—	118	2.8	14	0.9	17	2.0
Single-person households	10,125	48.7	1,407	22.2	3,197	68.6	2,664	63.5	2,878	69.3	121	7.6	609	72.1

[a]The sums of the household types do not match the numbers in the "Total" row because a household can have more than one of the characteristics.
[b]Due to changes in the Supplemental Nutrition Assistance Program Quality Control (SNAP QC) data, the definition of disabled changed in 2003. Beginning with the 2003 report, we are only able to identify households that contain a disabled person.
[c]Households not containing children, elderly individuals, or disabled nonelderly individuals.
—No sample households are found in this category.
Note: TANF = Temporary Assistance for Needy Families.

SOURCE: Mark Strayer, Esa Eslami, and Joshua Leftin, "Table 3.2. Household Composition and Selected Characteristics of Participating Households, Fiscal Year 2011," in *Characteristics of Supplemental Nutrition Assistance Program Households: Fiscal Year 2011*, U.S. Department of Agriculture, Food and Nutrition Service, November 2012, http://www.fns.usda.gov/ora/MENU/Published/snap/FILES/Participation/2011Characteristics.pdf (accessed January 21, 2013)

TABLE 4.8

Characteristics of SNAP recipient households, 1989–2011

Time period	Total households (000)	Percentage of households with:									
		Zero gross income	Zero net income[b]	Minimum benefit	Elderly individuals	Children	Disabled individuals[c]	AFDC/ TANF	Earnings	SSI	Any noncitizen
Fiscal year 1989	7,217	7.1	18.3	7.5	19.3	60.4	9.1	41.9	19.6	20.6	9.8
Fiscal year 1990	7,811	7.4	19.3	5.0	18.1	60.3	8.9	42.0	19.0	19.6	10.3
Fiscal year 1991	8,863	8.3	20.5	4.1	16.5	60.4	9.0	40.5	19.8	18.6	11.8
Fiscal year 1992	10,059	9.6	21.9	3.6	15.4	62.2	9.5	39.5	20.2	18.4	10.4
Fiscal year 1993	10,791	9.7	23.7	4.0	15.5	62.1	10.7	39.4	20.6	19.4	11.6
Fiscal year 1994	11,091	10.2	23.8	4.5	15.8	61.1	12.5	38.1	21.4	21.4	10.7
Fiscal year 1995	10,883	9.7	25.0	4.3	16.0	59.7	18.9	38.3	21.4	22.6	10.7
Fiscal year 1996	10,552	10.2	24.9	4.5	16.2	59.5	20.2	36.6	22.5	24.1	10.5
Fiscal year 1997	9,452	9.2	22.7	6.6	17.6	58.3	22.3	34.6	24.2	26.5	8.4
Fiscal year 1998	8,246	8.8	20.8	8.3	18.2	58.3	24.4	31.4	26.3	28.1	4.3
Fiscal year 1999	7,670	8.5	20.6	9.7	20.1	55.7	26.4	27.3	26.8	30.2	6.0
Fiscal year 2000	7,335	8.4	20.1	10.9	21.0	53.9	27.5	25.8	27.2	31.7	6.4
Fiscal year 2001	7,450	9.4	22.2	11.2	20.4	53.6	27.7	23.1	27.0	31.8	5.4
Fiscal year 2002	8,201	10.5	24.3	10.7	18.7	54.1	27.0	20.9	28.0	29.5	5.2
Fiscal year 2003	8,971	12.7	27.7	7.0	17.1	55.1	22.1	17.2	27.5	26.3	5.4
Fiscal year 2004	10,069	13.1	29.7	5.9	17.3	54.3	22.7	16.2	28.5	26.8	6.2
Fiscal year 2005	10,852	13.7	30.0	5.2	17.1	53.7	23.0	14.5	29.1	26.4	6.2
Fiscal year 2006	11,313	14.1	31.0	6.2	17.9	52.0	23.1	13.0	29.5	26.8	6.1
Fiscal year 2007	11,561	14.7	31.4	6.6	17.8	51.0	23.8	12.1	29.6	27.7	5.7
Fiscal year 2008	12,464	16.2	33.6	6.7	18.5	50.6	22.6	10.6	28.9	26.2	5.6
Fiscal year 2009	14,981	17.6	36.0	4.1	16.6	49.9	21.2	9.7	29.4	23.6	5.9
Fiscal year 2010	18,369	19.7	38.3	3.8	15.5	48.7	19.8	8.0	29.9	20.9	5.9
Fiscal year 2011	20,803	20.0	39.4	4.2	16.5	47.1	20.2	7.6	30.5	20.2	5.8

Note: SNAP = Supplemental Nutrition Assistance Program. AFDC = Aid to Families with Dependent Children. TANF = Temporary Assistance for Needy Families. Beginning with 2003, the weighting of the Supplemental Nutrition Assistance Program Quality Control (SNAP QC) data reflects adjustments to Food and Nutrition Service (FNS) Program Operations counts of households to account for receipt of benefits in error or for disaster assistance. Beginning with 2005, the weighting process was revised so that weighted SNAP QC data match adjusted Program Operations counts of households, individuals, and benefit amounts. Beginning with the 2009 report, we extended this methodology to the 2003 and 2004 data. We also incorporated corrected SNAP Program Operations data from Missouri for every year from 2003 to 2008. Therefore, statistics for these years may vary slightly from those presented in reports prior to 2009.

[a]Fiscal year analysis files were not developed for the years before 1989.

[b]Beginning in 2004, net income is not calculated for Minnesota Family Investment Program (MFIP) households or Social Security Income (SSI)—CAP households in States that use standardized SSI—CAP benefits.

[c]The substantial increase in 1995 and decrease in 2003 are in part a result of the changes in definition of a disabled household. Prior to 1995, disabled households were defined as households with SSI but no members over age 59. In 1995, that definition changed to households with at least one member under age 65 who received SSI, or at least one member age 18 to 61 who received Social Security, veterans benefits, or other government benefits as a result of a disability. Due to changes in the SNAP QC data in 2003, the definition of a disabled household changed again, to households with either SSI income or a medical expense deduction and without an elderly person, and households with a nonelderly adult who does not appear to be working and is receiving Social Security, veterans benefits, or workers' compensation.

SOURCE: Mark Strayer, Esa Eslami, and Joshua Leftin, "Table A.26. Comparison of Participating Households with Key SNAP Household Characteristics for Fiscal Years 1989 to 2011," in *Characteristics of Supplemental Nutrition Assistance Program Households: Fiscal Year 2011*, U.S. Department of Agriculture, Food and Nutrition Service, November 2012, http://www.fns.usda.gov/ora/MENU/Published/snap/FILES/Participation/2011Characteristics.pdf (accessed January 21, 2013)

of food assistance, but studies have shown that those families whose incomes are far below the poverty line see significant increases in well-being due to SNAP.

UNEMPLOYMENT COMPENSATION

The U.S. Department of Labor's Bureau of Labor Statistics (BLS), which collects data on the labor force (the total number of employed and unemployed people), defines an unemployed person as someone who is jobless, looking for a job, and available for work. Those who are jobless but not looking for work are not considered unemployed; they are classified as not being part of the labor force. The unemployment rate, as it is publicized each month in the media, is often mistakenly assumed to represent the number of jobless workers who have filed for unemployment compensation. Many workers who are jobless, actively looking for work, and available for work, however, have either come to the end of their unemployment benefits, are not eligible for benefits, or fail to apply

for benefits. The BLS's official unemployment rate, then, is derived not from unemployment compensation records but from the monthly Current Population Surveys conducted in partnership with the Census Bureau. A separate agency of the Department of Labor, the Employment and Training Administration, maintains and publishes data on those who file claims for unemployment insurance.

Table 4.10 shows the differences, on a state by state basis, between total unemployment and insured unemployment. As the data indicate, the insured unemployed made up only a fraction of the total unemployed in most states in the third quarter of 2012, a time when unemployment remained high nationally in the aftermath of the Great Recession. California, for example, the state with the largest civilian labor force in the United States, had an unemployment rate of 10.3% at that time, but the unemployment rate among those qualifying for unemployment compensation was only 3.4%. Similar gaps were in evidence in other states experiencing high unemployment,

TABLE 4.9

Recipients of SNAP benefits, by selected demographic characteristic, 2011

Participant characteristic	Total participants		Female participants		Male participants		Pro-rated benefits[b]	
	Number (000)	Percent[a]	Number (000)	Percent[a]	Number (000)	Percent[a]	Dollars (000)	Percent
Total	**44,148**	**100.0**	**24,936**	**56.5**	**19,212**	**43.5**	**5,838,193**	**100.0**
Age								
Child	19,927	45.1	9,809	22.2	10,118	22.9	2,580,620	44.2
Preschool (4 or less)	6,780	15.4	3,313	7.5	3,466	7.9	928,628	15.9
School age (5–17)	13,147	29.8	6,496	14.7	6,651	15.1	1,651,992	28.3
Nonelderly adult	20,452	46.3	12,643	28.6	7,809	17.7	2,824,272	48.4
18–35	10,617	24.0	6,947	15.7	3,670	8.3	1,482,522	25.4
36–59	9,835	22.3	5,695	12.9	4,139	9.4	1,341,750	23.0
Elderly individual (60 or more)	3,770	8.5	2,485	5.6	1,285	2.9	433,301	7.4
Citizenship								
U.S. born citizen	41,007	92.9	23,011	52.1	17,996	40.8	5,418,614	92.8
Naturalized citizen	1,379	3.1	893	2.0	486	1.1	184,586	3.2
Refugee	349	0.8	186	0.4	164	0.4	46,430	0.8
Other noncitizen	1,412	3.2	846	1.9	566	1.3	188,460	3.2
Unknown	1	0.0	0	0.0	0	0.0	104	0.0
Citizen children living with noncitizen adults[c]	3,741	8.5	1,785	4.0	1,956	4.4	529,016	9.1
Nondisabled adults age 18–49 in childless households[d]	4,486	10.2	1,927	4.4	2,559	5.8	778,211	13.3
Race and Hispanic status[e]								
White, not Hispanic[f]	15,255	34.6	8,685	19.7	6,570	14.9	1,930,409	33.1
African American, not Hispanic[g]	10,160	23.0	5,918	13.4	4,242	9.6	1,371,781	23.5
Hispanic, any race[h]	6,814	15.4	3,707	8.4	3,107	7.0	928,238	15.9
Asian, not Hispanic[i]	1,138	2.6	636	1.4	502	1.1	163,058	2.8
Native American, not Hispanic[j]	1,587	3.6	902	2.0	685	1.6	216,840	3.7
Multiple races reported, not Hispanic[k]	107	0.2	59	0.1	48	0.1	16,150	0.3
Race unknown[l]	9,087	20.6	5,029	11.4	4,058	9.2	1,211,716	20.8

Note: FY = Fiscal year. SNAP = Supplemental Nutrition Assistance Program.
[a]Percent of all participants.
[b]Pro-rated benefits equal the benefits paid to households multiplied by the ratio of participants with selected characteristic to total household size.
[c]Noncitizens may be inside or outside the SNAP unit.
[d]These participants are subject to work requirements and a time limit.
[e]New codes to allow reporting of multiple races were implemented beginning in April 2007. We have grouped the new codes together to form general race and ethnicity categories. Reporting of race and ethnicity is voluntary under the new format and was missing for 21 percent of participants in FY 2011. Because of these changes, FY 2011 race and ethnicity distributions are not comparable to distributions for years prior to FY 2007.
[f]This category includes the following values: white; white, not of Hispanic origin.
[g]This category includes the following values: black or African American; (blackor African American) and white; black, not of Hispanic origin.
[h]This category includes the following values: Hispanic; (Hispanic or Latino) and (American Indian or Alaska Native); (Hispanic or Latino) and Asian; (Hispanic or Latino) and (black or African American); (Hispanic or Latino) and (Native Hawaiian or other Pacific Islander); (Hispanic or Latino) and white; (Hispanic or Latino) and (American Indian or Alaska Native) and white; (Hispanic or Latino) and Asian and white; (Hispanic or Latino) and (black or African American); (Hispanic or Latino) and (American Indian or Alaska Native) and (black or African American); (Hispanic or Latino) and Respondent reported more than one race and does not fit into the listed values.
[i]This category includes the following values: Asian; Native Hawaiian or other Pacific Islander; Asian and white; Asian or Pacific Islander.
[j]This category includes the following values: American Indian or Alaska Native; (American Indian or Alaska Native) and White; (American Indian or Alaska Native) and (black or African American); American Indian or Alaska Native (old value).
[k]This category includes individuals who reported more than one race and who do not fit into any previously mentioned value.
[l]This category includes the following values: Unknown; Not recorded on the application for this individual; The application was not found during the quality control review, therefore racial/ethnic data is not available.

SOURCE: Mark Strayer, Esa Eslami, and Joshua Leftin, "Table A.23. Gender and SNAP Benefits of Participants by Selected Demographic Characteristic," in *Characteristics of Supplemental Nutrition Assistance Program Households: Fiscal Year 2011*, U.S. Department of Agriculture, Food and Nutrition Service, November 2012, http://www.fns.usda.gov/ora/MENU/Published/snap/FILES/Participation/2011Characteristics.pdf (accessed January 21, 2013)

such as Nevada (11.9% total unemployed and 3% insured unemployed), Rhode Island (10.5% and 3%), Georgia (9.1% and 2.1%), and Florida (9% and 2%). Although the unemployment insurance program provides a key form of support for covered workers, a large number among the total labor force do not qualify for benefits.

Who Receives Unemployment Insurance Benefits?

In 2010 the Employment and Training Administration released a wide range of reports resulting from a landmark five-year study of the unemployment compensation program. Conducted by the research firm

IMPAQ International, the study assessed many aspects of the program, including the characteristics of those receiving unemployment insurance (UI) benefits, between the 1950s and 2007. In "UI Benefits Study: Recent Changes in the Characteristics of Unemployed Workers," (August 2009, http://wdr.doleta.gov/research/FullText_Documents/UI%20Benefits%20Study%20-%20Recent%20Change%20in%20Characteristics%20of%20Unemployed%20Workers.pdf), Marios Michaelides of IMPAQ provides an overview of gender, racial, and ethnic disparities in unemployment and the collection of unemployment compensation over that period. The

TABLE 4.10

Unemployment compensation recipiency rates by state, third quarter 2012

State	IUR (%)	TUR (%)	Covered employment[a]	Civilian labor force	Total unemployment	Insured unemployment	
						Regular programs[b]	All programs[c]
Alabama	2.1	8.3	1,751	2,161	180.1	36.9	52.8
Alaska	3.2	6.7	296	371	24.8	9.7	16.7
Arizona	2.5	8.4	2,365	3,013	253.3	57.9	95.0
Arkansas	2.9	7.1	1,121	1,388	98.6	32.9	40.0
California	3.4	10.3	14,345	18,421	1,901.0	483.5	874.9
Colorado	1.9	7.8	2,162	2,742	214.4	41.3	76.9
Connecticut	3.4	8.9	1,586	1,913	170.4	55.1	93.7
Delaware	2.4	6.9	390	439	30.2	9.4	14.6
District of Columbia	0.9	8.9	499	360	31.9	4.3	7.2
Florida	2.0	9.0	7,183	9,353	841.2	143.3	264.3
Georgia	2.1	9.1	3,690	4,785	434.4	76.2	195.9
Hawaii	2.3	5.9	560	643	37.9	12.7	19.6
Idaho	2.1	6.7	580	780	52.3	12.4	20.2
Illinois	2.6	8.8	5,434	6,622	580.3	140.3	239.9
Indiana	1.8	7.9	2,715	3,166	251.6	48.2	90.3
Iowa	1.5	4.9	1,420	1,646	81.3	22.3	32.2
Kansas	2.0	6.1	1,278	1,491	90.3	26.1	37.3
Kentucky	2.1	8.3	1,697	2,080	171.7	35.9	64.7
Louisiana	1.9	7.2	1,821	2,091	150.1	34.8	42.9
Maine	1.9	6.9	546	717	49.6	10.7	17.6
Maryland	2.6	6.9	2,324	3,103	213.2	61.0	91.6
Massachusetts	3.0	6.5	3,114	3,483	224.7	93.6	154.5
Michigan	2.3	9.3	3,786	4,706	435.7	88.9	176.0
Minnesota	1.7	5.6	2,544	2,995	168.3	44.1	64.6
Mississippi	2.8	9.3	1,049	1,339	124.2	29.8	49.9
Missouri	2.0	7.0	2,514	3,002	210.2	50.1	86.0
Montana	2.1	5.5	403	515	28.6	8.6	13.0
Nebraska	1.4	3.8	881	1,021	39.2	12.3	18.1
Nevada	3.0	11.9	1,096	1,370	162.9	33.1	61.8
New Hampshire	1.7	5.5	593	745	41.0	9.9	12.7
New Jersey	3.7	9.7	3,669	4,604	444.9	138.5	273.2
New Mexico	2.5	6.6	743	927	61.2	18.5	28.8
New York	3.1	8.7	8,308	9,628	838.2	262.5	513.9
North Carolina	2.8	9.5	3,774	4,700	446.3	105.7	203.0
North Dakota	0.6	2.7	384	395	10.6	2.2	2.8
Ohio	1.7	6.9	4,854	5,813	401.8	85.3	144.5
Oklahoma	1.7	5.0	1,466	1,815	91.4	24.5	35.3
Oregon	3.0	8.3	1,576	1,986	165.7	48.0	85.1
Pennsylvania	3.9	8.0	5,389	6,557	526.5	209.8	338.4
Puerto Rico	4.0	14.3	912	1,265	181.3	36.7	70.1
Rhode Island	3.0	10.5	430	562	59.2	13.3	23.1
South Carolina	2.2	9.1	1,746	2,150	195.9	39.2	74.9
South Dakota	0.6	4.2	376	448	18.9	2.2	2.7
Tennessee	1.4	8.2	2,561	3,124	256.6	36.3	69.6
Texas	1.7	7.0	10,319	12,665	882.7	174.4	293.7
Utah	1.2	5.5	1,149	1,364	75.0	13.7	19.4
Vermont	1.9	5.1	290	360	18.2	5.4	7.1
Virgin Islands	4.6		42			1.9	2.6
Virginia	1.4	5.8	3,391	4,353	253.6	46.6	66.9
Washington	2.4	8.2	2,737	3,507	287.5	68.1	118.6
West Virginia	2.6	7.1	677	805	57.0	18.0	26.0
Wisconsin	2.9	6.9	2,595	3,083	212.8	76.6	119.0
Wyoming	1.3	5.0	263	309	15.3	3.5	4.8
United States	2.5	8.1	127,395	155,619	12,613.0	3,156.2	5,548.5

IUR = Insured unemployment rate.
TUR = Total unemployment rate.
Note: Blank cells indicate that information is unavailable.
[a]Wages and covered employment lag the rest of the data summary information by 6 months.
[b]Includes state unemployment insurance (UI), unemployment compensation for federal employees (UCFE), and unemployment complensation for ex-service members (UCX).
[c]Includes extended unemployment compensation (EUC08) + extended benefits (EB).

SOURCE: Adapted from "Labor Force Information by State (Levels in Thousands) for CYQ 2012.3," in *Unemployment Insurance Data Summary*, U.S. Department of Labor, Employment and Training Administration, 2012, http://www.workforcesecurity.doleta.gov/unemploy/content/data_stats/datasum12/DataSum_2012_3.pdf (accessed January 21, 2013)

report finds that, after controlling for industry and occupation differences:

1. women have higher unemployment rates than men but are equally likely to receive UI benefits,

2. the racial unemployment gap is smaller than in earlier years but remains substantial, yet nonwhites are only marginally more likely to receive UI benefits than whites, and

TABLE 4.11

Unemployment rate, by demographic characteristics and job type, selected years 1953–2007

	1953–57	1963–67	1973–77	1983–87	1993–97	2003–07
Population	4.2	4.6	6.7	7.5	5.8	5.2
Male	4.0	4.0	6.1	7.5	5.8	5.3
Female	4.8	5.7	7.8	7.5	5.7	5.1
White	4.1	4.1	6.1	6.5	5.0	4.6
Nonwhite	8.6	8.6	11.8	14.1	10.0	8.2
Non-Hispanic	—	—	6.6	7.3	5.4	5.0
Hispanic	—	—	9.9	10.9	9.3	6.4
Industry						
Manufacturing	—	—	7.2	8.2	5.5	6.4
Trade	—	—	7.5	7.6	6.6	6.4
Services	—	—	5.1	5.0	4.3	4.3
Construction	—	—	11.1	11.6	9.2	7.4
Other	—	—	4.0	4.9	3.7	3.9
Occupation						
White collar	—	—	—	3.8	3.4	3.5
Blue collar	—	—	—	9.6	7.5	6.7

Note: Each number represents the average of Current Population Survey monthly values for the referenced period.

SOURCE: Marios Michaelides and Peter Mueser, "Table 2. Unemployment Rate, by Demographic Category and Job Type," in *UI Benefits Study: Recent Changes in the Characteristics of Unemployed Workers*, U.S. Department of Labor, Employment and Training Administration, August 2009, http://wdr.doleta.gov/research/FullText_Documents/UI%20Benefits%20Study%20-%20Recent%20Change%20in%20Characteristics%20of%20Unemployed%20Workers.pdf (accessed February 15, 2013)

3. there is a dramatic convergence in the unemployment rates between Hispanics and non-Hispanics, although Hispanics remain less likely to receive UI benefits.

Table 4.11 shows the historic changes in the unemployment rate for different demographic groups. Although there was a sizable gap in the unemployment rate for men and women from 1953 to 1957, that gap closed by the mid-1980s, and in the period 1993 to 2007 the unemployment rate for women was slightly less than that for men. The gap in the unemployment rate for white and nonwhite workers remained wide over the course of those same 54 years, however. The unemployment rate for white workers averaged 4.1% between 1953 and 1967, while the unemployment rate for nonwhite workers averaged 8.6%. By the first decade of the 21st century, the gap had closed only marginally, with 4.6% of white workers and 8.2% of nonwhite workers experiencing unemployment during the years 2003 through 2007. Moreover, the gap had widened in the interim, peaking in the mid-1980s, when 6.5% of white workers were unemployed compared with 14.1% of nonwhite workers. The gap between non-Hispanic workers and Hispanic workers closed more significantly: from a difference of 3.3 percentage points during the mid-1970s to a 1.4 point separation during the years 2003 through 2007.

The explanations for these phenomena are complex. Uneven distribution in different industries and occupations likely explains some portion of the changing dynamic between unemployment for men and unemployment for women. Some of the industries and occupations subject to the highest levels of unemployment over time,

such as the construction industry, are heavily dominated by men. By contrast, women are far more likely to work in white-collar jobs than men. Thus, even though women may face lingering disadvantages due to workplace bias, their overall unemployment rate has converged with that of men.

By contrast, as Table 4.12 shows, between 1992 and 2007 nonwhites and whites were approximately equally likely to work in blue-collar versus white-collar jobs, but nonwhites were far more likely to be unemployed in all occupation categories. Thus, the gap in the employment rate cannot be attributed to the differing concentrations of whites and nonwhites in various industries. Instead, social factors are likely to play a role in the disparity.

Nonwhite workers, in spite of their significantly higher rates of unemployment in almost all occupations between 1992 and 2007, were not substantially more likely than white workers to receive unemployment compensation. (See Figure 4.5.) As Michaelides writes, "Since UI is only available to the experienced labor force, we might expect higher unemployment among experienced nonwhites to lead to greater level of UI receipt. On the other hand, however, even in the same industries and occupations nonwhites suffer greater employment instability and lower earnings, making them less likely to meet states' minimum earnings or employment requirements. They may also be more likely to separate from jobs under circumstances that make them ineligible for benefits."

Hispanics, too, were overrepresented among the unemployed in the years surveyed by Michaelides and the Department of Labor. The trend of Hispanic

TABLE 4.12

Employment distribution and unemployment rate across occupations, by race, 1992–2007

	Experienced unemployment rate		Employment distribution	
	Whites	Nonwhites	Whites	Nonwhites
Blue collar occupations	**7.2%**	**11.2%**	**40%**	**43%**
Construction workers	10.9%	18.7%	6%	4%
Farming, fishing, and forestry workers	9.5%	18.6%	2%	1%
Other blue collar occupations	7.1%	10.5%	15%	18%
Other service-related occupations	6.2%	10.3%	13%	17%
Mechanics and repairers	4.1%	6.5%	4%	3%
White collar occupations	**3.1%**	**5.7%**	**60%**	**57%**
Sales occupations	4.6%	10.2%	12%	10%
Office and administrative support	3.9%	6.9%	14%	16%
Engineers and scientists	2.7%	3.5%	5%	5%
Professional specialty occupations	2.6%	4.2%	4%	4%
Corporate executive officers/managers	2.3%	3.1%	13%	9%
Health care occupations	2.1%	4.3%	6%	8%
Teachers and social workers	1.3%	2.8%	6%	5%

Note: Occupation categories are mutually exclusive.

SOURCE: Marios Michaelides and Peter Mueser, "Table 6. Employment Distribution by Race, across Occupations: Averages of March CPS Supplement Values, 1992–2007," in *UI Benefits Study: Recent Changes in the Characteristics of Unemployed Workers*, U.S. Department of Labor, Employment and Training Administration, August 2009, http://wdr.doleta.gov/research/FullText_Documents/UI%20Benefits%20Study%20-%20Recent%20Change%20in%20 Characteristics%20of%20Unemployed%20Workers.pdf (accessed February 15, 2013)

FIGURE 4.5

Unemployment compensation receipt rate, by race, 1992–2007

[Actual and adjusted for industry-occupation]

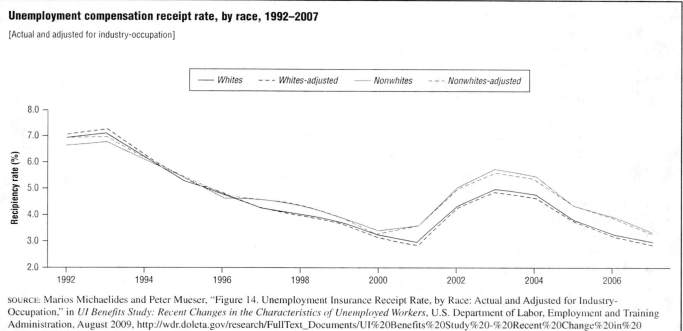

SOURCE: Marios Michaelides and Peter Mueser, "Figure 14. Unemployment Insurance Receipt Rate, by Race: Actual and Adjusted for Industry-Occupation," in *UI Benefits Study: Recent Changes in the Characteristics of Unemployed Workers*, U.S. Department of Labor, Employment and Training Administration, August 2009, http://wdr.doleta.gov/research/FullText_Documents/UI%20Benefits%20Study%20-%20Recent%20Change%20in%20 Characteristics%20of%20Unemployed%20Workers.pdf (accessed February 15, 2013)

unemployment relative to the group's presence in the overall labor force had begun to resemble that of the trend between women and men, however, in the later years considered in the study. The proportion of Hispanics among the unemployed grew more rapidly than the proportion of Hispanics in the labor force in the 1980s and 1990s, but by 2000 the proportion of Hispanics among the unemployed had stopped increasing,

even though the proportion of Hispanics in the labor force continued to grow. (See Figure 4.6.)

Hispanics' likelihood of receiving unemployment compensation has changed over time. In the early 1990s, Hispanics were more likely to receive unemployment benefits than non-Hispanics, in keeping with the fact that they experienced unemployment at a higher rate than non-Hispanics. After 2000, however, non-Hispanic

FIGURE 4.6

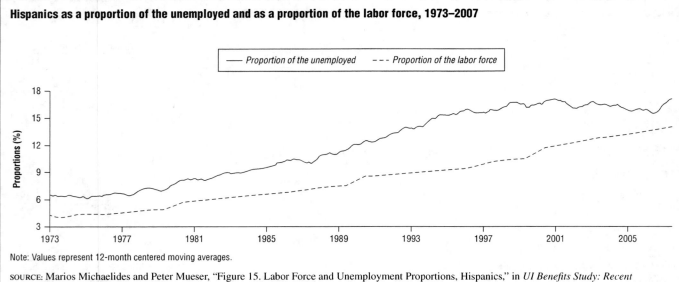

Hispanics as a proportion of the unemployed and as a proportion of the labor force, 1973–2007

Note: Values represent 12-month centered moving averages.

SOURCE: Marios Michaelides and Peter Mueser, "Figure 15. Labor Force and Unemployment Proportions, Hispanics," in *UI Benefits Study: Recent Changes in the Characteristics of Unemployed Workers*, U.S. Department of Labor, Employment and Training Administration, August 2009, http://wdr .doleta.gov/research/FullText_Documents/UI%20Benefits%20Study%20-%20Recent%20Change%20in%20Characteristics%20of%20Unemployed%20 Workers.pdf (accessed February 15, 2013)

workers became marginally more likely to receive unemployment compensation than Hispanics, even though Hispanics were more likely to be unemployed. Michaelides hypothesizes that this gap, which is not explained by differing distributions across industries, may be attributable to unfamiliarity, on the part of some Hispanic workers, with U.S. laws regarding their eligibility for unemployment benefits.

In the years following the period studied by Michaelides and the Labor Department, unemployment rose dramatically as a result of the Great Recession, and many of the same trends described in the report persisted. Nonwhites and Hispanics continued to be overrepresented among the unemployed. As Table 4.13 indicates, the 2012 unemployment rate for white male workers aged 16 years and older was 8.2% and for Asian-American male workers of the same age it was 5.8%, compared with 15% for African-American male workers and 9.9% for Hispanic male workers. Overall, women were slightly less likely to be unemployed than men in 2012; the unemployment rate for women aged 16 and older was 7.9%, and for men it was 8.2%. There was substantial variation among female unemployment across demographic categories, roughly in keeping with trends among the male workforce. Approximately 7% of white women and 6.1% of Asian-American women were unemployed, compared with 12.8% of African-American women and 10.9% of Hispanic women. Across all categories, single people were generally more likely to be unemployed than married people, with the never-married proportion of each demographic group experiencing dramatically higher rates of unemployment than any other subset.

SUPPLEMENTAL SECURITY INCOME

SSI is a means-tested income assistance program that was created in 1972 to provide monthly cash assistance to senior citizens, blind people, and disabled individuals. A number of requirements must be met to receive financial benefits from SSI. First, a person must meet the program criteria for age, blindness, or disability. In addition, because SSI is a means-tested program, only those who meet the income eligibility requirements receive payments. Total SSI payments to all recipients grew steadily from $5.1 billion in 1974 to $49.5 billion in 2011. (See Table 4.14.) During that period, the number of SSI recipients grew from 3.2 million to 8.1 million. (See Table 4.15). According to the CBPP's "Introduction to the Supplemental Security Income (SSI) Program" (January 10, 2011, http://www.cbpp.org/cms/index.cfm?fa= view&id=3367), this growth has come as a result of the program's shifting emphasis. SSI's main function in its early years was to supplement the incomes of elderly beneficiaries of the primary Social Security program, whose official name is Old Age, Survivors and Disability Insurance (OASDI). Since that time, SSI has become a broader anti-poverty program, serving as a primary resource for children and adults who are both poor and disabled.

Who Receives Supplemental Security Income Benefits?

Of the 8.1 million recipients in 2011, approximately 6.9 million (84.6%) were disabled, and 1.2 million (14.6%) were aged; less than 1% (69,033) were blind. (See Table 4.16.) Among these three eligibility categories, the disabled and the blind received the highest

TABLE 4.13

Unemployed persons by selected demographic characteristics, 2010 and 2011

[Numbers in thousands]

Marital status, race, Hispanic or Latino ethnicity, and age	Men				Women			
	Unemployed		Unemployment rates		Unemployed		Unemployment rates	
	2011	2012	2011	2012	2011	2012	2011	2012
Total, 16 years and over	**7,684**	**6,771**	**9.4**	**8.2**	**6,063**	**5,734**	**8.5**	**7.9**
Married, spouse present	2,671	2,274	5.8	4.9	2,031	1,915	5.6	5.3
Widowed, divorced, or separated	1,186	1,005	11.1	9.4	1,420	1,286	9.7	8.7
Never married	3,827	3,492	15.1	13.7	2,612	2,533	12.5	11.8
White, 16 years and over	**5,631**	**4,931**	**8.3**	**7.4**	**4,257**	**3,985**	**7.5**	**7.0**
Married, spouse present	2,081	1,764	5.3	4.6	1,630	1,539	5.3	5.1
Widowed, divorced, or separated	903	767	10.3	8.8	1,060	947	9.2	8.3
Never married	2,648	2,399	13.4	12.2	1,567	1,499	10.5	9.9
Black or African American, 16 years and over	**1,502**	**1,292**	**17.8**	**15.0**	**1,329**	**1,252**	**14.1**	**12.8**
Married, spouse present	385	303	11.1	8.4	218	200	7.8	6.8
Widowed, divorced, or separated	217	177	16.0	13.3	265	252	11.8	10.9
Never married	899	812	24.8	22.1	846	800	19.3	17.5
Asian, 16 years and over	**269**	**249**	**6.8**	**5.8**	**250**	**234**	**7.3**	**6.1**
Married, spouse present	135	122	5.2	4.4	130	111	6.2	4.8
Widowed, divorced, or separated	20	25	6.4	7.2	42	37	9.0	6.3
Never married	113	102	10.9	8.5	78	86	9.2	8.9
Hispanic or Latino ethnicity, 16 years and over	**1,527**	**1,383**	**11.2**	**9.9**	**1,102**	**1,130**	**11.8**	**10.9**
Married, spouse present	606	498	8.6	6.9	421	396	10.0	8.6
Widowed, divorced, or separated	175	166	10.5	9.3	217	243	10.7	11.0
Never married	745	720	15.3	14.2	464	491	15.1	13.8
Total, 25 years and over	**5,623**	**4,821**	**7.9**	**6.8**	**4,490**	**4,234**	**7.3**	**6.8**
Married, spouse present	2,590	2,207	5.7	4.9	1,910	1,815	5.4	5.1
Widowed, divorced, or separated	1,141	961	10.9	9.2	1,353	1,229	9.5	8.6
Never married	1,892	1,654	12.3	10.6	1,227	1,189	10.0	9.4
White, 25 years and over	**4,137**	**3,555**	**7.1**	**6.1**	**3,181**	**3,003**	**6.5**	**6.1**
Married, spouse present	2,013	1,710	5.3	4.5	1,528	1,459	5.1	4.9
Widowed, divorced, or separated	871	737	10.2	8.6	1,009	904	9.0	8.2
Never married	1,253	1,107	10.6	9.4	645	640	7.8	7.7
Black or African American, 25 years and over	**1,082**	**883**	**15.2**	**12.3**	**951**	**878**	**11.9**	**10.6**
Married, spouse present	378	292	11.1	8.3	207	188	7.6	6.6
Widowed, divorced, or separated	208	167	15.7	13.0	254	242	11.5	10.7
Never married	496	424	20.9	17.9	490	448	15.9	14.2
Asian, 25 years and over	**217**	**198**	**6.0**	**5.0**	**209**	**187**	**6.8**	**5.4**
Married, spouse present	132	121	5.1	4.4	127	108	6.1	4.7
Widowed, divorced, or separated	19	24	6.2	7.0	41	35	9.0	6.1
Never married	65	53	9.0	6.4	41	44	7.3	6.9
Hispanic or Latino ethnicity, 25 years and over	**1,068**	**941**	**9.5**	**8.1**	**788**	**805**	**10.2**	**9.5**
Married, spouse present	582	476	8.6	6.9	386	367	9.6	8.4
Widowed, divorced, or separated	163	153	10.2	8.9	203	222	10.5	10.5
Never married	324	312	11.4	10.6	200	216	11.4	10.8

Note: Estimates for the above race groups (white, black or African American, and Asian) do not sum to totals because data are not presented for all races. Persons whose ethnicity is identified as Hispanic or Latino may be of any race. Updated population controls are introduced annually with the release of January data.

SOURCE: "24. Unemployed Persons by Marital Status, Race, Hispanic or Latino Ethnicity, Age, and Sex," in *Labor Force Statistics from the Current Population Survey*, U.S. Department of Labor, Bureau of Labor Statistics, February 5, 2013, http://bls.gov/cps/cpsaat24.htm (accessed February 15, 2013)

average monthly payments from SSI in 2011, at $519.38 and $520.29, respectively. Aged beneficiaries received an average monthly payment of $397.62. (See Table 4.17.) Approximately 4.8 million (58.9%) of SSI beneficiaries were between the ages of 18 and 64; just under 1.3 million (15.7%) were aged 17 and younger; and roughly 2.1 million (25.4%) were 65 or older. The share of SSI recipients who were 65 or older declined dramatically between 1974 and 2011, from 61% to 25%. The program's growth, then, was primarily a result of an increasing number of disabled children and adults aged 18 to 64.

Among the different age groups, children received the highest average monthly payment from SSI, due largely to an absence of other income sources. (See Figure 4.7.)

Few of those collecting SSI claimed any earned income in 2011. As Figure 4.8 shows, although adult beneficiaries between the ages of 18 and 64 were most likely to have earned income in addition to their SSI income, only 4.8% of the beneficiaries in this category had earned income. Over one-third (33.9%) of all SSI beneficiaries, by contrast, also collected benefits from

TABLE 4.14

Total Supplemental Security Income (SSI) payments, by eligibility category, selected years 1974–2011

[In thousands of dollars]

Year	Total	Federal SSI	Federally administered state supplementation
All recipients			
1974	5,096,813	3,833,161	1,263,652
1975	5,716,072	4,313,538	1,402,534
1980	7,714,640	5,866,354	1,848,286
1985	10,749,938	8,777,341	1,972,597
1990	16,132,959	12,893,805	3,239,154
1995	27,037,280	23,919,430	3,117,850
1996	28,252,474	25,264,878	2,987,596
1997	28,370,568	25,457,387	2,913,181
1998	29,408,208	26,404,793	3,003,415
1999	30,106,132	26,805,156	3,300,976
2000	30,671,699	27,290,248	3,381,451
2001	32,165,856	28,705,503	3,460,353
2002	33,718,999	29,898,765	3,820,234
2003	34,693,278	30,688,029	4,005,249
2004	36,065,358	31,886,509	4,178,849
2005	37,235,843	33,058,056	4,177,787
2006	38,888,961	34,736,088	4,152,873
2007	41,204,645	36,884,066	4,320,579
2008	43,040,481	38,655,780	4,384,701
2009	46,592,308	42,628,709	3,963,606
2010	48,194,514	44,605,122	3,589,392
2011	49,520,299	45,999,647	3,520,652
Aged			
1974	2,414,034	1,782,742	631,292
1975	2,516,515	1,842,980	673,535
1980	2,617,023	1,860,194	756,829
1985	2,896,671	2,202,557	694,114
1990	3,559,388	2,521,382	1,038,006
1995	4,239,222	3,374,772	864,450
1996	4,282,498	3,449,407	833,091
1997	4,303,529	3,479,948	823,581
1998	4,166,231	3,327,856	838,375
1999	4,445,687	3,524,355	921,332
2000	4,540,045	3,597,516	942,530
2001	4,664,076	3,708,527	955,549
2002	4,802,792	3,751,491	1,051,301
2003	4,856,875	3,758,070	1,098,805
2004	4,894,070	3,773,901	1,133,324
2005	4,964,627	3,836,625	1,128,002
2006	5,115,911	3,953,106	1,162,804
2007	5,301,277	4,113,424	1,187,853
2008	5,378,921	4,180,786	1,198,135
2009	5,569,078	4,499,045	1,070,033
2010	5,453,906	4,529,485	924,422
2011	5,430,932	4,535,873	895,059

SOURCE: "Table 7.A4. Total Federally Administered Payments, by Eligibility Category, Selected Years 1974–2011," in *Annual Statistical Supplement to the Social Security Bulletin, 2012*, U.S. Social Security Administration, Office of Retirement and Disability Policy, February 2013, http://www.socialsecurity.gov/policy/docs/statcomps/supplement/2012/7a.html (accessed January 21, 2013)

OASDI. Not surprisingly, those SSI beneficiaries most likely to receive OASDI benefits were age 65 or older; 56.3% of SSI beneficiaries in that age group collected OASDI payments, compared with 31.3% of SSI beneficiaries aged 18 to 64 and 7.6% of SSI beneficiaries under age 18.

Although SSI benefits are not enough to lift recipients out of poverty, the CBPP and others credit the program with a high level of effectiveness in lifting recipients out of extreme poverty, or 50% of the poverty line.

TABLE 4.15

Number of recipients of SSI payments, by eligibility category, selected years 1974–2011

Month and year	Total*	Federal SSI	Federally administered state supplementation	State supplementation only
All recipients				
January 1974	3,215,632	2,955,959	1,480,309	259,673
December				
1975	4,314,275	3,893,419	1,684,018	420,856
1980	4,142,017	3,682,411	1,684,765	459,606
1985	4,138,021	3,799,092	1,660,847	338,929
1990	4,817,127	4,412,131	2,058,273	404,996
1995	6,514,134	6,194,493	2,517,805	319,641
2000	6,601,686	6,319,907	2,480,637	281,779
2001	6,688,489	6,410,138	2,520,005	278,351
2002	6,787,857	6,505,227	2,461,652	282,630
2003	6,902,364	6,614,465	2,467,116	287,899
2004	6,987,845	6,694,577	2,497,589	293,268
2005	7,113,879	6,818,944	2,242,112	294,935
2006	7,235,583	6,938,690	2,268,579	296,893
2007	7,359,525	7,061,234	2,302,130	298,291
2008	7,520,501	7,219,012	2,343,599	301,489
2009	7,676,686	7,422,879	2,339,346	253,807
2010	7,912,266	7,655,667	2,385,933	256,599
2011	8,112,773	7,866,390	2,389,113	246,383
Aged				
January 1974	1,865,109	1,690,496	770,318	174,613
December				
1975	2,307,105	2,024,765	843,917	282,340
1980	1,807,776	1,533,366	702,763	274,410
1985	1,504,469	1,322,292	583,913	182,177
1990	1,454,041	1,256,623	649,530	197,418
1995	1,446,122	1,314,720	663,390	131,402
2000	1,289,339	1,186,309	622,668	103,030
2001	1,264,463	1,164,825	620,952	99,638
2002	1,251,528	1,151,652	611,395	99,876
2003	1,232,778	1,132,947	602,807	99,831
2004	1,211,167	1,110,757	601,078	100,410
2005	1,214,296	1,112,779	584,787	101,517
2006	1,211,656	1,108,925	590,575	102,731
2007	1,204,512	1,101,440	595,555	103,072
2008	1,203,256	1,100,188	600,909	103,068
2009	1,185,959	1,100,626	587,766	85,333
2010	1,183,853	1,098,752	588,307	85,101
2011	1,182,106	1,101,427	584,518	80,679

SSI = Supplemental Security Income.
*Includes retroactive payments.

SOURCE: "Table 7.A3. Number of Recipients of Federally Administered Payments, by Eligibility Category, January 1974 and December 1975–2011, Selected Years," in *Annual Statistical Supplement to the Social Security Bulletin, 2012*, U.S. Social Security Administration, http://ssa.gov/policy/docs/statcomps/supplement/2012/7a.pdf (accessed February 15, 2013)

TABLE 4.16

Number of SSI recipients, total payments, and average monthly payment, by eligibility category, December 2011

		Category			Age		
Source of payment	Total	Aged	Blind	Disabled	Under 18	18–64	65 or older[a]
				Number of recipients			
Total	**8,112,773**	**1,182,106**	**69,033**	**6,861,634**	**1,277,122**	**4,777,010**	**2,058,641**
Federal payment only	5,723,660	597,588	41,045	5,085,027	1,025,120	3,546,247	1,152,293
Federal payment and state supplementation	2,142,730	503,839	24,045	1,614,846	250,425	1,105,867	786,438
State supplementation only	246,383	80,679	3,943	161,761	1,577	124,896	119,910
Total with—							
Federal payment	7,866,390	1,101,427	65,090	6,699,873	1,275,545	4,652,114	1,938,731
State supplementation	2,389,113	584,518	27,988	1,776,607	252,002	1,230,763	906,348
				Total payments[b] (thousands of dollars)			
Total	**4,389,872**	**471,847**	**36,718**	**3,881,307**	**812,295**	**2,744,100**	**833,478**
Federal payments	4,090,280	396,173	31,608	3,662,500	798,660	2,577,066	714,555
State supplementation	299,591	75,674	5,110	218,808	13,635	167,034	118,923
				Average monthly payment[c] (dollars)			
Total	**501.64**	**397.62**	**520.29**	**519.38**	**601.38**	**517.45**	**403.23**
Federal payments	481.31	358.51	475.87	501.58	592.26	498.50	367.34
State supplementation	118.57	128.03	175.87	114.55	50.26	124.32	129.74

Note: Totals do not necessarily equal the sum of rounded components.
[a]Includes approximately 14,500 blind and 862,100 disabled persons aged 65 or older.
[b]Includes retroactive payments.
[c]Excludes retroactive payments.

SOURCE: "Table 7.A1. Number of Recipients of Federally Administered Payments, Total Payments, and Average Monthly Payment, by Source of Payment, Eligibility Category, and Age, December 2011," in *Annual Statistical Supplement to the Social Security Bulletin, 2012*, U.S. Social Security Administration, http://ssa.gov/policy/docs/statcomps/supplement/2012/7a.pdf (accessed February 15, 2013)

TABLE 4.17

Average monthly SSI payment by eligibility category, selected years 1975–2011

[In dollars]

Year	Total	Federal SSI	Federally administered state supplementation
All recipients			
1975	106.33	90.59	61.72
1980	161.92	138.14	95.17
1985	218.09	193.77	99.39
1990	276.45	241.52	127.83
1995	335.45	312.83	98.66
2000	378.82	351.48	112.50
2001	393.96	366.31	113.65
2002	407.42	376.76	127.53
2003	417.16	383.59	138.38
2004	428.29	395.36	138.07
2005	439.09	406.50	156.30
2006	454.75	423.05	156.24
2007	468.36	437.05	156.56
2008	477.79	447.00	156.23
2009	498.75	476.33	124.96
2010	500.69	478.73	124.29
2011	501.64	481.31	118.57
Aged			
1975	86.72	73.77	57.38
1980	126.66	105.69	95.60
1985	164.01	141.41	103.58
1990	208.26	170.74	136.31
1995	250.27	220.15	109.62
2000	299.69	258.12	128.46
2001	314.22	271.13	130.89
2002	330.04	280.86	146.17
2003	342.28	287.10	160.02
2004	350.53	295.13	160.44
2005	360.25	303.29	170.39
2006	373.05	316.48	170.64
2007	384.15	327.06	171.69
2008	393.46	336.03	172.29
2009	399.14	357.86	134.96
2010	399.75	358.32	134.95
2011	397.62	358.51	128.03

SOURCE: "Table 7.A5. Average Monthly Federally Administered Payment, by Eligibility Category, December 1975–2011," in *Annual Statistical Supplement to the Social Security Bulletin, 2012*, U.S. Social Security Administration, http://ssa.gov/policy/docs/statcomps/supplement/2012/7a .pdf (accessed February 15, 2013)

FIGURE 4.7

SSI payment amounts, by age, 2011

[Average monthly]

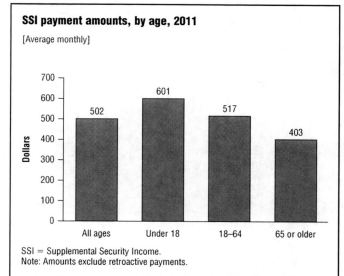

SSI = Supplemental Security Income.
Note: Amounts exclude retroactive payments.

SOURCE: "Payment Amounts, by Age, December 2011," in *Fast Facts & Figures About Social Security, 2012*, Social Security Administration, Office of Retirement and Disability Policy, Office of Research, Evaluation, and Statistics, August 2012, http://www.ssa.gov/policy/ docs/chartbooks/fast_facts/2012/fast_facts12.pdf (accessed January 21, 2013)

FIGURE 4.8

SSI recipients with other income, 2011

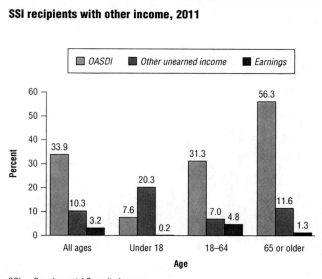

SSI = Supplemental Security Income.
OASDI = Old-age, Survivors, and Disability Insurance.

SOURCE: "Other Income, December 2011," in *Fast Facts & Figures about Social Security, 2012*, Social Security Administration, Office of Retirement and Disability Policy, Office of Research, Evaluation, and Statistics, August 2012, http://www.ssa.gov/policy/docs/chartbooks/ fast_facts/2012/fast_facts12.pdf (accessed January 21, 2013)

CHAPTER 5
CHARACTERISTICS OF THE HOMELESS

AUTHORITATIVE ESTIMATES OF HOMELESSNESS

The Facts Are Hard to Determine

Broad national assessments of homelessness were undertaken by several agencies and organizations during the 1980s and mid-1990s, including *A Report to the Secretary on the Homeless and Emergency Shelters* (1984) by the U.S. Department of Housing and Urban Development (HUD), Martha R. Burt and Barbara E. Cohen's *America's Homeless: Numbers, Characteristics, and Programs That Serve Them* (1989), and Martha R. Burt et al.'s *Homelessness: Programs and the People They Serve* (December 1999, http://www.urban.org/UploadedPDF/homelessness.pdf). In 2002 Burt et al. summarized in *Evaluation of Continuums of Care for Homeless People* (May 2002, http://www.huduser.org/publications/pdf/continuums_of_care.pdf) the difficulty of addressing homelessness without a continuing census or other governmental program to track the homeless population.

In 2001 Congress directed HUD to begin collecting nationwide data on homelessness. In response, the agency began compiling a report each year, called the *Annual Homeless Assessment Report* (*AHAR*), consisting primarily of a point-in-time (PIT) count of the homeless. Other important features of the *AHAR* are data on shelter availability and occupancy levels and longitudinal data collected in the Homeless Management Information Systems (HMIS), the electronic system that the agency and local officials maintain. In November 2012 HUD released a final version of *The 2011 Annual Homeless Assessment Report to Congress* (https://www.onecpd.info/resources/documents/2011AHAR_Final Report.pdf). Also in November 2012, HUD released a preliminary version of its 2012 PIT-count data, *The 2012 Point-in-Time Estimates of Homelessness: Volume 1 of the 2012 Annual Homeless Assessment Report*. HUD's data are nationally representative samples, rather than full counts. Regardless, they are considered the most accurate counts of the homeless population that are generally available.

Several other organizations periodically collect data on the homeless population. The Association of Gospel Rescue Missions (AGRM), which runs more than 100 missions located in inner cities, regularly undertakes its own surveys of those whom it serves. AGRM missions do not serve the homeless exclusively, but approximately 83% of its clients were homeless in 2012. Therefore, AGRM's annual surveys supplement rather than rival the more comprehensive and focused HUD data, but there are broad similarities between the two data sets.

Additionally, the National Alliance to End Homelessness (NAEH) has collected information and analyzed HUD data in ways that enable a broader understanding of homelessness in the United States. In 2007 the organization compiled data from 461 local Continuum of Care PIT counts from across the nation and published an estimate of the national homeless population in *Homelessness Counts: Changes in Homelessness from 2005 to 2007* (January 12, 2009, http://www.endhomelessness.org/content/article/detail/2158). The NAEH has used HUD data to build on its 2005–07 analysis in a series of annual research reports, *The State of Homelessness in America*. In *The State of Homelessness in America 2012* (January 2012, http://www.endhomelessness.org/page/-/files/file_FINAL_The_State_of_Homelessness_in_America_2012.pdf), the NAEH notes that, according to HUD data, on a single January night in 2011, 636,017 people experienced homelessness in the United States. (See Figure 5.1.) Of these, 392,316 (62%) were sheltered, and 243,701 (38%) were unsheltered. Nearly two-thirds (399,836, or 63%) were homeless individuals, and 236,181 (37%) were members of homeless families, who together formed 77,186 family households. An estimated 67,495 (11%) of the homeless

FIGURE 5.1

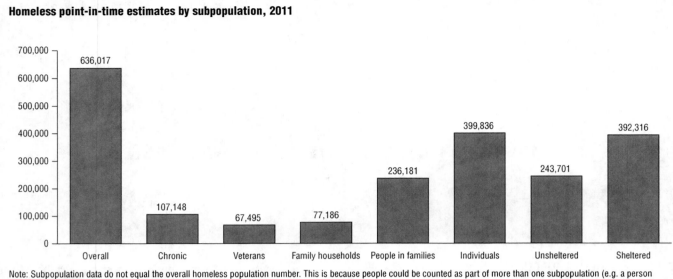

Homeless point-in-time estimates by subpopulation, 2011

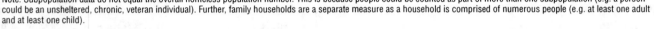

Note: Subpopulation data do not equal the overall homeless population number. This is because people could be counted as part of more than one subpopulation (e.g. a person could be an unsheltered, chronic, veteran individual). Further, family households are a separate measure as a household is comprised of numerous people (e.g. at least one adult and at least one child).

SOURCE: Peter White, "Figure 1.1. Homeless Population and Subpopulations, 2011," in *The State of Homelessness in America 2012*, National Alliance to End Homelessness, January 2012, http://www.endhomelessness.org/page/-/files/4361_file_FINAL_The_State_of_Homelessness_in_America_2012.pdf (accessed January 22, 2013)

were veterans, and 107,148 (17%) homeless people were chronically homeless (that is, they had been homeless continuously for a year or had experienced four episodes of homelessness during the previous three years).

The NAEH did not include a count of unaccompanied homeless youth in its *State of Homelessness in America* reports, observing that no comprehensive national data exist for this subset of the homeless population because the HUD PIT counts fail to survey unsheltered youth effectively. The organization further notes that, although the HUD PIT data has limitations, including variations in methodology both among the individual communities that collect the data and across time within individual communities, it remained the most reliable data set relating to homelessness, as it was the only count that included both the sheltered and the unsheltered homeless populations.

How Numbers Are Used

Common conceptions of the homeless usually involve images of people, including children, who live on the street permanently and sleep in cars, under bridges, and in cardboard boxes. There are, of course, people in this category, but they are the minority among the homeless. HUD, the NAEH, and other experts call such people the chronically homeless, and as the above PIT data indicate, the number of chronically homeless in 2011 was estimated at 107,148 people, less than one-fifth of the overall homeless population. (See Figure 5.1.) Most of the homeless are not chronically homeless but

are temporarily without a residence. After some period of homelessness, during which they often occupy emergency or transitional shelters, they find a more permanent home of their own or move in with relatives. Those living with relatives or "doubled-up" (the Census Bureau defines doubled-up households as those including one or more persons over the age of 18 who is not enrolled in school and is not the householder, spouse, or cohabiting partner of the householder) are considered homeless by some advocacy groups, but they are not included as part of the homeless population in HUD's PIT counts.

The prevailing official definition of the homeless population is the group of people who are, on any day, without proper shelter. When agencies or the media cite numbers in the 600,000 to 800,000 range, they mean the size of the homeless population at any one point in time. Individuals are continuously joining this population, and others are leaving it. If all people who are homeless at some point during a given year were counted, the number would reach between 2.5 million and 3.5 million individuals, as indicated by Burt et al. in *Evaluation of Continuums of Care for Homeless People*. The researchers estimated this number by using counts of the number of people who sought homeless services during one week in October 1996. During that week an estimated 36,900 individuals began spells of homelessness, whereas the total number of people in the homeless population in any one week in 1996 was estimated to be 444,000. The annual projection assumed that each week 36,900 people became homeless and an equal number phased out of the homeless status. Thus, multiplying 36,900 by 52 weeks in the year, and then adding that amount to 444,000, produced the count of 2.3 million people who were homeless at least once in 1996. This number does not mean that there were 2.3 million homeless people during the entire span of 1996.

In *The 2011 Annual Homeless Assessment Report to Congress*, HUD notes that it conducted a count of all homeless individuals who used a shelter during 2011. Approximately 1.5 million individuals, or 1 out of every 201 U.S. residents, used an emergency shelter or transitional housing. This count underrepresents the number of women because the residents of domestic violence shelters are not reported. It also does not include the unsheltered homeless population. In *The State of Homelessness in America 2012*, the NAEH estimates that the odds of experiencing homelessness, whether sheltered or unsheltered, were approximately 1 in 194 for the general population of the United States in a given year.

The NAEH further notes, however, that the odds of experiencing homelessness are far greater for certain subpopulations. Veterans who live in poverty are the most likely group to experience homelessness; a person fitting this description had an estimated 1 in 10 chance of being homeless in a given year, as of 2012. Young people who had aged out of foster care, according to the NAEH, had approximately a 1 in 11 chance of experiencing homelessness in a given year; and people who were living doubled-up had a 1 in 12 chance of experiencing homelessness. (Many people who eventually become homeless attempt to live in a doubled-up housing situation before moving to a shelter or the streets.) Finally, newly released prisoners are among the most likely members of society to experience homelessness. In 2012 the NAEH estimated the odds that a person recently discharged from prison would experience homelessness in a given year at 1 in 13.

Counting Homeless Children

In *Education for Homeless Children and Youths Program: Data Collection Summary* (June 2012, http://center.serve.org/nche/downloads/data_comp_0909-1011.pdf), the National Center for Homeless Education (NCHE) states that 1,065,794 children who experienced homelessness at some point during the year were enrolled in school during the 2010–11 school year. (See Table 5.1.) This number was almost certainly much lower than the number of children who actually experienced homelessness during that period, as the homeless status of children does not always come to the attention of school officials, and many homeless children are not enrolled in school. Regardless, the number had risen substantially with the so-called Great Recession of 2007 to 2009 and its aftermath. In 2006–07, the number

of homeless children enrolled in schools was 679,724; in 2007–08 it was 794,617; and in 2008–09 it was 956,914. The number of homeless children in schools dropped slightly in 2009–10, to 939,903, before climbing above 1 million 2010–11.

In *America's Youngest Outcasts: State Report Card on Child Homelessness* (December 2011, http://www.homelesschildrenamerica.org/media/NCFH_America Outcast2010_web_032812.pdf), Ellen L. Bassuk et al. of the National Center on Family Homelessness update a groundbreaking study first published in 1999. Bassuk et al. use data collected by local education agencies as mandated by the McKinney-Vento Homeless Assistance Act to estimate the number of U.S. children who experience homelessness each year. Child homelessness is a particular problem, according to the report, in the South and Southwest, regions where poverty levels tend to be higher and social welfare programs provide less coverage, than in the North and Northeast. In the previous edition of *America's Youngest Outcasts*, published in 2009 based on data from 2006, the number of homeless children was estimated at 1.5 million, or 1 in 50 American children. This total was abnormally high because of the displacement of hundreds of thousands of families in the aftermath of Hurricanes Katrina and Rita, and by 2007 the number had dropped to 1.2 million. With the Great Recession, however, the number of children experiencing homelessness climbed again, reaching 1.6 million in 2010, or 1 in 45 American children.

This rapid increase in the number of homeless children came in spite of the federal government's Homelessness Prevention and Rapid Re-Housing Program, which spurred a substantial increase, over the same period, in the supply of housing available to those at risk of homelessness. Additionally, Bassuk et al. note that the total number of homeless children in 2010 was likely artificially low, due to changes in data collection procedures in California. The state was among the hardest-hit by the Great Recession, and yet it reported decreases in the number of homeless children even as all regions of the nation were reporting increases. This disparity was of particular concern given that in the two previous counts undertaken by the center, California accounted for approximately 25% of the entire national population of homeless children.

PROFILES OF THE HOMELESS
Gender and Race

Studies of homeless people and surveys of officials knowledgeable about homeless clients conducted since the 1990s show similar patterns of gender and racial data for the homeless, although the percentages vary from study to study.

HUD reports in *The 2011 Annual Homeless Assessment Report to Congress* that in 2011, about 37% of the sheltered homeless population was female and 63% was

TABLE 5.1

Total homeless children enrolled in school, by state, school years 2008–09, 2009–10, and 2010–11

	Total enrolled SY0809	Percent of total enrolled SY0809	Total enrolled SY0910	Percent of total enrolled SY0910	Total enrolled SY1011	Percent of total enrolled SY1011	Percent change between SY0809 and SY0910	Percent change between SY0910 and SY1011	Percent change between SY0809 and SY1011 (3 year)
Total enrolled all states in LEAs with and without subgrants	956,914	100	939,903	100	1,065,794	100	−2	13	11
Total enrolled by state									
Alabama	12,859	1.3	16,287	1.7	18,910	1.8	27	16[b]	47
Alaska	3,401	0.4	4,218	0.4	4,451	0.4	24	6[b]	31
Arizona	25,336	2.6	30,815	3.3	31,312	2.9	22	2[b]	24
Arkansas	6,344	0.7	8,107	0.9	9,625	0.9	28	19[b]	52
Bureau of Indian Education	2,088	0.2	1,867	0.2	1,857	0.2	−11	−1[c]	−11
California[d]	288,233	30.1	193,796	20.6	220,738	20.7	−33	14[b]	−23
Colorado	15,834	1.7	18,408	2.0	20,624	1.9	16	12[b]	30
Connecticut	2,387	0.3	2,716	0.3	2,942	0.3	14	8[b]	23
Delaware	2,598	0.3	2,843	0.3	3,486	0.3	9	23[a]	34
District of Columbia	950	0.1	2,499	0.3	3,058	0.3	163	22[a]	222
Florida[d]	40,967	4.3	48,695	5.2	55,953	5.2	19	15[b]	37
Georgia	24,079	2.6	26,428	2.8	31,804	3.0	10	20[a]	32
Hawaii	1,739	0.2	2,966	0.3	2,320	0.2	71	−22[c]	33
Idaho	2,710	0.3	4,342	0.5	4,774	0.4	60	10[b]	76
Illinois	26,688	2.8	33,367	3.6	38,900	3.6	25	17[b]	46
Indiana	10,364	1.1	12,248	1.3	13,419	1.3	18	10[b]	29
Iowa	6,824	0.7	6,631	0.7	7,046	0.7	−3	6[b]	3
Kansas	6,700	0.7	8,452	0.9	8,995	0.8	26	6[b]	34
Kentucky	22,626	2.4	23,104	2.5	33,966	3.2	2	47[a]	50
Louisiana	25,362	2.7	25,223	2.7	23,211	2.2	−1	−8[c]	−8
Maine	1,300	0.1	1,158	0.1	991	0.1	−11	−14[c]	−24
Maryland	10,676	1.1	13,158	1.4	14,136	1.3	23	7[b]	32
Massachusetts	12,269	1.3	13,090	1.4	14,247	1.3	7	9[b]	16
Michigan	18,706	2.0	22,189	2.4	30,671	2.9	19	38[a]	64
Minnesota	7,590	0.8	9,221	1.0	11,076	1.0	21	20[a]	46
Mississippi	8,525	0.9	7,499	0.8	10,150	1.0	−12	35[a]	19
Missouri	14,350	1.5	16,654	1.8	19,940	1.9	16	20[a]	39
Montana	1,308	0.1	1,445	0.2	1,507	0.1	10	4[b]	15
Nebraska	1,752	0.2	2,188	0.2	2,674	0.3	25	22[a]	53
Nevada	8,670	0.9	8,841	0.9	9,319	0.9	2	5[b]	7
New Hampshire	2,130	0.2	2,573	0.3	3,160	0.3	21	23[a]	48
New Jersey	7,890	0.8	6,250	0.7	5,665	0.5	−21	−9[c]	−28
New Mexico	8,380	0.9	9,432	1.0	11,449	1.1	13	21[a]	37
New York[d]	76,117	8.0	82,409	8.8	90,506	8.5	8	10[b]	19
North Carolina	18,693	2.0	21,019	2.2	18,022	1.7	12	−14[c]	−4
North Dakota	1,149	0.1	836	0.1	870	0.1	−27	4[b]	−24
Ohio	16,059	1.7	19,113	2.0	21,849	2.1	19	14[b]	36
Oklahoma	12,139	1.3	15,910	1.7	17,450	1.6	31	10[b]	44
Oregon	18,051	1.9	19,954	2.1	21,632	2.0	11	8[b]	20
Pennsylvania	12,438	1.3	18,204	1.9	18,531	1.7	46	2[b]	49
Puerto Rico	4,064	0.4	4,464	0.5	4,727	0.4	10	6[b]	16
Rhode Island	1,099	0.1	996	0.1	977	0.1	−9	−2[c]	−11
South Carolina	8,738	0.9	10,820	1.2	10,590	1.0	24	−2[c]	21
South Dakota	1,794	0.2	1,512	0.2	1,883	0.2	−16	25[a]	5
Tennessee	9,836	1.0	11,458	1.2	13,958	1.3	16	22[a]	42
Texas[d]	80,940	8.5	76,095	8.1	85,155	8.0	−6	12[b]	5
Utah	14,016	1.5	15,702	1.7	23,048	2.2	12	47[a]	64
Vermont	662	0.1	785	0.1	915	0.1	19	17[b]	38
Virginia	12,768	1.3	14,223	1.5	16,420	1.5	11	15[b]	29
Washington	20,780	2.2	21,826	2.3	26,048	2.4	5	19[b]	25
West Virginia	4,257	0.4	4,817	0.5	6,630	0.6	13	38[a]	56
Wisconsin	10,955	1.1	12,029	1.3	13,370	1.3	10	11[b]	22
Wyoming	724	0.1	1,021	0.1	837	0.1	41	−18[c]	16
Total enrolled all states	956,914	100	939,903	100	1,065,794	100	−2	13	11

Notes: LEA = Local Education Agency. SY = School year.
[a]States had an increase in the number of homeless students enrolled of 20% or more between SY 2009–10 and SY 2010–11.
[b]States had an increase in the number of homeless students enrolled of 19% or less between SY 2009–10 and SY 2010–11.
[c]States showed a decrease in the number of homeless students enrolled between SY 2009–10 and SY 2010–11.
[d]States constitute the largest percentages of the total homeless students enrolled.

SOURCE: "Table 3. Total Enrolled in LEAs with and without McKinney-Vento Subgrants (1.9.1.1), Three-Year Comparison by State," in *Education for Homeless Children and Youths Program: Data Collection Summary*, National Center for Homeless Education, June 2012, http://center.serve.org/nche/downloads/data_comp_0909-1011.pdf (accessed January 22, 2013)

FIGURE 5.2

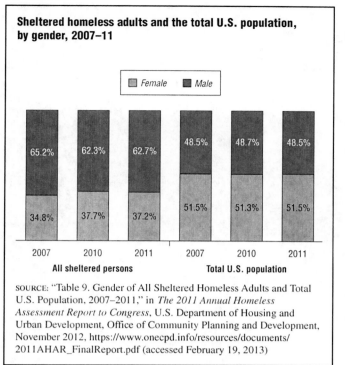

Sheltered homeless adults and the total U.S. population, by gender, 2007–11

SOURCE: "Table 9. Gender of All Sheltered Homeless Adults and Total U.S. Population, 2007–2011," in *The 2011 Annual Homeless Assessment Report to Congress*, U.S. Department of Housing and Urban Development, Office of Community Planning and Development, November 2012, https://www.onecpd.info/resources/documents/2011AHAR_FinalReport.pdf (accessed February 19, 2013)

FIGURE 5.3

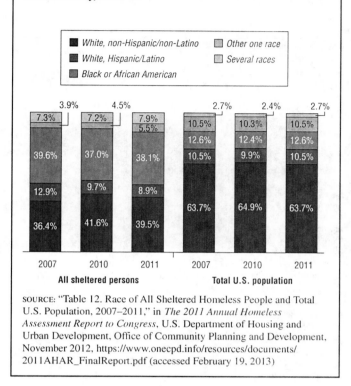

Sheltered homeless people and the total U.S. population, by race/ethnicity, 2007–11

SOURCE: "Table 12. Race of All Sheltered Homeless People and Total U.S. Population, 2007–2011," in *The 2011 Annual Homeless Assessment Report to Congress*, U.S. Department of Housing and Urban Development, Office of Community Planning and Development, November 2012, https://www.onecpd.info/resources/documents/2011AHAR_FinalReport.pdf (accessed February 19, 2013)

male. (See Figure 5.2.) Males, then, are overrepresented in the homeless population relative to the general population, but they are even more significantly overrepresented in the homeless population relative to the poor population. In 2011 approximately 58% of adults below the poverty line were women. The fact that, among the poor, men disproportionately tend to become homeless was likely influenced by their inability to qualify for TANF benefits, their higher rates of substance abuse relative to women, and the greater likelihood that they have been incarcerated.

The gender balance among the sheltered homeless population shifted slightly during and after the Great Recession, however. Between 2007 and 2011 the share of women among the sheltered homeless increased from 34.8% to 37.2%, which was consistent with a simultaneous increase in the share of families among the overall homeless population. (See Figure 5.2.) Most homeless families are headed by single adult women.

African-Americans are overrepresented among the homeless population as well. HUD indicates that in 2011, although African-Americans represented 12.6% of the total U.S. population, they accounted for 38.1% of the sheltered homeless population. (See Figure 5.3.) Approximately 39.5% of the sheltered homeless population in 2011 was non-Hispanic white, and approximately 8.9% was Hispanic/Latino. Among the factors contributing to the overrepresentation of African-Americans among the homeless population is the fact that homelessness is concentrated in urban areas, where African-Americans are similarly overrepresented.

In the press release "Survey Points to Needs of Iraq, Afghanistan Veterans" (November 13, 2012, http://www.agrm.org/NewsBot.asp?MODE=VIEW&ID=343), which presents the findings of its 2012 survey, the AGRM notes that men made up 72% of those seeking services at its missions in 2012. (See Table 5.2.) The AGRM shows an increase in the female portion of the mission client population between 2008 and 2012, from 26% of the total mission population to 28%. Of those seeking service at AGRM missions, 81% were individuals. Among those seeking service as part of a family, the percentage of women with children was 51%, down from 66% in 2008. Men with children constituted 11% of those seeking service as a family, intact families with children constituted 16%, and couples constituted 23%.

The AGRM indicates that the race and ethnic makeup of the homeless population seeking services stayed relatively stable between 2011 and 2012. The white (50%) and African-American (34%) portions of those seeking AGRM services was steady during that time, and the Hispanic/Latino portion of its clients rose slightly from 9% to 10%.

Family Structure

In *The 2011 Annual Homeless Assessment Report to Congress*, HUD notes that 63.4% of homeless

TABLE 5.2

Demographic overview of the homeless population served by Association of Gospel Rescue Missions, 2008–12

[Individuals surveyed: 18,776; Participating missions: 115; Families with children: 2,189; Individuals in long-term rehab: 5,306]

	2012	2011	2010	2009	2008
Gender (of total mission population)					
Male	72%	74%	75%	75%	74%
Female	28%	26%	25%	25%	26%
Age groups (of total mission population)					
Under 18	7%	7%	9%	9%	12%
18–25	9%	9%	9%	8%	9%
26–35	18%	18%	15%	17%	18%
36–45	23%	25%	22%	25%	26%
46–65	39%	39%	40%	38%	31%
65+	3%	3%	4%	3%	4%
Race/ethnic groups (of total mission population)					
White/Caucasian	50%	50%	—	—	—
Black or African American	34%	34%	—	—	—
Hispanic, Latin, or Spanish origin	10%	9%	—	—	—
Asian	1%	1%	—	—	—
American Indian or Alaskan Native	2%	2%	—	—	—
Native Hawaiian or other Pacific Islander	0%	0%	—	—	—
Other or 2+ races	3%	3%	—	—	—
Single individuals (of total mission population)	81%	86%	—	—	—
Women/children/families (of family units identified)					
Couples	23%	20%	12%	13%	15%
Women with children	51%	52%	57%	60%	66%
Men with children	11%	12%	9%	9%	5%
Intact families	16%	17%	22%	18%	14%
Veteran status (of total mission population)					
Veterans (male)	13%	13%	16%	19%	18%
Veterans (female)	2%	1%	4%	4%	3%
Of veterans identified:					
Served in Korea	3%	5%	—	—	—
Served in Vietnam	21%	25%	—	—	—
Served in Persian Gulf	16%	13%	—	—	—
Iraq or Afghanistan War	12%	6%	—	—	—
Homeless status (of total mission population)					
Not currently homeless	17%	17%	—	—	—
Currently homeless	83%	83%	—	—	—
Of currently homeless:					
Less than 3 months	30%	31%	—	—	—
3 to 6 months	24%	21%	—	—	—
6 months to 1 year	20%	20%	—	—	—
More than 1 year	27%	27%	—	—	—
Never before homeless	34%	35%	37%	37%	33%
Homeless once previously	26%	24%	25%	25%	24%
Homeless twice previously	17%	17%	16%	16%	18%
Homeless three-plus times previously	22%	24%	22%	22%	25%
Other information (of total mission population)					
Struggles with mental illness	30%	30%	—	—	—
Victim of physical violence in last 12 months	24%	21%	15%	17%	18%
Prefer spiritual emphasis in services	81%	80%	82%	83%	76%
Comes daily to the mission	84%	82%	84%	80%	77%

SOURCE: "Snapshot Survey Homeless Statistical Comparison," in *Survey Points to Needs of Iraq, Afghanistan Veterans*, Association of Gospel Rescue Missions, November 13, 2012, http://www.agrm.org/NewsBot.asp?MODE=VIEW&ID=343 (accessed January 15, 2013)

households consisted of one person, usually a single adult man, whereas in the U.S. population at large, only 13% of households consisted of only one person. Similarly, only 16% of homeless households consisted of four or more people, compared with 43% of households in the general population. The percentage of single-person homeless households had, however, been on the decline since 2007, when 70.3% of homeless households consisted of only one person. This decline was a function primarily of an increase in homeless families beginning in 2007. Although the number of homeless people in families did not increase in the years that followed, it remained high relative to the levels of family homelessness prior to the Great Recession. The number of sheltered homeless people in families increased yearly from 473,541 in 2007 to 567,334 in 2010, before declining slightly to 537,414 in 2011. (See Figure 5.4.)

FIGURE 5.4

FIGURE 5.5

Sheltered homeless people in families, 2007–11

SOURCE: "Table 50. Estimates of Sheltered People in Families during a One-Year Period, 2007–2011," in *The 2011 Annual Homeless Assessment Report to Congress*, U.S. Department of Housing and Urban Development, Office of Community Planning and Development, November 2012, https://www.onecpd.info/resources/documents/2011AHAR_FinalReport.pdf (accessed February 19, 2013)

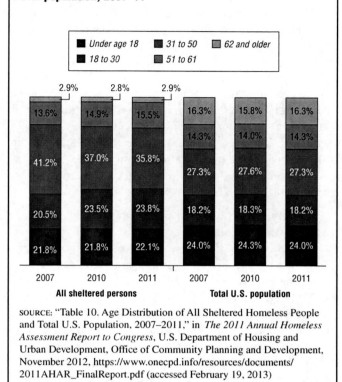

Age distribution of sheltered homeless people and of total U.S. population, 2007–11

SOURCE: "Table 10. Age Distribution of All Sheltered Homeless People and Total U.S. Population, 2007–2011," in *The 2011 Annual Homeless Assessment Report to Congress*, U.S. Department of Housing and Urban Development, Office of Community Planning and Development, November 2012, https://www.onecpd.info/resources/documents/2011AHAR_FinalReport.pdf (accessed February 19, 2013)

Among homeless families in 2011, 79.3% of adults were women. By comparison, in the general U.S. population, 54.5% of adults in families were women and 45.5% were men. Small families were much more common among the homeless than among the general population; 24.8% of homeless families consisted of only two people (one parent and one child), and 30% consisted of three people. In the general U.S. population, only 4.2% of families consisted of two people, and 21.1% consisted of three people. Likewise, larger families were much less common among the homeless than among the general population. Whereas 22% of homeless families consisted of four people and 23.2% of five or more people, 33.5% of families in the general population consisted of four people and 41.3% of five or more.

Age

The age distribution of the sheltered homeless population was relatively consistent between 2007 and 2011, according to HUD. (See Figure 5.5.) In 2007, 21.8% of sheltered homeless people were under age 18, 20.5% were aged 18 to 30, 41.2% were aged 31 to 50, 13.6% were aged 51 to 61, and 2.9% were aged 62 or older. In 2011, 22.1% of sheltered homeless people were under age 18, 23.8% were aged 18 to 30, 35.8% were aged 31 to 50, 15.5% were aged 51 to 61, and 2.9% were aged 62 or older. Compared with the total U.S. population, the numbers of children, of adults aged 18 to 30, and of adults aged 51 to 61 in the sheltered homeless population were approximately proportionate. Adults aged 31 to 50,

by contrast, were substantially overrepresented in the sheltered homeless population between 2007 and 2011, and adults aged 62 and older were significantly underrepresented in the sheltered homeless population.

HOMELESS CHILDREN. Homeless children have always received special attention from the public and from welfare agencies. In the terminology of previous centuries, children are considered "worthy poor" (that is, "worthy" of help from society) because they have no control over their financial circumstances.

HUD estimated that 341,040 homeless children were sheltered in 2011. Of these, 321,548 (94%) were members of families who were sheltered together. The remaining 19,492 children fall into the category of "unaccompanied youth," a category that HUD's PIT studies are generally believed to undercount dramatically. According to the NAEH in *The State of Homelessness in America 2012*, the most widely accepted estimate of unaccompanied youth numbers comes from a 1999 U.S. Department of Justice initiative, the National Incidence Studies of Missing, Abducted, Runaway, and Throwaway Children, which estimated the "runaway and throwaway" categories—equivalent to unaccompanied homeless children—at 1.7 million over the course of one year. As the NAEH notes, however, "Approximately 1.3 million of these children returned home within one week, not all of these children became homeless, and the data is outdated, so this information also lacks accuracy."

The NCHE collects estimates of homeless children from selected school district records. The data exclude infants as the HUD estimates do not, but the data include some children of preschool age. Also unlike HUD, the NCHE counts as homeless those students who are living doubled-up and in hotels and motels. Accordingly, the NCHE arrives at a much larger estimate of the number of homeless children—1,062,928 during the 2010–11 school year, up dramatically from 2007–08, when the organization counted 773,832 homeless children—even though its count of sheltered homeless children is smaller than HUD's.

Slightly fewer than one-fifth (187,675) of homeless students were sheltered, according to the NCHE count, 5% (55,388) were living in hotels or motels, and 5% (51,897) were unsheltered during the 2010–11 school year. (See Figure 5.6.) Much of the disparity between the 2011 HUD count of 341,040 sheltered homeless children in 2011 and the NCHE count of 1,062,928 can be attributed to the inclusion in the latter of children who were living doubled-up. During the 2010–11 school year, the NCHE estimated that 767,968 students, or 72% of the total number of students it classified as homeless, were doubled-up. This number was up dramatically from 606,764 during the 2008–09 school year. Although

HUD does not count doubled-up children as homeless, the agency notes the highly elevated risk of homelessness to which doubled-up families and individuals are subject. Although HUD found that the homeless population had leveled off after increasing rapidly at the beginning of the Great Recession, the growing number of doubled-up children between 2008 and 2011 suggested ongoing cause for concern among child-welfare advocates.

Much of the increase in homeless and precariously housed children was due to the economic recession that began in December 2007. Michelle D. Anderson reports in "Schools Facing Rise in Homeless Students" (*Christian Science Monitor*, April 12, 2011) that the handful of schools around the nation that serve exclusively homeless children were facing a growing enrollment due to the rise in foreclosures and unstable housing conditions in 2011. For example, Anderson notes that the Monarch School in San Diego, California, saw a 74% increase in enrollments between 2008 and 2011, and the Children First Academy in Phoenix, Arizona, saw the number of children on its waitlist quadruple and its enrollment increase between 12% and 18% annually.

It should be noted that, even though the NCHE counts many children (those who are doubled-up or living in hotels and motels) who do not appear in the HUD data, there are also numerous classes of at-risk children who do not appear in the NCHE report. In addition to its exclusion of infants too young to attend preschool, the ability of the NCHE to measure the homeless population is limited by the fact that many school-age homeless children do not attend school. For example, in *2007 Greater Los Angeles Homeless Count* (2007, http://www.lahsa.org/docs/homelesscount/2007/LAHSA.pdf), a survey of homeless respondents in Los Angeles, California, the Los Angeles Homeless Services Authority finds that 11% of homeless families with school-age children stated their children were not attending school in 2007.

When homeless children do attend school, they have less than optimal conditions for educational achievement. Ellen L. Bassuk et al. indicate in *America's Youngest Outcasts 2010: State Report Card on Child Homelessness* that homeless children are far more likely than other children to be subject to traumatic stresses associated with abuse, neglect, and domestic violence, as well as with issues related to the loss of home and safety. Homeless children are also more likely than other children to have chronic or acute medical conditions that severely limit their ability to learn and achieve. "They go hungry at twice the rate of other children," according to Bassuk et al. "They have three times the rate of emotional and behavioral problems, such as anxiety, depression, sleep problems, withdrawal, and aggression." As reported in *America's Youngest Outcasts 2010*, approximately 40% of homeless children change schools at least once per

FIGURE 5.6

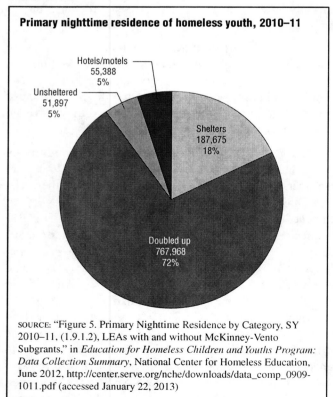

Primary nighttime residence of homeless youth, 2010–11

Hotels/motels
55,388
5%

Unsheltered
51,897
5%

Shelters
187,675
18%

Doubled up
767,968
72%

SOURCE: "Figure 5. Primary Nighttime Residence by Category, SY 2010–11, (1.9.1.2), LEAs with and without McKinney-Vento Subgrants," in *Education for Homeless Children and Youths Program: Data Collection Summary*, National Center for Homeless Education, June 2012, http://center.serve.org/nche/downloads/data_comp_0909-1011.pdf (accessed January 22, 2013)

year, and an estimated 28% change schools two times or more in a single school year. The rate at which homeless children display delayed development is four times higher than that among other students, and they are categorized as learning-disabled at twice the rate of the student population at large. A homeless child is twice as likely to score lower on a standardized test than a child with secure housing, three times as likely to be assigned to a special-education class, and eight times as likely to be a candidate for repeating a grade.

Military Background

Homeless veterans are another subpopulation of particular concern to many Americans and policy makers. Many ordinary people and policy makers believe that some level of gratitude and support is owed to those who serve the country in wartime. Additionally, the trauma of combat and the difficulty of reintegrating into civilian life leave veterans at an increased risk of homelessness relative to the general population. As the 100,000 Homes Campaign, an affiliate of the U.S. Department of Veterans Affairs (VA) committed to finding homes for 100,000 veterans, notes in its *National Survey of Homeless Veterans in 100,000 Homes Campaign Communities* (November 2011, http://www.va.gov/HOMELESS/docs/NationalSurveyofHomelessVeterans _FINAL.pdf), veterans represent less than 9% of the total population, but they make up 15.2% of the homeless population surveyed. Additionally, veterans tend to remain homeless for longer than nonveterans. The 100,000 Homes Campaign found that the veterans it surveyed had been homeless for an average of 5.8 years, compared with 3.9 years for the homeless nonveterans it surveyed. Homeless veterans were also more likely than homeless nonveterans to have health conditions such as liver disease, kidney disease, HIV/AIDS, frequent frostbite, and tri-morbidity (a combination of mental illness, physical illness, and substance-abuse problems). Homeless veterans were also much more likely than homeless nonveterans to be 60 years old or older.

HUD and the VA work together to generate accurate estimates of the population of homeless veterans, and their PIT counts of veterans are believed to be among their most accurate estimates. In *The 2011 Annual Homeless Assessment Report to Congress*, HUD estimates the homeless veteran population on a single January night in 2011 was 67,495, or 14% of the total homeless population. (See Figure 5.7.) Of these veterans, 40,033 (59%) were sheltered, and 27,462 (41%) were unsheltered. This represented a 10.7% decrease in the number of homeless veterans since 2010, when HUD counted 76,329 homeless veterans; and the number of unsheltered veterans decreased particularly rapidly, from 32,892 in 2010. The estimated number of veterans who were homeless at any point in 2011 (141,449) had also declined since

FIGURE 5.7

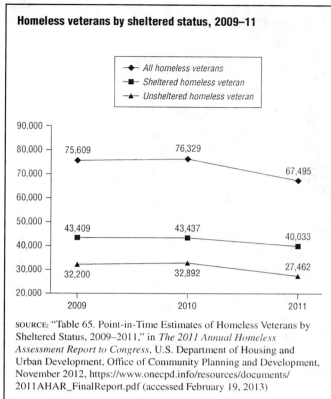

Homeless veterans by sheltered status, 2009–11

SOURCE: "Table 65. Point-in-Time Estimates of Homeless Veterans by Sheltered Status, 2009–2011," in *The 2011 Annual Homeless Assessment Report to Congress*, U.S. Department of Housing and Urban Development, Office of Community Planning and Development, November 2012, https://www.onecpd.info/resources/documents/2011AHAR_FinalReport.pdf (accessed February 19, 2013)

2009, when 149,636 veterans found themselves homeless at some point in the year. A measure of the declines in veteran homelessness was attributable to the Homelessness Prevention Fund, part of the American Recovery and Reinvestment Act of 2009, which included specific funds for fighting homelessness among veterans.

The gender distribution of homeless veterans remained relatively constant between 2009 and 2011, according to HUD; 92.5% of homeless veterans were male in 2009, and 90.2% were male in 2011. More than 80% of homeless veterans were between the ages of 31 and 61 during the period 2009 through 2011, although the distribution shifted within this category. In 2009 an estimated 44.6% of homeless veterans were aged 31 to 50, and 38.1% were aged 51 to 61; by 2011, 39.1% of homeless veterans were aged 31 to 50, and 42.3% were aged 51 to 61. The proportion of homeless veterans aged 62 and older increased slightly during this time, from 8.9% to 9.5%, as did the proportion of homeless veterans aged 18 to 30, from 8.4% to 9.1%.

WHERE THE HOMELESS LIVE

Table 5.3 shows the distribution of the U.S. homeless population by state in 2009 and 2011, using data from HUD's PIT counts. Although the homeless population declined by approximately 1.1% nationally between 2009 and 2011, the pattern across individual states and

TABLE 5.3

Overall homelessness by state, 2009 and 2011 and percentage change

State	Overall homeless population, 2011	Overall homeless population, 2009	Homeless population change, 2009 to 2011	2011 rate of homelessness (Homeless people per 10,000 in general population)
Alabama	5,558	6,080	−8.59%	12
Alaska	2,128	1,992	6.83%	30
Arizona	10,504	14,721	−28.65%	16
Arkansas	3,424	2,852	20.06%	12
California	135,928	133,129	2.10%	36
Colorado	15,116	15,268	−1.00%	30
Connecticut	4,456	4,605	−3.24%	12
Delaware	1,035	1,130	−8.41%	12
District of Columbia	6,546	6,228	5.11%	108
Florida	56,687	55,599	1.96%	30
Georgia	20,975	20,360	3.02%	22
Hawaii	6,188	5,782	7.02%	45
Idaho	2,199	1,939	13.41%	14
Illinois	14,009	14,055	−0.33%	11
Indiana	6,196	6,984	−11.28%	10
Iowa	3,134	3,380	−7.28%	10
Kansas	2,511	1,892	32.72%	9
Kentucky	6,034	5,999	0.58%	14
Louisiana	9,291	12,504	−25.70%	20
Maine	2,447	2,444	0.12%	18
Maryland	10,208	11,698	−12.74%	18
Massachusetts	16,664	15,482	7.63%	25
Michigan	13,185	14,005	−5.86%	13
Minnesota	7,495	7,718	−2.89%	14
Mississippi	2,306	2,797	−17.55%	8
Missouri	8,989	6,959	29.17%	15
Montana	1,768	1,196	47.83%	18
Nebraska	3,548	3,718	−4.57%	19
Nevada	10,579	14,478	−26.93%	39
New Hampshire	1,469	1,645	−10.70%	11
New Jersey	14,137	13,169	7.35%	16
New Mexico	3,601	3,475	3.63%	17
New York	63,445	61,067	3.89%	33
North Carolina	12,896	12,918	−0.17%	13
North Dakota	603	773	−21.99%	9
Ohio	13,030	12,700	2.60%	11
Oklahoma	4,625	4,838	−4.40%	12
Oregon	17,254	17,309	−0.32%	45
Pennsylvania	15,096	15,096	0.00%	12
Rhode Island	1,070	1,607	−33.42%	10
South Carolina	5,093	4,473	13.86%	11
South Dakota	826	731	13.00%	10
Tennessee	9,113	10,532	−13.47%	14
Texas	36,911	36,761	0.41%	15
Utah	3,130	3,795	−17.52%	11
Vermont	1,144	1,214	−5.77%	18
Virginia	8,816	8,852	−0.41%	11
Washington	20,439	22,782	−10.28%	30
West Virginia	2,211	1,667	32.63%	12
Wisconsin	5,785	6,525	−11.34%	10
Wyoming	1,038	515	101.55%	18
United States	**636,017**	**643,067**	**−1.10%**	**21**

SOURCE: Peter White, "Table 1.1. Overall Homelessness," in *The State of Homelessness in America 2012*, National Alliance to End Homelessness, January 2012, http://www.endhomelessness.org/page/-/files/4361_file_FINAL_The_State_of_Homelessness_in_America_2012.pdf (accessed January 22, 2013)

the District of Columbia was far from uniform. Nearly half of the states (24) and the District of Columbia reported increases in homelessness over the period, and the variation among states' individual PIT counts was extreme. Rhode Island, for example, experienced a 33% decrease in homelessness between 2009 and 2011, whereas Wyoming registered an increase in homelessness of 102% during the same time.

Of the total 1.5 million people who sought refuge in a homeless shelter during 2011, according to HUD,

1,041,863 were in principal cities (the main population centers in metropolitan areas) and 458,652 were in suburbs or rural areas. (See Table 5.4.) The sheltered homeless in cities were more likely to be members of a minority group than were the sheltered homeless in suburban and rural areas. Hispanic/Latino people constituted approximately 18% of the urban homeless population, compared with 10.1% of the suburban/rural homeless population; and 42.1% of the urban homeless were African-American, compared with 29.3% of the suburban/rural homeless

TABLE 5.4

Characteristics of the sheltered homeless population, by geography, 2011

Characteristic	Principal cities	Suburban and rural
Number of homeless people	1,041,863	458,652
Gender of adults		
Female	34.7%	43.3%
Male	65.2%	56.7%
Ethnicity		
Non-Hispanic/non-Latino	82.0%	90.0%
Hispanic/Latino	18.0%	10.1%
Race		
White, non-Hispanic/non-Latino	33.6%	52.8%
White, Hispanic/Latino	9.9%	6.6%
Black or African American	42.1%	29.3%
Other one race	6.0%	4.5%
Several races	8.4%	6.8%
Age		
Under age 18	20.6%	25.5%
18 to 30	23.1%	25.3%
31 to 50	36.8%	33.4%
51 to 61	16.3%	13.5%
62 and older	3.2%	2.3%
People by household size		
1 person	66.3%	56.9%
2 people	9.5%	10.8%
3 people	9.5%	13.5%
4 people	7.2%	9.0%
5 or more people	7.5%	9.8%
Disabled (adults only)		
Yes	37.0%	39.5%
No	63.0%	60.5%

SOURCE: "Table 17. Characteristics of All Sheltered Homeless People by Geography, 2011," in *The 2011 Annual Homeless Assessment Report to Congress*, U.S. Department of Housing and Urban Development, Office of Community Planning and Development, November 2012, https://www.onecpd.info/resources/documents/2011AHAR_FinalReport.pdf (accessed February 19, 2013)

population. A higher proportion of the sheltered homeless population was female in suburban and rural areas (43.3%) than in principal cities (34.7%). This was consistent with the fact that the sheltered homeless population in suburban and rural areas included a higher proportion of families than the urban homeless population. Homeless individuals tend overwhelmingly to be male, whereas the heads of homeless families tend to be female.

Rural Homelessness

The bulk of the homeless population resides in cities, so most studies have been focused on urban areas. Common images of homelessness also create the impression that this problem exists only on city sidewalks. Rural homelessness, however, is a very real problem. In fact, as the NAEH indicates in "Rural Homelessness" (2012, http://www.endhomelessness.org/pages/rural), three of the areas with the highest homeless rates in the United States are rural. Rural and urban areas have similar rates of poverty (while the suburban poverty rate is significantly lower), and the same structural issues, such as a

lack of affordable housing and a lack of income, tend to drive both urban and rural homelessness. Rural communities, however, are often much less equipped to serve their homeless populations. There are fewer official shelters, and the transportation infrastructure necessary for the homeless to access services is often lacking. There are also fewer public places (e.g., heating grates, subways, or train stations) where the homeless can find temporary shelter or relief from the elements. Therefore, the rural homeless are more likely to live in a car or camper, or with relatives in overcrowded or rundown housing, than in shelters or typical unsheltered locations. Finding the rural homeless, then, is more difficult for investigators of the problem, so it is possible that they are typically undercounted in HUD and other surveys.

The National Coalition for the Homeless (NCH) reports in the fact sheet "Rural Homelessness" (July 2009, http://www.nationalhomeless.org/factsheets/rural.html) that the rural homeless are more likely to be white, female, married, and currently working than are the urban homeless. They are also more likely to be homeless for the first time and generally experience homelessness for a shorter period than the urban homeless. Furthermore, the NCH notes that domestic violence is more likely to be a cause of homelessness in rural areas and that alcohol or substance abuse is less likely to be a cause. In addition, those living in rural areas have fewer employment opportunities, typically earn lower wages, and remain unemployed for longer periods than do people living in metropolitan areas—factors which all contribute significantly to the entrenched problem of rural homelessness.

Burt et al. determine in *Homelessness* that in 1996, 21% of all homeless people in their study lived in suburban areas, and 9% lived in rural communities. The rural homeless surveyed were more likely to be working, or to have worked recently, than the urban homeless; 65% of the rural homeless had worked for pay during the previous month. Homeless people living in rural areas were also more likely to be experiencing their first spell of homelessness (60%). In 55% of the cases the homeless period lasted three months or less.

In *Hard to Reach: Rural Homelessness and Health Care* (October 2001, http://www.nhchc.org/wp-content/uploads/2012/02/October2001HealingHands.pdf), Patricia A. Post of the National Health Care for the Homeless Council argues that rural residents typically deal with a lack of permanent housing not by sleeping on the streets, like their urban counterparts, but by first moving in with a series of friends; second, by moving into abandoned shacks, cars, or campgrounds; and finally, by moving to cities in search of employment. They also differ from urban homeless people in other ways: Rural homeless people have less education, typically hold temporary jobs with no benefits, are less likely to receive government assistance or have health insurance, and are more likely to have been incarcerated.

Several types of rural areas generate higher-than-average levels of homelessness, including regions that:

- Are primarily agricultural—residents often lose their livelihood because of either a reduced demand for farm labor or a shrinking service sector

- Depend on declining extractive industries, such as mining or timber

- Are experiencing economic growth—new or expanding industrial plants often attract more job seekers than what can be absorbed

- Have persistent poverty, such as Appalachia and the rural South, where the young and able-bodied may have to relocate before they can find work

TRENDS IN HOMELESSNESS

There is an undeniable connection between homelessness and poverty. People in poverty live from day to day, with little or no financial safety net for times when unforeseen expenses arise. If a family's resources are small, expenditures on necessities such as food, shelter, and health care have to be carefully decided and sometimes sacrifices have to be made. Should one spend money on food, a visit to the doctor, buying necessary medicines, or paying the rent? As of 2013, a person working 40 hours per week for 50 weeks per year at minimum wage ($7.25 per hour) would gross $290 per week, or $14,500 per year, below the poverty level for a family of two ($15,510 in 2013) and substantially below the poverty level for a family of three ($19,530). (See Chapter 3.) Being poor often means that an illness, an accident, or a missed paycheck could be enough to cause homelessness.

After large decreases in the poverty rate during the 1960s and 1970s, the poverty rate increased during the 1990s to a high of 15.1% in 1993. (See Figure 1.1 in Chapter 1.) As the U.S. economy expanded between 1994 and 2000, the poverty rate fell, but between 2001 and 2011 it rose steadily, both during the period of economic expansion in the middle of the decade and during the crisis years of the Great Recession and its aftermath. In 2011, 46.2 million people (15%) lived below the poverty line. Although rising poverty rates do not always correspond to rising homelessness rates, the poor are especially vulnerable to fluctuations in housing prices.

According to the Joint Center for Housing Studies (JCHS) of Harvard University in *America's Rental Housing—The Key to a Balanced National Policy* (May 2008, http://www.jchs .harvard.edu/sites/jchs.harvard.edu/files/rh08_americas _rental_housing.pdf), the foreclosure crisis in 2007 and

2008 pushed previous homeowners into the rental market, who then competed for a limited number of affordable housing units. The organization points out that "no single minimum-wage earner working 40 hours a week, 52 weeks a year, earns enough to cover the cost of a modest rental anywhere in the country." Low income and high-rent payments often result in substandard housing accommodation, doubled-up living, or living on the street or in a public shelter. The necessity of basic sustenance and medical care usually leaves little money to meet housing needs. People in poverty have further difficulties finding housing if they have previously defaulted on their rent or mortgage, resulting in homelessness. In an update of the 2008 report, the JCHS notes in *America's Rental Housing: Meeting Challenges, Building on Opportunities* (April 2011, http:// www.jchs.harvard.edu/sites/jchs.harvard.edu/files/americas rentalhousing-2011.pdf) that as the need for affordable housing has increased, the number of available low-cost rental units has declined, exacerbating the problem. For example, 11.9% of the vacant or for-rent units with rents below $400 per month in 1999 had been demolished by 2009. Other affordable units had been upgraded to higher rents, converted to nonresidential or seasonal uses, or abandoned, which reduced the number of for-rent units with rents below $400 per month by 28% between 1999 and 2009. The JCHS estimates that as of 2009, 18 million low-income renters were competing for only 11.6 million available, affordable units, creating a national supply gap of 6.4 million units.

The NAEH reports in *The State of Homelessness in America 2012*, that the number of poor households classified by HUD as "severely housing-cost burdened" (that is, households that spend more than half of their incomes on rent) increased from 5.9 million in 2009 to 6.2 million in 2010. (See Table 5.5.) Approximately 75% of all poor households who lived in rental properties were, during this time, severely housing-cost burdened. Additionally, unemployment rose from pre-recession levels below 5% to a peak of 10% in October 2009. Although the unemployment rate fell thereafter, it remained above 8% through most of 2012, leaving millions of people vulnerable to poverty and homelessness. The working poor, even when they kept their jobs, saw their wages stagnate: between 2009 and 2010 the average real annual income of the working poor rose by less than 1%, from approximately $9,300 to approximately $9,400. The foreclosure crisis continued well beyond the recession's official end, as well. In 2010, 1 out of 45 American houses was in foreclosure. (See Table 5.6.) In the states hardest-hit by the housing crisis, the foreclosure rate was far worse. In Nevada in 2010, for example, 1 of every 11 housing units was in foreclosure. All of these structural economic factors translated into a period during which poor Americans were exceptionally likely, by historical standards, to become homeless.

TABLE 5.5

National changes in economic factors that contribute to homelessness, 2009–10

Factor	2009	2010	Percent change 2009 to 2010
Severely housing cost burdened poor renter households	5,886,293	6,215,080	6 %
Unemployed people	14,265,000	14,825,000	4%
Average income of working poor people	$9,301	$9,413	1%
Residential units in foreclosure	2,824,674	2,871,891	2%

SOURCE: Peter White, "Table 2.4. National Changes in Economic Factors, 2009 to 2010," in *The State of Homelessness in America 2012*, National Alliance to End Homelessness, January 2012, http://www.endhomelessness.org/page/-/files/4361_file_FINAL_The_State_of_Homelessness_in_America_2012.pdf (accessed January 22, 2013)

EMPLOYMENT AND THE HOMELESS

It is extremely difficult for people to escape homelessness without a job. Yet, it is equally difficult for homeless people to find and keep good jobs. The NCH, in the fact sheet "Employment and Homelessness" (July 2009, http://www.nationalhomeless.org/factsheets/employment.html), enumerates a number of barriers to employment that homeless people routinely face:

• Lack of education

• Lack of competitive work skills

• Lack of transportation

• Lack of day care

• Disabling conditions

In addition, the homeless, like other workers, are subject to fluctuations in the labor market. The availability of jobs and the wages and benefits paid for those available jobs often determine whether or not people can remove themselves from homelessness. Many homeless are underemployed—that is, they would like to work full time but have been unsuccessful at finding full-time work.

Burt et al. indicate in *Homelessness* that in 1996, 44% of homeless respondents reported working during the previous month. Two percent earned income as self-employed entrepreneurs—by peddling or selling belongings; 42% of the homeless respondents worked for, and were paid by, an employer. HUD did not publish employment information in its *2011 AHAR*. However, the U.S. Conference of Mayors, in *Hunger and Homelessness Survey* (December 2012, http://usmayors.org/pressreleases/uploads/2012/1219-report-HH.pdf), reports that between September 2011 and August 2012, 17% of homeless adults in its 25 survey cities were employed.

Advocates for the homeless are concerned that unfavorable labor market conditions, including both high unemployment and stagnant wages, support continued homelessness. Prior to the recession, a minimum-wage worker who worked full time, year-round, made an income insufficient to support a family of three, and the recession placed additional downward pressure on those wages that rose above the federal minimum. Because most homeless people do not have more than a high school education and because a majority of the low-paying jobs go to those with at least a high school education, advocates worry that the available job opportunities for homeless people provide an insufficient base for exiting homelessness.

Regular work, which is characterized by a permanent and ongoing relationship between employer and employee, does not figure significantly in the lives and routines of most homeless people, as it is usually unavailable or inaccessible. Homelessness makes getting and keeping regular work difficult because of the lack of a fixed address, communication, and, in many cases, the inability to get a good night's sleep, clean up, and dress appropriately. Studies find that the longer a person is homeless, the less likely he or she is to pursue wage labor and the more likely he or she is to engage in some other form of work. For those who do participate in regular jobs, in most cases, the wages received are not sufficient to escape living on the street.

Homeless people earn money in a number of different ways. Some of the most common income-generating activities the homeless engage in are day labor, shadow work, institutionalized assistance, and the distribution of street newspapers. A discussion of each of these activities follows.

Day Labor

Day labor (wage labor secured on a day-to-day basis, typically at lower wages and changing locations) is somewhat easier for the homeless to secure than regular work. Tim Bartley and Wade T. Roberts state in "Relational Exploitation: The Informal Organization of Day Labor Agencies" (*WorkingUSA: The Journal of Labor and Society*, vol. 9, March 2006) that "popular and scholarly depictions of homelessness have often portrayed homeless individuals as disconnected from the world of work—implicitly or explicitly equating homelessness with joblessness.... Yet... homeless persons engage in far more paid work than usually assumed." In fact, the

TABLE 5.6

Foreclosed housing units by state, 2009–10

State	Foreclosed housing units, 2010	Foreclosed housing units, 2009	Change in foreclosure 2009 to 2010	2010 rate of foreclosure (1/x housing units)
Alabama	20,869	19,896	4.89%	103
Alaska	2,654	2,442	8.68%	104
Arizona	155,878	163,210	−4.49%	17
Arkansas	19,757	16,547	19.40%	66
California	546,669	632,573	−13.58%	25
Colorado	54,041	50,514	6.98%	40
Connecticut	21,705	19,679	10.30%	66
Delaware	4,727	3,034	55.80%	83
District of Columbia	2,153	3,235	−33.45%	133
Florida	485,286	516,711	−6.08%	18
Georgia	130,966	106,110	23.42%	31
Hawaii	12,425	9,002	38.02%	41
Idaho	19,088	17,161	11.23%	34
Illinois	151,304	131,132	15.38%	35
Indiana	44,172	41,405	6.68%	63
Iowa	8,663	5,681	52.49%	153
Kansas	11,415	9,056	26.05%	107
Kentucky	12,656	9,682	30.72%	152
Louisiana	15,753	11,750	34.07%	120
Maine	3,502	3,178	10.20%	200
Maryland	42,446	43,248	−1.85%	55
Massachusetts	36,092	36,119	−0.07%	76
Michigan	135,874	118,302	14.85%	33
Minnesota	31,315	31,697	−1.21%	74
Mississippi	5,280	5,402	−2.26%	240
Missouri	33,944	28,519	19.02%	78
Montana	3,307	1,373	140.86%	133
Nebraska	3,377	1,845	83.04%	233
Nevada	106,160	112,097	−5.30%	11
New Hampshire	7,703	7,210	6.84%	78
New Jersey	64,808	63,208	2.53%	54
New Mexico	11,133	7,212	54.37%	78
New York	43,913	50,369	−12.82%	182
North Carolina	40,151	28,384	41.46%	105
North Dakota	488	390	25.13%	642
Ohio	108,160	101,614	6.44%	47
Oklahoma	17,718	12,937	36.96%	92
Oregon	36,958	34,121	8.31%	44
Pennsylvania	51,278	44,732	14.63%	107
Rhode Island	5,246	5,065	3.57%	86
South Carolina	33,063	25,163	31.40%	62
South Dakota	1,244	765	62.61%	291
Tennessee	39,206	40,733	−3.75%	70
Texas	118,923	100,045	18.87%	81
Utah	32,520	27,140	19.82%	29
Vermont	393	143	174.83%	795
Virginia	51,588	52,127	−1.03%	64
Washington	43,856	35,268	24.35%	64
West Virginia	1,329	1,479	−10.14%	667
Wisconsin	39,920	35,252	13.24%	64
Wyoming	815	717	13.67%	302
United States	**2,871,891**	**2,824,674**	**1.67%**	**45**

SOURCE: Peter White, "Table 2.8. Residential Housing Units in Foreclosure," in *The State of Homelessness in America 2012*, National Alliance to End Homelessness, January 2012, http://www.endhomelessness.org/page/-/files/4361_file_FINAL_The_State_of_Homelessness_in_America_2012.pdf (accessed January 22, 2013)

Center for Urban Economic Development at the University of Illinois, Chicago, reports in "A Fair Day's Pay? Homeless Day Laborers in Chicago" (2000, http://www.urbaneconomy.org/node/35) that the majority of adults living in the shelters it studied worked at temporary, contingent, or day-labor jobs.

Day labor may involve unloading trucks, cleaning up warehouses, cutting grass, or washing windows. Day labor often fits the abilities of the homeless because transportation may be provided to the worksite, and appearance, work history, and references are less important than in regular employment. Day labor usually pays cash at quitting time, thus providing immediate pocket money. Day labor jobs are, however, by definition, without a future, and Bartley and Roberts point out the exploitation that many day laborers face. Because of the growth of day labor, agencies have sprung up to profit from making these informal arrangements more formal. Many of these agencies do not pay workers for the time they wait until being assigned or charge fees for equipment or check-cashing. In "In the Shadows, Day Laborers Left Homeless as Work Vanishes" (*New York Times*, January 1, 2010), Fernanda Santos reports that during the Great Recession of 2007–09 even day labor dried up, leaving people who had depended on that work even more likely to become homeless.

Shadow Work

Shadow work refers to methods of getting money that are outside the normal economy, some of them illegal. David Levinson, the editor of *Encyclopedia of Homelessness* (2004), explains that these methods include panhandling, scavenging, selling possessions, picking up aluminum cans and selling them, selling one's blood or plasma, theft, or peddling illegal goods, drugs, or services. A homeless person seldom engages in all these activities consistently but may turn to some of them as needed. Researchers estimate that 60% of homeless people engage in some shadow work. Shadow work is more common for homeless men than for homeless women. Theft is more common for younger homeless people.

In "Buddy, Can You Spare a Dime?: Homelessness, Panhandling, and the Public" (*Urban Affairs Review*, vol. 38, no. 3, 2003), Barrett A. Lee and Chad R. Farrell of Pennsylvania State University note that a mixture of institutionalized assistance, wage labor, and shadow work is typical of those who live on the streets. For example, Laura Christine Hein indicates in "Survival among Male Homeless Adolescents" (May 2006, http://etd.library.vanderbilt.edu/available/etd-03082006-112327/unrestricted/HeinDissertation.pdf) that homeless adolescents use a combination of strategies to survive, including accessing homeless services, robbing or stealing, prostitution, panhandling, dumpster diving, and working. Studies find that many homeless people are resourceful in surviving the rigors of street life and recommend that this resourcefulness be somehow channeled into training that can lead to jobs paying a living wage. However, the NCH notes in "Employment and Homelessness" that homeless people who have adapted to street life may likely need transitional socialization programs as well as programs that teach them marketable skills.

Institutionalized Assistance

A certain proportion of homeless people receive some form of institutionalized assistance. This would include institutionalized labor, such as that provided by soup kitchens, shelters, and rehabilitation programs that sometimes pay the homeless for work related to facility operation. The number of people employed by these agencies is a small percentage of the homeless population. In addition, the pay—room, board, and a small stipend—tends to tie the homeless to the organization rather than providing the means to get off the street.

Institutionalized assistance also includes income supplements that are provided by the government, family, and friends. Researchers indicate, however, that even though a considerable number of the homeless may receive some financial help from family or friends, it is usually small. Women seem to receive more help from family and friends and to remain on the streets for shorter periods than men. Cash from family and friends seems to decline with the amount of time spent on the street and with age.

Street Newspapers

In the United States, as well as in other countries, homeless people write, publish, and sell their own newspapers, which typically focus on poverty, homelessness, and related issues. Many street newspaper publishers belong to the North American Street Newspaper Association (NASNA), which was organized in Chicago in 1996. The NASNA holds an annual conference, offers business advice and services, and supports street newspaper publishers in the same way that any professional organization supports its membership. It also lobbies the government on homeless issues. As of 2013, NASNA (http://www.nasna.org/) had 31 members, 23 in the United States and eight in Canada.

Generally, the street newspapers are lent on credit to homeless vendors who then sell them for $1 each. At the end of the workday, the vendor pays the publisher the agreed-on price and pockets the remainder as profit. Although the income from selling street newspapers is unlikely, on its own, to provide a path back to permanent housing, it can provide people with crucial transitional funds as they prepare to embark on that path. Additionally, the activity of selling the newspapers can be a source of self-confidence and an aid in helping the homeless overcome the isolation they often feel. Many street newspapers accept submissions from the homeless themselves, including articles, letters, and artwork, offering an opportunity for self-expression that can further alleviate the feelings of marginalization common to many on the streets and in shelters. Finally, street newspapers dispel stereotypes about the homeless and offer a point of connection between them and the population at large.

EXITING HOMELESSNESS

According to Burt et al. in *Homelessness*, homeless people said in 1996 that the primary reason they could not exit homelessness is insufficient income. Of those clients surveyed, 54% mentioned employment-related reasons for why they remained homeless, 30% cited insufficient income, and 24% cited lack of a job.

Data used by Burt et al. show how little income the homeless earned in 1996; 81% of the "currently" homeless had incomes of less than $700 in the 30 days before the study, and the average monthly income was $367. Most of the homeless in the study were receiving their income from Aid to Families with Dependent Children (now Temporary Assistance for Needy Families). Of the formerly homeless people surveyed, the median (the middle value—half are higher and half are lower) monthly income of $470 would constitute an annual income of $5,640, an amount well below the poverty level for a single person ($7,740 in 1996). (For comparison purposes, it would be similar to earning approximately $8,410 in 2013, when the poverty level for a single person was $11,490.)

Daunting as such income barriers are to those attempting to exit homelessness, the task often requires more than income, especially in the case of the chronically homeless. Persistent medical assistance, sometimes for an entire lifetime, has to be available for the mentally ill or for people with addiction and substance abuse problems. Furthermore, without programs such as job training, assistance with general education, help with socialization skills, and counseling, the maintenance of a degree of independent life for the long term can be difficult for the chronically homeless.

Ultimately, government and other forms of assistance may be more effective at preventing homelessness in the first place than in helping to rehabilitate those who have been scarred by the traumas that come with life on the streets. In *The State of Homelessness in America 2012*, the NAEH notes that the Homelessness Prevention and Rapid Re-Housing Program created during the administration of President Barack Obama (1961–) appeared to have substantially forestalled continued increases in homelessness after the onset of the Great Recession. The program focused on preventing homelessness among those most at risk of it and on getting those on the verge of losing their homes into new homes as quickly as possible. The successes of the program demonstrated the effectiveness of addressing the risk of homelessness before it becomes a reality, but spending cuts at the national level threatened to undermine such successes and to increase the risk of homelessness for many vulnerable individuals and families.

CHAPTER 6
THE HOUSING PROBLEM

At one time a home was defined as a place where a family resided, but as American society changed, so did the definition of the term *home*. A home is now considered a place where one or more people live together, a private place to which they have legal right and where strangers may be excluded. It is the place where people keep their belongings and where they feel safe from the outside world. For housing to be considered a home, it should be permanent with an address. Furthermore, in the best of circumstances a home should not be substandard but should still be affordable. Many people would agree that a place to call home is a basic human right.

Those people who have no fixed address and no private space of their own are the homeless. The obvious solution to homelessness would be to find a home for everyone who needs one. There is enough housing available in the United States; as such, the problem lies in the affordability of that housing. Most of the housing in the United States costs far more than poor people can afford to rent or buy.

HIGH HOUSING COSTS AND HOMELESSNESS

Decades of research indicates that the primary cause of homelessness is the inability to pay for housing, which is itself caused by some combination of low income and high housing costs. Even though many other factors may contribute to homelessness, such as a low level of educational achievement or mental illness, addressing such problems will seldom bring someone out of homelessness in the absence of attention to the problem of housing affordability.

Homeless people and homeless families are similar to other poor people. Given the disparity between incomes at the lowest strata of society and the costs of housing in the 21st century, most people living near or below the poverty line are at risk of becoming homeless at least periodically. Most of the homeless, in turn, do not

stay homeless for long periods. These families and individuals are often able to return to permanent housing when they solve their income problems, for example through finding a job, or when they receive government or other assistance with housing.

For the chronically homeless, or those who experience long-term or repeated homelessness, other problems often must be addressed at the same time as housing affordability. In *The State of Homelessness in America 2012* (January 2012, http://b.3cdn.net/naeh/9892745b6de8a5ef59_q2m6yc 53b.pdf), the National Alliance to End Homelessness (NAEH) notes that in 2011 an estimated 107,148 people, or 17% of the total homeless population of 636,017, were chronically homeless (that is, they had been homeless continuously for a year or had experienced four episodes of homelessness during the previous three years). The chronically homeless have higher rates of chronic disabilities, substance abuse disorders, physical disabilities, human immunodeficiency virus (HIV), and acquired immunodeficiency syndrome (AIDS). Because of these disabilities and diseases, the only way to combat chronic homelessness, in the view of the NAEH and other advocacy groups, is by providing housing that is linked to other supportive services that address the wide array of medical and social problems with which this population struggles.

THE SCOPE OF THE HOUSING PROBLEM

The federal government establishes the official standard for low-income housing at 30% of a family's annual income. If a poor or near-poor household must spend more than 30% of its income on rent and utilities, its members risk being unable to afford other basic necessities. Low-income housing, then, is housing that is affordable to those in poverty based on this formula. In 2013 a family of two with an annual income of less than $15,510 was in poverty; a family of four was in poverty if its income was less than $23,550. (See Table 1.1 in

Chapter 1.) Thus, in 2013 a family of two generally qualified for low-income housing if its housing costs were more than 30% of $15,510 annually, or more than $387.75 per month; a family of four qualified if its housing costs were more than 30% of $23,550 annually, or more than $588.75 per month.

The price of rental units, however, has been on the rise since 1980, at the same time that the real income of renters has been declining. The Joint Center for Housing Studies (JCHS) of Harvard University finds in *The State of the Nation's Housing, 2010* (June 2010, http://www .jchs.harvard.edu/sites/jchs.harvard.edu/files/son2010.pdf) that in 2009 dollars renters in 1980 had a median (the middle value—half are higher and half are lower) income of $2,640 per month and a median gross rent (including rent and utilities) of $678. By 2009 gross rent had risen, but income had remained about the same. In that year renters had a median income of $2,664 per month and a median gross rent of $807.

According to the Census Bureau's American Community Survey, the median monthly gross rent for renter-occupied housing units was $871 in 2011. (See Table 6.1.) Although this represented a yearly rental expense of approximately 21% of the 2011 national median household income of $50,054, the median income for renters is far lower. According to the National Low Income Housing Coalition (NLIHC) in "Out of Reach 2012: Online Guide to Data Usage and Sources" (March 2012, http://nlihc.org/ sites/default/files/oor/2012-OOR-How-Where-Guide.pdf), the median income of renters was $33,363 in 2011; at this income level, the national median rent would require a household to allocate just over 31% of its income to housing. Moreover, as the NLIHC notes in *Out of Reach 2012: America's Forgotten Housing Crisis* (March 2012, http:// nlihc.org/oor/2012), one out of four renter households is classified as extremely low income. Extremely low income households had a median annual income during this time of approximately $20,210; at this income level and at the median rental price, a household would have to allot approximately 52% of its income to housing.

In 2011, according to the Census Bureau, almost half (49.3%) of all American renter households spent 30% or more of their income on housing, and well over half of all renters in California (54.5%), Connecticut (52%), Florida (56.2%), and Hawaii (53.5%) spent 30% or more of their income on housing. (See Table 6.2.) Additionally, rapidly increasing numbers of households (both renters and homeowners) were spending 50% or more of their income on housing. As the JCHS reports in *The State of the Nation's Housing, 2012*, the number of households that spent 50% or more of their income on housing and were therefore classified as having severe housing cost burdens rose by 6.4 million between 2001 and 2010. (See Figure 6.1.)

TABLE 6.1

Median monthly housing costs for renter-occupied housing units by state, 2011

Geographic area	Dollar
United States	**871**
Alabama	687
Alaska	1,049
Arizona	850
Arkansas	639
California	1,174
Colorado	900
Connecticut	1,021
Delaware	960
District of Columbia	1,216
Florida	949
Georgia	833
Hawaii	1,308
Idaho	689
Illinois	859
Indiana	707
Iowa	643
Kansas	709
Kentucky	626
Louisiana	747
Maine	747
Maryland	1,153
Massachusetts	1,034
Michigan	739
Minnesota	787
Mississippi	689
Missouri	708
Montana	650
Nebraska	673
Nevada	936
New Hampshire	939
New Jersey	1,135
New Mexico	729
New York	1,058
North Carolina	745
North Dakota	626
Ohio	692
Oklahoma	675
Oregon	840
Pennsylvania	786
Rhode Island	875
South Carolina	741
South Dakota	612
Tennessee	715
Texas	813
Utah	822
Vermont	849
Virginia	1,062
Washington	930
West Virginia	599
Wisconsin	739
Wyoming	759
Puerto Rico	442

SOURCE: Adapted from "GCT2514. Median Monthly Housing Costs for Renter-Occupied Housing Units (Dollars)," in *2011 American Community Survey 1-Year Estimates*, U.S. Census Bureau, 2012, http://factfinder2 .census.gov/faces/tableservices/jsf/pages/productview.xhtml?pid=ACS_11_ 1YR_GCT2514.US01PR&prodType=table (accessed January 22, 2013)

As Figure 6.2 shows, most of these households with severe housing cost burdens were poor or near-poor. The number of households with annual income of less than $15,000 who were severely housing cost burdened steadily rose between 2001 and 2010, from just over 8 million households to well over 10 million. By 2010, nearly 70% of all households at this income level had severe housing cost burdens. Households making between $15,000 and

TABLE 6.2

FIGURE 6.1

Percentage of renter-occupied units spending 30% or more of household income on rent and utilities, by state, 2011

Geographic area	Percent
United States	**49.3**
Alabama	46.8
Alaska	40.6
Arizona	47.4
Arkansas	45.6
California	54.5
Colorado	48.8
Connecticut	52.0
Delaware	49.8
District of Columbia	46.3
Florida	56.2
Georgia	49.6
Hawaii	53.5
Idaho	46.4
Illinois	49.2
Indiana	47.5
Iowa	43.4
Kansas	42.8
Kentucky	44.9
Louisiana	47.9
Maine	49.6
Maryland	50.6
Massachusetts	48.9
Michigan	51.0
Minnesota	47.3
Mississippi	46.3
Missouri	45.4
Montana	41.6
Nebraska	40.3
Nevada	49.3
New Hampshire	47.0
New Jersey	51.4
New Mexico	47.6
New York	51.3
North Carolina	47.9
North Dakota	38.0
Ohio	47.5
Oklahoma	43.0
Oregon	51.8
Pennsylvania	47.1
Rhode Island	47.9
South Carolina	47.3
South Dakota	35.6
Tennessee	47.0
Texas	46.1
Utah	47.8
Vermont	49.2
Virginia	46.5
Washington	48.0
West Virginia	38.7
Wisconsin	46.0
Wyoming	33.3
Puerto Rico	32.4

SOURCE: Adapted from "GCT2515. Percent of Renter-Occupied Units Spending 30 Percent or More of Household Income on Rent and Utilities," in *2011 American Community Survey 1-Year Estimates*, U.S. Census Bureau, 2012, http://factfinder2.census.gov/faces/tableservices/jsf/pages/productview .xhtml?pid=ACS_11_1YR_GCT2515.US01PR&prodType=table (accessed January 22, 2013)

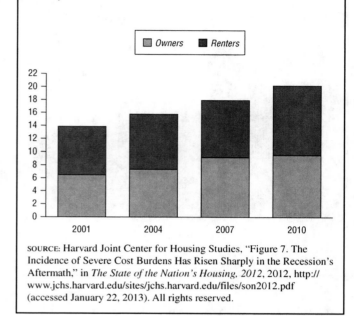

Incidence of severe housing cost burdens, selected years 2001–10

[Number of households paying more than half of pre-tax income for housing in millions]

SOURCE: Harvard Joint Center for Housing Studies, "Figure 7. The Incidence of Severe Cost Burdens Has Risen Sharply in the Recession's Aftermath," in *The State of the Nation's Housing, 2012*, 2012, http:// www.jchs.harvard.edu/sites/jchs.harvard.edu/files/son2012.pdf (accessed January 22, 2013). All rights reserved.

$29,999 a year were also disproportionately housing cost burdened. Nearly 6 million (approximately 30%) households in this income bracket had severe housing cost burdens, up from approximately 3.5 million (just over 20%) in 2001.

In *Out of Reach 2012*, the NLIHC introduces the notion of a "housing wage," or the level of income needed to obtain adequate, affordable housing in the U.S. rental market. Using the fair market rent (FMR; HUD's estimate of what a household seeking modest rental housing must expect to pay for rent and utilities) for a two-bedroom rental, the NLIHC notes that the hourly wage needed to pay for such an apartment while spending no more than 30% of one's income on rent was $18.25. However, the estimated average hourly wage of renters in the United States was $14.15, and the federal minimum wage was $7.25. The NLIHC notes that in no U.S. state was it possible in 2011 to pay for a two-bedroom FMR apartment on one minimum-wage income. The number of minimum-wage incomes necessary to afford such an apartment ranged from 1.3 in Puerto Rico to 4.4 in Hawaii. There are very few locations anywhere in the United States, moreover, where a single minimum-wage income will pay for even a one-bedroom apartment, and among extremely low income families, the odds of finding a studio or efficiency apartment in adequate repair are minimal. For a blind, disabled, or elderly person dependent on SSI, for example, there was not a single county in the United States where even the most modest of fair-market efficiency apartments was affordable in 2011.

Since 1991 HUD has released biannual reports to Congress on those renters who have what the agency terms "worst case housing needs." Renters with worst case needs are, according to the HUD definition, those with incomes below 50% of the area median income (the median income in the locality in which the individual

FIGURE 6.2

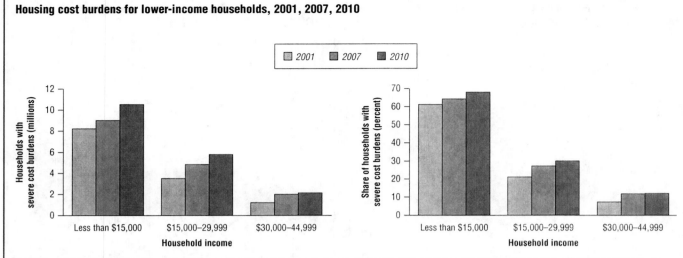

Housing cost burdens for lower-income households, 2001, 2007, 2010

Notes: Households with severe cost burdens spend more than 50 percent of pre-tax income on housing costs. Incomes are in constant 2010 dollars, adjusted for inflation by the Consumer Price Index for All Urban Consumers (CPI-U) for All Items.

SOURCE: Harvard Joint Center for Housing Studies, "Figure 31. The Great Recession Brought Housing Cost Burdens to Many More Lower-Income Households," in *The State of the Nation's Housing, 2012*, 2012, http://www.jchs.harvard.edu/sites/jchs.harvard.edu/files/son2012.pdf (accessed January 22, 2013).

lives) who receive no housing assistance from the government and who pay more than half of their income for housing, live in substandard conditions, or experience both of these housing problems. HUD's findings in *Worst Case Housing Needs 2011: A Report to Congress* (February 22, 2013, http://www.huduser.org/Publications/pdf/HUD-506_WorstCase2011.pdf) support the dire assessments of the JCHS and the NLIHC.

The HUD authors note that between 2009 and 2011 the overall economy was slowly recovering from the so-called Great Recession that began in 2007, but that the benefits of recovery had not begun to reach low-income renters. In fact, HUD notes, there had been "dramatic increases in worst case housing needs during the 2009–2011 period that cut across demographic groups, household types, and regions. This rise in hardship among renters is due to substantial increases in rental housing demand and weakening incomes that increase competition for already-scarce affordable units."

Between 2007 and 2011, the agency finds, the number of renters with worst case needs grew by an unprecedented 43.5%, from 5.9 million to 8.5 million. (See Figure 6.3.) Only 3% of those designated as having worst case needs qualified for the designation because of the inadequacy of their housing; 97% qualified because they were paying more than half of their income for rent. The increase in worst case housing needs affected virtually all household types and demographic groups. Among those with worst case needs in 2011, there were 3.2 million families with children, 1.5 million elderly households, and 3 million nonfamily households (households consisting of nonrelated

FIGURE 6.3

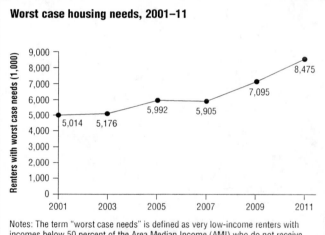

Worst case housing needs, 2001–11

Notes: The term "worst case needs" is defined as very low-income renters with incomes below 50 percent of the Area Median Income (AMI) who do not receive government housing assistance and who either paid more than half of their income for rent or lived in severely in adequate conditions, or who faced both of these challenges. The Department of Housing and Urban Development's (HUD's) estimates of worst case needs are based primarily on data from the American Housing Survey (AHS).

SOURCE: "Exhibit 1. Growth in Worst Case Housing Needs, 2001–2011," in *Worst Case Housing Needs 2011: Report to Congress, Summary*, U.S. Department of Housing and Urban Development, February 2013, http://www.huduser.org/Publications/pdf/HUD-506_WorstCase2011.pdf (accessed February 22, 2013)

people). Approximately one in six households with worst case housing needs in 2011 included a nonelderly disabled member, and such cases were rising dramatically. Between 2009 and 2011, the number of households both including a disabled person and experiencing worst case housing needs grew from 990,000 to 1.3 million.

TABLE 6.3

Existing one-family homes sold and price, by region, 1990–2010

[2,914 represents 2,914,000. Includes existing detached single-family homes and townhomes; excludes condos and co-ops. Based on data (adjusted and aggregated to regional and national totals) reported by participating real estate multiple listing services.]

Year	Homes sold (1,000)					Median sales price (dollars)				
	U.S.	Northeast	Midwest	South	West	U.S.	Northeast	Midwest	South	West
1990	2,914	513	804	1,008	589	97,300	146,200	76,700	86,300	141,200
1992	3,151	577	907	1,047	620	105,500	149,000	84,600	92,900	143,300
1993	3,427	614	961	1,167	685	109,100	149,300	87,600	95,800	144,400
1994	3,544	618	961	1,213	752	113,500	149,300	90,900	97,200	151,900
1995	3,519	615	940	1,212	752	117,000	146,500	96,500	99,200	153,600
1996	3,797	656	986	1,283	872	122,600	147,800	102,800	105,000	160,200
1997	3,964	683	1,004	1,356	921	129,000	152,400	108,900	111,300	169,000
1998	4,495	745	1,129	1,592	1,029	136,000	157,100	116,300	118,000	179,500
1999	4,649	728	1,145	1,704	1,072	141,200	160,700	121,600	122,100	189,400
2000	4,603	715	1,116	1,707	1,065	147,300	161,200	125,600	130,300	199,200
2001	4,735	710	1,154	1,795	1,076	156,600	169,400	132,300	139,600	211,700
2002	4,974	730	1,217	1,872	1,155	167,600	190,100	138,300	149,700	234,300
2003	5,446	770	1,323	2,073	1,280	180,200	220,300	143,700	159,700	254,700
2004	5,958	821	1,389	2,310	1,438	195,200	254,400	151,500	171,800	289,100
2005	6,180	838	1,411	2,457	1,474	219,000	281,600	168,300	181,100	340,300
2006	5,677	787	1,314	2,352	1,224	221,900	280,300	164,800	183,700	350,500
2007	4,939	723	1,181	2,053	982	217,900	288,100	161,400	178,800	342,500
2008	4,350	623	1,022	1,721	984	196,600	271,500	150,500	169,400	276,100
2009	4,566	641	1,067	1,745	1,113	172,100	243,200	142,900	155,000	215,400
2010	4,308	604	984	1,669	1,051	173,100	243,900	140,800	153,700	220,700

SOURCE: "Table 977. Existing One-Family Homes Sold and Price by Region: 1990 to 2010," in *The 2012 Statistical Abstract: The National Data Book*, U.S. Census Bureau, June 27, 2012, http://www.census.gov/compendia/statab/2012/tables/12s0978.pdf (accessed February 21, 2013). Data from National Association of Realtors, *Real Estate Outlook: Market Trends & Insights*.

Even with the decrease in home values brought about by the Great Recession, homeownership remained well beyond the reach of most low-income families. As Table 6.3 shows, the median price of existing one-family homes in the United States, which cost less on average than newly constructed homes, was $173,100 in 2010. Typically, a qualified homebuyer must pay 20% of his or her income in the form of a down payment. At the median 2010 sales price, then, a buyer would need $34,620 in cash to secure a loan. Then, depending on current interest rates for mortgages, which fluctuate over time, the same homeowner could expect to pay between $750 and $1,200 per month, not including property taxes, insurance, and other fees. The median sales price of existing apartments, whether condominiums or co-ops, was only marginally less than that of existing one-family homes, at $171,700 in 2010. (See Table 6.4.)

THE SHORTAGE OF AFFORDABLE HOUSING

In December 2000 Congress established the bipartisan Millennial Housing Commission to examine the role of the federal government in meeting the nation's housing needs. In *Meeting Our Nation's Housing Challenges* (May 30, 2002, http://permanent.access.gpo.gov/lps19766/www.mhc.gov/mhcfinal.pdf), the commission states that "there is simply not enough affordable housing. The inadequacy of supply increases dramatically as one moves down the ladder of family earnings. The challenge is most acute for rental housing in high-cost areas, and the most egregious problem is for the very poor."

In *Worst Case Housing Needs 2011*, HUD indicates that the supply of affordable housing for those renters at the lowest end of the income scale had been decreasing since 2003. (See Figure 6.4.) In 2011 only 65 units of adequate and affordable rental housing were available for every 100 very low-income renters and that only 36 such units were available for every 100 extremely low-income renters. This scarcity was worst in central cities and suburbs. HUD notes that the major causes of the increases in worst-case needs among very-low-income renters were shrinking incomes due to unemployment, a growing lack of federal rental assistance, and competition for affordable units. HUD further observes that competition for rental units increased primarily due to the foreclosure crisis and the high rate of unemployment, both of which persisted well beyond the end of the Great Recession. Although most of those who lost their homes were not at the lowest end of the income scale, almost all of them subsequently entered the rental market, increasing the competition and, as a consequence, the prices for rental homes and apartments. Likewise, many of those who lost their jobs during the recession went from being homeowners to being renters.

The JCHS reports in *State of the Nation's Housing, 2012* the number of renters earning $15,000 per year (roughly equivalent to a year's full-time employment at minimum wage) or less increased by 2.2 million in the years 2001 through 2010. During the same period, the number of rental units that people in this income group could afford declined by 470,000. (See Figure 6.5.) In 2001, there were 8.1 million

TABLE 6.4

Existing condos and co-ops, units sold and median sales price, by region, 1990–2010

[272 represents 272,000. Data shown here reflect revisions from prior estimates.]

	Units sold (1,000)					Median sales price (dollars)				
Year	U.S.	Northeast	Midwest	South	West	U.S.	Northeast	Midwest	South	West
1990	272	73	55	80	64	86,900	107,500	70,200	64,200	114,600
1995	333	108	66	96	63	89,000	92,500	90,700	67,800	114,800
2000	571	197	106	160	108	114,000	108,500	121,700	84,200	149,100
2003	732	250	146	211	125	168,500	178,100	162,600	126,900	222,400
2004	820	292	161	230	137	197,100	214,100	181,000	156,600	258,000
2005	896	331	177	245	143	223,900	245,100	189,100	187,300	283,800
2006	801	299	169	211	122	221,900	249,700	190,900	184,000	264,700
2007	713	283	146	182	102	226,300	256,100	195,200	185,100	263,300
2008	563	226	107	144	86	209,800	252,500	188,200	166,800	218,500
2009	590	227	96	169	98	175,600	232,800	157,100	132,700	162,100
2010	599	213	92	191	103	171,700	242,200	150,500	118,500	154,700

SOURCE: "Table 980. Existing Apartment Condos and Co-Ops—Units Sold and Median Sales Price by Region: 1990 to 2010," in *The 2012 Statistical Abstract: The National Data Book*, U.S. Census Bureau, June 27, 2012, http://www.census.gov/compendia/statab/2012/tables/12s0980.pdf (accessed February 21, 2013). Data from National Association of Realtors, *Real Estate Outlook; Market Trends & Insights*.

FIGURE 6.4

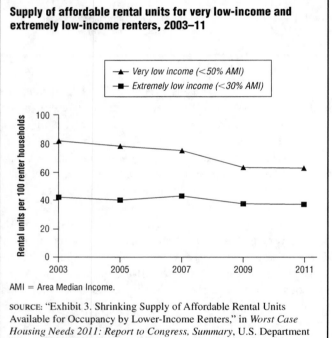

Supply of affordable rental units for very low-income and extremely low-income renters, 2003–11

AMI = Area Median Income.

SOURCE: "Exhibit 3. Shrinking Supply of Affordable Rental Units Available for Occupancy by Lower-Income Renters," in *Worst Case Housing Needs 2011: Report to Congress, Summary*, U.S. Department of Housing and Urban Development, February 2013, http://www.huduser.org/Publications/pdf/HUD-506_WorstCase2011.pdf (accessed February 22, 2013)

FIGURE 6.5

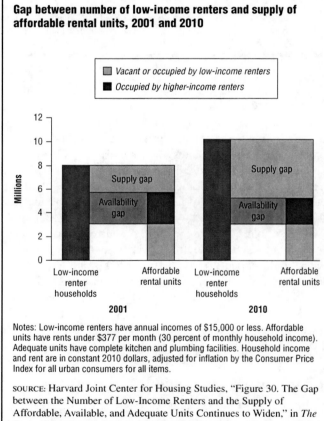

Gap between number of low-income renters and supply of affordable rental units, 2001 and 2010

Notes: Low-income renters have annual incomes of $15,000 or less. Affordable units have rents under $377 per month (30 percent of monthly household income). Adequate units have complete kitchen and plumbing facilities. Household income and rent are in constant 2010 dollars, adjusted for inflation by the Consumer Price Index for all urban consumers for all items.

SOURCE: Harvard Joint Center for Housing Studies, "Figure 30. The Gap between the Number of Low-Income Renters and the Supply of Affordable, Available, and Adequate Units Continues to Widen," in *The State of the Nation's Housing, 2012*, 2012, http://www.jchs.harvard.edu/sites/jchs.harvard.edu/files/son2012.pdf (accessed January 22, 2013). All rights reserved.

low-income renters and 5.7 million suitable rental units, and in 2010 there were more than 10.3 million low-income renters and 5.2 million suitable units. Compounding the problem, approximately 40% of the available affordable rental units were occupied by high-income renters in 2010.

The JCHS further notes that between 1999 and 2009, approximately 30% of rental units that cost less than $400 had been demolished or otherwise permanently removed from the low-cost housing market. Although the conventional wisdom suggests that over time, rents at a given property tend to decline due to wear and tear and other factors, allowing for a continuous supply of affordable rentals, this was not the case in aggregate over the decade 1999 to 2009. During that time, for every two units with asking prices that decreased so that they became affordable to low-income households, three units saw their rents increased so that they moved out of the affordable category.

The limited availability of affordable housing is a problem across the nation. According to Christiana McFarland, Casey Dawkins, and C. Theodore Koebel in *The State of America's Cities 2007, Local Housing Conditions and Contexts: A Framework for Policy Making* (2007), 32% of city officials believed general housing affordability was a major problem in their area and another 49% believed it was a moderate problem.

FEDERALLY SUBSIDIZED HOUSING

The federal government, operating primarily through HUD, has a number of housing programs that help poor and low-income people. Subsidized housing, like other social welfare programs aimed specifically at low-income individuals and families, is means-tested, or based on income thresholds. The qualifying income level—much like the definition of poverty—changes over time. Beneficiaries of housing assistance never receive cash outright. The benefits are therefore labeled "means-tested noncash benefits." In 2009, 11.1 million people, or 3.7% of the population, lived in subsidized housing. (See Table 6.5.)

HUD operates many different kinds of subsidized-housing programs, but there are two basic forms of subsidies: vouchers and public housing. There are, further, two main types of voucher programs: tenant based and project based. In tenant-based programs the voucher stays with the tenant when the tenant moves to another qualifying unit. In project-based programs the voucher is attached to a particular housing project and remains available for a new tenant when a unit is vacant. Families are directed to participating projects after they qualify. Tenants cannot automatically transfer their voucher from one project-based dwelling to another, but they may qualify for another tenant-based voucher after they move. Tenant-based vouchers have increasingly become the most common mechanism for delivering federal housing subsidies.

In its proposed 2013 budget, HUD allocated $16.7 billion of its total net budget of $44 billion to tenant-based rental assistance. Another $8.4 billion was allotted to project-based rental assistance, and $4.5 billion to the operating fund for the agency's public housing programs. When other ancillary expenditures in each of these core HUD program areas are tallied, the totals come to $19 billion for tenant-based programs, and $8.7 billion for project-based programs. (See Figure 6.6.) About $6.6 billion was earmarked for rental assistance and public housing programs.

TABLE 6.5

Persons living in households receiving selected noncash benefits, 2009

[In thousands (303,820 represents 303,820,000), except percent. Persons, as of March 2010, who lived with someone (a nonrelative or a relative) who received aid. Not every person tallied here received the aid themselves. Persons living in households receiving more than one type of aid are counted only once. Excludes members of the armed forces except those living off post or with their families on post. Population controls for 2009 based on Census 2000 and an expanded sample of households. Based on Current Population Survey.]

Age, sex, and race	Total	In household that received means-tested assistance[a]		In household that received means-tested cash assistance		In household that received food stamps		In household in which one or more persons were covered by Medicaid		Lived in public or authorized housing	
		Number	Percent	Number	Percent	Number	Percent	Number	Percent	Number	Percent
Total	303,820	92,005	30.3	19,608	6.5	34,377	11.3	74,457	24.5	11,098	3.7
Under 18 years	74,579	33,565	45.0	5,666	7.6	13,917	18.7	27,748	37.2	3,989	5.3
18 to 24 years	29,313	9,886	33.7	1,985	6.8	3,786	12.9	8,119	27.7	1,251	4.3
25 to 34 years	41,085	13,081	31.8	2,337	5.7	5,230	12.7	10,839	26.4	1,366	3.3
35 to 44 years	40,447	11,519	28.5	2,131	5.3	3,836	9.5	9,035	22.3	1,027	2.5
45 to 54 years	44,387	10,174	22.9	2,754	6.2	3,450	7.8	8,051	18.1	1,070	2.4
55 to 59 years	19,172	3,693	19.3	1,425	7.4	1,227	6.4	2,949	15.4	475	2.5
60 to 64 years	16,223	2,921	18.0	1,120	6.9	941	5.8	2,302	14.2	427	2.6
65 years and over	38,613	7,167	18.6	2,190	5.7	1,990	5.2	5,414	14.0	1,493	3.9
65 to 74 years	20,956	3,901	18.6	1,229	5.9	1,127	5.4	3,046	14.5	727	3.5
75 years and over	17,657	3,266	18.5	962	5.4	862	4.9	2,367	13.4	766	4.3
Male	149,237	43,163	28.9	9,087	6.1	15,242	10.2	34,954	23.4	4,388	2.9
Female	154,582	48,842	31.6	10,521	6.8	19,135	12.4	39,503	25.6	6,710	4.3
White alone[b]	242,047	64,190	26.5	12,420	5.1	21,966	9.1	52,480	21.7	5,618	2.3
Black alone[b]	38,556	19,606	50.9	5,252	13.6	9,666	25.1	15,197	39.4	4,445	11.5
Asian alone[b]	14,005	3,907	27.9	788	5.6	801	5.7	3,254	23.2	353	2.5
Hispanic[c]	48,811	26,037	53.3	4,246	8.7	9,200	18.8	21,359	43.8	2,311	4.7
White alone, non-Hispanic[b]	197,164	40,398	20.5	8,688	4.4	13,664	6.9	32,967	16.7	3,667	1.9

[a]Means-tested assistance includes means-tested cash assistance, food stamps, Medicaid, and public or authorized housing.
[b]Refers to people who reported specific race and did not report any other race category.
[c]People of Hispanic origin may be of any race.

SOURCE: "Table 543. Persons Living in Households Receiving Selected Noncash Benefits: 2009," in *Statistical Abstract of the United States: 2012*, U.S. Census Bureau, August 31, 2012, http://www.census.gov/compendia/statab/2012edition.html (accessed January 22, 2013)

FIGURE 6.6

Funding levels for major U.S. Department of Housing and Urban Development (HUD) programs, 2012 and 2013

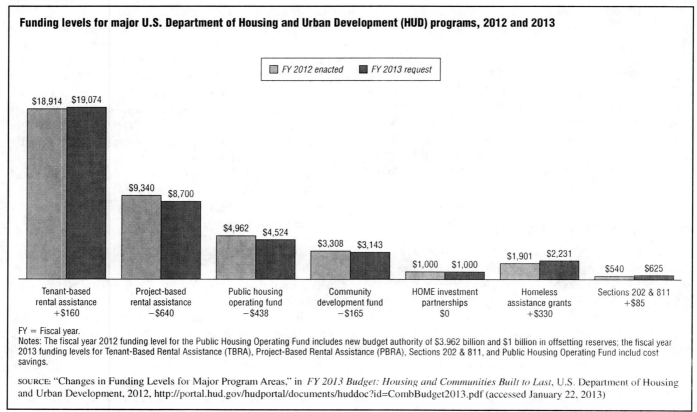

FY = Fiscal year.
Notes: The fiscal year 2012 funding level for the Public Housing Operating Fund includes new budget authority of $3.962 billion and $1 billion in offsetting reserves; the fiscal year 2013 funding levels for Tenant-Based Rental Assistance (TBRA), Project-Based Rental Assistance (PBRA), Sections 202 & 811, and Public Housing Operating Fund includ cost savings.

SOURCE: "Changes in Funding Levels for Major Program Areas," in *FY 2013 Budget: Housing and Communities Built to Last*, U.S. Department of Housing and Urban Development, 2012, http://portal.hud.gov/hudportal/documents/huddoc?id=CombBudget2013.pdf (accessed January 22, 2013)

Vouchers

Voucher programs, which make up the bulk of HUD's efforts to provide housing for low-income Americans, pay a portion of the rent for qualifying families. Only low-income families are eligible, specifically those with incomes lower than half of an area's median income. Under some circumstances, families with up to 80% of the local median income may also qualify; such cases may involve, for example, families that have been displaced by public housing demolition. The family pays 30% of its income toward the rent, and the voucher covers the remaining balance. Vouchers are issued by the local public housing agency (PHA), which executes assistance contracts with the landlord, who must also qualify.

Besides these two basic programs, HUD also has five other voucher programs. Conversion vouchers are used to help tenants relocate when public housing is demolished. Family unification vouchers are used to help families stay together. Homeownership vouchers assist families in purchasing a first home or another home if the family has not lived in a house in the past three years. Participants must be employed and have an income of at least minimum wage. Vouchers for people with disabilities and welfare-to-work vouchers assist the elderly or nonelderly disabled and families transitioning from welfare to work.

In all these programs the housing supplied is privately owned and operated, and the rents paid are at or below the

FMR. HUD determines the FMR in every locality of the nation by an annual survey of new rental contracts that have been signed during the past 15 months. In most cities the FMR is set at the 40th percentile of rents paid, meaning that 40% of renters paid a lower rent and 60% paid a higher rent; in certain cities the FMR is calculated at the 50th percentile. HUD has chosen the 40th percentile to increase housing choices while keeping budgets at reasonable levels. Table 6.6 presents the FMRs that were used by HUD in a sample of small and large cities throughout the country in 2013.

Of the cities shown in Table 6.6, the city with the highest average FMR was Honolulu, Hawaii, which had the country's highest FMR at the studio ($1,276), two-bedroom ($1,833), three-bedroom ($2,701), and four-bedroom ($3,100) price points. San Francisco, California, had the highest FMR for one-bedroom apartments, at $1,423. At the other end of the scale, Bismarck, North Dakota, had the lowest 2013 FMR levels of all the cities included, at all price points. The FMR for a studio in Bismarck was $443; for a one-bedroom apartment, $502; for a two-bedroom, $628; for a three-bedroom, $890; and for a four-bedroom, $1,050.

According to HUD's *Resident Characteristics Report* (2013, https://pic.hud.gov/pic/RCRPublic/rcrmain.asp), the average annual income for recipients of all types of vouchers was $12,770 between 2011 and 2013. Approximately

TABLE 6.6

Fair market rental rates for selected metropolitan areas, fiscal year 2013

Area definition	0 bedroom	1 bedroom	2 bedroom	3 bedroom	4 bedroom
Bismarck, ND	$443	$502	$628	$890	$1,050
Cincinnati-Middleton, OH-KY-IN	$445	$557	$740	$1,025	$1,129
Lexington-Fayette, KY	$458	$535	$700	$997	$1,116
Kansas City, MO-KS	$491	$632	$783	$1,073	$1,195
Albuquerque, NM	$507	$637	$780	$1,129	$1,381
Salt Lake City, UT	$564	$677	$839	$1,197	$1,408
Memphis, TN-MS-AR	$567	$648	$768	$1,049	$1,170
Dallas, TX	$585	$701	$887	$1,183	$1,429
Minneapolis-St. Paul-Bloomington, MN-WI	$592	$736	$920	$1,296	$1,529
Charlotte-Gastonia-Rock Hill, NC-SC	$607	$669	$793	$1,069	$1,326
Ann Arbor, MI	$630	$760	$901	$1,232	$1,596
New Orleans-Metairie-Kenner, LA	$637	$755	$935	$1,173	$1,420
Atlanta-Sandy Springs-Marietta, GA	$676	$737	$874	$1,158	$1,406
Portland, ME	$685	$816	$1,008	$1,334	$1,401
Las Vegas-Paradise, NV	$691	$864	$1,064	$1,568	$1,861
Gulfport-Biloxi, MS	$692	$714	$857	$1,102	$1,174
Orlando-Kissimmee-Sanford, FL	$697	$825	$983	$1,311	$1,586
Chicago-Joliet-Naper ville, IL	$717	$815	$966	$1,231	$1,436
Flagstaff, AZ	$733	$852	$1,066	$1,353	$1,724
Anchorage, AK	$745	$862	$1,104	$1,627	$1,955
Seattle-Bellevue, WA	$758	$897	$1,104	$1,627	$1,955
Philadelphia-Camden-Wilmington, PA-NJ-DE-MD	$788	$929	$1,119	$1,394	$1,496
Baltimore-Towson, MD	$846	$1,000	$1,251	$1,598	$1,740
Los Angeles-Long Beach, CA	$911	$1,101	$1,421	$1,921	$2,140
Boston-Cambridge-Quincy, MA-NH	$1,035	$1,156	$1,444	$1,798	$1,955
San Francisco, CA	$1,093	$1,423	$1,795	$2,438	$2,948
Washington-Arlington-Alexandria, DC-VA-MD	$1,130	$1,191	$1,412	$1,890	$2,374
New York, NY	$1,191	$1,243	$1,474	$1,895	$2,124
Honolulu, HI	$1,276	$1,392	$1,833	$2,701	$3,100

SOURCE: Adapted from "Schedule B. FY2013 Final Fair Market Rents for Existing Housing," in *Fair Market Rents*, U.S. Department of Housing and Urban Development, 2013, http://www.huduser.org/datasets/fmr/fmr2013f/FY2013F_SCHEDULE_B.pdf (accessed January 22, 2013)

69% of voucher recipients were classified as extremely low income, with incomes below 30% of their area's median; 18% were classified as very low income, with incomes below 50% of their area's median; 3% were classified as low income, with incomes below 80% of their area's median; and a fraction of a percent were classified as above low income, with incomes above 81% of their area's median. (There were no income data in the report for 9% of voucher recipients.)

During the first decade of the 21st century there was a pronounced shift of the subsidized population from public housing toward voucher housing. This represented a major change in the direction of federal policy, and in the view of many analysts, it foreshadows a continued shift toward increased privatization of housing subsidies. Among voucher types, tenant-based programs are least dependent on nonmarket forces; they do not require the participation of developers, many of whom complain that the construction and maintenance of low-income housing is less profitable than other types of construction. Tenant-based vouchers also give low-income people choices in housing, allowing poor families to be more flexible in the pursuit of job opportunities. Tenant-based voucher recipients can move to areas with better opportunities and transportation options, and in the aggregate this offers possibilities to avoid one of the unintended negative effects of public housing and some project-based subsi-

dies: the concentration and entrenchment of poverty in certain urban areas.

Public Housing

Although much maligned due to perceived failures in planning and upkeep—and not considered as central to HUD's mission as in earlier decades—the agency's provision of public housing remained an important source of assistance to some of the poorest U.S. families and individuals as of 2013. According to the agency's *Resident Characteristics Report*, nearly a million households with approximately 2.1 million members and an average annual income of $13,661 lived in public housing overseen by HUD between 2011 and 2013. Of these households, 68% were classified as extremely low income, with incomes below 30% of their area's median; 19% were classified as very low income, with income below 50% of their area's median; 8% were classified as low income, with incomes below 80% of their area's median; and 3% were classified as above low income, with incomes above 81% of their area's median. (There were no income data in the report for 2% of households residing in public housing.)

The management of public housing is handled by PHAs (sometimes called housing authorities) that have been established by local governments to administer HUD housing programs. The U.S. Housing Act of 1937 required that PHAs submit annual plans to HUD and declared that it was the policy of the United States "to vest in public housing agencies that perform well, the maximum amount of responsibility and flexibility in program administration, with appropriate accountability to public housing residents, localities, and the general public."

Thus, PHAs operate under plans that are approved by HUD and under HUD supervision, and the HUD budget's allotment to public housing programs flows through these PHAs. However, the PHAs are also expected to operate with some independence and to be accountable to their residents, local (or state) governments, and the public.

Not all PHAs have performed well, and HUD has been accused of lax supervision. PHAs and public housing generally reflect the distressed economic conditions of the population living in government-owned housing. Many PHAs have been charged with neglecting maintenance, tolerating unsafe living conditions for tenants, and conducting fraudulent or careless financial practices. In an effort to improve its accountability for the conditions of low-income housing, HUD implemented the Public Housing Assessment System (PHAS) in January 2000. The PHAS is used to measure the performance of PHAs. The assessment system consists of four primary components:

- Ensure, through physical inspection, that PHAs meet the minimum standard of being decent, safe, sanitary, and in good repair

- Oversee the finances of PHAs

- Evaluate the effectiveness of the management of PHAs

- Receive feedback from PHA residents on housing conditions

The U.S. Government Accountability Office (GAO) finds in "Major Management Challenges at the Department of Housing and Urban Development" (February 8, 2005, http://www.gao.gov/pas/2005/hud.htm) that in 2005 HUD continued to have major problems addressing the effective management of PHAs. It had made progress since implementing the PHAS. However, because "some of HUD's corrective actions are still in the early stages of implementation and additional steps are needed to resolve ongoing problems," its rental housing assistance programs remained "high risk." Nevertheless, David G. Wood of the GAO's Financial Markets and Community Investments notes in *Public Housing: Information on the Roles of HUD, Public Housing Agencies, Capital Markets, and Service Organizations* (February 15, 2006, http://www.gao.gov/new.items/d06419t.pdf) that in many cases HUD's enforcement actions against troubled PHAs (e.g., technical assistance and training or sanctions such as withholding of funding) resulted in some improvements.

In *Public Housing: HUD's Oversight of Housing Agencies Should Focus More on Inappropriate Use of Program Funds* (June 2009, http://www.gao.gov/new

.items/d0933.pdf), the GAO determines that HUD's reliance on single audits and the PHAS to identify inappropriate use and mismanagement of public housing funds limits HUD's ability to identify at-risk PHAs. For example, the GAO notes that between 2002 and 2006, 200 PHAs had written checks exceeding the amounts in their checking accounts by $25,000 or more. However, 75% of these agencies had received passing PHAS scores, raising questions about not only serious management issues by PHAs but also HUD's ability to adequately oversee them.

Other Housing Assistance Programs

In addition to its main voucher programs and public housing, HUD operates programs offering subsidized housing for people living with AIDS, elderly people, Native Americans and Native Hawaiians, and people with disabilities. The Prisoner Reentry Initiative, begun in 2005, helps former prisoners find housing and receive job training and other services.

Other federal programs aim to increase privately owned low-income housing stock. HUD's Federal Housing Administration (FHA) offers mortgage insurance for multifamily projects, tax credits to housing developers who provide a portion of their projects at low rents, and a Community Development Block Grant program that is used to rehabilitate housing within urban communities that have people with low and moderate income.

HUD maintains demographic and income data only on participants in its major programs. For that reason, information on the characteristics of participants in many other HUD subsidy programs aimed at low-income people is unavailable.

Rural Housing Programs

The U.S. Department of Agriculture's Rural Housing Service (RHS) administers a variety of rural housing programs. These programs make federal money available for housing in rural areas, which are considered places with populations of 50,000 or less. Eligibility for rural rental assistance is similar to that of subsidized urban programs. Other RHS programs include grants or low-interest loans to repair substandard housing, subsidized mortgages and down-payment assistance for low-income home ownership, and loans that help developers build multifamily housing for low-income residents. According to the *USDA Rural Development 2012 Progress Report* (March 1, 2013, http://www.rurdev.usda.gov/SupportDocuments/RD2012Progress Report.pdf), the USDA helps an average of 40,000 to 50,000 rural Americans purchase homes and offers subsidized housing to another 450,000 each year.

The RHS, like HUD, has been plagued by accusations of mismanagement. In "Rural Housing Service: Overview of Program Issues" (March 10, 2005, http://www.gao.gov/highlights/d05382thigh.pdf), the GAO states that "several issues prevent the agency from making the best use of resources," including the policy of grandfathering communities (which inhibits an accurate determination of metropolitan versus rural areas), the consistent overestimation of the RHS's rental assistance budget needs, insufficiently monitoring the use of the agency's funds, and the implementation of inaccurate data collection methods.

In *Rural Housing Service: Opportunities Exist to Strengthen Farm Labor Housing Program Management and Oversight* (March 2011, http://www.gao.gov/new .items/d11329.pdf), the GAO looks specifically at the Farm Labor Housing Loan and Grant Program, which supports the development of affordable housing for farm workers. The GAO finds the same type of management problems in this program that it has found in other RHS programs. The GAO states that the "RHS management processes have hindered the agency's ability to assure farmworkers access to decent and safe housing and compliance with program requirements." Specifically, the GAO notes that the RHS has difficulty determining whether farm labor housing borrowers are in compliance and that enforcement measures to bring borrowers back in compliance are insufficient. Also, because the RHS routinely overestimates its costs, it does not make available the full amount of low-interest financing to potential borrowers.

FORECLOSURE PREVENTION PROGRAMS

With the collapse of the housing market during the Great Recession, millions of Americans saw the values of their homes drop below what they owed on their mortgages, leaving it difficult or impossible to refinance or sell their homes. Even though the recession ended in mid-2009, many U.S. homeowners continued to struggle making their mortgage payments due to persistently high rates of unemployment, and as a result, foreclosures remained high for years afterward. Janna Herron reports in "Highest Number of Foreclosures in Forecast" (Associated Press, January 14, 2011) that more people were expected to lose their homes in 2011 than in any year since the crisis began. In *The State of the Nation's Housing, 2012*, the JCHS points to signs that the foreclosure epidemic had begun to abate by early 2012, as the share of mortgage loans that were 90 or more days delinquent had fallen from a high of 5.1% of mortgages to 3.1% in the first quarter of 2012. Nevertheless, the backlog of pending foreclosures, consisting in large part of borrowers who had not made payments in a year or more, remained high. Several new federal programs were established during and after the Great Recession to respond to the foreclosure crisis.

The FHA put in place an early delinquency intervention program to help up to 400,000 homeowners avoid foreclosure. Through the agency, lenders could offer formal forbearance agreements (agreements that lending institutions will delay foreclosing on a loan provided the borrowers perform certain agreed-on terms and conditions) to borrowers who were under 90 days in default of their loans. Loss mitigation (the process of attempting to collect past-due mortgage payments) programs were also put in place by the FHA to assist an additional 300,000 homeowners. Mortgage modifications, pre-foreclosure sales, and special forbearance agreements were also offered by the early delinquency intervention program.

A joint program offered by HUD and the U.S. Department of the Treasury, the Making Home Affordable program, was aimed at helping homeowners refinance or modify mortgages to make them more affordable. Part of the program was designed to specifically assist borrowers who owed more on their mortgage than their home was worth. In addition, HUD reoriented its free counseling programs that had previously helped consumers make well-informed decisions about taking on mortgages. By fiscal year (FY) 2010 most counseling services were geared toward helping homeowners avoid foreclosure.

In *Fiscal Years 2012–2013 Annual Performance Plan* (February 2012, http://portal.hud.gov/hudportal/documents/ huddoc?id=FY12-FY13APP.pdf), HUD notes that, between the onset of the Great Recession and early 2012, it had offered foreclosure relief to approximately 1.3 million homeowners by helping them refinance their mortgage loans. The agency also helped another 900,000 homeowners through its loss mitigation programs and its early delinquency interventions. HUD's goal through 2013 was to help another 700,000 troubled homeowners avoid foreclosure.

DIFFICULTIES IN MEETING HOUSING NEEDS

As HUD observes in *Worst Case Housing Needs 2011*, the scale of the housing problems faced by low-income renters in early 2013 was unprecedented. Increasing numbers of households with eroding incomes faced mounting competition for rental properties. Although subsidized housing had a good track record of providing basic security for low-income individuals and families, the existing government programs were incapable of meeting the needs of the country's poorest citizens. For every very low-income household that had rental assistance, there were two very-low-income households with worst case needs that could not obtain rental assistance. In spite of the high level of need, the political climate in the wake of the Great Recession tended more toward concerns about reducing government spending than toward expanding programs to aid vulnerable members of society.

Available Rental Assistance

The poor essentially have two options when pursuing rental assistance: low-income housing units that are operated by local PHAs and privately owned housing, whose owners accept Section 8 rental assistance vouchers (also called Housing Choice vouchers). The vouchers pay the difference between 30% of the renter's income and the fair market value of the rental. However, there are concerns that HUD is not committed to keeping private owners in the Section 8 program. The GAO indicates in *Project-Based Rental Assistance: HUD Should Update Its Policies and Procedures to Keep Pace with the Changing Housing Market* (April 2007, http://www.gao.gov/products/GAO-07-290) that between 2001 and 2005 only 92% of Section 8 rental assistance contracts were renewed, and even among those contracts that were renewed, there were 5% fewer units covered. Owners who left Section 8 did so to "seek higher rents in the private market or to convert their units into condominiums." According to the GAO, rents permitted under the voucher program have not kept pace with actual rents in many markets. The GAO suggests that some HUD policies, such as the one-for-one replacement policy that does not allow owners to reduce the total number of units in a property when a contract is renewed and therefore does not allow them to reconfigure a property and offer larger units, may compel private owners to leave the program. In addition, adjustments to rent are slow, administrative costs are high, and subsidy payments are often late, forcing some owners to leave the program. The GAO recommends that HUD modify some of its policies and address other concerns of private owners in the program to preserve Section 8 rental stock.

WAITING LISTS. Low-income people hoping for housing assistance from the federal government face other formidable obstacles, as well. Section 8 and public housing waiting lists are long and often closed in surveyed cities. For example, as reported in *Chicago Breaking News* ("Public Housing Wait List to Reopen after 10 Years," May 10, 2010), the Chicago Housing Authority reopened its waiting list for public housing between June 14 and July 9, 2010; it was the first time families could put themselves on the waiting list since 1999. Similarly, according to the New York City Housing Authority in *About NYCHA: Fact Sheet* (March 28, 2013, http://www.nyc.gov/html/nycha/html/about/factsheet.shtml), there were 167,353 families on the waiting list for public housing and 123,533 families on the waiting list for Section 8 housing as of March 27, 2013. The number of families waiting for public housing nearly equaled the number of total available public-housing apartments in the city (178,914 as of March 1, 2013), and the number of families on the Section 8 list exceed the number of apartments that were then rented through the Section 8 program in the city (92,561 as of January 1, 2013). Although 23,319 applicants were on both waiting lists, the mismatch between the supply of housing assistance and the unmet need for it was unmistakable.

Declining Housing Stock

The contracts that HUD establishes with private owners limit profits and often limit the monies that are put back into the property for repairs. As a result, the existing housing that is available to renters at the lowest income levels often suffers from a lack of upkeep. Neglected maintenance results in deterioration and sometimes removal from the housing inventory altogether.

In the fact sheet "Affordable Housing Shortage" (June 19, 2007, http://www.endhomelessness.org/content/article/detail/1658), the NAEH reports that funding for upkeep of existing public housing units decreased 25% between 1999 and 2006. Declines in the available stock of public housing continued in the years that followed.

FACTORS THAT INHIBIT CONSTRUCTION. Meanwhile, construction of low-income units has been hampered by community resistance, by regulations that increase the cost of construction, and by limits on federal tax credits that make new construction unprofitable.

These phenomena generally stem from the stigma conventionally associated with the occupants of public and subsidized housing. Many middle- and upper-income people resist the introduction of low-income housing in their communities out of a traditional "not in my backyard" (NIMBY) mentality, believing that such developments will bring rising crime, falling property values, and overcrowded classrooms. Many advocates for the poor contest such scenarios. For example, in *From NIMBY to Good Neighbors: Recent Studies Reinforce That Apartments Are Good for a Community* (May 1, 2006, http://www.nmhc.org/Content/ServeFile.cfm?FileID=5408), the National Multi Housing Council summarizes research showing that smart growth (long-term goals for managing the growth of a community) may depend on the development of more high-density housing, such as apartments. The council states, "The good news is that there is an ever-increasing body of research that indicates that apartments (including affordable apartments) are not a threat to local property values and are a net plus to communities."

Community resistance is not the only obstacle faced by those who would like to see new affordable-housing developments. Developers themselves complain that there is not sufficient profit to be made from building and operating low-income housing. To provide incentives to developers, the 1986 Low-Income Housing Tax Credit program gave the states $1.25 per capita (per person) in tax credits toward the private development of low-income housing. In "A New Era for Affordable Housing" (March 1, 2003, http://nreionline.com/news/developer/real_estate_new_era_affordable/), H. Lee Murphy reports on data from the National Council of State Housing Agencies indicating that construction hit a high in 1994, when 117,100 apartment units were built with the credits. Skyrocketing construction costs brought a decline in new construction, which reached a low of 66,900 units in 2000. In 2001 Congress raised the per capita allotment to $1.75 and provided that the formula would rise each

FIGURE 6.7

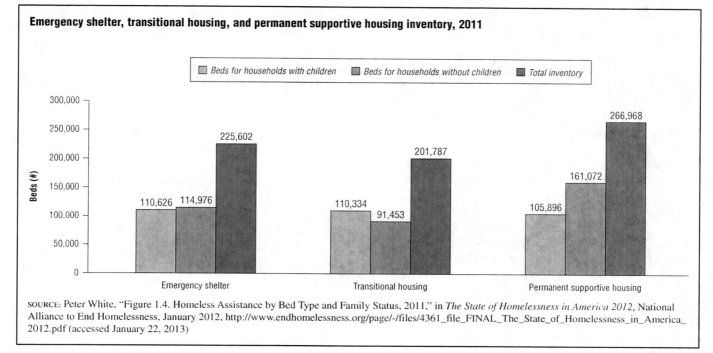

Emergency shelter, transitional housing, and permanent supportive housing inventory, 2011

SOURCE: Peter White, "Figure 1.4. Homeless Assistance by Bed Type and Family Status, 2011," in *The State of Homelessness in America 2012*, National Alliance to End Homelessness, January 2012, http://www.endhomelessness.org/page/-/files/4361_file_FINAL_The_State_of_Homelessness_in_America_2012.pdf (accessed January 22, 2013)

year with inflation. The tax credits financed the construction of 75,000 new units in 2001. HUD reports in "Low-Income Housing Tax Credits" (August 17, 2012, http://www.huduser.org/portal/datasets/lihtc.html) that between 1995 and 2010 an average of more than 1,400 projects and roughly 107,000 housing units per year were built because of the tax credit. However, this rate of construction still did not keep pace with the number of affordable housing units that are demolished each year.

WHERE THE HOMELESS LIVE

When faced with high rents and low housing availability, many poor people become homeless. What happens to them? Where do they live? Research shows that after becoming homeless, many people move around, staying in one place for a while, then moving on to another place. Many homeless people take advantage of homeless shelters at some point. Such shelters may be funded by the federal government, by religious organizations, or by other private homeless advocates.

Emergency Housing: Shelters and Transitional Housing

Typically, a homeless shelter provides dormitory-style sleeping accommodations and bathing facilities, with varying services for laundry, telephone calls, and other needs. Residents are often limited in the length of their stay and must leave the shelter during the day under most circumstances. By contrast, transitional housing is intended to bridge the gap between the shelter or street and permanent housing, with appropriate services to move the homeless

into independent living. It may be a room in a hotel or motel, or it may be a subsidized apartment. According to the NAEH in *The State of Homelessness in America 2012*, in 2011 there were 225,602 beds in emergency shelters and 201,787 beds in transitional housing available. (See Figure 6.7.) Primarily as a result of government efforts to combat homelessness during the Great Recession, the number of permanent supportive housing beds had increased by more than 40% since 2007, to 266,968 beds.

Illegal Occupancy

Poor neighborhoods are often full of abandoned buildings. Even the best-intentioned landlords cannot afford to maintain their properties in these areas. Many have let their buildings deteriorate or have simply walked away, leaving the fate of the building and its residents in the hands of the government. Despite overcrowding and unsafe conditions, many homeless people move into these dilapidated buildings illegally, glad for what shelter they can find. Municipal governments, which are overwhelmed by long waiting lists for public housing, by a lack of funds and personnel, and by an inadequate supply of emergency shelter beds, are often unable or unwilling to strictly enforce housing laws, allowing the homeless to become squatters rather than forcing them into the streets. Some deliberately turn a blind eye to the problem, knowing they have no better solution for the homeless.

The result is a multitude of housing units with deplorable living conditions—tenants bedding down in illegal boiler basements, sharing beds with children or in-laws, or sharing bathrooms with strangers. The buildings may have leaks and rot, rusted fire escapes, and rat and roach infestations. Given the alternative, many homeless people feel lucky to be sheltered at all.

As a result of the housing crisis that began in 2008, some homeless people began turning to foreclosed homes in their search for shelter. According to the article "Some Homeless Turn to Foreclosed Homes" (Associated Press, February 17, 2008), many homeless began moving into these vacant homes and became squatters. The article notes that "foreclosed homes often have an advantage over boarded-up and dilapidated houses that have been abandoned because of rundown conditions: Sometimes the heat, lights and water are still working." The article "Activist Moves Homeless into Foreclosures" (Associated Press, December 1, 2008) explains that in 2008 homeless people were squatting in foreclosed homes in southern Florida with the help of the national organization Take Back the Land. This group finds empty foreclosed properties, arranges to have the utilities turned on, and becomes a pseudo landlord. Taryn Wobbema reports in "City Foreclosures Open Space for Squatters" (MNDaily.com, March 4, 2009) that in Minneapolis, Minnesota, the Poor People's Economic Human Rights Campaign places homeless people in empty homes illegally.

In "Homeless Squatting in Foreclosed City Homes" (http://13wham.com, December 20, 2010), Rachel Barnhart indicates that in 2010 homeless squatters were moving into some of the 3,000 empty houses in Rochester, New York. The squatters were helped by Take Back the Land. Similar actions were taking place around the country. Take Back the Land explains in "US Senators Contact Take Back the Land–Rochester to Address the Housing Crisis" (http://www.takebacktheland.org/) that in March 2011 it staged a two-week-long community eviction defense by physically blocking authorities from removing Catherine Lennon and 10 extended family members from her Rochester home, which had been foreclosed. A SWAT team was eventually brought in to forcibly evict Lennon. In all, seven people were arrested. Intense media scrutiny led Representative Louise McIntosh Slaughter (1929–; D-NY) to intervene and ask the federal authorities to negotiate with Lennon. Although Bank of America and Fannie Mae, the federally subsidized mortgage-backed securities company, continued to press their foreclosure case, the negative publicity eventually led them to pursue a settlement that would allow Lennon and her family to stay in their home.

CHAPTER 7
DEALING WITH THE PROBLEM OF HOMELESSNESS

PUBLIC INTEREST IN HOMELESSNESS

Interest in and attitudes toward homelessness in the United States have changed over time. The mid- to late 1980s was a period of relatively high concern about homelessness. In 1986 the U.S. public demonstrated concern over the plight of the homeless by initiating the Hands across America fund-raising effort. Some 6 million people locked hands across 4,152 miles (6,682 km) to form a human chain across the country, bringing an outpouring of national attention and concern to the issue. That same year the comedians Robin Williams (1951–), Whoopi Goldberg (1955–), and Billy Crystal (1948–) hosted the HBO comedy special *Comic Relief* to help raise money for the homeless. The show was a success and became an annual event. Magazines, art shows, books, and songs turned the nation's attention toward homelessness. Well-funded research studies came out by the dozens. The country was awash in statistical information regarding the homeless. All these activities pointed to the widely held belief that people became homeless because of circumstances outside their control.

By 2013, however, national concern about homelessness had faded. *Comic Relief* could only be seen in reruns. The annual fund-raiser ran out of steam in 1996 except for a revival show two years later. After that, there was no resurgence of public interest in the homeless problem, even though the problem worsened due to the foreclosure crisis beginning in 2007 and remained at crisis levels in the years that followed, amid stubbornly high unemployment rates and a dwindling supply of affordable housing.

In "The Real Face of Homelessness" (*Time*, January 13, 2003), Joel Stein explores a change in the national mood about homelessness. This change in national mood corresponded with efforts to criminalize homelessness. For example, a campaign was launched in Philadelphia, Pennsylvania, to discourage giving money to panhandlers. In Orlando, Florida, people could be jailed for

sleeping on the sidewalk. In San Francisco, Proposition N ("Care Not Cash") reduced county housing support payments from $395 to $59 a month. In Dallas, Texas, the homeless complained that they were issued vagrancy tickets.

Moreover, as a result of the so-called Great Recession, the economic recession and housing crisis that began in late 2007, localities across the country started to report a huge surge in homelessness, even among populations previously considered middle class. Wendy Koch reports in "Homelessness up as Families on the Edge Lose Hold" (*USA Today*, April 6, 2009) that homelessness increased sharply in 2009 and that the demand for homeless services such as shelter requests was up dramatically. She quotes Nancy Radner, the head of the Chicago Alliance to End Homelessness, who said, "We're getting requests from people earning more than $30,000 a year, even $65,000. That's unprecedented." Arthur Delaney notes in "Recession Increasing Interest in Homelessness" (*Huffington Post*, March 27, 2009) that some observers suggested in 2009 that the lengthening reach of homelessness was increasing public interest in the problem once again. For example, the National Center on Family Homelessness states in "Public Education and Policy" (2010, http://www.familyhomelessness.org/publiceducation.php?p=ts) that more than 3,000 media stories had reported on its findings on U.S. homeless children in 2009.

Treating the Homeless as Criminals

Matthew Philips explains in "OK, Sister, Drop That Sandwich!: Cities Fight Panhandling by Outlawing Food Giveaways in Parks" (*Newsweek*, November 6, 2006) that in Orlando, Florida, city lawmakers passed ordinances in 2006 that made it illegal to feed large groups of people in public parks—making not only homelessness but also helping the homeless illegal. According to Forrest Norman in "Proposed Ordinance Targeting Shantytown Pulled"

(*Daily Business Review*, January 9, 2007), an ordinance in Miami, Florida, that would make it illegal for homeless people to sleep on vacant city-owned lots missed emergency passage in December 2006 by only one vote and was pulled from the agenda in January 2007 because city commissioners "needed more time to consider the ordinance" due to community support of the targeted shantytown. In "Lacey to Revisit Homeless Ordinance" (*Olympian*, January 20, 2009), Christian Hill indicates that in 2009 the city council of Olympia, Washington, debated an ordinance that would require churches to house homeless people indoors, rather than in tents. Hill notes in "Lawmaker Pens Homeless Bill" (*Olympian*, February 5, 2009) that in response, the Democratic state representative Brendan Williams (1968–) introduced legislation in the Washington House of Representatives that would limit localities' ability to impose regulations on churches who shelter homeless people. In "Los Angeles Accused of Criminalizing Homelessness" (Reuters, July 14, 2009), Steve Gorman reports that even in the midst of the recession, Los Angeles maintained its Safer City Initiative, a set of policies that, according to the initiative's critics, were designed to punish homelessness. For example, homeless people routinely receive tickets and are even arrested for small offenses such as jaywalking and loitering.

Addressing Homelessness Is a Low Priority

When asked, Americans in the 21st century state they continue to be troubled by the existence of homelessness. In *Americans' Worries about Economy, Budget Top Other Issues* (March 21, 2011, http://www.gallup.com/poll/146708/Americans-Worries-Economy-Budget-Top-Issues.aspx), Lydia Saad of the Gallup Organization indicates that in March 2011, 41% of Americans said they worry about hunger and homelessness a great deal, and 34% said they worry about it a fair amount. Only 26% said they are worried only a little or not at all. Dennis Jacobe of the Gallup Organization explains in *Americans on Housing Aid: Unfair but Necessary* (February 25, 2009, http://www.gallup.com/poll/116101/Americans-Housing-Aid-Unfair-Necessary.aspx) that in 2009, 51% of Americans believed that providing government assistance to homeowners who cannot pay their mortgage is unfair, but 59% believed such aid is necessary nonetheless. When the question was phrased another way and Americans were asked about "giving aid to homeowners who are in danger of losing their homes to foreclosure," and thus potentially facing homelessness, nearly two-thirds (64%) of Americans said they are in favor of the plan.

FEDERAL GOVERNMENT AID FOR THE HOMELESS

What should the role of the government be in combating homelessness? Some people believe it is the duty of the government to take care of all citizens in times of need. Others point out that government help has often been misdirected or inadequate; in some instances, it has even added to the problem. Some people assert that people in trouble should solve their problems themselves with the help of family or friends. Federal programs for the homeless reflect a consensus that limited government help is important and necessary, but that homeless people also need to help themselves.

Since 1860 the federal government has been actively involved with the housing industry, specifically the low-income housing industry. In 1860 the government conducted the first partial census of housing—by counting slave dwellings. Twenty years later the U.S. census focused on the living quarters of the rest of the population by conducting a full housing census. Since then the federal government has played an increasingly larger role in combating housing problems in the United States:

- 1937—the U.S. Housing Act established the Public Housing Administration (which was later merged into the Federal Housing Administration [FHA] and the U.S. Department of Housing and Urban Development [HUD]) to create low-rent housing programs across the country through the establishment of local public housing agencies.

- 1949—the Housing Act set the goals of "a decent home and a suitable environment" for every family and authorized an 810,000-unit public housing program over the next six years. Title I of the act created the Urban Renewal Program, and Title V created the basic rural housing program under the FHA, which put the federal government directly into the mortgage business.

- 1965—Congress established HUD. Its goal was to create a new rent supplement program for low-income households in private housing.

- 1974—the Housing and Community Development Act created a new leased-housing program that included a certificate (voucher) program, expanding housing choices for low-income tenants. The voucher program soon became known as Section 8, after the section of the act that established it.

THE MCKINNEY-VENTO HOMELESS ASSISTANCE ACT

Widespread public outcry over the plight of the homeless during the early 1980s prompted Congress to pass the Stewart B. McKinney Homeless Assistance Act of 1987. Congress renamed the act the McKinney-Vento Homeless Assistance Act in 2000 to honor Representative Bruce F. Vento's (1940–2000; D-MN) service to the homeless. The range and reach of the act has broadened over the years. Most of the money authorized by the act went, initially, toward the funding of homeless shelters.

The program also funded a Supportive Housing Program (SHP), a Shelter Plus Care Program (S+C), and the Single Room Occupancy Program (SRO) besides the Emergency Shelter Grants Program. Amendments to the act later enabled funding and other services to support permanent housing and other programs to help the homeless. HUD administers most McKinney-Vento funds.

In February 2007 the Homeless Emergency Assistance and Rapid Transition to Housing (HEARTH) Act was introduced in the U.S. House of Representatives to reauthorize the McKinney-Vento Homeless Assistance Programs; it was reintroduced in September 2008. The bill was passed in the House in October 2008 and was introduced in the U.S. Senate in April 2009. The Senate passed the bill and President Barack Obama (1961–) signed it into law in May 2009.

The HEARTH Act consolidated a number of HUD homeless assistance programs, expanded the definition of homelessness, and added new funds in areas including emergency shelter needs and rural housing. HEARTH requires the federal government to submit an annual plan to eliminate homelessness. In 2010 the U.S. Interagency Council on Homelessness released *Opening Doors: The Federal Strategic Plan to Prevent and End Homelessness* (June 2010, http://www.usich.gov/PDF/OpeningDoors _2010_FSPPreventEndHomeless.pdf), the first comprehensive federal plan on ending homelessness. In the introduction to the report, President Obama states that "veterans should never find themselves on the streets, living without care and without hope. It is simply unacceptable for a child in this country to be without a home." The plan outlines four goals: ending chronic homelessness within five years, preventing and ending homelessness among veterans within five years, preventing and ending homelessness for families and children within 10 years, and eventually eliminating homelessness altogether. The federal government aims to increase collaborative efforts among government and organizations, increase access to affordable housing, increase economic security, improve health, and revamp homeless services to better respond to crises.

In fiscal year (FY) 2013 HUD's budget for programs to help the homeless was $2.2 billion, an amount which marked a slight decrease over previous years. According to the agency's *FY 2013 Budget: Housing and Communities Built to Last* (February 2012, http://portal.hud.gov/ hudportal/documents/huddoc?id=CombBudget2013.pdf) over $1.9 billion of the total budget would go to the Continuum of Care Program (CoC), and another $286 million would go to the Emergency Solutions Grants (ESG) Program.

Continuum of Care

According to HUD in "Homeless Assistance Programs" (2013, http://portal.hud.gov/hudportal/HUD?src=/ program_offices/comm_planning/homeless), the purpose of the CoC program is to "promote communitywide commitment to the goal of ending homelessness; provide funding for efforts by nonprofit providers, and State and local governments to quickly rehouse homeless individuals and families while minimizing the trauma and dislocation caused to homeless individuals, families, and communities by homelessness; promote access to and effective utilization of mainstream programs by homeless individuals and families; and optimize self-sufficiency among individuals and families experiencing homelessness."

Nonprofit groups and local government entities applying for funds under these programs are expected to survey and assess local needs and to write a comprehensive plan for combating homelessness and meeting needs. Grant recipients are required to assess their clients' progress and make changes in the program in response to ongoing evaluation. Three major programs (SHP, S+C, and SRO) as well as some additional demonstration and rural efforts have developed over the years. Table 7.1 outlines the eligibility guidelines for the Supportive Housing and Shelter Care Programs within the larger CoC designation.

SUPPORTIVE HOUSING PROGRAM. The aim of the SHP is to provide housing and services that will enable homeless clients to achieve economic independence and control over their lives. In *Supportive Housing Program Fact Sheet* (2013, http://www.hudhre.info/index.cfm?do=viewSupportive HousingProgram), HUD explains that the SHP provides matching funds for the construction of new buildings for housing homeless people; it also provides funding for the acquisition or refurbishing of existing buildings. The program underwrites 75% of the operating cost, including administration, and up to 80% of the cost of support programs. These programs must help clients achieve independence by providing skills training, child care, education, transportation assistance, counseling, and job referrals. Elements of the program include transitional housing for 24 months, permanent housing for the disabled, supportive services without housing, havens for the hard-to-reach and the mentally ill, and other innovative programs to solve problems of homelessness.

SHELTER PLUS CARE PROGRAM. HUD notes in *Shelter Plus Care Fact Sheet* (2013, http://www.hudhre.info/ index.cfm?do=viewShelterPlusCare) that S+C helps agencies that specifically target the hardest-to-serve homeless: those with mental and physical disabilities living on the street or in shelters, including drug addicts and people who are suffering from acquired immunodeficiency syndrome (AIDS). The program provides rental assistance and supportive services; housing in this program can be in the form of group homes or individual units with supportive services. Grant funds must be matched with local dollars. Subsidies for projects are available for 10 years; assistance

TABLE 7.1

Eligibility requirements for HUD Continuum of Care homeless assistance

[Projects funded in fiscal year 2011 Continuum of Care (CoC) Competition—Supportive Housing Program and Shelter Plus Care Programs]

Eligibility by component

Supportive services only

Individuals and families defined as homeless under the following categories are eligible for assistance in Supportive Services Only projects:
- Category 1—Literally homeless
- Category 2—Imminent risk of homeless
- Category 3*—Homeless under other federal statutes
- Category 4—Fleeing/attempting to flee domestic violence

Safe havens

Individuals defined as homeless under the following categories are eligible for assistance in Safe Havens projects:
- Category 1—Literally homeless

SH projects have the following additional Notice of Funding Availability (NOFA) limitations on eligibility within Category 1:
- Must serve individuals only
- Individual must have a severe mental illness
- Individual must be living on the streets and unwilling or unable to participate in supportive services

Transitional housing

Individuals and families defined as homeless under the following categories are eligible for assistance in Transitional Housing projects:
- Category 1—Literally homeless
- Category 2—Imminent risk of homeless
- Category 3*—Homeless under other federal statutes
- Category 4—Fleeing/attempting to flee domestic violence

Permanent supportive housing

Individuals and families defined as homeless under the following categories are eligible for assistance in Permanent Supportive Housing projects:
- Category 1—Literally homeless
- Category 4—Fleeing/attempting to flee domestic violence

Permanent Supportive Housing projects have the following additional NOFA limitations on eligibility within Category 1:
- Individuals and families coming from Transitional Housing must have originally come from the streets or emergency shelter
- Individuals and families must also have an individual family member with a disability

Projects that are dedicated chronically homeless projects, including those that were originally funded as Samaritan Bonus Initiative Projects must continue to serve chronically homeless persons exclusively.

*Projects must be located within a CoC that has received HUD approval to serve this category.
Notes: HUD = Department of Housing and Urban Development.

SOURCE: Adapted from "The Homeless Definition and Eligibility for SHP, SPC, and ESG," U.S. Department of Housing and Urban Development, May 2012, https://www.onecpd.info/resources/documents/HomelessDefEligibility%20_SHP_SPC_ESG.pdf (accessed January 22, 2013)

to sponsors and tenants is available for five years. A range of supportive services for tenants must be funded through other sources. Rental assistance includes four types of contracts:

- Tenant-Based Rental Assistance—direct contract with a low-income tenant

- Project-Based Rental Assistance—building owner contracts

- Sponsor-Based Rental Assistance—contracts with nonprofit organizations

- Single-Room Occupancy–Based Rental Assistance—single-room occupancy contracts provided by public housing authorities

SINGLE ROOM OCCUPANCY PROGRAM. According to HUD in *Section 8 Moderate Rehabilitation Program for Single-Room Occupancy Dwellings for Homeless Individuals Fact Sheet* (2013, http://www.hudhre.info/index.cfm?do=viewSroProgram), single-room occupancy housing is housing in a dormitory-style building where each person has his or her own private room but shares kitchens, bathrooms, and lounges. SRO housing is generally the

cheapest type of housing available in a given locality. Funding is intended to encourage the establishment and operation of such housing and thus to help unaccompanied homeless individuals move into a permanent housing situation. Subsidy payments fund a project for a period of 10 years in the form of rental assistance in amounts equal to the rent, including utilities, minus the portion of rent payable by the tenants.

OTHER PROGRAM COMPONENTS. Other programs folded under the Continuum of Care designation by HUD include demonstration programs for safe havens for the homeless, innovative homeless programs, and rural homeless housing programs.

Emergency Solutions Grants Program

The Emergency Solutions Grants (ESG) Program (formerly the Emergency Shelter Grants Program) is HUD's formula grant program administered as a part of its community planning and development grant program. In the fact sheet *Emergency Solutions Grants (ESG) Program* (2013, https://www.onecpd.info/resources/documents/EmergencySolutionsGrantsProgramFactSheet.pdf), HUD explains that the program "provides funding to: (1) engage homeless individuals and families living on the street; (2) improve the number and quality of emergency shelters for homeless individuals and families; (3) help operate these shelters; (4) provide essential services to shelter residents; (5) rapidly re-house homeless individuals and families; and (6) prevent families and individuals from becoming homeless." Recipients of funding are states, large cities, urban counties, and U.S. territories that have filed consolidated community development plans with HUD. Federal funds are matched, to varying degrees, by these government recipients, and then money either flows to constituent government offices or nonprofit organizations dealing with the homeless. City and county recipients are required to match federal funds either with cash or in-kind contributions that can include new staff or volunteer efforts, donated buildings and materials, or the value of building leases. States do not have to match the first $100,000 of ESG funding, but the benefits of the exemption must go to sub-recipients (government offices or nonprofits) that are not capable of generating matching funds. Territories do not have to provide any matching funds. Table 7.2 details the eligibility guidelines for those receiving assistance under the ESG program.

Title V

HUD notes in *Title V—Federal Surplus Property for Use to Assist the Homeless Fact Sheet* (2013, http://www.hudhre.info/index.cfm?do=viewTitleV) that it maintains information about and publishes listings of federal properties categorized as unutilized, underutilized, in excess, or in surplus. States, local governments, and nonprofit organizations can apply to use such properties to house the homeless. Title V does not provide funding; it provides properties to agencies for housing use on an "as is" basis, and it offers leases free of charge for between one and 20 years. Groups must pay their own operating and repair costs.

Veterans Affairs Supportive Housing

Since 2008 Congress has allocated funding to HUD for the specific purpose of reducing the prevalence of homelessness among U.S. veterans. As HUD notes in *Veterans Affairs Supportive Housing (HUD-VASH) Fact Sheet* (2013, http://www.hudhre.info/index.cfm?do=viewHudVash Program), the program is a partnership with the Department of Veterans Affairs (VA), whereby homeless veterans are offered rental assistance in combination with case management and clinical care at VA medical centers and clinics. Most of the vouchers providing rental assistance are tenant-based, but project-based vouchers are issued on case-by-case basis.

EDUCATION FOR HOMELESS CHILDREN AND YOUTH

In response to reports that over 50% of homeless children were not attending school regularly, Congress enacted the McKinney-Vento Homeless Assistance Act's Education for Homeless Children and Youth program in

TABLE 7.2

Eligibility requirements for HUD Emergency Solutions Grants homeless assistance

Eligibility by component

Street outreach

Individuals defined as homeless under the following categories are eligible for assistance in street outreach:
- Category 1—Literally homeless
- Category 4—Fleeing/attempting to flee domestic violence (where the individual or family also meets the criteria for Category 1)

Street outreach projects have the following additional limitations on eligibility within Category 1:
- Individuals and families must be living on the streets (or other places not meant for human habitation) and be unwilling or unable to access services in emergency shelter

Emergency shelter

Individuals and families defined as homeless under the following categories are eligible for assistance in emergency shelter projects:
- Category 1—Literally homeless
- Category 2—Imminent risk of homeless
- Category 3—Homeless under other federal statutes
- Category 4—Fleeing/attempting to flee domestic violence

Rapid re-housing

Individuals defined as homeless under the following categories are eligible for assistance in rapid re-housing projects:
- Category 1—Literally homeless
- Category 4—Fleeing/attempting to flee domestic violence (where the individual or family also meets the criteria for category 1)

Homelessness prevention

Individuals and families defined as homeless under the following categories are eligible for assistance in homelessness prevention projects:
- Category 2—Imminent risk of homeless
- Category 3—Homeless under other federal statutes
- Category 4—Fleeing/attempting to flee domestic violence

Individuals and families who are defined as at risk of homelessness are eligible for assistance in homelessness prevention projects.

Homelessness prevention projects have the following additional limitations on eligibility with homeless and at risk of homeless:
- Must only serve individuals and families that have an annual income below 30% of area median income

SOURCE: Adapted from "The Homeless Definition and Eligibility for SHP, SPC, and ESG," U.S. Department of Housing and Urban Development, May 2012, https://www.onecpd.info/resources/documents/HomelessDefEligibility%20_SHP_SPC_ESG.pdf (accessed January 22, 2013)

1987. The program ensures that homeless children and youth have equal access to the same free, appropriate education that is provided to other children. Education for Homeless Children and Youth also provides funding for state and local school districts to implement the law. States are required to report estimated numbers of homeless children and the problems encountered in serving them. The act includes the following guidelines:

- Homeless children cannot be segregated.

- Transportation has to be provided to and from schools of origin if requested (a school of origin is the school the student attended when permanently housed, or the school in which the student was last enrolled).

- In case of a placement dispute, immediate enrollment is required pending the outcome.

- Local education agencies must put the "best interest of the child" first in determining the feasibility of keeping children in their school of origin.

- Local education agencies must designate a local liaison for homeless children and youth.

- States have to subgrant 50% to 75% of their allotments under Education for Homeless Children and Youth competitively to local education agencies.

At the time the McKinney-Vento Homeless Assistance Act was passed, only an estimated 57% of homeless children were enrolled in school. By 2000 the percentage had increased to 88%. The National Center on Family Homelessness estimates in "Homeless Children: America's New Outcasts" (March 2004, http://www.ucdenver .edu/academics/colleges/ArchitecturePlanning/discover/ centers/CYE/Publications/Documents/outcasts.pdf) that in 2004 about 80% of homeless children attended school. In *Education for Homeless Children and Youths Program* (April 2009, http://www2.ed.gov/programs/ homeless/data-comp-04-07.pdf), the National Center for Homeless Education (NCHE) notes that during the 2007–08 school year 794,617 homeless children were enrolled in school across the nation, up 114,893 from the year before, most likely due to the worsening housing crisis and rising unemployment. The numbers of homeless children in schools climbed throughout the Great Recession and its aftermath, as the NCHE notes in its 2012 installment of *Education for Homeless Children and Youths Program* (June 2012, http://center.serve .org/nche/downloads/data_comp_0909-1011.pdf). Nearly 1.1 million homeless children were enrolled in schools during the 2010–11 school year, an increase of 13% over 939,903 homeless students in 2009–10.

In implementing the McKinney-Vento legislation, school districts found that barriers arose in areas such as residency, guardian requirements, incomplete or missing documentation (including immunization records and birth certificates), and transportation. Consequently, some school districts established separate schools for homeless children. According to Kristen Kreisher in "Educating Homeless Children" (*Children's Voice*, September–October 2002), in 2001 there were an estimated 40 separate schools for the homeless in 19 states, and even though separate schools were outlawed with the 2002 reauthorization of the McKinney-Vento Homeless Assistance Act, those schools that already existed were allowed to remain.

Transportation became an issue for school districts providing education to homeless students. Nicole Brode reports in "New York's School Choice Leaves More Homeless Children with Hour-Plus Commutes" (*Knight-Ridder/Tribune Business News*, February 10, 2003) that 34% of the 226 students in one New York homeless shelter faced commutes of longer than an hour because their parents had opted to keep the children in the same schools they had attended before they became homeless, a right guaranteed by the new law. In "Homeless Kids Lack School to Call Home" (*Chicago Tribune*, February 13, 2009), Carlos Sadovi notes that homeless children must either change schools often or face commutes of up to several hours. According to Kathleen Kingsbury in "Keeping Homeless Kids in School" (*Time*, March 12, 2009), in March 2009, when nearly 1 out of 10 children in Minneapolis, Minnesota, was homeless, children faced commutes of an hour or more.

RESTRICTIVE ORDINANCES

Gentrification, the conversion of low-value neighborhoods to high-value neighborhoods, has transformed many American inner cities since the 1990s, with serious consequences for the poor and the homeless. Gentrification typically displaces earlier—and usually poorer—residents and often destroys ethnic communities. Even though gentrification has positive aspects—reduced crime, new investment in the community, and increased economic activity— these benefits are typically enjoyed by the newcomers while the existing residents are marginalized. When a neighborhood is gentrified, the long-term population can suffer due to the lack of affordable housing. As more and more privately owned, federally subsidized apartment buildings and former "skid rows" were gentrified at the end of the 20th century and beginning of the 21st century, more of the poorest people were forced into homelessness. Furthermore, the visible homeless are often viewed as a blight on the quality of life of the new residents. The presence of homeless people can drive away tourists and frustrate the proprietors of local businesses.

Accordingly, since the 1990s, there has been an increase in the enactment of laws and ordinances intended to regulate the activities of homeless people. Advocates for the homeless contend that such practices deny the homeless their most basic human, legal, and political rights.

Criminalizing Homelessness

Homeless people live in and move about public spaces, and many Americans believe society has a right to control or regulate what homeless people can do in these shared spaces. A city or town may introduce local ordinances or policies that are designed to restrict homeless people's activities, remove their belongings, or destroy their nontraditional living places.

Some local ordinances prevent homeless people from sleeping on the streets or in parks, even though there may not be enough shelter beds to accommodate every homeless person every night. The homeless may be turned out of shelters to fend for themselves during the day, yet local ordinances prevent them from loitering in public places or resting in bus stations, libraries, or public buildings. Begging or picking up cans for recycling may help the homeless to support themselves, yet often there are restrictions against panhandling or limits on the number of cans they can redeem. To see the homeless bathe or use the toilet in public makes people uncomfortable; consequently, laws are passed to prohibit such activities.

Other localities pass ordinances that target homeless people in the hopes of driving them from the community. According to the National Law Center on Homelessness and Poverty (NLCHP) in *Criminalizing Crisis: The Criminalization of Homelessness in U.S. Cities* (November 2011, http://www.nlchp.org/content/pubs/11.14.11%20Criminalization%20Report%20&%20Advocacy%20Manual,%20FINAL1.pdf), of 234 cities surveyed in 2011, 33% prohibited sitting or lying in some public places; 40% prohibited camping in some places, and 22% prohibited it citywide; 56% prohibited loitering in some places, and 19% prohibited it citywide; and 53% prohibited begging in some places and prohibited "aggressive" panhandling, while 23% had citywide prohibitions against panhandling. Since the NLCHP's 2009 report, there had been a 7% increase in prohibitions on panhandling, a 7% increase in prohibitions on camping, and a 10% increase in prohibitions on loitering. The NLCHP had seen similar increases in prohibitions between its 2006 and 2009 report, suggesting that the trend toward the criminalization of homelessness was steadily gaining momentum. Table 7.3 provides a breakdown of the

TABLE 7.3

Prohibited conduct in selected cities, 2011

	Begging in public places city-wide	Begging in particular public places	"Aggressive" panhandling	Sleeping in public city-wide	Sleeping in particular public places	Camping in public places city-wide	Camping in particular public places	Loitering, loafing, vagrancy city-wide	Loitering, loafing in particular public places	Obstructing sidewalks or public places
Albuquerque, NM		X	X		X		X		X	X
Anchorage, AK		X	X				X			X
Atlanta, GA		X	X		X		X		X	X
Baltimore, MD		X	X					X		X
Boston, MA		X	X		X				X	X
Charleston, SC			X	X		X		X	X	X
Charlotte, NC		X	X		X				X	X
Chicago, IL		X	X						X	
Cincinnati, OH		X	X				X		X	X
Cleveland, OH		X	X		X				X	X
Dallas, TX		X	X	X			X		X	X
Des Moines, IA		X						X	X	X
Denver, CO		X	X		X		X		X	X
Detroit, MI	X							X	X	X
Hartford, CT	X	X	X					X	X	X
Honolulu, HI			X		X		X		X	
Houston, TX		X	X				X	X	X	
Indianapolis, IN		X	X		X		X	X		X
Las Vegas, NV		X	X		X		X			X
Los Angeles, CA		X	X		X		X		X	X
Louisville, KY	X	X	X	X	X			X	X	X
Miami, FL		X	X	X			X		X	X
Minneapolis, MN		X	X			X	X		X	X
New Orleans, LA	X			X	X		X			X
New York, NY	X		X			X			X	
Newark, NJ	X	X	X				X		X	X
Philadelphia, PA		X	X				X		X	X
Phoenix, AZ		X	X	X		X			X	X
Portland, OR		X				X			X	X
Salt Lake City, UT	X				X		X		X	X
San Francisco, CA		X	X		X		X		X	X
Seattle, WA		X		X	X		X		X	X
Washington, DC		X	X		X	X		X		X

SOURCE: Adapted from "Prohibited Conduct Chart," in *Criminalizing Crisis: The Criminalization of Homelessness in U.S. Cities*, National Law Center on Homelessness and Poverty, November 2011, http://www.nlchp.org/content/pubs/11.14.11%20Criminalization%20Report%20&%20Advocacy%20Manual,%20FINAL1.pdf (accessed January 22, 2013)

activities common among homeless people that are prohibited in selected U.S. cities.

Exacerbating the Problem

In *Criminalizing Crisis*, the NLCHP notes that 73% of its survey respondents, who were drawn not only from the ranks of the homeless but from those who provide services to them, reported arrests and/or citations for public urination or defecation; 55% reported arrests or citations for camping or sleeping in public; 53% reported arrests or citations for panhandling; 20% reported arrests or citations for public storage of belongings; and 19% reported arrests or citations for sitting on sidewalks. (See Figure 7.1.) At the same time, 80% of respondents observed that their cities lacked adequate shelter space, public restrooms, and storage options that would allow the homeless to avoid such behaviors.

Criminalizing Crisis includes numerous firsthand accounts of how prosecution of the homeless deepens their problems rather than helping them escape homelessness. For example, a survey respondent in Los Angeles described being arrested on an outstanding warrant and held in jail for 90 days, during which time he lost his Section 8 housing; he was homeless for four years afterward. A service provider in Wenatchee, Washington, told the NLCHP, likewise, about a homeless family that was in the concluding stages of obtaining a two-bedroom apartment when the father was arrested for public urination. In police custody, he missed a scheduled appointment with the landlord, and the apartment was rented to someone else. The family remained homeless months later. Even in the absence of such missed opportunities, an arrest record makes it more difficult for a homeless person—already at a pronounced disadvantage in the job market—to find employment.

The NLCHP additionally argues that police intervention makes it more difficult for those who serve the homeless to do their jobs. Outreach workers must build relationships over time with the homeless, who can be extremely wary and hard to locate. When police conduct sweeps of areas where the homeless gather, service providers lose track of their clients and become unable to do their jobs. The result, of course, is that more of the homeless miss out on the crucial help that might get them off the streets and into permanent jobs and housing. Additionally, many NLCHP respondents reported the loss of essential property during police sweeps, such as important documents and identification. The absence of identification makes it impossible to get a job, and replacing a birth certificate or state-issued identification card takes time and costs money. Many service providers do not have the time or available funding to solve such problems, even when the affected individual is a good candidate for employment.

Arresting the homeless places exorbitant burdens on the criminal justice system and communities, as well. Approximately 39% of the homeless have a mental disorder, according to the NLCHP, so when police are ordered to apprehend them, they are often intervening in situations of mental-health crises, which lie well beyond the scope of their training. The time and

FIGURE 7.1

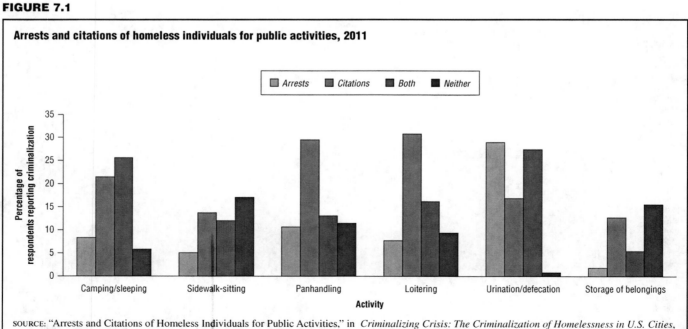

Arrests and citations of homeless individuals for public activities, 2011

Legend: Arrests | Citations | Both | Neither

(y-axis) Percentage of respondents reporting criminalization

(x-axis) Activity: Camping/sleeping | Sidewalk-sitting | Panhandling | Loitering | Urination/defecation | Storage of belongings

SOURCE: "Arrests and Citations of Homeless Individuals for Public Activities," in *Criminalizing Crisis: The Criminalization of Homelessness in U.S. Cities*, National Law Center on Homelessness and Poverty, November 2011, http://www.nlchp.org/content/pubs/11.14.11%20Criminalization%20Report%20&%20Advocacy%20Manual,%20FINAL1.pdf (accessed January 22, 2013)

resources directed toward arresting the homeless for simply being homeless could, as some observers note, be spent deterring dangerous criminals.

In addition to the allocated police manpower, arresting the homeless results in court costs and the cost of housing them in jail. A 2003 study in Alachua County, Florida, for example, found that the total cost to the police and courts of arresting a homeless person on a minor offense was $600, an amount that would go a long way toward providing housing for that person. In 2011, according to the NLCHP, it cost Eugene, Oregon, $379 to arrest, book, and hold someone in jail for one day, whereas the median rent in the city was $774 per month. Officials in Buncombe County, North Carolina, followed 37 chronically homeless individuals for three years and found that the individuals collectively accounted for 1,271 arrests. These arrests and the subsequent expense to jails cost municipal authorities approximately $370,000, or $10,000 per individual. The same 37 individuals received $120,000 worth of emergency medical care and $425,000 worth of hospitalization, for a total medical bill average of $5,500 per person.

Numerous studies have shown that it is much cheaper to house the homeless either in emergency shelters or in long-term supportive housing than in city or county jails, prisons, or mental institutions. A 2004 study in Utah described by the NLCHP, for example, found that shelter costs for one homeless person in Salt Lake City cost $6,600, versus $25,500 to house someone in the Salt Lake County Jail for a year, $35,000 in a state prison, and $146,730 in the state mental hospital. Even in the absence of disabilities or mental illness, studies have shown that providing permanent housing through subsidies is more cost-effective than other methods of addressing the problems of homelessness. In 2003 the Congressional Budget Office (CBO) estimated that providing a homeless person with Section 8 housing for a year cost less than half of what HUD paid at the time to shelter that same person through its ESG program. The effort and money spent on bringing the homeless into the courthouse, the NLCHP maintains, would provide more than enough resources to address the nation's lack of affordable housing.

The Rationale for Restrictive Ordinances

Local officials often restrict homeless people's use of public space to protect public health and safety—either of the general public, the homeless themselves, or both. Dangers to the public have included tripping over people and objects on sidewalks, intimidation of passersby caused by aggressive begging, and the spreading of diseases. Many people believe the very presence of the homeless is unsightly and their removal improves the appearance of public spaces. Other laws are based on the need to prevent crime. New York's campaign is based on the broken windows theory of the criminologists James Q. Wilson

(1931–1997) and George L. Kelling (1935–), who discuss this theory in "Broken Windows" (*Atlantic Monthly*, March 1982). They argue that allowing indications of disorder, such as a broken window or street people, to remain unaddressed shows a loss of public order and control, as well as apathy in a neighborhood, which breeds more serious criminal activity. Therefore, keeping a city neat and orderly should help prevent crime.

These are all legitimate concerns to some degree. The problem, critics say, is that rather than trying to eliminate or reduce homelessness by helping the homeless find housing and jobs, most local laws try to change the behavior of the homeless by punishing them. They target the homeless with legal action, ignoring the fact that many would gladly stop living on the streets and panhandling if they had any feasible alternatives. Even though these laws may be effective in the sense that the shanties are gone and homeless people are not allowed to bed down in subway tunnels or doorways, the fact remains that homelessness has not been eradicated. Homeless people have simply been forced to move to a different part of town, have hidden themselves, or have been imprisoned.

Alternative Strategies

While the trend toward criminalizing homelessness showed no signs of abating, as of 2013, some communities have experimented with alternative approaches. As the NLCHP reports, in 2010 the City of Seattle, Washington, reversed a law that had allowed the homeless to be banned from private businesses such as stores or coffee shops, even when they were not violating standards of conduct established by the business. Meanwhile, the City of Portland, Oregon, has been experimenting with solar-powered 24-hour toilets for the homeless, with an innovative design and durable materials that offer measurable improvements in public health and safety over ordinary toilets, most of which close after business hours. Instances of public urination and defecation have fallen, and no increases in crime have been reported, as a result of the toilets' installation. In 2010 the City of Puyallup, Washington, recognizing its shortfall of shelter beds for the homeless, allowed religious organizations to set up temporary encampments where the homeless can legally sleep and keep their possessions. The City of Minneapolis, along with Hennepin County, Minnesota, have likewise recognized the financial and human waste involved with arresting and incarcerating the homeless. In an attempt to cut public costs, city and county officials have begun working with service providers, allowing police calls that are not obviously in need of a criminal-justice response to be answered by homeless outreach workers. Between 2007 and 2009, as a result of the program, the city and county saw homeless arrests fall by 14%.

CONSTITUTIONAL RIGHTS OF THE HOMELESS

The U.S. Constitution and its amendments, especially the Bill of Rights, guarantee certain freedoms and rights to all U.S. citizens, including the homeless. As more and more cities move to deal with homelessness by aggressively enforcing public place restrictions, the restrictions are increasingly being challenged in court as unconstitutional. Sometimes a city ordinance is declared unconstitutional; at other times a court finds that there are special circumstances that allow the ordinance to stand.

Ordinances affecting the homeless can violate their rights in many ways. Numerous court challenges claim that the laws in question are unconstitutionally broad or vague. Others claim that a particular law denies the homeless equal protection under the law or violates their right to due process, as guaranteed by the Fifth and 14th Amendments. There are also cases based on a person's right to travel, and others that claim restrictions on the homeless constitute "cruel and unusual punishment," which is prohibited by the Eighth Amendment. Many cities have ordinances against panhandling, but charitable organizations freely solicit in public places. As a result, according to those challenging the ordinances, the right to free expression under the First Amendment is available to organizations but denied to the homeless.

The appearance of poverty should not deny an individual's right against unreasonable search and seizure, as guaranteed by the Fourth Amendment. Often, homeless people's property (such as camping gear or personal possessions) has been confiscated or destroyed without warning because it was found on public property. The state of homelessness is such that even the most personal living activities have to be performed in public. Denying activities that are necessary for survival may infringe on an individual's rights under the Eighth Amendment.

The 14th Amendment's right to equal protection under the law may be at issue when the homeless are cited for sleeping in the park, but others lying on the grass sunning themselves or taking a nap during a picnic, for instance, are not.

Testing the Constitutionality of Laws in Court

Some court cases test the law through civil suits, and others challenge the law by appealing convictions in criminal cases. Many advocates for the homeless, or the homeless themselves, challenge laws that they believe infringe on the rights of homeless people.

NO BED, NO ARREST. The concept of "no bed, no arrest" first arose out of a 1988 class action suit filed by the Miami Chapter of the American Civil Liberties Union on behalf of about 6,000 homeless people living in Miami, Florida. The city had a practice of sweeping the homeless from the areas where the Orange Bowl Parade and other related activities were held. The complaint in *Pottinger v. City of Miami* (S.D.Fla. 810 F. Supp. 1551 [1992]) alleged that the city had "a custom, practice and policy of arresting, harassing and otherwise interfering with homeless people for engaging in basic activities of daily life—including sleeping and eating—in the public places where they are forced to live. Plaintiffs further claim that the City has arrested thousands of homeless people for such life-sustaining conduct under various City of Miami ordinances and Florida Statutes. In addition, plaintiffs assert that the city routinely seizes and destroys their property and has failed to follow its own inventory procedures regarding the seized personal property of homeless arrestees and homeless persons in general."

The U.S. District Court for the Southern District of Florida ruled in *Pottinger* that the city's practices were cruel and unusual, in violation of the Eighth Amendment's ban against punishment based on status (only the homeless were being arrested). Furthermore, the court found the police practices of taking or destroying the property of the homeless to be in violation of the Fourth and Fifth Amendments' rights of freedom from unreasonable seizure and confiscation of property.

The city appealed the district court's judgment. Ultimately, a settlement was reached in which Miami agreed that a homeless person who is observed committing a "life-sustaining conduct" misdemeanor may be warned to stop, but if there is no available shelter, no warning is to be given. If there is an available shelter, the homeless person is to be told of its availability. If the homeless person accepts assistance, no arrest is to take place.

In *In re Eichorn* (81 Cal. Rptr. 2d 535 [Cal. App. Dep't. Super. Ct. 2000]), James Eichorn challenged his arrest for sleeping outside a county office building in Santa Ana, California. He attempted to prove, per the "no bed, no arrest" policy, that on the night he was arrested there were no shelter beds available. However, the court would not allow a jury to consider his necessity defense, and Eichorn was subsequently convicted and lost his appeal. Eichorn's lawyer then filed a writ of habeas corpus. The appeals court found that Eichorn should have been allowed to present his necessity defense, and the conviction was set aside and remanded back to the municipal court. Subsequently, the district attorney decided not to retry him. In essence, the case reaffirmed the "no bed, no arrest" policy.

In *Sipprelle v. City of Laguna Beach* (No. 8:2008cv01447 [2008]), a group of homeless people challenged a city ordinance in Laguna Beach, California, that prohibits sleeping in public places. The complaint states that the police prohibit the homeless from carrying out life-sustaining activities, including sleeping in public places, when there are no shelter beds available. The lawsuit was successful when the city council repealed the ordinance in June 2009.

SLEEPING OUTDOORS. Sarasota, Florida, passed a series of ordinances after 2000 that were designed to criminalize sleeping outdoors; two were overturned by state courts. A third ordinance made it illegal to sleep outdoors on either private or public property without permission of the property owner or the city manager if one of the following conditions existed: many personal objects were present (indicating the person is homeless), the person is cooking or maintaining a fire, the person is digging, or the person states he or she is homeless. This law survived the constitutionality test in *City of Sarasota v. McGinnis* (No. 2005 MO 16411 NC [Fla. Cir. Ct. 2005]). Nevertheless, Sarasota's ordinance against sleeping outdoors was found unconstitutional in *City of Sarasota v. Nipper* (No. 2005 MO 4369 NC [Fla. Cir. Ct. 2005]), in which the court found that the law punished innocent conduct and left too much discretion in the hands of the police.

LOITERING OR WANDERING. In 2000 homeless street dwellers and shelter residents of the Skid Row area (the plaintiffs) sought a temporary restraining order (TRO) against the Los Angeles Police Department (the defendant), claiming that their First and Fourth Amendment rights were being violated. The plaintiffs alleged that they were being stopped without cause and their identification demanded on threat of arrest; that they were being ordered to "move along" even though they were not in anyone's way; that their belongings were being confiscated; and that they were being ticketed for loitering. In *Justin v. City of Los Angeles* (No. CV-00-12352 LGB, 2000 U.S. Dist. Lexis 17881 [C.D. Cal. December 5, 2000]), Judge Lourdes G. Baird (1935–) denied a TRO that would have prevented the defendant from asking the plaintiffs to "move along." The TRO was granted with reference to the following actions when in the Skid Row area:

- Detention without reasonable suspicion
- Demand of identification on threat of arrest
- Searches without probable cause
- Removal from sidewalks unless free passage of pedestrians was obstructed
- Confiscation of personal property that was not abandoned
- Citation of those who may "annoy or molest" if interference was reasonable and free passage of pedestrians was not impeded

LIVING IN AN ENCAMPMENT. In 1996 advocates for the homeless sought an injunction against a Tucson, Arizona, resolution barring homeless encampments from city-owned property on Eighth Amendment and equal protection grounds. In *Davidson v. City of Tucson* (924 F. Supp. 989), the court held that the plaintiffs did not have standing to raise a cruel and unusual punishment claim, as they had not been convicted of a crime and no

one had been arrested under the ordinance. The equal protection claim failed because the court did not consider homeless people a suspect class and the right to travel did not include the right to ignore trespass laws or remain on property without regard to ownership.

A Sarasota law prohibited camping on public and private property between sunset and sunrise. Five homeless people challenged the law, arguing that it punished innocent conduct and was unconstitutionally vague. The circuit court found in *City of Sarasota v. Tillman* (No. 2003 CA 15645 NC [Fla. Cir. Ct. 2004]) that the law was unconstitutional for criminalizing the noncriminal act of sleeping.

PANHANDLING. One of the notable court cases addressing panhandling involved Jennifer Loper, who moved from her parents' suburban New York home to beg on the streets of New York City. From time to time she and her friend William Kaye were ordered by police to move on, in accordance with the city ordinance, which stated: "A person is guilty of loitering when he: '(1) Loiters, remains or wanders about in a public place for the purpose of begging.'" In 1992 Loper and Kaye sued the city, claiming that their free speech rights had been violated and that the ordinance was unconstitutional. A district court declared the ordinance unconstitutional on First Amendment grounds. On appeal, the police department argued that begging has no expressive element that is protected by the First Amendment. In *Loper v. New York City Police Department* (999 F.2d 699 [2d Cir. 1993]), the U.S. Court of Appeals for the Second Circuit declared the city's ban on begging invalid, noting that the regulations applied to sidewalks, which have historically been acknowledged to be a public forum. The court agreed that the ban deprived beggars of all means to express their message. Even if a panhandler does not speak, "the presence of an unkempt and disheveled person holding out his or her hand or a cup to receive a donation itself conveys a message of need for support and assistance."

In *Chase v. City of Gainesville* (2006 WL 2620260 [N.D. Fla. Sept. 11, 2006]), a group of homeless people challenged the constitutionality of three antisolicitation laws in Gainesville. Two of the laws prohibited holding signs on sidewalks or by the side of the road soliciting donations, while the third law required anyone seeking charitable contributions on sidewalks or roadways to obtain a permit. The homeless people argued that soliciting donations should be protected under the First Amendment. The court granted a preliminary injunction and in September 2006 the lawsuit was settled, which included a permanent injunction against enforcement of the three laws.

ZONING THE HOMELESS OUT OF DOWNTOWN. In 1998 Alan Mason, a homeless man, sought an injunction, damages, and relief against the city of Tucson and the city police for zoning homeless people. The suit alleged that homeless people were arrested without cause, were charged with misdemeanors, and were then released only if they agreed to stay away from the area where they had been arrested. Mason himself had been restricted from certain downtown areas, such as federal, state, and local courts (including the court in which his case was tried); voter registration facilities; a soup kitchen; places of worship; and many social and transportation agencies.

The plaintiff argued that such restrictions violated his constitutional right to travel, deprived him of liberty without due process in violation of the Fifth Amendment, and implicated the equal protection clause of the 14th Amendment. In *Mason v. Tucson* (D. Arizona, 1998), the district court granted a temporary injunction against enforcing the law, saying the zone restrictions were overbroad. The case was subsequently settled out of court.

SLEEPING ON SIDEWALKS. In 2006 a federal appeals court in Pasadena, California, ruled that ordinances against homeless people "sitting, lying, or sleeping" on sidewalks are unconstitutional. In *Jones v. City of Los Angeles* (444 F.3d 1118 [9th Cir.]), the court ruled that Los Angeles enforced the law only against homeless people, therefore criminalizing "the status of homelessness," which violated the Eighth Amendment. It was the first time in more than a decade that a law criminalizing homelessness had been struck down in court.

CHAPTER 8
HEALTH CARE

HEALTH OF POOR PEOPLE
Connection between Poor Health and Poverty

In *Health, United States, 2011* (May 2012, http://www.cdc.gov/nchs/data/hus/hus11.pdf), the National Center for Health Statistics (NCHS) points out that adults in poverty are more likely than other adults to have health problems and to be uninsured, and that on average they have shorter life spans than the nonpoor. Likewise, the NCHS notes, children in poverty have elevated risks for poor health and teen pregnancy and are more likely than nonpoor children to be uninsured.

Although the correlation between poverty and health problems is well established, less consensus exists about the specific nature of the cause and effect relationship. The NCHS approaches the issue through the lens of socioeconomic status (SES), a measure that takes into account income, education, and employment characteristics. Low levels of education, low income, marginal employment status, and poor health reinforce one another in numerous ways. Those with low levels of education are more likely to have low-paying and low-status jobs or to be unemployed. Low-paying and low-status jobs can pose health risks that higher-status jobs do not, and because they are less likely to provide health insurance benefits, they correlate with lower access to preventive health care, including vaccinations. Additionally, low levels of education, which are common among the impoverished, can result in a lack of awareness about the health effects of certain lifestyle choices. Low SES correlates with behaviors that adversely affect health, including tobacco use and physical inactivity, and low-SES children and adults often live in low-income neighborhoods that are lacking in resources for promoting healthy lifestyles. Both the poor and the near-poor are more likely to be uninsured than those in higher economic brackets, and therefore they often seek medical care only when health issues have reached a crisis stage.

Low-SES women are less likely to use contraception to prevent pregnancy than are high-SES women, and when pregnant, they are less likely to receive satisfactory prenatal care.

ADULTS. In *Health, United States, 2011*, the NCHS highlights some specific health challenges common among low-SES adults. According to the NCHS, poor adults are more likely than adults above the poverty line to suffer from disabilities, defined as one or more of the following: "movement difficulty, emotional difficulty, sensory (seeing or hearing) difficulty, cognitive difficulty, self-care (ADL or IADL [measures of an individual's ability to satisfy basic daily activities]) limitation, social limitation, or work limitation." In 2010 one-quarter of all adults aged 18 to 64 were disabled according to the above definition, but more than 40% of impoverished adults in the same age group were disabled. Poor seniors were also more likely to be disabled than seniors in other income categories. Approximately 60% of all adults aged 65 and older had disabilities in 2010, compared with roughly 75% of poor adults in the same age group. As Figure 8.1 shows, adults' disability status is closely correlated with income: among those with incomes between 100% and 199% of poverty, disability is less common than among those in poverty but more common than among those with incomes between 200% and 399% of poverty. Adults aged 18 to 64 whose incomes are at 400% or more of poverty are approximately half as likely to be disabled as poor adults in the same age group. The same basic pattern holds among the elderly.

The NCHS also notes the alarming prevalence of depression among adults aged 20 and older who live in poverty. As Figure 8.2 shows, between 2005 and 2010, 17% of those 20 years of age and older who lived below the poverty line reported symptoms that led them to be classified as clinically depressed, compared with 10% of those whose incomes fell between 100% and 199% of

FIGURE 8.1

The prevalence of disability among adults, by age and percentage of poverty level, 2000–10

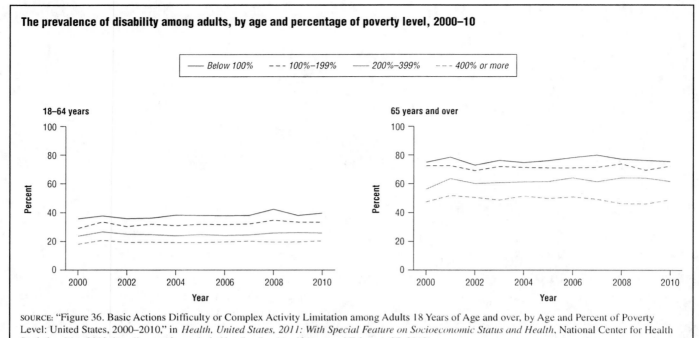

SOURCE: "Figure 36. Basic Actions Difficulty or Complex Activity Limitation among Adults 18 Years of Age and over, by Age and Percent of Poverty Level: United States, 2000–2010," in *Health, United States, 2011: With Special Feature on Socioeconomic Status and Health*, National Center for Health Statistics, May 2012, http://www.cdc.gov/nchs/data/hus/hus11.pdf (accessed February 27, 2013)

FIGURE 8.2

Depression among adults 20 years of age and older, by age and percentage of poverty level, 2005–10

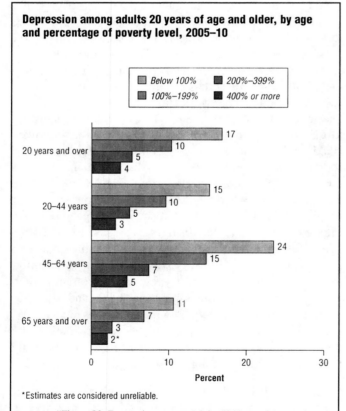

*Estimates are considered unreliable.

SOURCE: "Figure 33. Depression among Adults 20 Years of Age and over, by Age and Percent of Poverty Level: United States, 2005–2010," in *Health, United States, 2011: With Special Feature on Socioeconomic Status and Health*, National Center for Health Statistics, May 2012, http://www.cdc.gov/nchs/data/hus/hus11.pdf (accessed February 27, 2013)

poverty, 5% of those whose incomes were between 200% and 399% of poverty, and 4% of those whose incomes reached 400% of poverty or greater. Adults between the ages of 45 and 64 were more likely to suffer from depression than adults in any other age group, and those who were both poor and between the ages of 45 and 64 suffered from depression more frequently than any other subgroup, at a rate of 24%. As the NCHS notes, depression at all income levels correlates with "increased morbidity and mortality, reduced productivity, and poorer quality of life." As with physical disabilities, the NCHS suggests that depression may be both a cause and a consequence of low SES. Those with low incomes and low levels of educational attainment may be at greater risk of developing depression, and depression is likely to reduce one's ability to excel on the job, resulting in deepened or sustained poverty.

The NCHS further reports in *Health, United States, 2011* that in midlife the poor are substantially more prone to develop one or more chronic conditions than those living above poverty level. People with more than one of the following health problems—heart disease, high blood pressure, stroke, emphysema, cancer, diabetes, asthma, bronchitis, kidney disease—present particular complications to health care professionals, increasing both the amount of treatment typically required and the expense of that treatment. As Figure 8.3 shows, in both 1999–2000 and 2009–10, adults in poverty between ages 45 and 64 were substantially more likely to have more than one chronic condition than were adults in the same age group with different income profiles. Between the

FIGURE 8.3

Prevalence of two or more chronic conditions among adults ages 45–64, by percentage of poverty level, 1999–2000 and 2009–10

Below 100%   200%–399%
100%–199%   400% or more

1999–2000
31
24
17
12

2009–2010
33
30
21
16

Percent

Note: Selected chronic conditions include ever told had heart disease, diabetes, cancer, hypertension (told at least twice), stroke, or emphysema; or told in last year had chronic bronchitis or kidney disease; or reported having an asthma attack in past year.

SOURCE: "Figure 35. Two or More Selected Chronic Health Conditions among Adults 45–64 Years of Age, by Percent of Poverty Level: United States, 1999–2000 and 2009–2010," in *Health, United States, 2011: With Special Feature on Socioeconomic Status and Health*, National Center for Health Statistics, May 2012, http://www.cdc.gov/nchs/data/hus/hus11.pdf (accessed February 27, 2013)

FIGURE 8.4

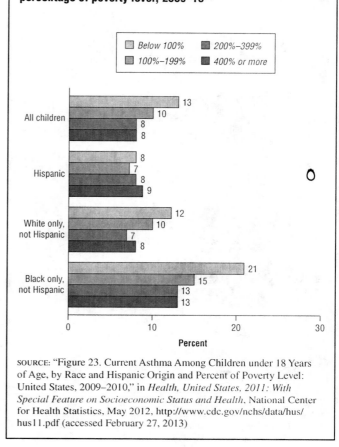

Asthma among children, by race and Hispanic origin and percentage of poverty level, 2009–10

Below 100%   200%–399%
100%–199%   400% or more

All children
13
10
8
8

Hispanic
8
7
8
9

White only, not Hispanic
12
10
7
8

Black only, not Hispanic
21
15
13
13

Percent

SOURCE: "Figure 23. Current Asthma Among Children under 18 Years of Age, by Race and Hispanic Origin and Percent of Poverty Level: United States, 2009–2010," in *Health, United States, 2011: With Special Feature on Socioeconomic Status and Health*, National Center for Health Statistics, May 2012, http://www.cdc.gov/nchs/data/hus/hus11.pdf (accessed February 27, 2013)

two survey periods, moreover, the NCHS found that the likelihood of those middle-aged adults living at 100% to 199% of poverty to develop more than one chronic condition closely approached the likelihood of the middle-aged poor to develop more than one chronic condition. The prevalence of more than one chronic condition among all adults aged 45 to 64 living above poverty increased between the two survey periods more than it did among adults living below the poverty line. However, in 2009–10, middle-aged adults living below poverty were still more than twice as likely to suffer from two or more chronic conditions as adults of the same age group with incomes of more than 400% of poverty.

CHILDREN. The NCHS also highlights certain specific health challenges common among low-SES children in *Health, United States, 2011.* Asthma, a chronic condition that causes difficulty with breathing, occurs at significantly higher rates among certain demographic groups of poor children than among other poor children, as well as occurring at higher rates among poor children than among higher-income children. As Figure 8.4 shows, among all children in poverty, asthma occurred at a rate of 13% in 2009–10, compared with 10% for children whose household income was between 100% and 199% of poverty and

8% for all children above 200% of poverty. The prevalence of childhood asthma at different income levels varied substantially among different demographic groups, however. Hispanic children showed no significantly greater disposition for asthma in poverty than at other income levels, but among white non-Hispanics, 12% of poor children suffered from asthma, compared with 10% of children with household incomes between 100% and 199% of poverty, 7% at 200% to 399% of poverty, and 8% above 400% of poverty. Among African-American children, asthma was more prevalent at all income levels, and children in poverty were substantially more likely to have been diagnosed with the condition: 21% of African-American children below the poverty line had asthma, compared with 15% at 100% to 199% of poverty and 13% at 200% of poverty and above.

Attention-deficit/hyperactivity disorder (ADHD), one of the most common neurobehavioral conditions among children, also shows meaningful variations among different income groups and among different demographic groups. As with asthma, there is a statistically significant correlation between poverty and childhood prevalence of ADHD, as well as significant variation between Hispanic and non-Hispanic children. Figure 8.5 shows that 13% of all

FIGURE 8.5

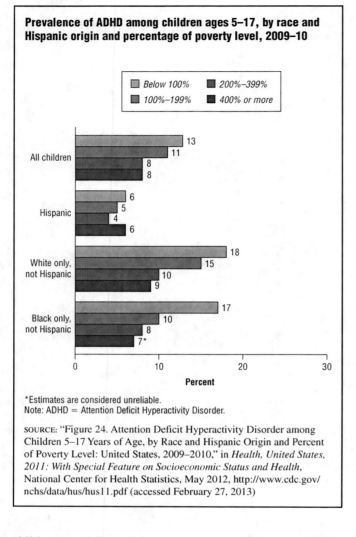

Prevalence of ADHD among children ages 5–17, by race and Hispanic origin and percentage of poverty level, 2009–10

Below 100%   200%–399%
100%–199%   400% or more

*Estimates are considered unreliable.
Note: ADHD = Attention Deficit Hyperactivity Disorder.

SOURCE: "Figure 24. Attention Deficit Hyperactivity Disorder among Children 5–17 Years of Age, by Race and Hispanic Origin and Percent of Poverty Level: United States, 2009–2010," in *Health, United States, 2011: With Special Feature on Socioeconomic Status and Health*, National Center for Health Statistics, May 2012, http://www.cdc.gov/nchs/data/hus/hus11.pdf (accessed February 27, 2013)

children aged 5 to 17 in poverty had ADHD in 2009–10, compared with 11% of children at 100% to 199% of poverty and 8% of children at 200% of poverty and above. Among Hispanic children, poverty was not a predictor of the prevalence of ADHD, but among non-Hispanic whites the condition was far more common among children below poverty (18%) and at 100% to 199% of poverty (15%) than among children above 200% of poverty (9%–10%). Among African-American children, those in poverty were by far the most likely (17%) to suffer from ADHD, but the prevalence among those at 100% to 199% more closely resembled the prevalence among African-American children in higher income brackets.

Poverty and Access to Health Care

The NCHS notes in *Health, United States, 2011* that poor and near-poor people have reduced access to medical care. In 2010, 23.4% of those living below the poverty level reported either not receiving care or delaying care because of cost. (See Figure 8.6.) Perhaps surprisingly, an even greater percentage of those living just above the poverty line (24%) reported either not receiving care or

FIGURE 8.6

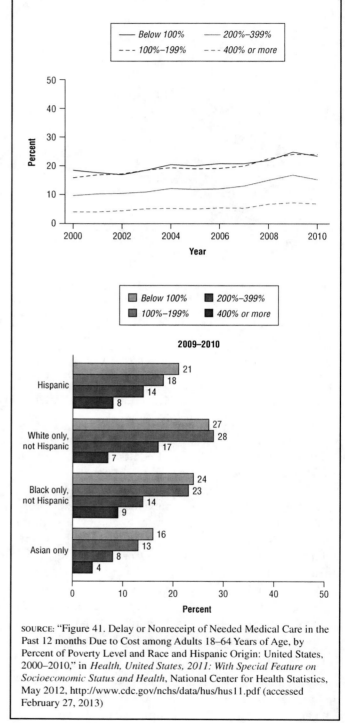

Delay or nonreceipt of medical care in the past 12 months due to cost among adults ages 18–64, by percentage of poverty level and race and Hispanic origin, 2000–10

Below 100%   200%–399%
100%–199%   400% or more

2009–2010

Below 100%   200%–399%
100%–199%   400% or more

SOURCE: "Figure 41. Delay or Nonreceipt of Needed Medical Care in the Past 12 months Due to Cost among Adults 18–64 Years of Age, by Percent of Poverty Level and Race and Hispanic Origin: United States, 2000–2010," in *Health, United States, 2011: With Special Feature on Socioeconomic Status and Health*, National Center for Health Statistics, May 2012, http://www.cdc.gov/nchs/data/hus/hus11.pdf (accessed February 27, 2013)

delaying care because of cost. This income group had additionally shown the largest increase, over the period 2000 to 2010, in unmet medical needs, with the percentage of those who delayed or did not receive needed medical care rising from 15.8% in 2000 to 24% in 2010.

As the NCHS observes, the presence or absence of health insurance is a major factor in whether or not a person has unmet medical needs, but insurance coverage plans vary widely, with lower-cost plans often excluding treatments or requiring higher levels of co-payment from the policyholder. As health care costs rose at unprecedented rates in the first decade of the 21st century, even some individuals who were insured were forced to postpone or forego care due to cost issues. Accordingly, the percentage of those at 200% to 399% of poverty who had unmet medical needs rose significantly between 2000 and 2010, in concert with the percentages of the poor and near-poor who had unmet needs. In 2000, 9.6% of people at this level of income had unmet medical needs; by 2010 the figure reached 15.2%. Among those at 400% of poverty and above, 6.8% had unmet medical needs in 2010.

Children in poverty were also more likely than higher-income children to have unmet medical needs, but due in large part to the Children's Health Insurance Program (CHIP), which will be discussed later in this chapter, the gap between poor and nonpoor children narrowed significantly between 2000 and 2010. In 2000, 22% of children below poverty and 21.7% of children at 100% to 199% of poverty had no health insurance coverage. By 2010 the figures for the two groups had been lowered to 10.6% and 12.7%, respectively, representing a substantial increase in the number of children able to access preventive care and to have their health needs met.

HEALTH INSURANCE

The scope of health issues regarding the impoverished and homeless in the United States is related in part to the number of uninsured Americans. People without insurance are less likely to seek medical care. When they do seek medical care, they are more likely to go to an emergency department, which leads to skyrocketing health care costs, thus reinforcing the pattern of unaffordability that forced them to forego or delay care in the first place. Figure 8.7

FIGURE 8.7

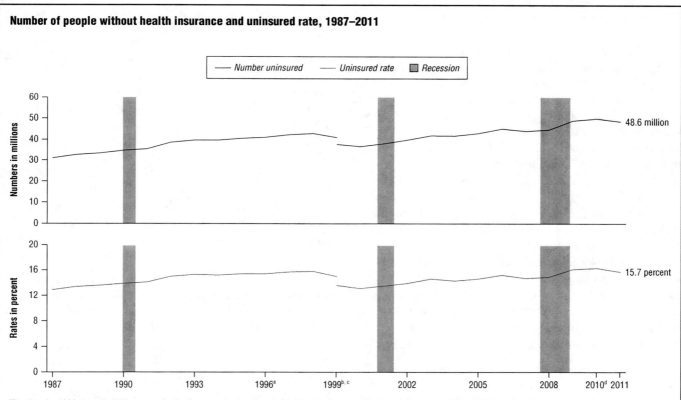

Number of people without health insurance and uninsured rate, 1987–2011

aThe data for 1996 through 1999 were revised using an approximation method for consistency with the revision to the 2004 and 2005 estimates.
bImplementation of Census 2000-based population controls occurred for the 2000 Annual Social and Economic (ASEC) Supplement, which collected data for 1999. These estimates also reflect the results of follow-up verification questions, which were asked of people who responded "no" to all questions about specific types of health insurance coverage in order to verify whether they were actually uninsured. This change increased the number and percentage of people covered by health insurance, bringing the Current Population Survey (CPS) more in line with estimates from other national surveys.
cThe data for 1999 through 2009 were revised to reflect the results of enhancements to the editing process.
dImplementation of 2010 Census population controls.
Note: Respondents were not asked detailed health insurance questions before the 1988 CPS. The data points are placed at the midpoints of the respective years.

SOURCE: Carmen DeNavas-Walt, Bernadette D. Proctor, and Jessica C. Smith, "Figure 8. Number Uninsured and Uninsured Rate: 1987 to 2011," in *Income, Poverty, and Health Insurance Coverage in the United States: 2011*, U.S. Census Bureau, September 2012, http://www.census.gov/prod/2012pubs/p60-243.pdf (accessed January 15, 2013)

FIGURE 8.8

Number of children and nonelderly adults without health insurance, 2007–11

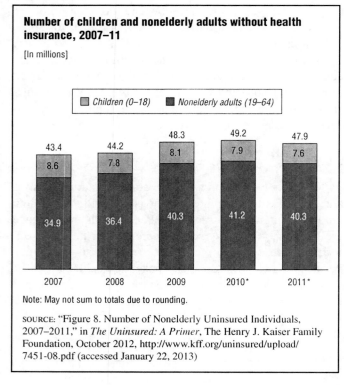

[In millions]

Note: May not sum to totals due to rounding.

SOURCE: "Figure 8. Number of Nonelderly Uninsured Individuals, 2007–2011," in *The Uninsured: A Primer*, The Henry J. Kaiser Family Foundation, October 2012, http://www.kff.org/uninsured/upload/7451-08.pdf (accessed January 22, 2013)

FIGURE 8.9

Health insurance coverage of nonelderly persons by race and Hispanic origin, 2011

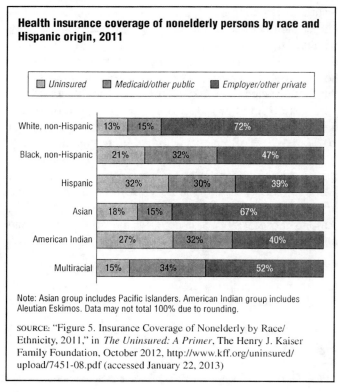

Note: Asian group includes Pacific Islanders. American Indian group includes Aleutian Eskimos. Data may not total 100% due to rounding.

SOURCE: "Figure 5. Insurance Coverage of Nonelderly by Race/Ethnicity, 2011," in *The Uninsured: A Primer*, The Henry J. Kaiser Family Foundation, October 2012, http://www.kff.org/uninsured/upload/7451-08.pdf (accessed January 22, 2013)

shows that the number of uninsured people rose sharply during the so-called Great Recession, which lasted from late 2007 to mid-2009, and then leveled off at historically high rates in the post-recession years. As the Henry J. Kaiser Family Foundation (KFF) reports in *The Uninsured: A Primer: Key Facts about Americans without Health Insurance* (October 2012, http://www.kff.org/uninsured/upload/7451-08.pdf), the number of nonelderly uninsured (a category that includes children) rose sharply between 2007 and 2010, from 43.4 million to 49.2 million. (See Figure 8.8.) The KFF notes that the increase in the numbers of the uninsured was driven primarily by high unemployment, which resulted in many Americans' loss of employer-sponsored health coverage. Because many who lost coverage in this way were not poor enough to qualify for Medicaid or CHIP, which are means-tested programs, they went without coverage. With slowly improving employment conditions, some of those who had lost insurance regained it in the post-recession years.

In 2011 Hispanic people were the most likely to be uninsured. Almost a third (32%) of Hispanics were uninsured, followed by Native Americans (27%) and non-Hispanic African-Americans (21%). (See Figure 8.9.) By contrast, 18% of Asian-Americans and 13% of non-Hispanic whites were uninsured. Not coincidentally, these two groups were by far the most likely to have employer-sponsored health care coverage. Approximately 67% of Asian-Americans and 72% of whites had coverage through their jobs, compared with 39% of Hispanics, 40% of Native Americans, and 47% of African-Americans.

Figure 8.10 shows that the likelihood of being uninsured correlates closely with income, and that dramatic disparities in the uninsured rate occurred well above poverty level in the years 1999 to 2011. Approximately 7.8% of those making more than $75,000 per year were uninsured in 2011. Those making between $50,000 and $74,999, meanwhile, were almost twice as likely (15.4%) to be uninsured, and those making between $25,000 and $49,999 were almost three times as likely (21.5%) to be uninsured as those making $75,000 or more. One-quarter (25.4%) of those making less than $25,000 were uninsured. Moreover, in all income categories, the uninsured rate was higher in 2011 than it had been in 1999.

From 2009 to 2011 the national uninsured rate averaged 16%, but there was dramatic variation among state rates. (See Table 8.1.) Approximately 1 out of 5 people in California (19.5%), Florida (20.7%), Georgia (19.7%), Nevada (21.6%), and New Mexico (20.6%) were uninsured during these years. Texas had by far the highest uninsured rate between 2009 and 2011, at 24.6%. Other states had much lower rates, including Hawaii (7.6%), Maine (9.7%), Minnesota (9%), Vermont (9.1%), and Wisconsin (9.6%). Massachusetts had by far the lowest uninsured rate (4.4%), the result of a state law requiring most individuals to carry health insurance. In general, states in the South and West had the highest uninsured rates, whereas midwestern and northeastern states had the lowest. (See Figure 8.11.)

In spite of gains made in the uninsured rate among children since 2000, children in poverty remained much

FIGURE 8.10

Uninsured rate by real household income, 1999–2011

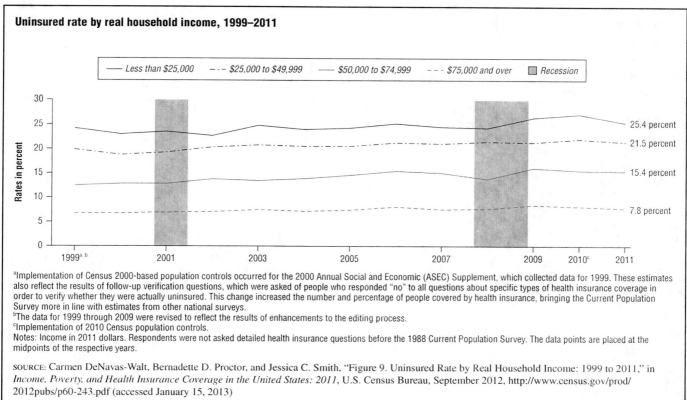

[a]Implementation of Census 2000-based population controls occurred for the 2000 Annual Social and Economic (ASEC) Supplement, which collected data for 1999. These estimates also reflect the results of follow-up verification questions, which were asked of people who responded "no" to all questions about specific types of health insurance coverage in order to verify whether they were actually uninsured. This change increased the number and percentage of people covered by health insurance, bringing the Current Population Survey more in line with estimates from other national surveys.
[b]The data for 1999 through 2009 were revised to reflect the results of enhancements to the editing process.
[c]Implementation of 2010 Census population controls.
Notes: Income in 2011 dollars. Respondents were not asked detailed health insurance questions before the 1988 Current Population Survey. The data points are placed at the midpoints of the respective years.

SOURCE: Carmen DeNavas-Walt, Bernadette D. Proctor, and Jessica C. Smith, "Figure 9. Uninsured Rate by Real Household Income: 1999 to 2011," in *Income, Poverty, and Health Insurance Coverage in the United States: 2011*, U.S. Census Bureau, September 2012, http://www.census.gov/prod/2012pubs/p60-243.pdf (accessed January 15, 2013)

more likely than children in general to be uninsured in 2011 (13.8% versus 9.4%), and the uninsured rate was similarly high for children in all income groups making below $75,000. (See Figure 8.12.) Additionally, the uninsured rate among children varied significantly by race. Hispanic children (15.1%) were far more likely to be uninsured than African-American children (10.2%), Asian-American children (9.1%), or non-Hispanic white children (6.8%).

Health Care Reform

Barack Obama (1961–) campaigned for the presidency in 2008 with a pledge to reform the health care system in order to provide accessible health care for all Americans. Once President Obama took office in January 2009, he signed into law the reauthorization of the Children's Health Insurance Program (CHIP), providing coverage for an additional 4 million children in the years that followed. The American Recovery and Reinvestment Act of 2009, which was signed into law in February 2009, included $1 billion to digitize medical records and provide information on treatments to doctors, measures intended to reduce health care costs.

These health care policies were minor, however, compared to the comprehensive health reform law the Obama administration shepherded through Congress in early 2010. Known as the Affordable Care Act (ACA), the measure was signed into law on March 23, 2010, and phased in over the subsequent four years. In 2010 a Patient's Bill of Rights was implemented, providing consumer protections in the insurance market and outlawing a number of notorious industry practices. Also beginning in 2010, insurance companies were required to begin offering free coverage for a number of preventive health measures, and small businesses offering health care coverage to their employees could take advantage of tax credits. In 2011 an expansion of Medicare benefits kicked in, an experimental center for testing new health care delivery mechanisms began operating, and measures aimed at controlling premium increases among private insurers took effect. The major elements of the law that went into effect in 2012 were a program incentivizing increased quality of treatment for Medicare patients and new rules allowing for the standardization and streamlining of medical billing through the use of electronic records. In 2013 an expansion of Medicaid benefits went into effect, and the law's centerpiece, the establishment of a national Health Insurance Marketplace in which individuals not covered by their employers would be able to purchase their own health plans, was scheduled to begin enrolling participants. The Health Insurance Marketplace was scheduled to open in 2014, and insurers at that point would be subject to strict limits on their ability to deny coverage to individuals. Also in 2014, the Medicaid eligibility threshold was scheduled to be raised to 133% of the poverty level; in practical terms, this meant that millions of Americans would become newly eligible for the program.

TABLE 8.1

Number and percentage of people without health insurance coverage by state, 2008–09, 2010–11, and 2009–11

[Numbers in thousands. People as of March of the following year.]

States	Total	3-year average (2009–2011)[a]		2-year average percentage uninsured		
		Uninsured		2008–2009	2010[b]–2011	Change (2010–2011 average less 2008–2009 average)[c]
		Number	Percentage	Percentage	Percentage	
United States	**306,554**	**49,146**	**16.0**	**15.5**	**16.0**	**0.5**
Alabama	4,728	708	15.0	14.0	14.3	0.3
Alaska	698	125	18.0	18.4	18.2	−0.2
Arizona	6,422	1,183	18.4	19.0	18.2	−0.8
Arkansas	2,883	528	18.3	18.3	18.0	−0.3
California	37,242	7,250	19.5	18.7	19.6	0.8
Colorado	4,981	714	14.3	14.9	14.3	−0.6
Connecticut	3,528	364	10.3	10.2	9.9	−0.3
Delaware	894	103	11.5	11.9	10.7	−1.2
District of Columbia	605	68	11.3	10.9	10.6	−0.3
Florida	18,802	3,898	20.7	20.6	20.2	−0.3
Georgia	9,604	1,889	19.7	18.8	19.3	0.5
Hawaii	1,318	100	7.6	7.3	7.8	0.4
Idaho	1,554	266	17.1	15.3	18.0	2.8
Illinois	12,725	1,853	14.6	13.2	14.8	1.6
Indiana	6,389	831	13.0	12.5	12.7	0.2
Iowa	3,013	332	11.0	9.9	11.1	1.2
Kansas	2,783	361	13.0	12.3	13.1	0.8
Kentucky	4,290	642	15.0	15.8	14.6	−1.2
Louisiana	4,455	820	18.4	17.0	20.3	3.3
Maine	1,313	128	9.7	10.1	9.7	−0.4
Maryland	5,771	765	13.3	12.3	13.3	1.0
Massachusetts	6,542	288	4.4	4.6	4.5	−0.2
Michigan	9,744	1,241	12.7	12.2	12.7	0.5
Minnesota	5,244	471	9.0	8.1	9.5	1.3
Mississippi	2,904	528	18.2	17.5	18.6	1.1
Missouri	5,924	857	14.5	13.5	14.4	0.9
Montana	983	169	17.2	15.4	18.2	2.8
Nebraska	1,811	222	12.3	11.1	12.8	1.7
Nevada	2,686	580	21.6	19.3	22.0	2.7
New Hampshire	1,301	140	10.8	10.0	11.3	1.4
New Jersey	8,710	1,319	15.1	13.9	15.5	1.7
New Mexico	2,029	419	20.6	21.9	20.5	−1.4
New York	19,147	2,636	13.8	13.8	13.6	−0.1
North Carolina	9,441	1,617	17.1	16.5	16.7	0.2
North Dakota	660	73	11.1	10.9	11.3	0.3
Ohio	11,372	1,551	13.6	12.5	13.7	1.2
Oklahoma	3,714	646	17.4	15.9	17.1	1.2
Oregon	3,815	602	15.8	16.6	14.9	−1.7
Pennsylvania	12,586	1,369	10.9	10.3	10.9	0.6
Rhode Island	1,038	125	12.0	11.5	11.8	0.2
South Carolina	4,571	860	18.8	16.2	19.7	3.6
South Dakota	803	106	13.2	12.6	13.0	0.4
Tennessee	6,306	899	14.3	14.7	13.9	−0.8
Texas	25,173	6,194	24.6	25.0	24.2	−0.8
Utah	2,774	393	14.2	13.0	14.2	1.2
Vermont	621	56	9.1	9.4	9.0	−0.4
Virginia	7,889	1,051	13.3	12.2	13.7	1.5
Washington	6,754	920	13.6	12.3	14.2	1.9
West Virginia	1,825	254	13.9	14.1	14.2	—
Wisconsin	5,636	539	9.6	9.1	9.9	0.8
Wyoming	555	93	16.8	14.3	17.5	3.2

—Represents or rounds to zero.
[a]Both 2009 and 2010 data are consistent with 2011 data through implementation of census 2010-based population controls.
[b]2010 data are consistent with 2011 data through implementation of census 2010-based population controls.
[c]Details may not sum to totals because of rounding.

SOURCE: Carmen DeNavas-Walt, Bernadette D. Proctor, and Jessica C. Smith, "Number and Percentage of People without Health Insurance Coverage by State Using 2- and 3-Year Averages: 2008–2009, 2010–2011, and 2009–2011," in *Income, Poverty, and Health Insurance Coverage in the United States: 2011, Tables and Figures*, U.S. Census Bureau, September 2012, http://www.census.gov/hhes/www/hlthins/data/incpovhlth/2011/race.xls (accessed January 22, 2013)

The functioning of the ACA's Health Insurance Marketplace was dependent on a so-called individual mandate, a requirement that all adults either purchase insurance or pay a penalty. Under the existing health insurance system of the time, individuals often could not get affordable insurance policies if they were not covered by their employers because the pool of applicants for individual policies often included a disproportionate number of

FIGURE 8.11

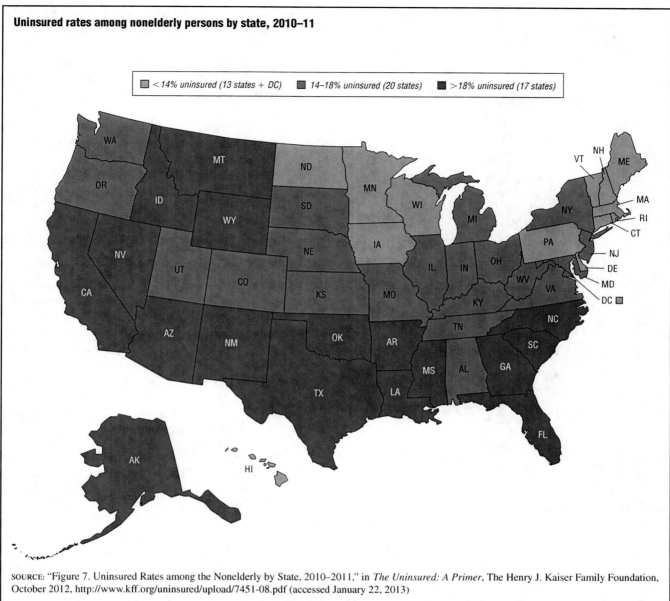

Uninsured rates among nonelderly persons by state, 2010–11

<14% uninsured (13 states + DC)   14–18% uninsured (20 states)   >18% uninsured (17 states)

SOURCE: "Figure 7. Uninsured Rates among the Nonelderly by State, 2010–2011," in *The Uninsured: A Primer*, The Henry J. Kaiser Family Foundation, October 2012, http://www.kff.org/uninsured/upload/7451-08.pdf (accessed January 22, 2013).

people with existing medical problems. Insurers thus charged correspondingly high premiums to ensure an acceptable level of profit. According to the architects of the individual mandate, however, if the young and healthy would enter the overall pool of the insured, the costs of insuring the sick would be balanced out by the costs of insuring the healthy. All individuals could therefore count on being able to get health insurance at all stages of their lives, whether or not their employers offered coverage, and insurance companies would still enjoy a profitable business model.

The concept of the individual mandate originated in conservative political think tanks and was supported by various Republican politicians during the 1990s and the first decade of the 21st century. A fierce partisan battle

engulfed the passage of the ACA, however, and after its passage, Republican groups mounted legal challenges hinging on the constitutionality of the mandate. The issue reached the U.S. Supreme Court, and in a 5–4 decision that Adam Liptak of the *New York Times* ("Supreme Court Upholds Health Care Law, 5–4, in Victory for Obama," June 28, 2012) called "the most significant federalism decision since the New Deal and the most closely watched case since Bush v. Gore in 2000," the court ruled that the mandate was constitutional and that the health care law could proceed toward full implementation.

Medicaid

Medicaid, which is authorized under Title XIX of the Social Security Act, is a federal-state program that provides

FIGURE 8.12

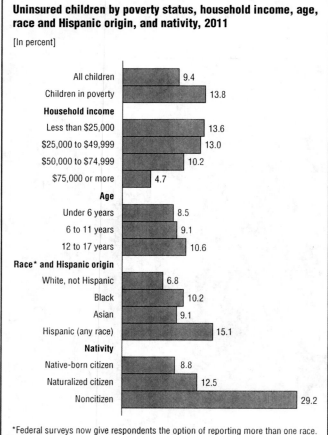

Uninsured children by poverty status, household income, age, race and Hispanic origin, and nativity, 2011

[In percent]

All children	9.4
Children in poverty	13.8
Household income	
Less than $25,000	13.6
$25,000 to $49,999	13.0
$50,000 to $74,999	10.2
$75,000 or more	4.7
Age	
Under 6 years	8.5
6 to 11 years	9.1
12 to 17 years	10.6
Race* and Hispanic origin	
White, not Hispanic	6.8
Black	10.2
Asian	9.1
Hispanic (any race)	15.1
Nativity	
Native-born citizen	8.8
Naturalized citizen	12.5
Noncitizen	29.2

*Federal surveys now give respondents the option of reporting more than one race. This figure shows data using the race-alone concept. For example, Asian refers to people who reported Asian and no other race.

SOURCE: Carmen DeNavas-Walt, Bernadette D. Proctor, and Jessica C. Smith, "Figure 10. Uninsured Children by Poverty Status, Household Income, Age, Race and Hispanic Origin, and Nativity: 2011," in *Income, Poverty, and Health Insurance Coverage in the United States: 2011*, U.S. Census Bureau, September 2012, http://www .census.gov/prod/2012pubs/p60-243.pdf (accessed January 15, 2013)

medical insurance for low-income people who are aged, blind, disabled, or members of families with dependent children and for certain other pregnant women and children. Within federal guidelines, each state designs and administers its own program. For this reason, there may be considerable differences from state to state as to who is covered, what type of coverage is provided, and how much is paid for medical services. Many states calculate eligibility based on the official poverty level, and many go beyond the minimum requirements established by the federal government when it comes to coverage of children. States receive federal matching payments based on their Medicaid expenditures and the state's per capita (per person) income. The federal match ranges from 50% to 80% of Medicaid expenditures.

Medicaid eligibility was historically linked to receipt of, or eligibility to receive, benefits under other welfare programs such as Aid to Families with Dependent Children or Supplemental Security Income (SSI), but legislation gradually extended coverage during the 1980s and 1990s. In 1986 benefits were extended to low-income children and pregnant women not on welfare; states were required to cover children less than six years of age and pregnant women with family incomes below 133% of the federal poverty level. Pregnant women in this group were only covered for medical services related to their pregnancies, and then their children received full Medicaid coverage. The states were authorized to cover children under one year old and pregnant women with incomes more than 133%, but not more than 185%, of the poverty level.

Changes in eligibility standards also allowed aged and disabled people receiving Medicare whose incomes were below 100% of the poverty level to collect benefits, and following the welfare reform of 1996, states were authorized to deny Medicaid benefits to adults who lose Temporary Assistance for Needy Families benefits because they refuse to work. However, poor pregnant women and children were exempted from this provision. In addition, the welfare law required state plans to ensure Medicaid for children receiving foster care or adoption assistance, and it gave states the option to use Medicaid to provide health care coverage to low-income working parents. Previously, even when the income of working households was below the federal poverty line, parents were ineligible for publicly funded health insurance.

Another major expansion of Medicaid came with the passage of the ACA in 2010. Beginning in 2014, a uniform national eligibility standard would go into effect, extending coverage to almost all Americans under age 65 whose incomes fell below 133% of the poverty line. Expected to result in the extension of health care coverage to approximately 17 million uninsured Americans, the ACA Medicaid expansion was complicated somewhat by a June 2012 Supreme Court ruling on the law. Although the Medicaid expansion was not struck down by the court, the justices required that states be allowed to opt out of the expansion and forego the additional federal funds that would pay for it, while still retaining their previous levels of federal Medicaid funding. As of February 2013, 14 state legislatures had opted out of the Medicaid expansion. Opposition to the Medicaid expansion, as with the opposition to the ACA in general, was strongest in the South, where most states chose not to expand coverage even though they had among the highest uninsured rates and the highest poverty rates in the country.

In 2011, prior to the expansion of the program under the terms of the ACA, 16.5% of the total population, about 50.8 million Americans, were covered by Medicaid, up from 15.8% (48.5 million) in 2010. (See Table 8.2.) These levels marked the highest rate of Medicaid participation since the late 1980s. As Figure 8.13 shows, 71% of poor children received health coverage through Medicaid or

TABLE 8.2

Coverage by type of health insurance, 2010 and 2011

[People as of March of the following year]

Coverage type	2010[a]	2011
Any private plan[b]	64.0	63.9
Any private plan alone[c]	52.5	52.0
Employment-based[b]	55.3	55.1
Employment-based alone[c]	45.7	45.1
Direct-purchase[b]	9.9	9.8
Direct-purchase alone[c]	3.7	3.6
Any government plan[b]	31.2	32.2
Any government plan alone[c]	19.7	20.4
Medicare[b]	14.6	15.2
Medicare alone[c]	4.7	4.9
Medicaid[b]	15.8	16.5
Medicaid alone[c]	11.1	11.5
Military health care[b, d]	4.2	4.4
Military health care alone[c, d]	1.3	1.3
Uninsured	16.3	15.7

[a]Implementation of Census 2010-based population controls.
[b]The estimates by type of coverage are not mutually exclusive; people can be covered by more than one type of health insurance during the year.
[c]The estimates by type of coverage are mutually exclusive; people did not have any other type of health insurance during the year.
[d]Military health care includes Tricare and CHAMPVA (Civilian Health and Medical Program of the Department of Veteran Affairs), as well as care provided by the Department of Veterans Affairs and the military.

SOURCE: Carmen DeNavas-Walt, Bernadette D. Proctor, and Jessica C. Smith, "Table 8. Coverage by Type of Health Insurance," in *Income, Poverty, and Health Insurance Coverage in the United States: 2011*, U.S. Census Bureau, September 2012, http://www.census.gov/prod/2012pubs/p60-243.pdf (accessed January 15, 2013).

FIGURE 8.13

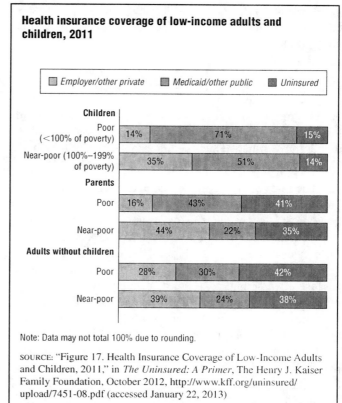

Health insurance coverage of low-income adults and children, 2011

Note: Data may not total 100% due to rounding.

SOURCE: "Figure 17. Health Insurance Coverage of Low-Income Adults and Children, 2011," in *The Uninsured: A Primer*, The Henry J. Kaiser Family Foundation, October 2012, http://www.kff.org/uninsured/upload/7451-08.pdf (accessed January 22, 2013)

other public sources (such as the closely related CHIP program, discussed later in this chapter) in 2011, as did 51% of near-poor children. Because of stricter eligibility guidelines for adults, however, only 43% of poor parents and 22% of near-poor parents received Medicaid benefits; and only 30% of poor adults without children and 24% of near-poor adults without children received Medicaid benefits. These poor and near-poor adults were the Americans most likely to be uninsured in 2011: 41% of poor parents and 42% of near-poor childless adults had no health coverage, while 35% of near-poor parents and 38% of near-poor childless adults had no health coverage. In states that did not opt out of the ACA's Medicaid expansion, most of these adults would become newly eligible for Medicaid benefits in 2014.

As the Urban Institute (UI) reports in *Medicaid* (http://www.urban.org/health_policy/medicaid/index.cfm), Medicaid spending grew explosively during the first decade of the 21st century. Total expenditures on the program were $205.7 billion in 2000; by 2006, prior to the Great Recession, spending had reached $314.5 billion. Although the program, like other social welfare efforts, was often characterized as wasteful or unnecessary, and though many argued that it represented an example of out-of-control government spending, the UI maintains that "The real reasons for high growth rates [in the program] are: increases in enrollment due in part to eroding employer-

sponsored insurance and increasing income inequality; increases in the incidence of and recognition of disability; and health care inflation." The UI further notes that, based on its examination of cost issues, coverage of the poor under Medicaid costs less than coverage of the same poor people under private insurance plans.

State Child Health Insurance Program

The Balanced Budget Act of 1997 set aside $24 billion over five years to fund the State Child Health Insurance Program (CHIP) in an effort to reach children who were uninsured. This was the nation's largest children's health care investment since the creation of Medicaid in 1965. The Children's Health Insurance Program Reauthorization Act was signed into law by President Obama in February 2009, extending and expanding the existing CHIP. CHIP requires states to use the funding to cover uninsured children whose families earn too much for Medicaid but too little to afford private coverage. States may use this money to expand their Medicaid programs, design new child health insurance programs, or create a combination of the two. The expanding legislation was expected to provide coverage to an additional 6.5 million children.

States must enroll all children who meet Medicaid's eligibility requirements in the Medicaid program rather than in CHIP. They are not allowed to use CHIP to replace existing health coverage. In addition, states must decide on what kind of cost-sharing, if any, to require of low-income families without keeping them from accessing the program. The only federal requirement is that cost-sharing cannot exceed 5% of family income.

HEALTH OF THE HOMELESS

Poor people can be catapulted into homelessness because of the expenses and missed work caused by health problems. Homelessness itself causes a person's health to deteriorate further. Thus, health problems are frequently both a cause and a consequence of homelessness.

The rates of both chronic and acute (short-term) health problems are disproportionately high among the homeless population. Except for obesity, strokes, and cancer, homeless people are far more likely than housed people to suffer from every category of chronic health problems. Other serious illnesses, such as tuberculosis (TB), are almost exclusively associated with the unhealthy living conditions brought on by poverty, and the homeless are especially vulnerable to them. In general, experts agree that homeless people suffer from more types of illnesses, for longer periods, and with more harmful consequences than housed people. Meanwhile, delivery of health care is complicated by a patient's homeless status, making management of chronic diseases such as diabetes, human immunodeficiency virus (HIV), and hypertension more difficult.

Street living comes with a set of health conditions that living in a home does not. Homeless people fall prey to parasites, frostbite, leg ulcers, and infections. They are also at greater risk of physical and psychological trauma resulting from muggings, beatings, and rape. With no safe place to store belongings, the proper storage or administration of medications becomes difficult. In addition, some homeless people with mental disorders may use drugs or alcohol to self-medicate, and those with addictive disorders are more susceptible to HIV and other communicable diseases.

Homeless people may also lack the ability to access some of the basic rituals of self-care: bed rest, good nutrition, and good personal hygiene. Infections that are easy to prevent among those able to clean themselves thoroughly and frequently can pose persistent threats to the homeless. Additionally, the ability to rest and recuperate, which is often essential for the recovery process, is almost impossible for homeless people. Not only must they spend time locating places to sleep and food to eat, in many cities it is literally illegal for them to rest. As discussed in Chapter 7, ordinances prohibiting sleeping or lying down in public have become increasingly common in the United States. As a result of these and other factors, relatively minor illnesses go untreated among the homeless until they develop into major emergencies, requiring expensive acute care treatment and long-term recovery.

Not surprisingly, then, studies find that homelessness increases the risk of death. James J. O'Connell of the Boston Health Care for the Homeless program reviews in *Premature Mortality in Homeless Populations: A Review of the Literature* (December 2005) the literature concerning the connection between homelessness and mortality. He finds that "a remarkable consistency . . . transcends borders, cultures and oceans: homeless persons are 3–4 times more likely to die than the general population." In addition, he notes that the average age of death of homeless people in the studies reviewed was between 42 and 52 years, despite a life expectancy of about 80 years in the United States. These premature deaths were highly associated with the coexistence of acute and chronic medical conditions with either mental illness or substance abuse. In "Homelessness as an Independent Risk Factor for Mortality: Results from a Retrospective Cohort Study" (*International Journal of Epidemiology*, March 21, 2009), David S. Morrison of the University of Glasgow concludes that homelessness itself is an independent risk factor for death; it appears to substantially increase mortality risk from specific causes.

Ailments of Homeless People

Local studies offer revealing glimpses into common health conditions among the homeless. For example, *Connecticut Counts 2009: Point-in-Time Homeless Count* (August 18, 2009, http://www.cceh.org/pdf/count/2009_pit _report.pdf), a 2009 Connecticut count of homeless people, finds that 36% of sheltered single adults, 35% of unsheltered single adults, and 17% of sheltered adults in families had been hospitalized for mental health issues. Additionally, 72% of unsheltered single adults, 54% of sheltered single adults, and 17% of sheltered adults in families had been in detox or rehab for substance abuse; and 39% of sheltered single adults, 30% of unsheltered single adults, and 17% of sheltered adults living in families had a chronic, limiting health condition. Approximately 7% of sheltered single adults, 5% of sheltered adults living in families, and 2% of unsheltered single adults had HIV or AIDS. In an update to the 2009 report, *Portraits of Homelessness in Connecticut 2010* (February 2011, http:// www.cceh.org/files/publications/portraits_full.pdf), 39% of single adults and 22% of adults in families "reported suffering from a health condition that limits their ability to work, get around and care for themselves." More than half (54%) of adults without children reported having been in a hospital or rehabilitation facility for substance abuse and nearly two-fifths (38%) of adults without children reported having been hospitalized for mental health issues.

A similar portrait of the health care problems faced by the homeless emerges in the *2007 San Mateo County Homeless Census and Survey* (May 2007, http://www.red woodcityhousing.org/pdf/2007_SMCO_Homeless_Census _and_Survey.pdf), conducted in San Mateo County, California, by the group Housing Our People Everyday. Over half (57%) of respondents reported being depressed, 35%

reported having a mental illness, 33% reported they abused drugs, 31% reported they abused alcohol, and 26% reported experiencing post-traumatic stress disorder. More than a third (35%) reported having a physical disability, 28% reported chronic physical health problems, and 2% reported having HIV/AIDS. In an update of the survey conducted in 2011, the *2011 San Mateo County Homeless Census and Survey* (May 4, 2011, http://www.co.sanmateo.ca.us/Attach ments/humanservices/Files/Homlessness/2011%20Census% 20and%20Survey.pdf), 79% of homeless respondents reported at least one disability such as alcohol or drug problems (56%), chronic health issues (43%), or physical disability (32%); 28% reported suffering from mental illness, and 21% reported experiencing post-traumatic stress disorder.

TUBERCULOSIS. Several kinds of acute, nonspecific respiratory diseases are common among homeless people. These diseases are easily spread through group living in overcrowded shelters without adequate nutrition. TB, a disease at one time almost eliminated from the general population in the United States, is a persistent affliction among the homeless. This disease is associated with exposure, poor diet, alcoholism, injection drug use, HIV, and other illnesses that lower the body's resistance to infection. TB is spread by long personal contact, making it a potential hazard not only to shelter residents but also to the general public.

Clinical data from federally funded Health Care for the Homeless (HCH) programs find prevalence rates for TB to be much higher among the homeless population than among the overall general population. For example, Bonnie D. Kerker et al. find in "A Population-Based Assessment of the Health of Homeless Families in New York City" (*American Journal of Public Health*, vol. 101, no. 3, March 2011) that rates of TB infection among homeless families were three times higher than among low-income families. Maryam B. Haddad et al. report in "Tuberculosis and Homelessness in the United States, 1994–2003" (*Journal of the American Medical Association*, vol. 293, no. 22, June 8, 2005) that many of the risk factors for TB in the United States overlap with the risk factors associated with homelessness, including having a history of incarceration or substance abuse. An additional contributing factor was the emergence of drug-resistant strains of TB. Experts report that to control the spread of TB, the homeless population must receive frequent screenings for TB and the infected must get long-term care and rest.

In *Reported Tuberculosis in the United States 2011* (October 2012, http://www.cdc.gov/tb/statistics/reports/ 2011/pdf/report2011.pdf), the Centers for Disease Control and Prevention (CDC) note that by 2011 the number of TB cases had dropped to the lowest levels since it began conducting surveys of those afflicted with the disease. In that year, there were 9,946 new cases of TB reported in the United States, and the CDC was able to determine the homelessness status of those afflicted in 9,814 of these cases. Based on this sample, 5.8% of those with TB were homeless, even though only 1% of the total U.S. population was homeless. (See Table 8.3.) Although the raw number of homeless people with TB had declined significantly since 1993, in combination with declines in the overall number of TB cases, the rate at which the homeless contracted TB had declined more slowly, from 7.5% in 1993 to 5.8% in 2011. Also, as Table 8.3 shows, there was significant variation in the prevalence of the problem from state to state. For example, of the 60 cases in Alaska in which homeless status could be determined, 14 (23.3%) were homeless; and 10% or more of those with TB were homeless in a number of states, including Georgia (10%), Maine (11.1%), Michigan (10.6%), and Mississippi (12.4%). California had the highest number of TB cases among the homeless, at 124, although the homeless represented a smaller percentage of the overall TB caseload (5.7%) than in these other states.

A campaign for increased public awareness, particularly among members of the medical community, was launched in 1990 to identify and screen those at the greatest risk for TB. Some researchers, such as Mary Lashley of Towson University in "A Targeted Testing Program for Tuberculosis Control and Prevention among Baltimore City's Homeless Population" (*Public Health Nursing*, vol. 24, no. 1, January–February 2007), and Maryann Duchene of Backus Home Health Care in Norwich, Connecticut, in "Infection Control in Soup Kitchens and Shelters" (*Home Healthcare Nurse*, vol. 28, no. 8, September 2010), tested pilot programs to better identify and treat homeless people infected with TB. Other studies, such as Jacqueline Peterson Tulsky et al. in "Can the Poor Adhere? Incentives for Adherence to TB Prevention in Homeless Adults" (*International Journal of Tuberculosis and Lung Disease*, vol. 8, no. 1, January 2004), and Adeline Nyamathi et al. in "Efficacy of Nurse Case-Managed Intervention for Latent Tuberculosis among Homeless Subsamples" (*Nursing Research*, vol. 57, no. 1, January–February 2008), investigated how best to help homeless adults adhere to treatment for latent TB infection.

SKIN AND BLOOD VESSEL DISORDERS. Frequent exposure to severe weather, insect bites, and other infestations make skin lesions fairly common among the homeless. Being forced to sit or stand for extended periods, as is common among the homeless, can result in chronic edema (swelling of the feet and legs), varicose veins, and skin ulcerations. The homeless are also more prone than the housed to conditions that can lead to chronic phlebitis (inflammation of the veins). Additionally, a person with circulatory problems who is forced, for example, to sleep sitting up in a doorway or in cramped conditions in a bus station or other public space

TABLE 8.3

Tuberculosis cases by homeless status, 2011

[Age ≥15:]

Reporting Area	Total cases	Cases with information on homeless status		Cases reported as being homeless[a]	
		No.	(%)	No.	(%)
United States	**9,946**	**9,814**	**(98.7)**	**565**	**(5.8)**
Alabama	150	150	(100.0)	9	(6.0)
Alaska	61	60	(98.4)	14	(23.3)
Arizona	242	209	(86.4)	15	(7.2)
Arkansas	81	81	(100.0)	8	(9.9)
California	2,193	2,167	(98.8)	124	(5.7)
Colorado	62	62	(100.0)	4	(6.5)
Connecticut	80	76	(95.0)	0	(0.0)
Delaware	21	21	(100.0)	0	(0.0)
District of Columbia	55	55	(100.0)	2	(3.6)
Florida	711	704	(99.0)	64	(9.1)
Georgia	321	319	(99.4)	32	(10.0)
Hawaii	122	107	(87.7)	9	(8.4)
Idaho	11	11	(100.0)	0	(0.0)
Illinois	342	339	(99.1)	33	(9.7)
Indiana	93	93	(100.0)	9	(9.7)
Iowa	39	39	(100.0)	2	(5.1)
Kansas	35	35	(100.0)	1	(2.9)
Kentucky	70	70	(100.0)	6	(8.6)
Louisiana	159	159	(100.0)	12	(7.5)
Maine	9	9	(100.0)	1	(11.1)
Maryland	218	217	(99.5)	13	(6.0)
Massachusetts	188	187	(99.5)	8	(4.3)
Michigan	163	160	(98.2)	17	(10.6)
Minnesota	127	127	(100.0)	2	(1.6)
Mississippi	89	89	(100.0)	11	(12.4)
Missouri	91	86	(94.5)	4	(4.7)
Montana	8	8	(100.0)	0	(0.0)
Nebraska	21	21	(100.0)	2	(9.5)
Nevada	85	85	(100.0)	4	(4.7)
New Hampshire	11	11	(100.0)	1	(9.1)
New Jersey	317	316	(99.7)	7	(2.2)
New Mexico	48	48	(100.0)	4	(8.3)
New York State[b]	206	202	(98.1)	3	(1.5)
New York City	675	661	(97.9)	16	(2.4)
North Carolina	228	227	(99.6)	15	(6.6)
North Dakota	6	6	(100.0)	0	(0.0)
Ohio	138	133	(96.4)	3	(2.3)
Oklahoma	82	79	(96.3)	6	(7.6)
Oregon	73	73	(100.0)	7	(9.6)
Pennsylvania	249	248	(99.6)	5	(2.0)
Rhode Island	25	25	(100.0)	2	(8.0)
South Carolina	133	132	(99.2)	8	(6.1)
South Dakota	14	14	(100.0)	0	(0.0)
Tennessee	148	148	(100.0)	11	(7.4)
Texas	1,227	1,227	(100.0)	59	(4.8)
Utah	32	32	(100.0)	2	(6.3)
Vermont	7	7	(100.0)	0	(0.0)
Virginia	213	213	(100.0)	1	(0.5)
Washington	188	188	(100.0)	9	(4.8)
West Virginia	12	12	(100.0)	0	(0.0)
Wisconsin	63	62	(98.4)	0	(0.0)
Wyoming	4	4	(100.0)	0	(0.0)
American Samoa[c]	3	3	(100.0)	0	(0.0)
Fed. States of Micronesia[c]	99	99	(100.0)	7	(7.1)
Guam[c]	67	67	(100.0)	3	(4.5)
Marshall Islands[c]	108	108	(100.0)	0	(0.0)
N. Mariana Islands[c]	26	26	(100.0)	0	(0.0)
Puerto Rico[c]	49	49	(100.0)	3	(6.1)
Republic of Palau[c]	8	8	(100.0)	0	(0.0)
U.S. Virgin Islands[c]	...	...	...	...	...

Notes: Homeless within past 12 months of TB diagnosis. Percentage based on 52 reporting areas (50 states, New York City, and the District of Columbia). Counts and percentages shown only for reporting areas with information reported for ≥75% of cases. Ellipses indicate data not available.
[a]Percent of those with known status.
[b]Excludes New York City.
[c]Not included in U.S. totals.

SOURCE: "Table 29. Tuberculosis Cases and Percentages by Homeless Status, Age >15: Reporting Areas, 2011," in *Reported Tuberculosis in the United States, 2011*, U.S. Department of Health and Human Services, Centers for Disease Control and Prevention, October 2012, http://www.cdc.gov/tb/statistics/reports/2011/pdf/report2011.pdf (accessed January 23, 2013)

can develop open lacerations that may become infected or maggot-infested if left untreated.

The inability of the homeless to clean themselves as frequently as those in the general population leads them to suffer from various forms of dermatitis (inflammation of the skin) at disproportionate rates. These inflammations frequently arise as a result of infestations of lice or scabies (a contagious skin disease caused by a parasitic mite that burrows under the skin to deposit eggs, causing intense itching). Additionally, an inability to bathe regularly increases the opportunity for infection to develop in cuts and other lacerations.

HIV/AIDS. The CDC notes in *Diagnoses of HIV Infection and AIDS in the United States and Dependent Areas, 2011: HIV Surveillance Report, Volume 23* (February 2013, http://www.cdc.gov/hiv/surveillance/resources/reports/2011 report/index.htm) that in 2011 there were an estimated 49,273 new cases of HIV infection. It also notes that an estimated 19,343 people with HIV diagnoses died in 2010; among these, an estimated 15,529 people had been diagnosed with AIDS. In addition, at the end of 2010 an estimated 872,990 people were living with HIV infection, and 487,692 people were living with AIDS in the United States.

The National Alliance to End Homelessness points out in the fact sheet "Homelessness and HIV/AIDS" (August 10, 2006, http://www.endhomelessness.org/library/entry/fact-sheet-homelessness-and-hiv-aids) that HIV/AIDS is more prevalent in homeless populations. As many as 3.4% of homeless people were HIV positive at the time the fact sheet was assembled, a rate that is three times higher than that of the general population. The high costs of medical care may even put individuals with HIV/AIDS at a greater risk of homelessness. Furthermore, the homeless life poses a grave threat to the health of those with HIV/AIDS, whose immune systems are compromised by the disease. Shelter conditions expose people to dangerous infections, and exposure to the elements and malnutrition exacerbate chronic illness. In addition, homeless people have difficulty obtaining and using common HIV/AIDS medications.

According to "Study: Disparity between Rich and Poor Mortality: Poor, Disadvantaged People Develop AIDS Faster" (*AIDS Alert*, vol. 18, no. 8, August 2003), a study of AIDS patients in San Francisco, California, poor people die more quickly from AIDS than do those with more financial resources. Within five years of diagnosis, fewer than 70% of people living in the city's poorest neighborhoods were still alive, compared with more than 85% of people who lived in the richest neighborhoods. Poor people with HIV usually have a number of co-occurring disorders, such as drug dependence, mental illness, and unstable housing arrangements. The lack of affordable and appropriate housing can be an acute crisis for these individuals, who need a safe shelter that provides protection and comfort, as well as a base from which to receive services, care, and support.

MENTAL ILLNESS AND SUBSTANCE ABUSE. Before the 1960s people with chronic mental illness were often committed involuntarily to state psychiatric hospitals. The development of medications that could control the symptoms of mental illness coincided with a growing belief that involuntary hospitalization was warranted only when a mentally ill person posed a threat to him- or herself or to others. Gradually, large numbers of mentally ill people were discharged from hospitals and other treatment facilities. Because the community-based treatment centers that were supposed to take the place of state hospitals were often either inadequate or nonexistent, many of these people ended up living on the streets.

In "Prevalence and Risk Factors for Homelessness and Utilization of Mental Health Services among 10,340 Patients with Serious Mental Illness in a Large Public Mental Health System" (*American Journal of Psychiatry*, vol. 162, no. 2, February 2005), David P. Folsom et al. find that 15% of patients treated for serious mental illness were homeless at some point during a one-year period. Twenty percent of patients with schizophrenia, 17% of patients with bipolar disorder, and 9% of patients with depression were homeless. Folsom and his coauthors find that mentally ill people are at a much higher risk of homelessness than the general population. The researchers emphasize that homelessness among the mentally ill was associated with two other factors: substance use disorders and a lack of Medicaid insurance. Folsom et al. state, "Although it would be naive to assume that treatment for substance use disorders and provision of Medicaid insurance could solve the problem of homelessness among persons with serious mental illness, further research is warranted to test the effect of interventions designed to treat patients with dual diagnoses and to assist homeless persons with serious mental illness in obtaining and maintaining entitlement benefits."

Experts debate the rate of mental disorders among homeless populations, but they generally agree that it is greater among the homeless than the general population. In "The Prevalence of Mental Disorders among the Homeless in Western Countries: Systematic Review and Meta-regression Analysis" (*PLoS Medline*, vol. 5, no. 12, December 2, 2008), Seena Fazel et al. analyze data from 29 surveys of the homeless in Western countries to find the prevalence of mental disorders in this population. The researchers find that the most common mental disorders were alcohol and drug dependence. The prevalence rates of psychosis and depression ranged from 2.8% to 42.3%. Fazel et al. conclude that the prevalence of substance abuse disorder, psychotic disorders, and depression are higher among the homeless population than among the general population.

Mentally ill homeless people present special problems for health care workers. They may not be as cooperative and motivated as other patients. Because of their limited resources, they may have difficulty getting transportation to treatment centers. They frequently forget to show up for appointments or to take medications. The addition of drug abuse can make them unruly or unresponsive. Among people with severe mental disorders, those at greatest risk of homelessness are both the most severely ill and the most difficult to help.

The National Alliance on Mental Illness states in "Dual Diagnosis and Integrated Treatment of Mental Illness and Substance Abuse Disorder" (2011, http://www.nami.org/Template.cfm?Section=By_Illness&Template=/TaggedPage/TaggedPageDisplay.cfm&TPLID=54&ContentID=23049) that mental illness and substance abuse frequently occur together; clinicians call this dual diagnosis. Experts explain that in the absence of appropriate treatment, people with mental illness often resort to self-medication—that is, using alcohol or drugs to silence the voices in their head or to calm the fears that torment them. Approximately 50% of individuals with severe mental disorders also abuse drugs or alcohol. Homeless people with dual diagnoses are frequently excluded from mental health programs because of treatment problems created by their substance abuse and are excluded from substance abuse programs due to problems in treating their mental illness. Experts note that the lack of an integrated system of care plays a major role in these people's recurrent homelessness and stress that transitional or assisted housing initiatives for homeless substance abusers must realistically address the issue of abstinence and design measures for handling relapses that do not place people back on the streets.

THE HEALTH OF HOMELESS CHILDREN

The National Center on Family Homelessness reports in "Children" (2010, http://www.familyhomelessness.org/children.php?p=ts) that 1 out of every 45 American children experiences homelessness each year. The organization points out that homeless children tend to have both acute and chronic health problems and that the stress and trauma in their lives has profound developmental effects. They are sick four times more often than housed children, with four times as many respiratory infections, twice as many ear infections, and five times as many gastrointestinal illnesses as housed children. They are four times more likely to have asthma, more likely to be obese, and twice as likely to go hungry than housed children. They also have three times more emotional and behavioral problems than housed children.

In "Policy Statement: Providing Care for Immigrant, Homeless, and Migrant Children" (*Pediatrics*, vol. 115, no. 4, April 2005), the American Academy of Pediatrics reviews the literature on the health of homeless children. The policy statement enumerates many health effects of homelessness, including homeless children's increased predisposition to experience poor health or fair health than are other children. In particular, homeless children have more trauma-related injuries, a greater incidence of sinus infections, anemia, asthma, eczema, visual and neurologic deficits, and digestive disorders. In addition, obesity and hunger are common. Unaccompanied youth as well as children in families living on the streets are at a higher risk of experiencing violence or victimization.

John C. Buckner of the Harvard Medical School also summarizes the results of several studies of homeless children's mental and physical health in "Understanding the Impact of Homelessness on Children: Challenges and Future Research Directions" (*American Behavioral Scientist*, vol. 51, no. 6, February 2008). He finds that both homeless and low-income housed children have higher rates of physical and mental health problems than do other children. He also notes that most studies find that homeless children evidence greater health problems than do low-income housed children.

VICTIMS OF VIOLENCE
Violence toward Homeless Women

Homeless women are at a high risk of interpersonal violence. According to Ellen Bassuk, Ree Dawson, and Nicholas Huntington in "Intimate Violence in Extremely Poor Women: Longitudinal Patterns and Risk Markers" (*Journal of Family Violence*, vol. 21, no. 6, August 2006), almost two-thirds of 280 homeless and extremely poor housed women had experienced intimate partner violence during their lifetime. Women who had been molested during childhood, who had inadequate emotional support from professionals, or who had poor self-esteem were the most likely to have experienced intimate partner violence in the past 12 months.

In "Correlates of Adult Assault among Homeless Women" (*Journal of Health Care for the Poor and Underserved*, vol. 21, no. 4, November 2010), Angela L. Hudson et al. find that some homeless women are more likely than others to experience violence. Noting that "homeless women are highly susceptible to victimization," the researchers cite research that finds that a third of homeless women reported experiencing sexual assault within the past year and another third reported being physically assaulted within the past year. Hudson et al. studied homeless women in Los Angeles, California, to uncover relationships among homeless women's psychological functioning, past victimization, and the likelihood of adult victimization. They determine that mental illness and low self-esteem were important risk factors for physical and sexual victimization among the homeless women in their study. Physical victimization was also associated with a history of physical abuse as a child, and sexual victimization was associated with a history of sexual abuse as a child. Current and previous substance abuse as well as involvement in the sex trade placed homeless women at great risk for physical and sexual victimization.

Suzanne L. Wenzel et al. find in "Sexual Risk among Impoverished Women: Understanding the Role of Housing Status" (*AIDS and Behavior*, vol. 11, supplement 6, November 2007) that impoverished women who are homeless or who have been recently victimized are also more likely to engage in risky sexual behavior that can lead to HIV infection. The researchers indicate that homeless African-American and Hispanic women had from two to five times greater odds of engaging in risky sexual behavior than women who were housed.

Hate Crimes

In *Hate Crimes against the Homeless: The Brutality of Violence Unveiled* (December 2012, http://www.national homeless.org/publications/hatecrimes/hatecrimes2011 .pdf), the National Coalition for the Homeless (NCH) notes that in 2011 there was an increase in the number of hate-motivated violent deaths among the homeless, and that among these deaths, an increasing number were classified as serial murders. The NCH also pointed out that, increasingly, violence against the homeless was committed by juveniles as young as 13 years old. In all, between 1999 and 2011, the NCH documents 1,289 acts of violence against the homeless (of which 339 resulted in death) that were believed to have been committed on the basis of prejudice or the ease with which the homeless can be targeted. Of the 1,289 violent acts catalogued, 72% were committed by people under 30 years old and 97% by males.

Although there were a number of local- and state-level hate-crime laws that protected the homeless, there was no federal classification for hate crimes against the homeless, which limited the ability to curtail the trend toward violence at the national level. The NCH consistently lobbied for such legislation, noting that in 2011, after Florida passed a state-level hate-crimes law including the homeless as a protected subset of the population, there was a significant decrease in the number of documented hate-motivated crimes against the homeless.

HEALTH CARE FOR THE HOMELESS

Martha R. Burt et al. analyze in *Homelessness: Programs and the People They Serve* (December 1999, http://www.urban.org/UploadedPDF/homelessness.pdf) the results of the 1996 National Survey of Homeless Assistance Providers and Clients, the only survey of its kind (studies of the homeless tend to focus on local populations). The researchers note that in the year preceding the survey 25% of the clients studied had needed medical attention but were not able to see a doctor or a nurse. They also reveal that newly housed people were even less likely to receive medical help when needed.

Burt et al. attribute the higher rate of health problems among newly housed people to several factors, including:

- The loss of convenient health care in centers or shelters
- The habit of enduring untreated ailments
- A lack of health care benefits (which is common among people below the poverty level)

In "The Behavioral Model for Vulnerable Populations: Application to Medical Care Use and Outcomes for Homeless People" (*Health Services Research*, vol. 34, no. 6, February 2000), Lillian Gelberg, Ronald M. Andersen, and Barbara D. Leake report the results of a study on the prevalence of certain disease conditions among homeless adults, which revealed that 37% suffered from functional vision impairment; 36% experienced skin, leg, and foot problems; and 31% tested positive for TB. The researchers indicate that homeless people who had a community clinic or a private physician as a regular source of care exhibited better health outcomes. Gelberg, Andersen, and Leake also suggest that clinical treatment of the homeless be accompanied by efforts to help them find permanent housing.

As the Kaiser Commission on Medicaid and the Uninsured reports in *Medicaid Coverage and Care for the Homeless Population: Key Lessons to Consider for the 2014 Medicaid Expansion* (September 2012, http://www .kff.org/medicaid/upload/8355.pdf), very few homeless people received benefits under Medicaid prior to the program's 2014 expansion. Homeless children were often eligible for Medicaid, and in some cases parents qualified, but for most homeless adults, eligibility depended on establishing disability status and qualifying for SSI, which is a painstaking process. Additionally, many homeless individuals distrust public systems and institutions, and mental illness and substance-abuse problems further complicate the process of applying for public assistance. Advocates and service providers looked to the Medicaid expansion as a major opportunity for meeting the health care needs of the homeless, and the expansion's simplification of eligibility and enrollment promised to increase the population's participation in the program. However, as the Kaiser Commission notes, the ability to successfully enroll homeless individuals in Medicaid and ensure that they received necessary treatment would remain a challenge requiring significant one-on-one assistance.

Federally funded outreach and assistance of a similar kind was already available under the HCH program, authorized under Title VI of the McKinney-Vento Homeless Assistance Act. In the Obama administration's 2013 budget, HCH programs, which were operated by the Department of Health and Human Services, were allotted $258 million, up from $232 million the previous year and well in excess of the $171 million requested for 2010.

The goal of the HCH programs is to improve the health of homeless individuals and families by improving access to primary health care and substance abuse services. The HCH programs provide outreach, counseling to clients explaining available services, case management, and referrals to services such as mental health treatment, housing, benefits, and other critical supports. Access to around-the-clock emergency services is available, as is help in establishing eligibility for assistance and obtaining services under entitlement programs.

Nonprofit private organizations and public entities, including state and local government agencies, may apply for grants from the program. The grants may be used to continue to provide services for up to one year to individuals who have obtained permanent housing if services were provided to them when they were homeless.

IMPORTANT NAMES
AND ADDRESSES

**American Public Human Services
Association**
1133 19th St. NW, Ste. 400
Washington, DC 20036
(202) 682-0100
FAX: (202) 289-6555
URL: http://www.aphsa.org/

Association of Gospel Rescue Missions
7222 Commerce Center Dr., Ste. 120
Colorado Springs, CO 80919
(719) 266-8300
1-800-473-7283
FAX: (719) 266-8600
E-mail: info@agrm.org
URL: http://www.agrm.org/

Center for Law and Social Policy
1200 18th St. NW, Ste. 200
Washington, DC 20036
(202) 906-8000
FAX: (202) 842-2885
URL: http://www.clasp.org/

Center for the Study of Social Policy
1575 Eye St. NW, Ste. 500
Washington, DC 20005
(202) 371-1565
FAX: (202) 371-1472
E-mail: info@cssp.org
URL: http://www.cssp.org/

Center on Budget and Policy Priorities
820 First St. NE, Ste. 510
Washington, DC 20002
(202) 408-1080
FAX: (202) 408-1056
E-mail: center@cbpp.org
URL: http://www.cbpp.org/

Children's Defense Fund
25 E St. NW
Washington, DC 20001
1-800-233-1200
E-mail: cdfinfo@childrensdefense.org
URL: http://www.childrensdefense.org/

Child Welfare League of America
1726 M St. NW, Ste. 500
Washington, DC 20036
(202) 688-4200
FAX: (202) 833-1689
URL: http://www.cwla.org/

Feeding America
35 E. Wacker Dr., Ste. 2000
Chicago, IL 60601
1-800-771-2303
FAX: (312) 263-5626
URL: http://www.feedingamerica.org/

Food Research and Action Center
1875 Connecticut Ave. NW, Ste. 540
Washington, DC 20009
(202) 986-2200
FAX: (202) 986-2525
URL: http://www.frac.org/

Habitat for Humanity International
121 Habitat St.
Americus, GA 31709-3498
1-800-422-4828
URL: http://www.habitat.org/

Homes for the Homeless
50 Cooper Sq., 4th Fl.
New York, NY 10003
(212) 529-5252
FAX: (212) 529-7698
E-mail: info@hfhnyc.org
URL: http://www.hfhnyc.org/

Housing Assistance Council
1025 Vermont Ave. NW, Ste. 606
Washington, DC 20005
(202) 842-8600
FAX: (202) 347-3441
E-mail: hac@ruralhome.org
URL: http://www.ruralhome.org/

**Institute for Research on Poverty
University of Wisconsin, Madison**
1180 Observatory Dr.
3412 William H. Sewell Social Sciences
Bldg.
Madison, WI 53706-1320

(608) 262-6358
FAX: (608) 265-3119
E-mail: djohnson@ssc.wisc.edu
URL: http://www.irp.wisc.edu/

**Joint Center for Housing Studies
Harvard University**
1033 Massachusetts Ave., 5th Fl.
Cambridge, MA 02138
(617) 495-7908
FAX: (617) 496-9957
URL: http://www.jchs.harvard.edu

Kaiser Family Foundation
2400 Sand Hill Rd.
Menlo Park, CA 94025
(650) 854-9400
FAX: (650) 854-4800
URL: http://www.kff.org/

National Alliance of HUD Tenants
42 Seaverns Ave.
Boston, MA 02130
(617) 267-9564
FAX: (617) 522-4857
E-mail: naht@saveourhomes.org
URL: http://www.saveourhomes.org/

National Alliance on Mental Illness
3803 N. Fairfax Dr., Ste. 100
Arlington, VA 22203
(703) 524-7600
FAX: (703) 524-9094
URL: http://www.nami.org/

National Alliance to End Homelessness
1518 K St. NW, Ste. 410
Washington, DC 20005
(202) 638-1526
FAX: (202) 638-4664
E-mail: naeh@naeh.org
URL: http://www.endhomelessness.org/

**National Association for the Education
of Homeless Children and Youth**
PO Box 26274
Minneapolis, MN 55426

(866) 862-2562
FAX: (763) 545-9499
E-mail: info@naehcy.org
URL: http://www.naehcy.org/

National Center for Children in Poverty
215 W. 125th St., 3rd Fl.
New York, NY 10027
(646) 284-9600
FAX: (646) 284-9623
E-mail: info@nccp.org
URL: http://www.nccp.org/

National Coalition for Homeless Veterans
333½ Pennsylvania Ave. SE
Washington, DC 20003-1148
(202) 546-1969
1-800-VET-HELP
FAX: (202) 546-2063
E-mail: info@nchv.org
URL: http://www.nchv.org/

National Coalition for the Homeless
2201 P St. NW
Washington, DC 20037
(202) 462-4822
FAX: (202) 462-4823
E-mail: info@nationalhomeless.org
URL: http://www.nationalhomeless.org/

National Health Care for the Homeless Council
PO Box 60427
Nashville, TN 37206-0427
(615) 226-2292
FAX: (615) 226-1656
URL: http://www.nhchc.org/

National Housing Conference and the Center for Housing Policy
1900 M St. NW, Ste. 200
Washington, DC 20036
(202) 466-2121

FAX: (202) 466-2122
URL: http://www.nhc.org/

National Housing Law Project
703 Market St., Ste. 2000
San Francisco, CA 94103
(415) 546-7000
FAX: (415) 546-7007
URL: http://www.nhlp.org/

National Law Center for Children and Families
305 Harrison St. SE, 3rd Fl.
Leesburg, VA 20175
(703) 548-5522
E-mail: info@nationallawcenter.org
URL: http://www.nationallawcenter.org/

National Law Center on Homelessness and Poverty
1411 K St. NW, Ste. 1400
Washington, DC 20005
(202) 638-2535
FAX: (202) 628-2737
URL: http://www.nlchp.org/

National League of Cities
1301 Pennsylvania Ave. NW, Ste. 550
Washington, DC 20004
1-877-827-2385
URL: http://www.nlc.org/

National Low Income Housing Coalition
727 15th St. NW, 6th Fl.
Washington, DC 20005
(202) 662-1530
FAX: (202) 393-1973
URL: http://www.nlihc.org/

National Rural Housing Coalition
1331 G St. NW, 10th Floor
Washington, DC 20002
(202) 393-5229
FAX: (202) 393-3034

E-mail: nrhc@ruralhousingcoalition.org
URL: http://ruralhousingcoalition.org/

National Women's Law Center
11 Dupont Cir. NW, #800
Washington, DC 20036
(202) 588-5180
FAX: (202) 588-5185
E-mail: info@nwlc.org
URL: http://www.nwlc.org/

Rural Policy Research Institute University of Missouri, Columbia
214 Middlebush Hall
University of Missouri–Columbia
Columbia, MO 65211
(573) 882-0316
FAX: (573) 884-5310
URL: http://www.rupri.org/

Urban Institute
2100 M St. NW
Washington, DC 20037
(202) 833-7200
URL: http://www.urban.org/

U.S. Conference of Mayors
1620 Eye St. NW
Washington, DC 20006
(202) 293-7330
FAX: (202) 293-2352
E-mail: info@usmayors.org
URL: http://www.usmayors.org/

U.S. Interagency Council on Homelessness
Federal Center SW
409 Third St. SW, Ste. 310
Washington, DC 20024
(202) 708-4663
FAX: (202) 708-1216
E-mail: usich@usich.gov
URL: http://www.usich.gov/

RESOURCES

The federal government is the premier source of facts on many issues related to social welfare, including poverty, employment, the welfare system, housing, and homelessness. A variety of government agencies and departments provide detailed data related to these issues in the form of published reports, their official websites, and searchable databases.

Data gathered by the U.S. Census Bureau was particularly central to compiling this book. Some excellent sources of information from the Census Bureau are *2011 American Community Survey 1-Year Estimates* (2012), *America's Families and Living Arrangements: 2012* (November 2012), *Current Population Survey (CPS), 2012 Annual Social and Economic Supplement* (September 2012), *Custodial Mothers and Fathers and Their Child Support: 2009* (December 2011), *Dynamics of Economic Well-Being: Poverty, 2004–2006* (March 2011), *The Emergency and Transitional Shelter Population: 2010* (September 2012), *Income, Poverty, and Health Insurance Coverage in the United States: 2011* (September 2012), *The Research Supplemental Poverty Measure: 2010* (November 2011), *The Research Supplemental Poverty Measure: 2011* (November 2012), and *Statistical Abstract of the United States: 2012* (2012).

The U.S. Department of Labor's Bureau of Labor Statistics (BLS) provides valuable data on wages and work patterns in its searchable website portal *Databases, Tables & Calculators by Subject* and its *Labor Force Statistics from the Current Population Survey*, on which it collaborates with the Census Bureau. The BLS likewise offers details about low-income workers in *A Profile of the Working Poor, 2010* (March 2012) and about minimum-wage workers in *Characteristics of Minimum Wage Workers: 2011* (March 2012). The Department of Labor's Employment and Training Administration offers data on unemployment compensation claims in *Unemployment Insurance Data Summary* (2012), and it offers detailed historical data pertaining to the recipients of unemployment compensation in *UI Benefits Study: Recent Changes in the Characteristics of Unemployed Workers* (August 2009).

The U.S. Department of Housing and Urban Development (HUD) is the source for much valuable data on homelessness, housing affordability, and subsidized housing programs. Among the HUD publications used in this book are *The 2011 Annual Homeless Assessment Report to Congress* (November 2012), *The 2012 Point-in-Time Estimates of Homelessness: Volume I of the 2012 Annual Homeless Assessment Report* (November 2012), *FY 2013 Budget Summary* (2012), and *Worst Case Housing Needs 2011: Report to Congress* (February 2013).

Important data on federal nutrition programs came from the U.S. Department of Agriculture's (USDA) Food and Nutrition Service, which provides detailed tables about the National School Lunch Program, the School Breakfast Program, the Supplemental Nutrition Assistance Program, and the Special Supplemental Food Program for Women, Infants, and Children. Additionally, the USDA's Economic Research Service provides data on those Americans whose food needs either go unmet or are in danger of going unmet in *Household Food Security in the United States in 2011* (September 2012).

Other valuable data came from the U.S. Department of Health and Human Services' (HHS) Office of Family Assistance, in particular the report *Temporary Assistance for Needy Families Program (TANF): Ninth Report to Congress* (June 2012). The Centers for Disease Control and Prevention (CDC), which is also a part of HHS, was a valuable source of data on health care and illness. The CDC's National Center for Health Statistics report *Health, United States, 2011: With Special Feature on Socioeconomic Status and Health* (May 2012) offers particularly useful insights into the connections between poverty and health.

Other important government data sources include the Federal Interagency Forum on Child and Family Statistics in *America's Children in Brief: Key National Indicators of Well-Being, 2012* (2012), the Social Security Administration in *Annual Statistical Supplement, 2012* (February 2013), and the U.S. House of Representatives

Committee on Ways and Means in *Background Material and Data on the Programs within the Jurisdiction of the Committee on Ways and Means (Green Book)* (2012).

Many different organizations study the poor and homeless. Notable among them for its many large studies on poverty and homelessness is the Urban Institute (UI). UI publications were a major source of information for this volume, especially *America's Homeless II: Populations and Services* (February 2000), *Child Care Subsidies and TANF: A Synthesis of Three Studies on Systems, Policies, and Parents* (2006), "A Decade of Welfare Reform: Facts and Figures—Assessing the New Federalism" (June 2006), *Federal Programs for Addressing Low-Income Housing Needs: A Policy Primer* (December 2008), "Government Work Supports and Low-Income Families: Facts and Figures" (July 2006), "The Great Recession, Unemployment Insurance, and Poverty" (April 2010), *Homelessness: Programs and the People They Serve—Findings of the National Survey of Homeless Assistance Providers and Clients* (December 1999), "How Has the TANF Caseload Changed over Time?" (March 2012), "Jobs in an Uncertain Economy: A Research Focus of the Urban Institute" (2010), "SNAP's Role in the Great Recession and Beyond" (July 2012), and *Welfare Rules Databook: State TANF Policies as of July 2011* (August 2012).

The Center on Budget and Policy Priorities (CBPP) is an organization that advocates for the interests of the poor in debates on federal budget and tax policies. CBPP publications that were useful in compiling this book include "Chart Book: TANF at 16" (August 22, 2012), "Contrary to 'Entitlement Society' Rhetoric, over Nine-Tenths of Entitlement Benefits Go to Elderly, Disabled, or Working Households" (February 10, 2012), "How States Have Spent Federal and State Funds under the TANF Block Grant" (August 7, 2012), "Implementing the TANF Changes in the Deficit Reduction Act" (February 2007), "Income Gaps between Very Rich and Everyone Else More Than Tripled in Last Three Decades, New Data Show" (June 2010), "Introduction to the Supplemental Security Program" (January 10, 2011), "Introduction to Unemployment Insurance" (February 6, 2013), "Many States Cutting TANF Benefits Harshly Despite High Unemployment and Unprecedented Need"

(October 3, 2011), "Policy Basics: State Earned Income Tax Credits" (December 5, 2012), "TANF Responded Unevenly to Increase in Need during Downturn: Findings Suggest Needed Improvements When Program Reauthorized" (January 25, 2011), "Policy Basics: An Introduction to TANF" (March 2009), and *State Earned Income Tax Credits: 2010 Legislative Update* (December 2010).

Additional information on the national homeless population came from a variety of organizations including the Association of Gospel Rescue Missions (AGRM), the National Alliance to End Homelessness (NAEH), the National Center for Homeless Education (NCHE), the National Coalition for the Homeless (NCH), the National Law Center on Homelessness & Poverty (NLCHP), and the U.S. Conference of Mayors (USCM). The NAEH's *The State of Homelessness in America 2012* (January 2012) analyzes national and state level homeless counts from the Department of Housing and Urban Development and explores economic and demographic drivers of homelessness. The NCHE's *Education for Homeless Children and Youths Program: Data Collection Summary* (June 2012) presents data collected by school systems regarding the population of homeless children enrolled in the nation's public schools. The NLCHP's *Criminalizing Crisis: The Criminalization of Homelessness in U.S. Cities* (November 2011) surveys American cities' increasing tendency to pass laws and ordinances prohibiting a wide range of conduct that is characteristic of homeless populations. The NCH's *Hate Crimes against the Homeless: The Brutality of Violence Unveiled* (December 2012) addresses the rise of hate-motivated violence against the homeless. *Hunger and Homelessness Survey: A Status Report on Hunger and Homelessness in America's Cities, a 25-City Survey* (December 2012) by the USCM and "Survey Points to Needs of Iraq, Afghanistan Veterans" (November 2012) by the AGRM also provide valuable information on the homeless population.

Finally, the Joint Center for Housing Studies of Harvard University, Health Care for the Homeless, the National Coalition for Homeless Veterans, the National Multi Housing Council, the Henry J. Kaiser Family Foundation, and UNICEF's Innocenti Research Centre all provided important data and analysis on the issues covered in this volume.

INDEX

McKinney-Vento Homeless Assistance Act, 130–133
   subsidized housing, 121–125, 122*f*
   vouchers program, 125–126
   worst case housing needs renters, 117–118
U.S. Department of Veterans Affairs, 107, 133

V

Vehicle asset limits, 67
Veterans, 104*t*, 107, 107*f*, 133
Violence against the homeless, 156–157
Vouchers, housing, 122–123, 125–126

W

Wages. *See* Income and earnings; Minimum wage
Waiting lists, housing assisting, 126
War on Poverty, 1, 2, 10
Wealth disparities, 11–12, 12*t*
Welfare assistance
   allocation percentages, by group, 78*f*
   caseload composition, 77–78
   eligible families, numbers of, 35, 42
   households and family status, 43*t*–45*t*
   maximum TANF benefits, by state, 60*f*
   noncash benefits, 121*t*

poverty measurement, 7–8
program participation of households for persons in poverty, 46*t*–48*t*
recipient characteristics, 42
recipient trends, 59*f*
SSI, 74–75, 92–94
SSI payments, by age, 97(*f*4.7)
SSI payments, by eligibility category, 94*t*–97*t*
SSI recipients with other income, 97(*f*4.8)
TANF caseload, 58*t*
TANF children, 80(*t*4.3)
TANF recipient demographics, 78–80, 79*t*
TANF recipients, by state, 78*f*
unemployment compensation, 87–92
See also Food assistance
Welfare reform
   caseload composition, 77–78
   history, 1–2
   Personal Responsibility and Work Opportunity Reconciliation Act, 57, 59–62, 80
White-collar unemployment, 90, 91*t*
WIC. *See* Special Supplemental Food Program for Women, Infants, and Children
Williams, Brendan, 130

Williams, Robin, 129
Wilson, James Q., 137
Women
   victimization of homeless women, 156–157
   welfare assistance recipients, 42
   working poor, 51
Work experience, 32
Workers
   female-to-male earnings, 14*f*
   income and earnings, 11–12, 13*t*
   minimum wage, 73–74, 73*t*, 75*t*
Working poor
   characteristics, 51, 52*t*, 53–54
   homelessness, 111–113, 111*t*
   housing issues, 110
   poverty, 32, 42*t*, 54*t*, 55*t*
   Temporary Assistance for Needy Families, 78*f*, 80(*t*4.4)
Worst case housing needs, 117–118, 118(*f*6.3), 119

Y

Youth. *See* Children and youth

Z

Zoning ordinances, 139–140

CPSIA information can be obtained
at www.ICGtesting.com
Printed in the USA
FFOW04n0933280913

9 781569 957929